THE CORRESPONDENCE OF
KING GEORGE THE THIRD

FROM 1760 TO DECEMBER 1783

MACMILLAN AND CO., Limited
LONDON · BOMBAY · CALCUTTA · MADRAS
MELBOURNE

THE MACMILLAN COMPANY
NEW YORK · BOSTON · CHICAGO
DALLAS · SAN FRANCISCO

THE MACMILLAN CO. OF CANADA, Ltd.
TORONTO

THE CORRESPONDENCE OF
KING GEORGE THE THIRD

FROM 1760 TO DECEMBER 1783

PRINTED FROM THE ORIGINAL PAPERS
IN THE ROYAL ARCHIVES AT WINDSOR CASTLE,
ARRANGED AND EDITED

BY

THE HON. SIR JOHN FORTESCUE
LL.D., D.LITT.

IN SIX VOLUMES

VOL. II

1768–JUNE 1773

MACMILLAN AND CO., LIMITED
ST. MARTIN'S STREET, LONDON

1927

COPYRIGHT

PRINTED IN GREAT BRITAIN
BY R. & R. CLARK, LIMITED, EDINBURGH

INTRODUCTION

THE present volume opens with the year 1768 ; and the
first incident in it brings forward again the prostration
of Chatham.   There was a question of passing a Charter
through the office of the Lord Privy Seal, who, since
the matter at issue was contentious, might be required
to hear both parties concerned.   Chatham being utterly
unfit for business of any kind, the difficulty was sur-
mounted by putting the Privy Seal for the moment into
commission ; the King at the same time writing him a
generous and considerate letter, to assure him that the
mere name of Chatham was sufficient to keep the
Ministry alive, and praying him not to think of retirement
(582-585).   Then, once again, we are plunged into riots
and disorders, and all the wearisome turmoil of Wilkes's
election for Middlesex.   The King was for dealing
firmly with mischievous riots upon principle, though
careful not to provoke them by unnecessary display of
force (607) ; but really, as he said, there were so few
troops in the country that it was difficult to meet the
daily calls made for them by the civil magistrates (625).
It is not sufficiently recognised that, when members of
Parliament declaimed against the maintenance of a
standing Army, they were declaiming also against the
only police force which stood between England and
anarchy. Men of substance evidently instigated and
supported the prosecutions of civil magistrates and

officers who did their duty by firing on the mob (634);
and in the violence of faction they took no account of
the danger which they were promoting to themselves
as well as to the Government.

These disorders lasted until July, and, meanwhile,
trouble was increasing in America. The Assembly of
Massachusetts had addressed circulars to the other
Colonies urging them to join in resisting the import
duties imposed by the British Parliament in 1767, and
the news from Virginia was still more alarming; so much
so that Lord Hillsborough recommended that men-of-
war and marines should be held ready for emergencies
(637, 638). General Sir Jeffery Amherst was Governor
of Virginia, drawing the emoluments in reward for his
military services, but not residing in the Colony; and,
since the circumstances demanded a resident Governor,
he was called upon to resign, the King promising him
adequate compensation. To the King's great surprise, Amherst declined to do so (643, 646), and as
another Governor had already been appointed, Amherst
took great offence. This was awkward, for Amherst
was a protégé of Chatham; and another of Chatham's
friends, Lord Shelburne, was also in disfavour, for he
was laying himself out to thwart every measure that
originated with his chief, the Duke of Grafton (651, 653).
Minister after Minister declared to the King that it was
impossible for Shelburne to continue as Secretary of
State, but Lord Chancellor Camden was morbidly
nervous as to the possible effects of Shelburne's removal
upon Chatham (660). The King decided that Shelburne
must resign, and that Grafton himself must see Lady
Chatham and break the news to her in such fashion as
should disarm any displeasure of her lord (661). Grafton
duly waited upon her ladyship, but failed to elicit from
her any opinion as to the manner in which Chatham

would receive the news of Shelburne's resignation, whereupon the King decided that Shelburne must none the less go (664). Three days later Chatham wrote to Grafton, resigning his office as Lord Privy Seal, nominally upon the ground of his health, but without dissembling his discontent over the treatment of Shelburne and Amherst (666). The King was taken aback, and wrote himself to Chatham urging him to reconsider his decision, but in vain, though the King was comforted by the fact that Chatham now alleged illness as the only motive for his retirement (667, 669, 670, 671). But the event reacted upon other members of the Government besides Shelburne, notably upon Lord Chancellor Camden and Lord Granby; and Grafton declared that it would be impossible for him to remain at the head of the Government if Camden resigned. Lord Hertford tendered his good offices (682, 685); Lord Hillsborough offered to vacate his post, if it would be of any convenience (683); and the difficulty by one means or another was adjusted, though the papers throw no light on the final stages of the process (686).

Meanwhile in May great excitement had been caused by the purchase of Corsica by France from the Genoese. Lord Rochford, the British Ambassador at Paris, was instructed to remonstrate as strongly as possible, and, as this proved fruitless, Grafton sent an emissary, Captain Dunant, to concert arrangements with the leader of the insurgents, General Paoli, who had successfully resisted the Genoese and hoped for British aid in resisting the French (642-645). The situation was so perilous it was thought necessary to warn the King's brother, Henry Frederick, Duke of Cumberland, not to proceed on a voyage, upon which he had already started, for the Mediterranean (652-657). Grafton was prepared to meet all requests of Paoli except a declaration in

his favour, which, as Grafton said, was equivalent to
a declaration of war against France. "I cannot think,"
wrote the King, "under the present State of Debt, for
the sake alone of the island of Corsica to begin acts of
hostilities against France" (653); so though arms and
money were sent to the insurgents, nothing serious came
of it; and the King, as we shall find in 1787, took to
heart this lesson. But wars and rumours of wars by
no means died down immediately. The Hereditary
Prince of Brunswick, greatly distinguished during the
Seven Years' War, wrote to ask for military employment
in Hanover, which was politely refused (728, 733).
The King privately inquired of Sir Joseph Yorke, his
trusty envoy at the Hague, as to the help that might be
expected of the United Provinces in case of war. He
received a long and not very satisfactory reply, the
Dutch having since 1748 lived on their old reputation as
a Maritime Power and being in fact impotent (736, 738).
Lastly, Paoli represented at length the advantages that
would accrue to England by annexation of Corsica (741),
but all to no purpose. Admiral Sir Charles Saunders
might say in Parliament that it would be better to go
to war with France than consent to her taking possession
of Corsica; and the opinion of so good an officer was
not lightly to be set aside. But the King thought
differently, and no doubt he was right.

The papers of 1769 are remarkably scanty, and with
one important exception (701) make little or no reference
to the steady growth of disaffection at Boston, nor even
to the wretched business of Wilkes. They are equally
silent as to Chatham's last interview with the King on
the 7th of July, as to the great man's reappearance in
Parliament, and as to his speech condemning the refusal
of the House of Commons to admit Wilkes. There are
no details of the crumbling of the Duke of Grafton's

administration ; and without any warning we come straight upon the King's invitation to Lord North to become First Lord of the Treasury (745). The report on the debate, when all the obnoxious duties in America were repealed, with the historic exception of that upon tea, is very brief, and provokes no answer from the King (762). Sovereign and Minister are far more occupied with the business of Wilkes and the remonstrance of the City of London (771-773, 792, 793, 797-802). But the Opposition was busy enough in Parliament (788, 789). Then without any warning the spectre of war suddenly rises (816), in consequence of the dispute with Spain about the Falkland Islands. The question of press-warrants came up in connection with the manning of the fleet, and the City of London, losing its head in the eagerness of faction, prepared its usual artillery of address, petition and remonstrance, a proceeding which the King condemned as puerile (832, 833). But the danger was very great, for conflict with Spain signified almost certainly war with France also, and the fleet was not in a satisfactory condition (846). One of the Ministers, Lord Weymouth, was for accepting war and attacking France at once in the East Indies (833). The King, on the other hand, with little hope of peace, laboured earnestly for it (835) ; but Weymouth was so bent upon his own project, that he declared it impossible for him to remain in the Cabinet (848-855). At Christmas peace still seemed hopeless ; and the King thought it worth while to make a copy in his own hand of a project for an attack on Ferrol, an enterprise which was tried without success twenty years later (875). On the 3rd of January 1771, the Spanish Ambassador learned with the greatest dismay that the British Minister at Madrid had been recalled, and begged that fresh orders might be sent to stay him (876). This was done after

some hesitation (895, 896), for the King did not fancy
ordering the Minister to return to Madrid unless he were
sure that the result would be peace. All was satis-
factorily settled, thanks chiefly to the fall of the Duc de
Choiseul in France ; and it need only be added that
the Mr. Harris whose name figures so prominently in
the whole transaction is that very able diplomatist
who later became Lord Malmesbury.

There was much discussion as to the succession to
Lord Weymouth. Lord Sandwich was first thought
of (856), then Lord Hillsborough, who declined upon
the ground that " he was a very bad Frenchman " ;
then Lord Suffolk (882, 883), then Lord Halifax,
Lord Hardwicke, and Lord Dartmouth (885-890, 893),
the choice ultimately falling upon Halifax. At the
same time Thurlow and Wedderburn became respectively Attorney- and Solicitor-General (866), and Henry
Bathurst, Lord Chancellor (898).

Immediately afterwards came the incident, concerning the publication of debates in Parliament, which
led to a collision between the House of Commons and
the City of London, and ended in the ignominious defeat
of the House. The King, it will be seen (913), at once
saw the danger of making a serious affair of it, and
though fully of opinion that the " lawless method of
publishing debates in the papers should be put a stop
to ", was for throwing the burden upon the " broader
shoulders " of the House of Lords. However, the
Commons insisted upon mismanaging the matter themselves. The Lord Mayor set the asserted privileges of
the House at defiance, and the King could see no alternative but for the House to take up the challenge. But
he did so reluctantly. " You know very well ", he
wrote to North, " I was averse to meddling with the
Printers, but now there is no retracting—the honour

of the Commons must be supported " (937). It seems to have been due in some measure to the King's wise counsel that the Commons did not insist upon the appearance of Wilkes at the bar of the House (938). The course of the business may be followed through the index, and need not further detain us. It may only be remarked that at one moment it brought Lord North into peril of his life from the mob, and that the King thereupon, with characteristic courage, went down to Westminster in person to give his assent to Bills (946).

On the 7th of June 1771 Lord Halifax died ; whereupon Lord Suffolk succeeded him as Secretary of State to the Northern Department, and the Duke of Grafton took over the Privy Seal from Suffolk, declining a seat in the Cabinet, which he considered to contain too many men already (959, 964).

The papers now show various indications of nervousness over a rupture with France. One document concerns the fortifications of Portsmouth (971). Among others are a letter of information as to the French forces in the East (973), a long account of the state and resources of Saxony, carefully copied by the King with his own hand (977), a memorandum by the King on the work of the English dockyards (979), two lengthy reports as to the defences of Portsmouth and the manner of meeting a French invasion by Captain Guy Carleton, the future Lord Dorchester (986, 990), and a curious paper about the Court of France under the reign of Madame du Barry (1008). If George III. had one feeling stronger than another, it was intense distrust of France.

The year 1772 brought to the King a succession of domestic worries. His brother, Henry Frederick, after many love affairs, married a Mrs. Horton, a widow and a sister of the Colonel Luttrell who had been elected for

Middlesex, illegally, in place of Wilkes. His brother, William Henry, Duke of Cumberland, announced his marriage, some years before, with the Countess Dowager of Waldegrave. His sister, Caroline Matilda, queen to the contemptible Christian VII., King of Denmark, was imprisoned by her husband for alleged misconduct with Count Struensee. It seemed at one moment as if the incident might lead to war (1055). The King banished his brothers from the Court, and sent a message to Parliament to recommend the passing of a Royal Marriage Bill. He also despatched a man-of-war to bring his sister home (1082). But yet another sorrow fell upon him through the death of his mother, the Princess Dowager, on the 8th of February (1013). She had, ever since her son's accession, been the butt of cowardly attacks from politicians, and had borne them all in silence, not, it is to be conjectured, unmixed with contempt. A curious complication in her obsequies was that the Lord Chamberlain at this same moment lost his daughter-in-law and sought for that reason to be excused from his duties, but in vain (1016-1018). The Princess Dowager died intestate, and the King took out letters of administration to appoint Lord North her executor (1016). Some curious details as to her possessions will be found (1111, 1165, 1191), with a list of her clothes (1166), which will not be without interest for some readers.

After some less important affairs, such as Joseph Banks's quarrel with his accommodation on board ship for his coming voyage with Captain Cook (1065, 1070, 1103), and a little squabble on administrative business between Lord Rochford and Lord North, which was tactfully composed by the King (1098-1100), we come to the reorganisation of the business of the American Department upon its transfer from Lord Hillsborough to Lord Dartmouth (1113, 1115, 1120). Incidentally we find General Paoli in England, and Lord North telling him that the English subsidy to the Corsicans in Tuscany must presently be stopped (1075). And then we come to a more serious matter—the revolution in Sweden—of which the advent was early reported to England by the British Minister at Stockholm (1087-1092). The King did not greatly value friendship with Sweden, unless to thwart the designs of France (917). As it happened, there was already a point of friction with the latter power (1102) which might be heated by the progress of events in Sweden, since one of the two factions leaned upon France, and the other (to which the King was not disposed to give great assistance) upon England and Russia (1122). As usual the King was firm in avoiding anything that might provoke war (1150, 1151). The movements of all French ships in the East were none the less carefully watched (1181), and the King, in reviewing the results of the first partition of Poland, even contemplated united action with France (1180). In the spring of 1773 the depredations of the Russian fleet in the Levant in consequence of the Russian war with Turkey seemed likely after all to bring about a collision with France, for her commerce in the Levant was suffering, and, if she took action at sea against Russia, England, as the Tsarina's ally, was bound to come to her rescue. The King took prompt measures to check France by preparing a sufficient fleet; the French very quickly took the hint (1228, 1231), and the danger passed away (1251).

The remainder of the papers, down to the end of June 1773, at which date this volume closes, are greatly occupied with the passing of Lord North's East India Bill through Parliament. East Indian affairs had a peculiar interest for the King, who evidently shared the

prejudice of all country squires against the " nabobs "
who had " shaken the pagoda tree " and come home
wealthy. Though acknowledging the great services of
Clive, he could not forgive him for "opening the door to
the fortunes we see daily made in that country" (1255).
There is a long paper as to the reconstitution of the East
India Company's powers in Bengal, which is worth
reading (1173). A long and elaborate analysis of intelligence respecting the movements of French naval
and military forces in the East suggests that there was
some anxiety over possible French aggression in that
quarter (1181). It is somewhat remarkable to note
Lord North's quiet report of the most momentous of
all his legislation in regard to the East Indies—the
exportation of tea to America and foreign parts (1232).
This seemingly innocent measure was designed to help
the East India Company to get rid of its huge stock of
tea, and provided for a drawback upon the duty that
might be imposed on it upon export to the American
Colonies. North never dreamed of it as evil or oppressive. He even regarded it as in some degree conciliatory;
but he reckoned without the smugglers of Boston. It
was the menace to their pockets which led to the scenes
of violence in Boston harbour, and which, provoking
retaliation as they did, led ultimately to the War of
Independence. We are, in deploring the breach with
America, a little too ready to forget that there were
other parts of the Empire which required attention as
well; that vast tracts of it had been newly won, and
that a measure designed for the benefit of one portion
aroused, quite unexpectedly, fierce resentment in another.
It was impossible even to grant toleration of the Roman
Catholic religion in Canada without giving bitter offence
to the New England Colonies. These papers at least
give some idea of the vast burden of work thrown on

the British Government while attempting to organise the new Empire.

For the rest, there is another instance of the aggression of the City of London, which neither North nor the King would take very seriously (1207, 1208, 1227). There is rather an interesting incident in the Levant which seemed likely to bring about war with France, a danger which the King averted, for once, by timely display of force (1221, 1222, 1224, 1225, 1228, 1231). There is a long and interesting paper on the state of Saxony (977), which the King thought worth transcription in his own hand. The King's care of the Army and his resistance to abuse of the purchase system may be traced in his correspondence with Lord Barrington. His interest in the Navy may be followed in the account of the preparations for his visit to Portsmouth Dockyard (*see under* George III.), though he resolutely opposed increase of the half-pay of Naval Captains (1193, 1194).

To come to smaller matters, there is a long letter concerning the project of a new bridge at Richmond, which should be of interest to local antiquarians (1206). There is a letter from the Royal Academy setting forth its laws and regulations (1179), in which we may note that " no needle-work, artificial flowers, cut paper, shell-work models in coloured wax, or any such performances, shall be admitted into the exhibition ". There are two papers on the state of the stage in London (872, 873), which should make attractive reading to students of the history of the drama, and these are supplemented by a petition of Samuel Foote (1131). As regards the King's own artistic collections, there is a letter from Lord Cowper from Florence advising the despatch of miniature copies of the " famous Gallery of Painters " (1189) ; the King's pretty answer (1210) saying that " the very curious and well executed copies of the Painters' Portraits in the

Florentine Gallery are much enhanced by the very genteel epistle that accompanied them ", and Lord Cowper's final letter (1223) hinting that the ribbon of the Garter—or, failing the Garter, of the Thistle— would make him the happiest man in the world. Lastly, if any Private Secretary, past or present, of a Prime Minister would like to study the methods of a persistent peerage-hunter one hundred and fifty years ago, he might turn up the name of George Pitt in the index, and read his letters.

by the said Officers in Rank until, by Death or Promotion without Purchase, other Officers may succeed to bear the said Deduction in the Room of the Officers recommended in the above Succession.

I am, with great Respect, Your Lordship's Most obedient Humble Servant   TOWNSHEND.

No. 576—*Lord Hertford to the King.*

Lord Hertford presumes, and He hopes without taking an improper liberty to express by the earliest occasion their Majesties great goodness in the appointment of Lady Hertford to the Queen's Bedchamber ; He cannot though He has the happiness of such frequent access to the King express such sentiments at a publick Levee nor would It become Him to trouble his Majesty too often in the Closet ; This morning when He had the honor of seeing the King He was unacquainted with the honor done to his Wife ; Lord Hertford is as sensible as a warm and grateful heart can make him to all the King's favors and goodness to Him & will endeavour to testifie it in every instance within his power by a suitable conduct.

GROSVENOR SQUARE
Janry. 7th 1768.

No. 577—*The King to Lord Hertford.*

QUEEN'S HOUSE *Jan. 7th* 1768
$\frac{m}{50}$ p^t 9 P.M.

Lord Hertford's attention in expressing his thankfulness at the Appointment of Lady Hertford to the Vacancy in the Queen's Bedchamber is duely remarked by Me, & I am pleased whenever any thing agreable to him is feesible as his Attachment to my Person has been uninterrupted ; the unfashionable propriety of Lady Hertford's conduct makes Her very fit for Her Employment.

No. 578—*Monsieur de Deinton to the King.*

SIRE—Peut-être me flatte-je trop de la gracieuse bonté et de la haute bienveillance de Votre Majesté en me persuadent que mon sort bon ou facheur qu'il est ne Lui soit pas tout à fait indifferent. C'est ce qui me fait esperer que la nouvelle, de m'être fiancé avez une demoiselle de Bulow ne Lui sera pas désagréable, et que Votre Majesté daignera honerer de Sa haute approbation cette demarche aussi necessaire et interessante pour ma proprieté et pour ma satisfaction. C'est une demarche Sire qui a bien couté a mon cœur toujours attaché au souvenir de ma femme defunte. Celui-ci m'est encore si sensible que je n'ai pu arreter les larmes quand j'ai parlé à ma fiancé de la defunte, de ses qualités et vertus, et combien j'avais été heureux dans l'union avec elle. Quoiqu'il m'en coute je dois supprimer tant il est possible ces idées et ne penser maintenant que de vivre heureux dans le mariage que je veux contracter, ses sentiments de pieté et de vertu suivis et confirmés par une bonne education je dois me flatter moyennant la benédiction divine que si mon bonheur n'est pas tout à fait le même qu'il n'a été dans mon premier mariage, il lui approchera beaucoup. Tant Je puis protester que passant au dessu de toutes vues d'interets Je n'ai eu egard qu'aux qualites personnelles a une bonne famille a une bonne education et aux parents pieux et vertueux. Que cet avis que mon devoir m'oblige de donner a Votre Majesté me prouve [?] en même temps l'honneur de Lui renouveller les sentiments de respect et de veneration avec lesquels Je serai toute ma vie Sire De Votre Majesté Le très humble très obéissant et très soumis Serviteur

E. G. DE DEINTON.

A STRELITZ
ce 15 *Janv.* 1768.

No. 579—*The Duke of Grafton to the King.*

GROS^R SQUARE Jany 20th 1768

$\dfrac{m}{55}$ past 9. A.M.

The Duke of Grafton presumes to ask his Majesty's final Commands in regard to Lord Weymouth & Lord Hillsborough,

as also Mr Rigby having the Honor of kissing his Majesty's hand
to day, which General Conway has no Sort of Objection to whatever. If approved of by the King, the Duke of Grafton will take
Care to have them acquainted with His Majesty's Pleasure.

No. 580—*The King to the Duke of Grafton.*

QUEENS HOUSE *Jan* 20 1768.

$\dfrac{m}{38}$ *pt* 10. A.M.

The above Gentlemen to be acquainted that their attendance
is expected this Day.

*Draft, written at the foot of the Duke of Grafton's
letter of same date.*

No. 581—*The King to the Duke of Grafton.*

QUEENS HOUSE *Jan* 22^d 1768. $\dfrac{m}{5}$ *pt* 8. P.M.

DUKE OF GRAFTON—The enclosed is the draft to Ld. Chatham
on which I desire to have Your opinion & the suggestion of any
alterations that may occur to You.

I saw Sir G. Macartney who gave Me the same extraordinary
reason for declining he had done Yesterday to You, but on my
scouting the idea He owned having received a letter from Mon^r
Pannin to urge him to resign the Commission, as the Empress
had been so pressed by the Relations of the Maid of Honour that
She would give a public refusal of him if He did not take this
hint, that Chernichew Should instantly set out to shew the desire
of the Empress for one of like Rank being nominated to Her
Court ; I told him I thought him wrong in giving the idle reason
he had, when He could give so weighty a one, & ordered him to
hint the truth to You & to Ld. Weymouth, tho begging both of
You not to make this public as it would be opening an affair
that had better be obliterated.

Draft, endorsed by the King.

No. 582—*The Duke of Grafton to the King.*

GROS^R SQUARE *Jan*^y 23^d 1768
½ *past* 8. A.M.

The Duke of Grafton entreats humbly his Majesty's Pardon, that he has deferred answering till this morning the Commands his Majesty in so gracious a Manner had laid upon him ; but returning home too late last night from Supping out, was the Occasion of it.

The most condescending Goodness of his Majesty must inevitably confirm Lord Chatham in the Desire he has expressed by Lady Chathams Letter (which the Duke of Grafton presumes to enclose) of putting the Privy Seal into Commission. He can not avoid presuming to congratulate his Majesty of this happy Issue from a Business so intricate, that the Duke of Grafton despaired of a fortunate turn, & only saw the many & great ill Consequences likely to follow, & materially to affect his Majesty's Administration.

Endorsed by the King.

No. 583—*The King to Lord Chatham.*

LORD CHATHAM—The D. of Grafton communicated to Me the letter He proposed sending to You on the unreasonable anxiety of a Lord concerned in the Warmley Charter ; as I have always chose to make You acquainted with my sentiments in my own words, I think it necessary to pursue that method on this most unpleasant Affair ; I see the necessity of the Affair being brought to a hearing & if Your health is not as yet so much reastablished as to enable You to do it ; I wish You would whom You would

Draft, unfinished.

No. 584—*The King to Lord Chatham.*

Printed. Chatham Corres. III. 318.

QUEENS HOUSE *Jan 23rd* 1768.

LORD CHATHAM—The Duke of Grafton communicated to Me Yesterday the letter he proposed sending to You on the unreasonable anxiety of a Lord concerned in the Warmley Charter; I think it proper on this occasion briefly to mention this affair; I have in conjunction with the Chancellor & Duke of Grafton staved off their having You pressed on this Subject as long as possible knowing that You are apprized that nothing less than ruin will befall the Persons engaged in this Copper Work unless almost immediately possessed of the Charter, & thinking that would stimulate You to give them as speedy a hearing as Your health would permit; but as there is no measure of keeping them any longer at rest, I wish You would take such steps as have been not unusual to conclude this unpleasant business; I am thoroughly convinced of the utility You are of to my service for tho confined to Your house, Your Name has been sufficient to enable my Administration to proceed; I therefore in the most earnest manner call on You to continue in Your Employment; indeed my conduct towards You since Your entering into my service gives Me a double right to expect this of You as well what You owe Your Country, & those who entered into my Service in conjunction with You & in particular the two above mentioned Ministers.   GEORGE R.

Endorsed by the King.

No. 585—*Lord Chatham to the King.*

Printed. Chatham Corres. III. 319.

[In Lady Chatham's handwriting.]

Lord Chatham begs to Lay Himself with all Duty and Submission at the Kings Feet, and Most Humbly to intreat His Majesty in his great Benignity and Goodness to pardon His

Servant the presuming to employ Another's hand to express to His Majesty his Obedience and Submission to His Majesty's Most Gracious Command, extreme Weakness and Illness rendering it totally impossible for him to use his Pen. Understanding last night, by a Letter from the Duke of Grafton, Your Majesty's most Gracious Pleasure with regard to a disabled, and, as he feard Useless Servant, [he] acquainted his Grace with his Most humble Acquiescence to the Expedient propos'd under your Majesty's most Gracious Approbation.

He has only to implore that Your Majesty in Your great Compassion will deign to receive his most humble Assurances of Unfeigned Zeal for Your Majesty's Service.

HAYS *Jan*ry 23d 1768
½ *past* 3 P.M.

Endorsed by the King.

No. 586—*Lord Shelburne to the King.*

[*23 January*, 1768.]

Lord Shelburne presumes to acquaint Your Majesty, that Mesrs Mason, Lambert & Legres Manufacturers in Spital Fields have been just with him, to set forth what has lately passed between the Master & Men, and to desire that the Guards might have orders to march there this night, as they had receiv'd undoubted Intelligence that a very considerable body propos'd assembling between one & two o'clock in the morning with a determin'd resolution to proceed to very great Violences—These Gentlemen have been with Sir Robert Darling the next Justice of the Peace, who advis'd them to come to the Secretary of State, as he could not call in any Military aid, till a Riot was actually commenc'd, and they are apprehensive in this case Great Mischief may be done before it's arrival.

As Lord Shelburne has never seen these Gentlemen before, & does not know their names, and therefore finds it difficult to Judge how far their Intelligence is to be depended on, Lord Shelburne presumes to submit it to your Majesty, whether it will not be sufficient to write to Colo Amherst, who happens to command at the Tower, to signifye your Majesty's commands to him to inquire into the particulars, and to take the proper measures to secure the quiet of that part of the Town, and for the support of the civil authority, taking care to avoid all unnecessary alarm at the same time, with any other orders Your Majesty Judges proper.

Saturday ½ after 6 P.M.

Endorsed by the King, Jan. 23ʳᵈ 1768.

No. 587—*The King to Lord Shelburne.*

QUEENS HOUSE *Jan 23ᵈ* 1768.
$$\frac{m}{5}.\ p^t\ 7.\ \text{P.M.}$$

LORD SHELBURNE—I thoroughly approve of Your writing to Colonel Amherst the Commandant at the Tower, the account that has been laid before You concerning the Supposed intention of the Weavers to commit this Night some outrage against their Masters; as that is the best method of preventing mischief without spreading any Allarm.

Draft, endorsed by the King.

No. 588—*Lord North to the King.*

3g: This should be 1778 - The reply's #2184 iv. 33

Lord North has the honour of inclosing some extracts of great importance from letters written to Mʳ Wentworth from France.

Lord North imagines that the news of Lord Chatham's separation from the Opposition must have come to his Majesty's ears, He believes the report to be perfectly true, as Mr Fitzroy is said to have been told this piece of intelligence last night by the D. of Richmond. Although Lord Chatham's age & infirmities do not render him able to be of so much service, or disservice to any party as he could formerly have been, nevertheless his abandoning the party with that reputation that he has acquired, & with all the popularity of his name, will be a very material blow to them, & they will certainly feel it in the opinion of many persons who revere the name & sentiments of Ld Chatham.

DOWNING STREET. *Feb^y* 1. [1768].

No. 589—*The Duke of Grafton to the King.*

HOUSE OF LORDS *Feby* 4th 1768

$$\frac{m}{35} \text{ past 7. P.M.}$$

The Duke of Grafton presumes to acquaint his Majesty that the Motion for the commitment of the East India Dividend Bill has been carried by a Majority of 73 to 35.

No. 590—*The Duke of Grafton to the King.*

GROSVENOR SQUARE *Feby.* 5th 1768

$$\frac{m}{45} \text{ past 8 A.M.}$$

The Duke of Grafton humbly entreats his Majesty's Forgiveness, if in his hurry he forgot to transmit to his Majesty the List of the Speakers, who were.

Lord Hardwicke	C
Lord Marchmont—	P
Lord Dartmouth	C
Lord Bathurst—	P
Lord Shelburne—	P
Duke of Richmond	C
Lord Hillsborough—	P
Lord Lyttleton—	C
L. Botetourt—	P
Duke of Grafton	P
Lord Temple—	C
Lord Weymouth—	C but in the most friendly manner.

The Duke of Grafton presumes to ask his Majesty's Pleasure, whether he may acquaint General Howard of his Majesty's gracious intentions of giving the Government of Chelsea to his Care.

No. 591—*The King to the Duke of Grafton.*

QUEENS HOUSE *Feb^y* 6*th* 1768 8 $\frac{m}{}$ *p^t* 8 A.M.

DUKE OF GRAFTON—I am desirous of knowing whether at the Meeting last Night any Opinion was formed to be submitted to Me of what seems most expedient to be done, on the most extraordinary state of the Irish House of Commons; if that be the case I will return earlier than usual from the Country to receive Lord Shelburne's Report, that the Messenger may be dispatched as soon as possible.

Draft.

No. 592—*The Duke of Grafton to the King.*

GROSVENOR SQUARE *Feb^y* 6*th*

1768 $\frac{m}{55}$ *pst* 8 A.M.

The Duke of Grafton in obedience to his Majesty's Commands, has the Honor to acquaint the King, that the different Lords of the Cabinet were of Opinion that before Monday Evening it would be dangerous to come to any Resolution, which, till then could not be duly considered on so delicate a Situation. They agreed solely to submit their Approbation of the intended temporary Alteration of the Garrisons of Gibraltar & Minorca for his Majesty's Decision, meaning also to meet on thursday next on the Affairs of Canada.

No. 593—*Lord North to the King.* 25 Feb 1769

[? *February,* 1768.]

Lord North has the honour of informing his Majesty that the Alteration proposed in the Nullum Tempus Bill was lost yesterday evening by 81 votes.

The Ayes were 124.
The Noes —— 205.

Speakers for the Amendment. The Attorney Genl The Sol^r Genl Mr Hussey, Sr George Maccartney & Mr Dyson. **Against** the Amendment. Mr Yorke, Mr Wedderburn, Mr Grenville, Mr Thos Townshend & Mr Burke.

No. 594—*The King to Lord North.*

Printed.   Donne I. 1.

LORD NORTH—Nothing can be more honourable for Administration than the Division this day, when not expected, and Mr Dowdeswell will not get great credit for so very weak a manœuvre.

QUEEN'S HOUSE
Feby 28th 1768.

$\frac{m}{2}$. p^t 9 A.M.

No. 595—*Lord North to the King.*

Lord North has the honour of informing his Majesty that after the report from the Secret Committee had been read today & order'd to be printed, Mr Hussey made a motion for an order to the Select Committee to enter immediately into an enquiry into the Conduct of the Directors concerning the declaration of the Dividend during the two last years, which, after some debate, he was persuaded to withdraw.

DOWNING STREET *Mar.* 9 [?] [1768] 7 *o'clock.*

No. 596—*The King to Lord Shelburne.*

QUEEN'S HOUSE *March* 13th 1768.
$\frac{m}{-}$ *past* 8. P.M.

LORD SHELBURNE—That You may with the greater precision explain my ideas to Lord Townshend on the Plan of Augmenting the Forces in Ireland I have now committed to paper the alterations I named to You this Day.

1. The Pay for the intended Establishment to take place from the 25th of this month at latest.

2. The Execution of this Plan not be begun till the 1st of December, which will enable money enough to be accumulated

to answer the expenses of Levy Money, Extra Cloathing & Arms.

3. Twenty two Regiments of Infantry to remain in Ireland furnishing a Detachment of Four Companies for the Isle of Mann.

4. & consequently Ireland to pay only five Regiments in Foreign Stations.

Draft.

No. 597—*Lord Hillsborough to the King.*

WHITEHALL *March* 27th 1768—

SIR—I have the honour to send for your Majesty's Perusal the Draughts of my Dispatch to General Gage, which I have endeavoured to prepare in such a manner as to answer your Majesty's Intention. But as this letter is of consequence, & the Draught to be sent in circulation before it goes to the General, I humbly presume to request your Majesty would be pleased to observe such parts as Your Majesty judges proper to have corrected or amended. I have the Honour also to send copies of the Minute and of the proposal laid before your Majesty, in case Your Majesty should wish to have recourse to them.

I have the honour to be with the most Entire Respect Sir Your Majesty's Most Dutyfull Subject & Most Obedient Servant

HILLSBOROUGH.

Endorsed by the King.

No. 598—*The King to Lord Hillsborough.*

QUEENS HOUSE *March* 27th 1768.

$\frac{m}{30} p^t$ 10. A.M.

LORD HILLSBOROUGH—I have perused with the utmost attention Your Draught to Major General Gage, as well as Circular to the American Governors, they both thoroughly meet with my Approbation; at the same time I cannot omit expressing the pleasure I feel at the ability with which You have restored the original opinion of the Majority at the Meeting without greatly deviating from the words of the Minute. The method that occurs to Me as best suited for Your obtaining the concurrence of the Majority in the mode You have digested this most weighty business, is the sending the above mentioned Draughts to each Individual that composed the meeting accompanied with a few lines desiring their opinions on the receipt of which You will transmit them to Me for my final Directions.

Draft, endorsed by the King.

No. 599—*Lord Barrington to the King.*

WAR OFFICE *March* 28*th* 1768.

A very great and riotous Mob having gone this morning to Brentford, it is not unreasonable to suppose they may attempt to do more mischief at their return : I have therefore given a hint to L. Colonel Hollingsworth who is the Officer on Guard to be alert ; and I have desired Lords Gower & Weymouth (who call'd on me, the same Idea having struck them) to take the proper measures for having a Civil Magistrate in the way this Evening. There is no sort of Intelligence to create the least suspicion of any form'd design but the mob if not prevented often does mischief which it did not intend.

I humbly hope your Majesty will not disapprove my Caution and will pardon my presumption in acquainting you with what I have done.   BARRINGTON.

L. General Hudson being the field Officer in waiting, I thought it best to speak to the Captain on Guard.

Since writing this I have seen Gen¹ Harvey who will have an Eye to what passes this Evening.

No. 600—*The King to Lord Barrington.*

QUEENS HOUSE *March* 28*th* 1768.
$$\frac{m}{35} p^t 5. \text{ P.M.}$$

LORD BARRINGTON—Nothing can more deserve my approbation than the prudential steps You have taken least the Mob should be inclined on their return from Brentford this Evening to commit any Outrages. I shall not stirr from home so that You may come or send to Me if any [thing] arises that requires my immediate Directions.

Draft.

No. 601—*The King to Lord Barrington.*

QUEENS HOUSE *March* 29th 1768.

$\frac{m}{37}$ *past Nine* A.M.

LORD BARRINGTON—Considering the Riotous conduct of the Populace last Night, it becomes the more highly necessary that every precaution be used that the Military be ready this Evening to keep the Peace if the Civil Magistrate should call for their Aid;

Draft.

No. 602—*Lord Barrington to the King.*

TUESDAY 29 *March* 1768 *past one.*

I was honour'd by your Majesty's most gracious Note of yesterday, and afterwards by another dated this morning which I recd. just as I was going to Lord Weymouth. I have seen him, & afterwards went to the War Office, to which I shall again return by two o'Clock. I hope to have settled every thing there time enough to attend your Majesty for your Commands at the Queen's house, soon after three. If I am kept longer I will not presume to trouble your Majesty there, but will write an Account of what is settled. Your Majesty may be assured that proper and sufficient military assistance will not be wanting, nor was it wanting yesterday. BARRINGTON.

No. 603—*Lord Barrington to the King.*

TUESDAY 29th *March* [1768] *near four oClock.*

Care has been taken that the Battⁿ in the Savoy shall be in readyness to answer any requisitions made by the Civil Magistrates in that part of the Metropolis. The Tower will furnish assistance to my Lord Mayor if he wants it. General Hudson will get as many of the Guards as he can together, I mean of those who are in quarters.

Colonel Mathews a very good Officer is on guard to day : I have seen him, & he will keep a very good look out.

I am my self persuaded that a very small force will if properly directed keep the peace ; but as no precaution should be omitted, I have desired Colonel Morison to draw up a proper Plan for bringing the Troops within three score miles, nearer to the Capital.

I have wrote a private Letter to Lord Cadogan to see that the Horse Guards and Grenadier Guards are ready in case they should be wanted. I apprehend the Gold Stick is the proper Channel.

I have fully appris'd Lord Weymouth of every thing I have done, & acquainted him where Military Aid may be had at a moments notice.

My greatest ambition is that your Majesty should approve my conduct, and if you are pleased to lay on me any Commands this Evening, I shall be ready to receive them at home. To morrow I shall not fail paying my duty to your Majesty at St James.

BARRINGTON.

No. 604—Mr. Powell to (?)

[? *March*, 1768.]
THURSDAY *pass* 4 *Clo.*

D^R SIR—That I might be perfect in my Acco^t I have been myself at Guildhall & attended the Casting up of the Poll, & the Numbers are as under. I saw M^r W—— go away with Sheriff & was told that He was taken into Custody, how or on what Account, or for the certainty I cannot Answer—I am happy in my ffriend Sr R. Ladbroke's Success, & am with great Respect Dr Sir, Your very obed^t Ser^v W. POWELL.

	Ladb	Harley	Beckf^d	Trecot^k	Glynn	Paterson	Wilks
1st day	81 –	64 –	59 –	60 –	57 –	59 –	29
2 –	563 –	562 –	449 –	446 –	429 –	304 –	143
Total	644 –	626 –	508 –	506 –	486 –	363 –	172

No. 605—*The Duke of Grafton to the King.*

GROSVENOR SQUARE. *March* 31st 1768

$\frac{m}{45}$ *past* 9 A.M.

The Duke of Grafton was on the Point of sending An Account of what has passed at the Meeting last Night to His Majesty, when he was honor'd with his Majesty's Commands. On the whole it was thought advisable to postpone the issuing the Proclamation, which, at this time, would only appear as finding fault only with the People for their Joy too riotously testifyed at the late Election, & in that consideration might committ rather than give weight to the Ministers of Government. Every Step of Precaution for the last Night's Security of the Town, as well as for the future was also directed to the Civil Magistrate, as also planned for the Military.

The Duke of Grafton presumes also to acquaint his Majesty that the Lord President & Lord Weymouth have agreed with him on the Necessity of summoning the Chancellor, Lord North &c & have fixed on tomorrow sen'night for their Meeting in London.

No. 606—*Lord Weymouth to the King.*

[? *April*, 1768.]

Having yesterday taken such precautions as I thought necessary on the first appearance of that riotous disposition of the People which has so unfortunately shewn itself, I wish'd to wait on Your Majesty this morning to lay before you the steps I had taken, & what happen'd last night as far as it has come to my knowledge, But Your Majesty being gone early to Richmond I was prevented. I shou'd be glad to have the honor of waiting on Your Majesty for a moment on your return, & I hope your Majesty will approve the utmost precaution & vigilance on this occasion, at the same time of giving as little suspicion of being alarm'd as possible, for tho' there may be but little danger of further disturbance, it is well to be quietly and cautiously prepared for the worst.   WEYMOUTH.

$\dfrac{m}{50}$ *past one.*

No. 607—*The King to the Duke of Grafton.*

QUEENS HOUSE *April* 9*th* 1768. $\dfrac{m}{5}$. p^t 5. P.M.

DUKE OF GRAFTON—The confidence I alone place in You makes it highly proper before You go to the Meeting of my principal Ministers this Evening, that You should be apprized of what has suggested itself to my mind on maturely reflecting upon this strange Affair. I am of opinion that those conversant in the Law must first declare what can legally be done, that once ascertained, I encline much to following that with vigour that Licentiousness may be curbed ; & a General Resolution to this effect is all I wish to be come to this Evening, the mode of effecting this to be defered for another meeting on Monday or Tuesday next ; if it should afterwards appear necessary, that Additional Troops be brought to the Capital. that can easily be affected & I have already taken some steps on that head that cannot spread allarm I am averse to making any show of Troops in the Streets on the Day of Opening the Term, for that naturally would draw a Concourse of People together but the Battaillon in Barracks at the Savoy may be kept there in readiness to be called upon at a minutes warning ; the same precaution may be had with regard to the Horse & Grenadier Guards without any noise whatever else occurs to Me I will mention when we meet to-morrow.

Draft.

No. 608—*Lord Hillsborough to the King.*

SIRE—I will certainly see the Duke of Grafton, & endeavour to get the Dispatch put into such a Shape as may answer your Majesty's Intentions, and at the same time satisfie His Grace. I can clearly perceive whence this trouble comes, & if I might shew your Majesty's Notes to the Duke probably I should succeed better, but this I shall not presume to do without your Majesty's permission. I shall ever be unable to express the High Sense I have of the great Goodness your Majesty condescends to shew to Sir Your Majesty's Most Dutyfull Subject & Most Humble & Obedient Servant   HILLSBOROUGH.

HANOVER SQUARE
10th *April* 1768—
    8. P.M—

Endorsed by the King.

No. 609—*The King to the Duke of Grafton.*

QUEENS HOUSE *April* 16th 1768.

$$\frac{m}{58} \text{ past } 9 \text{ A.M.}$$

DUKE OF GRAFTON—I return to You Mr Dyson's Paper which appears to Me drawn up with great knowledge of the proceedings of the House of Commons, & an uncommon precision in conveying the most efficacious as well as most proper mode of effecting the Expulsion.

Draft.

No. 610—*Orders for the Troops.*

The Tower, Savoy, and Tiltyard Guard will Supply Troops on the Requisition of the Civil Magistrates.

{ The Requisition from The Tower, must be made To
    Mr Rainsford, The Deputy Lieutenant.

{ From The Savoy, to Captain Goat of The First
    Regiment of Guards, or Officer who may Relieve
    him.

{ From The Tiltyard Guard, To The Commanding
    Officer.

A Party of 24 Horse Guards and 12 Grenadier Guards are also Ready to turn out Immediately.

{ The Requisition to be made To The Captain Com-
    manding att the Horse Guards.

If any more Troops are Wanted than what The Tower, Savoy, Tiltyard Guard, and Horse Guards can Supply—On application to the Secretary att War (att the War Office) Immediate orders will be Issued for that Purpose.

> An Orderly from The Gold Stick, and one from The Field Officer in Staff-waiting, are Attending att the War Office, in order to Convey any Orders (which may be Issued) with Immediate Dispatch.

20*th* *April* 1768.

No. 611—*Memorandum as to recruiting in Ireland.*

[? *April*, 1768.]

Directions to The Lord Lieutenant of Ireland, That The Greatest Diligance is to be Exerted, in order to Compleat The Corps which are on That Establishment, But att the Same time, All attention to be Given, That none but Proper Recruits are Inlisted, and That No man is to be Taken for The Regiments of Infantry, who is under Five Feet Six Inches & a Half High, Supposing That He is arrived att his full Growth.

Youths, who may not be of That Size (If not come to their full Growth) to be Inlisted, if They are well made, & Likely to Grow to it.

Orders to be Given to The Recruiting Officers, That They Most Strictly Observe The Regulation, as to not Exceeding One Guinea and a Half, as Bounty Money to Each Recruit, and That Whoever may Exceed it, will be Under His Majesty's Displeasure.

No. 612—*The Duke of Grafton to the King.*

GROSVENOR SQUARE *April* 22*d* 1768.

The Duke of Grafton presumes to acquaint His Majesty that Lord North & Lt. General Conway were desired to communicate to the Privy Counsellors & Men of Business in the House of

Commons the Desire of his Majesty's principal Servants jointly expressed that Mr Wilkes should not be allowed to sit in Parliament if it could be avoided by any Means justifiable by Law & the Constitution & conformable to the Proceedings of Parliament. There were doubts on the Expulsion since the Verdict was likely to be reversed ; but no difficulty to proceed to it, if to be defended by the Rules of the House.

No. 613—*The King to Lord North.*

Printed.   Donne I. 2.

QUEENS HOUSE *April* 25th 1768.

LORD NORTH—Tho entirely confiding in Your Attachment to my Person, as well as in Your hatred of every Lawless Proceeding yet I think it highly proper to apprize You that the Expulsion of Mr Wilkes appears to be very essential & must be effected ; & that I make no doubt when you lay this affair with Your usual precision before the meeting of the Gentlemen of the House of Commons this Evening, it will meet with the required Unanimity & vigour. The case of Mr Ward in the Reign of my Great Grand Father seems to point out the best method of proceeding on this occasion, as it will equally answer whether the Court should by that time have given Sentence ; or should he be attempting to obtain a Writ of Error. If there is any Man capable of forgetting his criminal Writings, I think his Speech in the Court of King's Bench on Wednesday last reason enough for to go as far as possible to expell him ; for he declared number 45 a paper that the Author ought to *glory in*, & the Blasphemous Poem, a mere *Ludicrous production*, but I will detain You no longer on this Subject ; & desire You will send Me word when the Meeting is over, the Result of what has passed, & also how soon You mean to dispatch a Messenger with an account of it to the Duke of Grafton as I will by the same Person send a letter to him.   GEORGE R.

No. 614—*The Duke of Grafton to the King.*

Gros^R Square *April* 25th 1768

$\frac{m}{30}$ *past* 6. P.M.

The Duke of Grafton humbly begs leave to assure his Majesty that nothing should have stopped his sending to his Majesty any authentic Account he had received from Westminster Hall. Mr Francis who is Mr Nuthall's Assistant, writes word that Mr Wilkes is gone to dine at Sr Joseph Mawbey's which being in Surrey will for a time, till they can get a Surrey Capias, prevent the present one from taking Effect. He adds that the Court would take no Cognizance of Mr W. till brought by the Process of the Court before them. This, the Duke of Grafton humbly presumes to think, will add but small Delay.

A Messenger will be immediately dispatched to Lt Gen: Conway with the Notice of the Meeting being put off till friday night, when the Duke of Grafton is confident of seeing him.

No. 615—*Lord Camden to the King.*

Sir—Upon my return home last night at Ten o'Clock from Lincoln's Inn I found Your Majesty's letter upon my Table & beg leave to return Your Majesty my most Humble Thanks for that goodness I have so often Experienced of Your Majesty's indulgence to my weekly excursions into the Country, assuring Your Majesty at the same time that neither that nor any other enjoyment shall ever detain me a moment when Your Majesty's service or Your Commands shall require my attendance elsewhere.

I have the Honour perfectly to agree with Your Majesty that the first meeting of the Next Parl^t ought to Pass in the same Manner that the first Session did in the year 1754, And as no such business is to be done wch requires a Speech from the Throne to introduce it, I sh^d think Your Majesty's Personal appearance unnecessary.

I did intend, S^r, upon this Idea to have taken Your Majesty's Pleasure for a Commission to open the Parl^t, But since I find by a letter from Ld Shelburne that a Notice is to be inserted to Night

in the Gazette of such a Commission, & that He & others of
Your Majesty's Principal Serv^{ts} are of the same Opinion for a
Commission, I have ordered it to be made out Forthwith.

Give me Leave, S^r to Subscribe myself with the most
Unfeigned Zeal & Loyalty Your Majesty's most Dutifull Devoted
& Obliged Subject.   CAMDEN.

> Ap^t 30. 1768.
> LINCOLN'S INN FIELDS.

Endorsed by the King.

No. 616—*Lord Weymouth to the King.*

S^T JAMES'S *May* 6th 1768.
3 *o'clock* P.M.

A Considerable number of Seamen assembled last night &
obliged most of the Ships in the River to strike their Yards and
top-masts, & said they wou'd allow no ship to sail till their
wages were raised, they came this day at two o'Clock thro'
Great George Street towards the Queen's House, finding the King
at Richmond they proposed going there ; & one who has a flag
mounted on the Rails before the Queen's House & hollowed out
for Richmond, they cry for Redress & seem to disclaim Wilkes,
however as Wilkes's affair is now before the King's Bench, there
are several of the Mob there. I sent directly to the Civil
Magistrates, & shall do every thing in my power to keep them
quiet. I hope they may not go on to Richmond 'till the
Magistrates come, but I thought proper to give your Majesty
this notice to prevent surprise. Justice Welch is Just come, &
I have sent to the War Office & to General Harvey.

Endorsed by the King.

No. 617—*Lord Weymouth to the King.*

May 9th 1768.

Upon receiving the enclosed I have written to Mr Ponton to
know his opinion with regard to an additional military force & the
proper manner of stationing them, in order to prevent immediate
mischief from these alarming circumstances. I have likewise

sent copies of the enclosed letter to the Chancellor the Duke of Grafton & Ld Shelburne to know their opinions if any thing further can be immediately done, of which note I send your Majesty an enclosed Copy. I really dread the consequence of these frequent alarms, but nothing shall be wanting on my part to prevent mischief if possible.

Endorsed by the King.

No. 618—*The Duke of Grafton to the King.*

GROSVENOR SQUARE *May* 12th

1768 $\frac{m}{33}$ *past* 6 P.M.

The Duke of Grafton has the Honor to acquaint his Majesty that the Duke of Northumberland moved an Address to his Majesty of thanks as also of assurance of Support in suppressing the Riots. He can not presume to mention for certain whether any Motion will be made farther than what is intended by a Mr Cavendish, who is to move that Mr Wilkes be brought to the Bar.

The Duke of Grafton continues bad with the head Ache, but this shall not prevent his paying his Duty tonight to his Majesty.

Endorsed by the King.

No. 619—*The Duke of Grafton to the King.*

GROSVENOR SQUARE *May* 13th

$\frac{m}{5}$ *past* 7 P.M.

The Duke of Grafton presumes to send inclosed the Letter he received from the Lord Chancellor from the House of Lords.

Lord Chamberlain shall be also acquainted that his Majesty has commanded the Duke of Grafton to say that the King would receive the Address at one tomorrow.

The Duke of Grafton humbly presumes to add that he shall think it his Duty to give his Majesty the earliest Information if any thing should prevent the King from fulfilling his most gracious Intentions.

Endorsed by the King.

No. 620—*Mr. Wood to the King.*

May 14*th* 1768.
10'*o Clock* P.M.

After a great deal of private negociation to day, not worth troubly your Majesty with now, I am informed that the Seamen are come to their senses ; they have order'd papers to be stuck up about White-Chapel & Wapping to acquaint their brother sailors that they are satisfied & ready to return to their business, & to advise them to do the same ; I cou'd not delay one moment giving your Majesty this agreable account.

Endorsed by the King.

No. 621—*Mr. Cressener to Lord Bute.*

MY LORD—According to my promise I have sent Your Lordship by the Duchess of Northumberland the Reductions and Incorporations made in the French Troops from the Peace to the 10th August 1764, I hope this work will be compleated in a few Months, and that I shall then be able to present Your Lordship with the List of the French and of their Allies imployed in the Siege of Minorca, in the Empire &c^t during the last war, in the mean time I have the honor to communicate to Your Lordship, l'Etat actuel des affaires generales concernant les finances du Roiaume de France et le detail general et specifique sur toutes les parties des finances du Roiaume de France, avec des observations politiques et interessantes tant sur la multiplicite onereuse des impots que de l'administration, et de la regie des dites finances : by this work it appears France contracted a debt of 1,306,236,236, livres from 1755 to the end of 1762, not including that they owe for the forage provisions, horses, carts &c^t furnished their Troops by the several Electors, Princes, and States of the Empire during all the last War, what was owing to the Kings Household, and to the several Contractors, the great anticipation of the revenus on many Provinces, the Plate carried into the Mint, and many other things. I flatter myself this will not be disagreable to Your Lordship, if You should have already seen it, it will at least prove my desire of making my Court, and of proving my gratitude.

I should be altogether unworthy of the protection you honored me with if I omitted profiting of this occasion to most humbly represent to Your Lordship how much it's the interest of the Maritime Powers and of the Elector of Hanover to gain the Friendship of the Elector of Cologne and to unite Him more closely to them to secure for his Successor such an Archbishop of Cologne and Bishop of Munster as may be agreable to those Powers, all that is required from Great Britain for this service amounts to no more than £15000, Ster. to be paid in three years, say £5000 a year, in the first 18 months the Ministry will be able to judge if this Money is well employed, and if the Effect answers their expectation, for the greatest part is to be distributed amongst the Prebends of the two Chapters, sure My Lord this is a very trifle if compared with the Advantage that will result from it.

the Courts of Vienna and Dresden spare nothing to gain those Chapters, and to fix them in the Interest of the Princes of the House of Saxony who are in the Church its impossible for me and the Dutch Minister to oppose with any hopes of success good words against such Offers as they make the Elector as well as the Canons of the two Chapters, I presume to mention this Affair to Your Lordship that I may not reproach myself here-after for having neglected any thing that might tend to frustrate the Enemys Scheme, or be of use to His Majesty. I beg the continuance of Your Lordships Bienveillance and that you'd be persuaded no One can be with higher Respect and Truth than.

My Lord. Your Lordships Most Faithfull most Devoted and most Humble Servant.   G. CRESSENER.

BONN 15 *May*
1768.

No. 622—*Lord Hertford to the King.*

Lord Hertford presumes to inform his Majesty that not having been able to prevail upon any other Dutchess or Marchioness to attend the funeral since the Dutchess of Grafton has declined it : He hopes his Majesty will approve his having taken the only method He could of supplying the vacancy in the numbers wanted by engaging Lady Harrington to be one of the Assistants in the place of the highest of that Rank who with his Majesty's approbation will become one of the Supporters to the chief Mourner which honor will now from her Rank if his Majesty has no objection devolve upon the Dutchess of Manchester; Lord Hertford has done every thing in his power to contribute to the Solemnity & dignity of the ceremony & is most concerned to have such frequent occasion to trouble his Majesty upon the difficulties which have occurred.

Lord Hertford has the honor of acquainting his Majesty that he has received a letter from Sr Charles Cottrell desiring Him to inform his Majesty that the Prince of Monaco will acknowledge it as a particular favor if his Majesty will permit Him to take leave of his Majesty on Wensday next as He is obliged to return to Paris.

GROSVENOR STREET
May 21st 1768.

No. 623—*The Duke of Grafton to the King.*

The Duke of Grafton not having an Opportunity this morning at St James's to ask his Majesty's Permission to profit of a few Days holy day by going on tuesday down to Wakefield Lodge; humbly presumes to hope that his Majesty will be graciously pleased to allow him to do it in this manner.

The Duke of Grafton would not desire to profit of these holy days, if he was not within reach of being called up at Six hours Distance, in case any Circumstance should turn out likely to disturb that Quiet State to which every thing promises fair to be returning.

The Duke of Grafton humble begs leave to add that he hopes he did not exceeding his Majesty's Commands, in assuring the Chancellor of the Exchequer that the King would have his Lordship express to the House in his Majesty's Name, the Desire of the Adjournment.

GROSV'NOR SQUARE *May* 22^d 1768.

$\frac{m}{35}$ *past* 2 P.M.

Endorsed by the King.

No. 624—*Lord Shelburne to the King.*

[*May,* 1768 ?]

Ld Shelburne presumes to trouble your Majesty with a Letter he has just receiv'd from Sir George Young, and to submit to your Majesty Whether I should signify to Lord Barrington Your Majesty's Pleasure, that some Troops should march immediately, and be quarter'd in the Towns recommended by Sir George Young.

WHITEHALL 4 *o'clock.*

No. 625—*The King to Lord Shelburne.*

[? *May,* 1768.]

LD. SHELBURNE—Y. must instantly acquaint the Secretary at War of ye disturbances in ye West y^t troops may be drawn from some other place to be quarter'd in y^e Towns propos'd by Sir G. Young ; there are in reality so few troops now in the Country y^t there is constantly a degree of difficulty in providing Troops on y^e daily calls Y^e Civil Magistrates are obliged to make for y^m in these very licentious days.

$\dfrac{m}{20}$ *pt.* 8 P.M.

Draft written on page of Lord Shelburne's preceding letter.

No. 626—*The Duke of Grafton to the King.*

GROSVENOR SQUARE *June* 10th 1768

$\dfrac{m}{55}$ *past* 8 A.M.

The Duke of Grafton presumes to acquaint his Majesty that the Lord Chancellor had last night as little Weight with Mr Townshend, as he had himself before. This occasions the Duke of Grafton humbly to submit to his Majesty's Consideration whether the different Reports, spread in the World on this Subject to shew that the Administration can be made to deviate on M^r

Townshend's Account from their Plan formed, can be so effectualey stopped as by Mr Rigby's having the Honor of kissing the King's hand to Day.

The Duke of Grafton will lose no Time in sounding Lord Clare's Sentiments & report them to his Majesty.

Endorsed by the King.

No. 627—*The Duke of Grafton to the King.*

GROSVENOR SQUARE *June* 11th 1768.

The Duke of Grafton humbly begs leave to acquaint his Majesty that Mr Rigby's Appointment may not get thro' the Offices in time for the next Month's Issue of Subsistence to the Forces, if it was to wait till Wednesday next; he has on that Account presumed to trouble his Majesty with it in this Manner.

Endorsed by the King.

No. 628—*The King to Lord Shelburne.*

RICHMOND LODGE *June* 17th 1768.

$$\frac{m}{45}. \ p^t \ 5. \ \text{P.M.}$$

LORD SHELBURNE—In consequence of Your request, I have heard the Duke of Grafton's objections to the appointing Lord Tankerville Envoy Extraordinary to the Court of Sardinia, which arise from thinking him too young for such a Commission; as You both differ so widely on this occasion & as at this conjuncture the pitching on a proper Successor to Mr Pitt is most material, I desire You will seperately talk the affair over with those usualy consulted on State Affairs previous to my coming to any decision.

Draft, endorsed by the King.

A second draft, unfinished.

No. 629—*The King to Lord Weymouth.*

RICHMOND LODGE *June* 18*th* 1768.

$\frac{m}{-}p^t.$

LORD WEYMOUTH—I have just received an Account from Mr Wood of the Sentence pronounced this day against Mr Wilkes, for which instance of his attention You will acquaint him with my Approbation.

Draft.

No. 630—[? *Mr. Wood to the King.*]

Wilkes was brought into Court quietly about Eight, the Court sat a Quarter before Nine ; Mr Justice Yates proceeded immediately to give Judgement, & having observed very fully & ably on the Nature of both Offences, viz. the North Britton, & the Essay on Woman, he pronounced Judgement on the first, £500. Fine ; & Ten Months Imprisonment ; & on the Second £500. Fine, & Twelve Months Imprisonment ; Upon the whole £1000. Fine, & Twenty Two Months Imprisonment. Mr Wilkes to give Security for his good Behaviour for Seven Years ; He is himself to be that Security as far as £1000. & to get Two Others to be Security for £500. each.—After this Wilkes pray'd for a Writ of Error, the Court referr'd him to the Attorney General, who said He would grant it upon his Application. He was reconducted to Prison, & by a little Management Things went off quietly, notwithstanding great Pains taken by His Friends to stir up & prepare the Mob for the Event of this Morning.

The Attorney General tells Mr Wood that Wilkes's Behaviour was more indecent than upon former Days ; He affected Ease & Indifference by picking His Teeth & talking to those near him while Mr Justice Yates was animadverting upon the Nature of His Crimes ; The Reason of the Ten Months Imprisonment for one of the Offences is because he has been Two Months in Prison already.—The Attorney General says that the Writ of Error will be granted this Day, but any Attempt for Bail will be ineffectual.

S^T JAMES'S

June 18*th* 1768. $\frac{m}{30}$. P.M.

No. 631—*Lord Hertford to the King.*

The Sardinian Minister having informed Lord Hertford that He had notified to the King the death of a Daughter of the Duke of Savoy, Lord Hertford presumes to submit it to his Majesty's choice whether He may not incline to have the mourning for that Princess worn at the same time with that ordered by his Majesty for the next week for her late Roial Highness the Princess Louisa in which case It may be necessary to have it inserted in the Gazette tomorrow : Lord Hertford did not hear it till this morning nor would He presume to trouble the King upon such an occasion at Richmond if He did not imagine It might be his Majesty's choice to shorten the mournings under such circumstances. Lord Hertford does not find in the office books any mournings which have been worn for a Grandaughter of the King of Sardinia, but in 1736, the Court went into the slightest mourning for an Infant & for a Princess of Portugal, which if his Majesty thinks sufficient precedents, The mourning ordered for the next week will be the same for both occasions & an advertisement in the Gazette expressing his Majesty's pleasure will be all that is necessary.

GROSVENOR STREET
Friday night, June 24th 1768.

No. 632—*Mr. Wood to the King.*

[9 *July*, 1768.]

The tryal of the Coal Heavers took up so much of this day that Justice Gillams tryal is put off till Monday ; Sir Henery Gould is to stay in town on this account & Mr Atty General has sent a letter by express, to open the Commission at York by Serjeant Aspinall ; Sr Richard Acton has also agreed to stay, & the Judges have sent to Lord Chief Justice Darker to beg the favour of his assistance on Monday. James Murphy & James Duggan, two Coal Heavers have been condemned, this day, to dye.——

$\frac{m}{30}$ *past* Eight.

Endorsed by the King, Mr Wood, July 9th, 1768.

No. 633—*Certificate.*

LONDON.

This is to Certify that Isebrand Vandermeer of Swart Waol in Holland late Master of the two Brothers Anthony and Cornelius came before me this Day and made Oath that he this Deponent was the only person who gave intelligence on the first of May 1747 to the late Lord Anson of the French Fleet Sailing out of the River Charante And this Deponent also upon his Oath further says that the Ship Tygor the next day was the Ship to whom he this Deponent gave the second information to And this Deponent further says he delivered a petition to the late Lord Anson in his Life time and also a Copy of his Journall in Dutch and another in English And this Deponent upon his Oath says that he was the only person that gave the Information aforesaid whereby the whole French Fleet Consisting of Seven Men of Warr and 30 Merchantman was taken and Destroyed And this Deponent further says he has never been able to shew himself on the Coast of France since this Deponents Name and person being fully Described in every public place and Town on the French Coast for the apprehending him for the above facts.

SWORN at the
Mansion House the
tenth day of JULY 1768— ⎱ ISEBRAND VAN DER MEER
Before me

THOMAS HARLEY
Mayor.

No. 634—*Mr. Wood to the King.*

[11 *July*, 1768.]

The Messenger has not been able to get at the Solicitor of the Treasury, at the old Baily, in order to have his account of Justice Gillam's tryal, but it appears that he has been honourably acquitted ; many of Mr Wilkes's friends were present & much disappointed ; one Derbyshire a bookseller swore that Mr Gillam told him he had orders from Government to kill a number of the Rioters, this Evidence being contradicted, & Mr Gillam acquitted, he demanded a Copy of his Indictment; this was strongly opposed by Serjeant Glynn, & as strenuously supported by Sr Fletcher Norton; the Judges agreed to grant it, Sr Henery Gould alone dissenting; this will probably discover those who were concern'd in the prosecution.

Endorsed by the King, July 11th, 1768.

No. 635.

15 *July* 1768.

An Arrangement of Apartments and Rooms at St. James's &c for the King of Denmark and His Majesty's Suite

The Prince of Wales's Apartments 5 Rooms and a Closet for The King

	No. of Rooms.	Numbered.	No. of Beds.	No. of Persons.	Rank of Person.
North East End of the Prince of Wales's Apartment & Council Chamber	2	....	1.	1.	A
Room going out of the Council Chamber	1	....	1.	1.	D.
Little Passage Room for the Baron Diede Occasionally					
Rooms leading to the Gallery	2	....	1.	1.	B.
Dr. Gisborne's Bed Chamber and Closet at the Back of The King's Bed	2	....	1.	1.	B.
Do. A Bed Chamber & Dressing Room up Another pair of Stairs......	2	....	1.	1.	B.
3 Garrets of Dr. Gisborne's for the Necessary Woman					
1 Garret of Dr. Gisborne's for a Valet	1	....	1.	1.	D.
Dr. Gisborne's Little Parlour & Grand Parlour ...	2	....	1.	1.	A.
The Necessary Woman's Large Room for a Dining Room.					

	No. of Rooms.	Numbered.	No. of Beds.	No. of Persons.	Rank of Person.
Dr. Gisborne's Kitchen for a Coffee Room					
Necessary Woman's 3 other Rooms................	3.	....	3.	3.	C.
Garret over The Prince of Wales's Apartment	5.	....	6.	12.	F.
	20.		16.	22.	
Mr. Constant's and Mr. Harris's Rooms	4.	....	4.	4.	C.
In the Baron's House					
Parlour No. 1 Best Apartment	3.	3, 4, 5.	1.	1.	A.
Valet to lie in the Passage Room	1.	2...	1.	1.	D.
Room with a Cane Blind to the Window	1.	6...	1.	1.	C.
Rice's Room	1.	7...	2.	2.	C.
Up One Pair of Stairs					
North West End Scarlet Flock Paper Gold Border & Room adjoining	2.	8, 9...	4.	4.	C.
Middle Room Green Paper	1.	10...	1.	1.	C.
South West Ends........	2.	11, 12	1.	1.	A.
Room adjoining & Closet..	1.	13...	1.	1.	D.
Room over Rice's Room..	1.	14...	2.	2.	C.
Long low Room	1.	15...	4.	7.	E.
Garrets	4.	16, 17, 18, 19	5.	9.	F.
The German Necessary Woman 1 Garret	42		43.	56.	

Rooms Wanted

His Highness hath   5 Rooms to Himself.

A His Exey: Count Bernstorff ..... 2 at least
A His Exey. Baron Schemelman ... 2
A His Exey. Count Moltke 2
   Baron Diede................. 1 Small One near Count Bernstorff without a Bed, if with One, so much the better.

A. Count Holk if not.............. 2 yet 1. at least & that near His Highness & handsome.

B. Baron Bulow .... 1 at least

B. Honble Mr Shumarker.......... 1 at least & that pretty near His Highness.

B. Honble Mr During.............. 1 at least.

C. Two Under Secretaries to C.Bstff. 2.

C. The Body Physician 1

C. .... Chaplain............. 1

C. .... Purser............... 1

C. ..Sergeant Surgeon 1

C. Secretary to the Treasurer....... 1

C. 10 Other Gentlemen belonging to His Highness's Household..... 5 at least

E. 7 Livery Servants to His Highness 3

F. 21 Livery Servant to the Prince.. 7 at least

D. Forgot for 4 Valets de Chambre to 4 Noblemen.............. } 4

So if possible 37 Rooms at least, each suitable to Each his Rank & Station in Life besides His Highness's own Five Rooms—

No. 636—*The King to Lord Hillsborough.*

RICHMOND LODGE
July 17^*th* 1768.

LORD HILLSBOROUGH—I have carefully weighed the enclosed Considerations & Propositions respecting the Island of Granada which meet with my Approbation ; & cannot possibly be objected to by any one but from motives of timidity or a desire of finding fault.

Draft, endorsed by the King.

No. 637—*Lord Hillsborough to the King.*

HANOVER SQUARE, 19^*th* *July* ¼ *past* 4 P.M.

SIR—I have this moment received the enclosed papers by Express from Governor Bernard, & think them of so much consequence that not a moment's time is to be lost in laying them before your Majesty, for your pleasure what I should do immediately. I presume your Majesty will command me to call together your most confidential Servants, & to lay these papers before them for their advice. Or whether your Majesty would be pleased to have me attend you first, to receive your Majesty's private thoughts before I see them ; I shall obey directly whatever yr Majesty is pleased to command. I have the Honour to be S^r Yr Majesty's Most Dutifull Subject   HILLSBOROUGH.

Endorsed by the King.

No. 638—*Lord Hillsborough to the King.*

WHITEHALL *July* 22^d 1768—
½ *past two* P.M.

SIR—The Dispatches I have now the Honour to send to your Majesty and which are just now arrived from Virginia, are still more alarming than those from Massachusetts Bay. Your Majesty will find the material parts of the Notes marked with pencil.—an Express is sent to the Duke of Grafton requesting His Grace will come to Town. As the loss of a few days in Exigencies of the important & dangerous nature that now press, may be of infinite consequence, I humbly submitt to your Majesty whether it may not be proper for me to write to the Lords of the Admiralty to signifie that I have your Majesty's commands to inform their Lordships that it is very probable your Majesty may have occasion for five or six Ships of War and a Body of Marines on very short notice, & that it is your Majesty's pleasure that they do prepare accordingly. But the propriety and expediency of this step I entirely submitt to your Majesty's better Judgement. I have the honour to be Sir Your Most Dutifull Subject   HILLSBOROUGH.

No. 639—*Lord Hertford to the King.*

Lord Hertford trusts to his Majesty's goodness & indulgence for forgiveness if He errs in giving his Majesty unnecessary trouble upon this occasion. He has just received the letter inclosed herewith from Monsieur Diede & as the Baron asked the liberty of occupying an appartment at St James's before the arrival of the King of Denmark He will not presume even upon this occasion to put a person of such Rank into any part of a palace inhabited by his Majesty & his family without his permission, though He is persuaded Monsieur Diede asks it merely for the sake of being better able to satisfie his Master's wishes, & does not foresee any inconvenience which can attend it, the different appartments which his Majesty has ordered for the use of the King of Denmark and his suite being all prepared.

Lord Hertford conversed with Mr Diede yesterday in obedience to his Majesty's commands & the Baron took upon Himself to answer that the King of Denmark would not wish to be met by any of the King's Servants upon the Road & that a compliment from his Majesty upon the King of Denmark's arrival in his appartments, from his Chamberlain would be thought perfectly respectful & sufficient : Such a person as Monsr Diede mentions in his letter to accompany the King of Denmark was not suggested by Lord Hertford.

Lord Hertford wishes upon this and every other occasion to testifie his obligations and attachment to the King by doing his duty & hopes his judgment will not betray Him in submitting everything as farr as the importance of it will justifie Him, to his Majesty's pleasure.

LONDON
Augt 5. 1768.
Past 7 *o'Clock*
in the evening.

No. 640—*The Duke of Grafton to the King.*

GROSVENOR SQUARE *Aug^t* 7th

1768 $\frac{m}{10}$ *past* 10 A.M.

The Duke of Grafton presumes to acquaint his Majesty that the inclosed was the Answer he received yesterday from the Bishop of Winchester, & that in Consequence of his Majesty's Commands that he sent off a Messenger immediately to the Bishop of Litchfield who is in Staffordshire.

Endorsed by the King.

No. 641—*The Duke of Grafton to the King.*

GROSVENOR SQUARE *Aug*^{t} 11th 1768
$\frac{m}{28}$ *past* 10 A.M.

The Duke of Grafton thinks it his Duty to lay the inclosed Letter before his Majesty, as he apprehends that the Step, alluded to by Sr Jeffery Amherst, will be the Resignation of his Regiment.

The Duke of Grafton presumes to ask the King's Commands, whether he should or should not apprize the Bishop of Litchfield & Coventry, that after the Levée tomorrow, his Majesty means to see that Prelate in the Closet after having confered so high & eminent a Trust on his Lordship.

He humbly submits this to his Majesty's Pleasure, least the Bishop should have left St James's as soon as he has had the honor of kissing the King's hand.

Endorsed by the King.

No. 642—*The Duke of Grafton to the King.*

GROSVENOR SQUARE *Aug*^{t} 13th 1768
late at night.

The Duke of Grafton thinks it his Duty to lose no Time in acquainting his Majesty that Captn Dunant is returned & presumes to inclose the Relation he has delivered to him of the Occurrences relating to his Commission from the Time the King saw the last Letter from Nice. Captn Dunant wrote from Paoli's own Dictating that Part which passed at their Interview. This Gentleman also picked up on his Return thro' France repeated Intelligence of a Delay on the part of that Crown from sending the farther Troops that were destined, & also, that Monsr de Chauvelin was not yet embarked. The Description Captn Dunant gives of the Climate & nature of the Country, requiring a stile of War peculiar to itself & to its Inhabitants, join'd to the eager zeal of the Corsicans hardened by the Difficulties & constant State of Danger they have lived in, & bear with cheerfulness, make the success of the french very doubtful; & that, which some timely Assistance prudently given may make very costly if it should not totally defeat their Purpose. But this the Duke of Grafton humbly is in hopes of receiving his Majesty's Commands upon so nice a Subject, when it has had his Majesty's maturest Consideration.

Endorsed by the King.

No. 643—*Lord Barrington to the King.*

CAVENDISH SQUARE *Aug^t* 14th 1768.

I had the honour yesterday to inform your Majesty that Sir Jeffrey Amherst would obey your Commands and wait your pleasure, since which He sent me word by M^r D'oyly that he should be in Town Wednesday morning : But in the afternoon I received a note which I humbly beg leave to send herewith.

I know that it has been complain'd of " that Sir Jeffrey " should be forced to say no to the King himself when it was no " secret to the Servants of the Crown what his motives and "resolutions were : " Perhaps the Note was intended to prevent that supposed hardship, or to ground more clearly a future publick complaint. I therefore drew up an answer which has been since amended & approved by the Duke of Grafton. I have ventured to send that likewise, that it may go to Sir Jeffrey tomorrow in case it shall be your Majesty's pleasure, after making such alterations in it as you may see fit.

I humbly conceive that leaving the Audience to Sir Jeffrey's option will prevent all possible ground of complaint, and leave your Majesty's gracious condecention intire ; but the whole is most dutifully submited to your Majesty. BARRINGTON.

Endorsed by the King.

No. 644—*The King to the Duke of Grafton.*

RICHMOND LODGE *Aug^t* 14th

1768. $\frac{m}{15}$ *past* 10 A.M.

DUKE OF GRAFTON—I have with the greatest Attention read the Relation Capt Dunant has wrote of the Occurrences Subsequent to his letter from Nice, the part dictated by General Paoli, shews the latter fully merits the opinion that has been formed of his Vigillance & Military Tallents I therefore wish You would call here on Me this Evening or tomorrow Morning, as I think every hour's delay is advantageous to the French & consequently must diminish the hopes of thwarting their rash & ill timed Desire of agrandizing themselves in the Mediterranean.

Draft, endorsed by the King.

No. 645—*Memorandum by the King.*

[14 *August*, 1768.]

1. Gen. Paoli is resolved to defend Corsica till he has spilt the last drop of his Blood.
2. The Corsicans eager to attack the French.
3. They have raised an extraordinary contribution of 4 per 1000. for paying additional Troops.
4. In every principal Port by a Signal of two Canons, 3, 4, or 5000. Men *can be* immediately assembled.
5. Money, Artillerie, Armed Vessels, portable Canons, & Firelock & *Bayonetts* are Wanting.
6. The General has a daily Report of the Motions of the French & of the *State* of his own Posts.

No. 646—*The King to Lord Barrington.*

RICHMOND LODGE *Aug^t* 14th 1768.

LORD BARRINGTON—The Note You have received from Sir Jeffrey Amherst is so very unlike that candour that has been one of the remarkable Attendants of him in every preceeding transaction of his Life, that I am not a little surprized at it; Your letter is very judiciously penned, & I think must inevitably overthrow whatever advantage was proposed to be gained by His Epistle.

No. 647—*Lord Hillsborough to the King.*

SIR—I have the honour to send Your Majesty Lord Botetourt's additional Instructions for Your Majesty to sign. I was obliged at Cabinet yesterday to consent to some verbal alterations from the Draught laid before your Majesty and approved by Lord Chancellor and the Duke of Grafton, in order to please General Conway and Lord Shelburne ; they are not of any consequence, & therefore I hope Your Majesty will not disapprove of what I have done—

I have the honour to be with the most devoted Respect Sir Your Majesty's Most Dutyfull Subject & Servant

HILLSBOROUGH.

HANOVER SQUARE
21^t *August* 1768.

No. 648—*Lord Hertford to the King.*

Lord Hertford has paid immediate obedience to the King's commands and being received by the King of Denmark his Danish Majesty expresses the highest sense of his Majesty's goodness & attention and has desired Him with his Majesty's best acknowledgements to inform the King that He finds himself at present much relieved.

Indeed He looks better ; The King of Denmark has taken something to-day by the Phisician's direction but proposes to take the air tomorrow ; The York Journey seems to be quite laid aside by the present indisposition.

LONDON

Augt 23 [1768] *at* $\dfrac{m}{30}$ *past one* P:M:

No. 649—*Lord Shelburne to the King.*

The Decyphering of the first of Mr Stuart's Letters having taken up so much time, and being found liable to a good deal of difficulty a Copy has been taken of the part of his last which is in Cypher, and will be sent Your Majesty as soon as it is done.

Lord Shelburne presumes to acquaint Your Majesty, that Lord Rochford is arriv'd, and proposes attending Your Majesty's Levée to morrow.

Tuesday Sepr 6th 1768 2 o'clock P.M.

No. 650—*The Duke of Grafton to the King.*

EUSTON *Sepr 11th* 1768.

The Duke of Grafton can not sufficiently express the grateful Sense he shall ever retain of his Majesty's most gracious Condescension towards him, of which he should esteem himself as most undeserving, if he had hinted a Wish of his to see Miss Jeffreys one of her Majesty's Maids of Honor to any one, without asking it as a Favor from their Majesties to himself. But he humbly begs leave to assure his Majesty that he never form'd such a Wish for Miss Jeffreys, whose Situation & Fortune in his humble Opinion, render that Honor less suited than to most other young Ladies ; and the Duke of Grafton presumes to add that he delivered the same Opinion to the Father, when he declined bearing his Request to His Majesty in favor of the Elder Sister.

Endorsed by the King.

No. 651—*The King to the Duke of Grafton.*

RICHMOND LODGE *Sep^t 15th* 1768.

DUKE OF GRAFTON—Having had a conversation of some consequence with the Lord Chancellor Yesterday, I think it material to make You acquainted with it, as otherwise his answer to the letter You proposed writing to him during Your stay at Euston, may appear not very intelligible ; He asked Me whether You & Lord Shelburne had in the least approached each other during his absence ; I very frankly said that Lord Shelburne manifestly still attempted to thwart every measure that originated from You, & seemed resolved to propose none himself, & that I believed He was lying by for some Popular occasion to resign with some degree of eclat ; that seeing this in a very strong light I had long declared to You that nothing could establish that harmony in the Cabinet which alone could give weight to measures taken either at home or abroad than the appointing a new Secretary to the Southern Department, He said He had long looked upon that measure as inevitable but that as the Lord who held that Employment had been recommended by Lord Chatham, He thought it best for Himself, to take a neuter part on this occasion, tho privately He could not conceal his thoughts to Me ; & that He must add, that Lord Shelburne had not only lost Your good opinion, but that of every one of the other active Members of the Cabinet ; & was even shy with Him, because He had not succeeded in raising doubts in his mind. I dropped the idea of Lord Rochford which seemed to please Him, as He could neither be called of the Bedford connection nor adverse to the Earl of Chatham, He then concluded with telling Me that the news from Hayes does not mend, & that He himself entirely despairs of seeing that able Man ever in a state of health to be of any farther use in Publick Affairs. The King of Denmark has desir'd us to give him a private Ball on Monday, to which I certainly should have invited You if You had been in Town but knowing You are not fond of those Entertainments I shall not expect You, but if You had previously intended being in Town that day I should be glad of seeing You.

Draft, endorsed by the King.

No. 652—*The Duke of Grafton to the King.*

EUSTON *Sep*[r] 15th 1768
¾ *pst.* 2 P.M.

The Duke of Grafton presumes to acquaint his Majesty that on receiving from the Earl of Shelburne S[r] Horace Mann's Letters as also M[r] Stewart's, both relating to Corsica ; he has taken the Liberty to send his Opinion in writing to his Lordship, wishing him to lay it before the Cabinet, in case his Lordship thinks it necessary to summons them on this Account, for the Duke of Grafton humbly begs Leave to observe to his Majesty that

Paoli's Wish in regard to Assistance is almost in every Point already gratifi'd except in the great Measure of all, A Declaration in their favor, which if once made by his Majesty will doubtless be considered at the same time as a Declaration of War against France, & be carried on accordingly.

If His Majesty would have the Duke of Grafton be in Town before tuesday next, he will set out on the shortest Notice.

The Duke of Grafton humbly submits to his Majesty whether the King would not think proper that Sr Edward Hawke should dispatch a Sloop to His Royal Highness the Duke of Cumberland, hoping that His Royal Highness would not proceed in the Mediterranean on Account of the many well expressed considerations in Sr Horace Mann's Letter.

Endorsed by the King.

No. 653—*The King to the Duke of Grafton.*

S^T JAMES'S *Sep^r* 16th 1768.

DUKE OF GRAFTON—On coming this instant to Town, I have received Your letter of Yesterday, & entirely join in opinion with You that everything that can with any degree of propriety be done for the assistance of the Corsicans has been already ordered ; for I am ready to declare it to the whole World, that I cannot think under the present State of Debt that it can be expedient, for the Sake alone of the Island of Corsica, to begin acts of hostilities against France, nor am I of opinion that we could now be in time to prevent Her from succeeding in the conquest of that Island ; does it not appear very extraordinary that Paoli should have continued so long silent when by the account he sent through the Channel of Sir Horace Mann, Mr de Choisseul has uninterruptedly avowed in the correspondence that Subsisted between them that the Conquest of the Island was intended, & now begin to call for our Assistance. You may certainly stay till tuesday at Euston & I will consult Sir Edward Hawke whether the D. of Cumberland will not be on his Return to Portsmouth previous to the possibility of an Express reaching him for that purpose.

Draft, endorsed by the King.

No. 654—*The King to Lord Shelburne.*

RICHMOND LODGE *Sep^t* 16th 1768.

LORD SHELBURNE—I omitted in discoursing with You this Day on the Subject of the last dispatch from Sir Horace Mann, mentioning that part that related to the Duke of Cumberland being at this time in the Mediterranean, which is so solid that I would have You write to Sir Edward Hawke to know how soon He expects the Venus & whether the sending a Sloop to order Her home would much anticipate Her return.

Draft.

No. 655—*Lord Shelburne to the King.*

Lord Shelburne has the honour to acquaint Your Majesty, that upon the receipt of Your Majesty's commands late last night, he immediately sent to Sir Edward Hawke, and finding that he was not return'd from Hampshire presum'd to send to Mr Stevens, whom he has seen this morning, and has since receiv'd from him both the Letters, which are submitted to Your Majesty.

Your Majesty is humbly requested to signifie Your Majesty's Pleasure, whether it be sufficient to send a general order for the Venus to return with His Royal Highness the Duke of Cumberland, or whether a particular Letter should be written to His Royal Highness or to Captn Barrington further explaining Your Majesty's commands.

Sir Edward Hawke is expected at Sunbury this Evening.

$\frac{3}{4}$ *after* 12. *p.m. Saturday Sep^t* 17. 1768.

No. 656—*The King to Lord Shelburne.*

RICHMOND LODGE *Sep^t* 17th 1768.

$\frac{m}{-} p^t$ 5 P.M.

LORD SHELBURNE—On the receipt of Your letter I have sent to Sir Edward Hawke at Sunbury, that He may write a private letter to Captain Barrington acquainting him with the reasons for hurrying his return, You will therefore direct Mr Stevens to keep the Boreas according to the order He has already Sent to Spithead, untill He receives directions from Sir Edward Hawke for Her Sailing.

No. 657—*The King to Sir Edward Hawke.*

RICHMOND LODGE *Sep^t* 17th 1768.

$\frac{m}{-}$ *p^t* 5. PM.

SIR EDWARD HAWKE—Having seen by some letters from Sir Horace Mann, that the French are very uncivil to a very unwarrantable degree to every Ship that comes near to Corsica, & thinking that my Brother the Duke of Cumberland might have some disagreable Scene if in his cruize He should meet with any of them, which naturally could not afterwards be so well adjusted between the two Courts, as the disputes between common Ships of War, I desire You will write a private letter to Captain Barrington acquainting him that in the present Situation of Affairs I think it best for my Brother to return after the first cruize to Port Mahon, the Boreas Frigate is detained at Spithead untill You have wrote, & then You will immediately dispatch that Vessel.

Draft.

No. 658—*The King to the Duke of Grafton.*

QUEENS HOUSE *Sep^t* 22^d 1768.

$\frac{m}{45}$ *p^t* 5 PM.

DUKE OF GRAFTON—After I had settled what business the two Secretaries had to lay before me this day ; I inquired when the Cabinet was to meet on the dispatches from Sir Horace Mann, on which he mentioned ten tomorrow morning, this gave Me a natural occasion to mention the necessity of filling up the Minister at the Court of Turin & asked him whether he had thought of a proper Person to which He replied, Lord Tankerville the only one He could Mention after what had passed ; this I said

surprized Me after the opinions of most of the other Confidential
Ministers were totally adverse to this ; that as he could not
recommend a proper Person, I proposed to Send Mr Lynch, to
which He seemed to acquiesce, but I find sends an Express
this Evening to summon Lieut. Gen. Conway to the meeting,
from some desire of mischief, I therefore desire You will see the
General when He comes to stave off anything disagreeable in
that quarter.

Draft, endorsed by the King.

No. 659—*The Duke of Grafton to the King.*

GROSVENOR SQUARE *Sep^t* 22^d 1768

$\frac{m}{35}$ *past* 6 P.M.

The Duke of Grafton humbly acknowledges the Gracious
Manner, with which his Majesty has been pleased to inform him
of the Discourse with the Secretarys of State on the subject of
appointing a Minister to the Court of Turin.   He will not fail to
obey his Majesty's Commands & endeavour to see Lieut: General
Conway, as soon as he arrives in Town, in case he comes, which
the Duke of Grafton greatly doubts.

Endorsed by the King.

No. 660—*The Duke of Grafton to the King.*

EUSTON *Oct^r* 2^d 1768

$\frac{m}{35}$ *past* 9 A.M.

The Duke of Grafton humbly presumes to inform his Majesty
of the Contents of a Letter he received a few Days ago from the
Lord Chancellor, on the Subject, which by the King's Command
the Duke of Grafton has never had from his thoughts since he
left London.   His Lordship's expresses that he sees plainly that
the Earl of Shelburne's Removal is determined ; that he thought
it unlucky, as he has some Reason to conjecture that Lord
Chatham, who is brooding over his own Suspicions & Discontent,

is persuaded that he is given up & abandoned. This Measure may fix his Opinion & bring on a Resignation that may lay the Lord Chancellor, as he observes under the greatest Difficulty. His Lordship states his Distress, his Wishes to retire even upon a scanty Income, provid'd the honorable Opportunity offered to justify it to his Majesty & to the professions he had made to the Duke of Grafton : then adding that this Step he would never take unless he should be so unfortunate to lose his Majesty's Favor & good Opinion. The Duke of Grafton will not trouble the King with observations on a Letter, which his Majesty's own Penetration will furnish so fully on these expressions from an honest & wellmeaning Servant of the Kings stating his Distresses on an occasion wherein he may foresee the aspersions that malice will throw out against the Lord Chancellor, as if he was concerned in undermining the Patron under whom he was first known to his Majesty. The Duke of Grafton may perhaps from a similitude of Situation feel this more strongly than an other ; and therefore will only presume to dwell on that Part which concerns the King's Affairs & the ill effect that the apprehended Resignation would bring to them at the opening of a new Parliament, & which could be the only means of giving any Eclat to the Earl of Shelburne, if he was no longer in the King's Services. The Decision of the Business is too delicate from these Circumstances for the Duke of Grafton to venture to lay his humble opinion before his Majesty : he has presumed only to state Consequences which the King, nor he himself had not foreseen as possible before the Receipt of the Lord Chancellor's Letter, & he humbly entreats his Majesty to give them that Consideration which the Importance of them to his Service make them deserve ; & humbly to assure his Majesty that, whenever the King shall be graciously pleased to express to the Duke of Grafton on which Side his Majesty sees the greatest Prejudice likely to fall on the Affair of Government, it shall then be the Duke of Grafton's Study to forward it with that Zeal & Duty with which he shall pursue every thing for the King's Service, Dignity & honor.

The Duke of Grafton did not mean to be in London till Saturday next, as it will be his last Absence, unless his Majesty commands him otherwise.

Endorsed by the King.

No. 661—*The King to the Duke of Grafton.*

RICHMOND LODGE *Oct.* 5*th* 1768.

DUKE OF GRAFTON—I have given the most mature consideration to Your letter of the 2ᵈ & cannot enter on the contents of it, without premising that the indecision that possesses You on this occasion is an additional proof of Your desire to be alone biassed by what shall appear most for my Service & the good of the Public, & that You suppress Your private feelings, which cannot but encrease my esteem & confidence in You.

The Lord Chancellor's letter indicates the feelings of an honest, amiable Man, but not of an enlarged mind, or much accustomed to Public concerns ; consequently it encreases my love of Him, tho it does not convey the idea of his being a great Statesman ; I therefore shall take up no time in combating his opinion, but shall lay down facts & reason on them, & I flatter myself propose a Plan that will be easy of execution & remove even the fear of the Lord Chancellor.

The Earl of Shelburne's continual attempt to thwart the measures of Administration, & in particular whatever springs from You, is the reason that has induced most of the Members of my Administration seperately to mention to Me the impossibility of his longer continuing in Office ; unless he changed his conduct ; the longer this is differed the more open his conduct has grown, so that I have been pressed to nominate to the Court of Turin an Envoy, contrary to his recommendation, he having previously notified through Count de Viry another Person as the one he meant to apply for, so that that Court is apprized of the little weight he can have even in his own Department ; tho He chuses to effect a cheerful acquiescence on this occasion, no one that is open to reason can be blinded by this, & must see he is only waiting for some popular moment to retire. My honour as well as the credit of my Administration requires that he should not be permitted to stay for such an event, therefore I would propose, that on Your return from Newmarket, You should go to Lady Chatham & explain in a concise Manner the plan on which You have acted since at my desire & at the earnest request of Her Lord You promised in Your last interview on the 4ᵗʰ of

June 1767. to continue in the Treasury, He engaging to defend whatever Steps You might find necessary to take during his confinement ; that in that conversation You had mentioned the necessity of removing Lord Shelburne if He did not change his plan of proceeding for that from the hour of Lord Chatham's illness he had rather been an Enemy than a part of Administration ; that whatever reason You might have at that time to form such an opinion, his Subsequent conduct had left no doubt of it, that this Step can be delayed no longer, that You acquainted her in confidence of the motives of Your conduct that She might on some favourable occasion drop the purport of it to Lord Chatham ; then mention what I have heard You express concerning that Great Man, & I cannot see any reason to fear Lord Chatham will act improperly, not indeed by what I have stated above has He any right to do it, this the Lord Chancellor owned to Me on friday ; if You see anything objectionable in this Plan, I am open to hear it, & am willing to make such alterations in it as may make it agreable to You, provided they do not extend to keeping an Enemy any longer in the Secret of Affairs.

Draft, endorsed by the King.

No. 662—*The Duke of Grafton to the King.*

NEWMARKETT *Oct^r* 6*^{th}* 1768

$\dfrac{m}{45}$ *past* 7 A.M.

The Duke of Grafton presumes to return his Majesty his most humble & grateful thanks for the King's Condescension in considering in so gracious a Manner the Motives that gave Rise to the Letter, which his Duty to his Majesty caused him to lay before the King, in order to state the possible Consequences of the Earl of Shelburne remaining in the Administration and of his removal from thence.

The Mode, his Majesty has been graciously pleased to direct, must solve every Difficulty with the Lord Chancellor, & the Duke of Grafton will instantly write to Lady Chatham to desire her Ladyship to appoint a time, when he may have that honor ; an answer to which the Duke of Grafton will be able to find on Saturday in London.

Endorsed by the King.

No. 663—*The Duke of Grafton to the King.*

GROSVENOR SQUARE *Oct^r* 10*th* 1768

$\frac{m}{45}$ *past* 8. A.M.

The Duke of Grafton presumes to acquaint his Majesty that, after a very long Conversation with Lady Chatham yesterday, he left her Ladyship without being able to draw from her Discourse any thing strong enough to decide clearly how far the Circumstance of the Earl of Shelburne's Removal will affect the Earl of Chatham's Situation in his Majesty's Service. The Duke of Grafton begged of her Ladyship to take the opportunity she should judge the most proper to assure his Lordship that as long as his Lordship's Conduct in the Ministry affected the Duke of Grafton only, He should go on as he had done to bear it with the utmost Temper & without complaint, remembering that it was Lord Chatham, who placed him there, but if his Duty to his Country as well as to his Majesty called him to advise his Removal, as he thought it did at this Time, that he did rely on the Earl of Chatham's Assurance to ascribe it to a necessity which the Welfare of the King's Affairs made indispensible. Her Ladyship said that on this head she knew Lord Chatham's. Sentiments, as he had often said on hearing the Report spread about, that if it took Place, he saw that his Majesty's Affairs would be most truly prejudiced by the loss of the Earl of Shelburne's Abilities. To which the Duke of Grafton could only reply that he sincerely lamented with her Ladyship the unlucky Circumstance ; & that he should & would join in the same Opinion with the Earl of Chatham, provided those Abilities were not on every occasion turned to thwart & not to assist his Majesty's Government ; the truth of which, if known to the Earl of Chatham, would undoubtedly cause his Lordship to judge differently on this Event.

Endorsed by the King.

No. 664—*The King to the Duke of Grafton.*

RICHMOND LODGE *Oct* 10*th* 1768
$\frac{m}{}$ *pt one* P.M.

DUKE OF GRAFTON—Nothing could more fully answer my
ideas than the very able manner in which You conducted
yesterday Your conversation with Lady Chatham, as in it You
shewed the attention & opinion You have ever had for her Lord,
at the same time not neglected what You owe to Me & to
the Public ; this has now thoroughly paved the way for what I
look upon as the greatest strengthening of Administration; on
Wednesday we will fix on the most eligible means of putting it
into execution ; the doing it above board & without any degree
of heat is what I most encline to.

Draft, endorsed by the King.

No. 665—*Lord Barrington to the King.*

BECKETT *October the* 12. 1768.

I received this morning by express a Letter from Lord Granby
which I humbly presume to enclose herewith to your Majesty.
If you are graciously pleased to permit that Colonel Mompesson
should sell out, & that the Succesion shall go in the Regiment
as Lord Granby recommends, may I humbly beg that your
Majesty's commands may be sent to me at the War Office, from
whence they will be immediately forwarded to me in order to be
obey'd. I sometimes fear that I am encouraged by your Majesty's
goodness to presume too much on such occasions as these, by
troubling you with Letters when I ought to attend you in Person :
Whenever I go too far, the least hint from your Majesty will
correct me.

I have never been an Advocate for such buying and selling as
Lord Granby now recommends ; but on this occasion I think
I may say that his former connections with the Mompesson
family will explain to the Army how he came to request the
favour he now begs of your Majesty, & it will be understood that

your indulgence is a personal gratification of your Commander in Chief, who certainly wishes what he desires with great earnestness.   BARRINGTON.

Enclosure.

Lord Granby to Lord Barrington.

SCARBRO' *October 5th* 1768.

MY DEAR LORD—Colonel Mompessons ill state of health makes him incapable of service, in consequence he has applied to me for my recommendation of him to his Majesty for leave to sell ; as Col: Mompesson has served twenty nine years I hope his Majesty will indulge his request.   As Major Ackland is a very good Officer as well as rank of Lt Colonel and the officers in succession old officers I beg you will recommend the succession in the regiment.   I must beg my Dear Lord you will get it done as soon as possible least any accident to Col: Mompesson should prevent his Children receiving any advantage from his long services as the Sale of his commission is I am affraid their only dependance my Dear Lord Yours very sincerely &c &c &c

GRANBY.

PS. Excuse haste going to dine with the corporation.

No. 666—*The Duke of Grafton to the King.*

GROS^R SQUARE *Oct^r* 13th 1768

$\frac{m}{5}$ *past* 8 A.M.

The Duke of Grafton thinks it his Duty to transmit to the King inclosed a Letter, which he received in the Afternoon yesterday from the Earl of Chatham ; as also the Copy of the Answer, which, as the Messenger waited, he was necessitated to make to the best of his Judgment, & which, he hopes, will not be disapproved of by his Majesty. The Duke of Grafton presumes to add his humble Opinion, that, if the Earl of Chatham should unfortunately persist in his Intention of resigning, it is well that no Step has been taken towards the Removal of the Earl of Shelburne, & that what has passed upon it is Conversation only

& even that confined to the very principal of his Majesty's
Servants : as the Duke of Grafton can not but think the
Difference to his Majesty's Affairs to be very wide, whether the
Earl of Chatham resigns on the Removal of the Earl of Shelburne,
or by the last Lord following the Resignation of the first. His
Majesty will be pleased to remark the Time chosen by Lord
Chatham to send his Letter, when he imagined that his Majesty
would have decided the Point. The Answer to it would be too
late to be delivered to his Lordship last Night : and, the Letter
being of so serious & important a Nature the Duke of Grafton
did not think it right to proceed to speak to Lord Weymouth
till he should this Day receive his Majesty's farther Commands.

Endorsed by the King.

Enclosure No. 1.

Lord Chatham to the Duke of Grafton.

HAYES *Wednesday Oct.* 12*th* 1768.

MY LORD—My extremely weak & broken state of health
continuing to render Me entirely useless to the King's Service,
I beg Your Grace will have the goodness to lay Me, with the
utmost Duty at His Majesty's Feet, together with my Humblest
Request that His Majesty will be Graciously pleased to grant Me
His Royal Permission to resign the Privy Seal. May I be allowed
at the same time to offer to His Majesty My deepest Sense of
His Majesty's long, most humane, & most Gracious Indulgence
towards Me, & to express My Ardent Prayers for His Majesty.

Tho unable to enter into business, give Me leave My Lord,
not to conclude without expressing to Your Grace that I cannot
enough lament the removal of Sir Jeffrey Amherst & that of
Lord Shelburne.

I will add no more to Your Grace's present trouble than to
desire Your Grace will accept my sincerest acknowledgements of
all Your goodness to Me.

I beg Your Grace to believe Me with the highest Esteem &
most perfect respect Your Grace's most faithfull & Most obedient
Humble Servant   CHATHAM.

Copy, in the King's handwriting.

Enclosure No. 2.

The Duke of Grafton to Lord Chatham.

GROSVENOR SQUARE *Oct^r* 12th 1768.

MY LORD—I feel too much concern on the Idea of any Circumstance, that can induce Your Lordship to retire, from Your Situation in the King's Service, from the prejudice it will bring to His Majesty's Affairs that if I had no other Reasons, I should even on this consideration beg leave to represent my Sentiments on an Event so unhappy for this Country. But My Lord, having myself some time ago given way to Your Entreaties to Me, to remain in my present Post, when Your Health was at least as bad as it is now, I have some Right to claim from You a Return of the same conduct, when I see as Your Lordship was pleased then to say, that nothing could be so truly serviceable to His Majesty's Affairs. Allow me to recall this Conversation & Assurance from Your Lordship to Your Recollection, & on the ground of it to entreat Your Lordship not to deprive His Majesty of that Support, which even the Hopes of Your Recovery gives to His Government.

Your Lordship's letter laments also a circumstance which I mentioned to Lady Chatham as one appearing to Me to be necessary & on which I intended humbly to submit my opinion to His Majesty : I lament it also as Lord Shelburne was recommended by Your Lordship, & give Me leave to say that in the same situation Your Lordship would have given the same Advice, which My honour as well as my Duty to the King will call Me to give. I could heartily have wished to have had an Opportunity of explaining to Your Lordship many important Subjects & amongst them how much Sir Jeffrey Amherst misconstrued the Intention of His Majesty & his Servants towards Him. But Your Lordship's health depriving Me of that satisfaction I could only impart to Lady Chatham in general the earnest wish I shall ever have for Your Recovery & that I have ever been & shall always remain &c. &c. GRAFTON.

Copy, in the King's handwriting.

No. 667—*The King to the Duke of Grafton.*

QUEENS HOUSE *Oct* 13th 1768. $\frac{m}{20}$ p^t 11. A.M.

DUKE OF GRAFTON—Tho I have within these eight Years met with enough to prevent my being much surprized at any thing that may happen, yet I cannot conceal the not having expected the letter You received the last Evening, from Lord Chatham, the impropriety of which is not a little encreased by the moment chosen for sending it, were I to detain You with every thought it gives rise to in my mind, no purpose could be answered by it, I will therefore alone remark the singularity of his entirely shutting himself up from the knowledge of the motives on which Administration act, & yet chusing without being called upon to express a disapprobation at the resignation of Sir Jeffrey Amherst & of the intended removal of Lord Shelburne, which he apprehends has already been put into execution. Your letter in answer is drawn up with all the regard You have inevitably expressed for him & with that dignity You owe to my Service & to Yourself. indeed I feel the greatest satisfaction from looking on You as on one in whom I can in the most entire Manner rely, & whom I sincerely value as a friend. the Distinction You judiciously make between Lord Chatham's resigning (if He persists in that I may say unfriendly part) in consequence of Lord Shelburne's removal or the latter quitting in consequence of the others taking that step, perfectly strikes Me in the same manner, I therefore think no step should further be taken untill I see You when I will also return the Lord Lieutenant's incoherent letter.

Draft, endorsed by the King.

No. 668—*The Duke of Grafton to the King.*

GROSVENOR SQUARE *Oct*^{r} 13th 1768

$\frac{m}{35}$ *past* 6. P.M.

The Duke of Grafton can not presume to add anything to the Letter, which his Majesty has deigned to send to him. He most heartily wishes that the Earl of Chatham may see by it the earnest Wish his Majesty is pleased to express for his Lordship's Continuance in the King's Service & that he may decide accordingly.

No. 669—*The King to Lord Chatham.*

Printed. Chatham Corres. III. 343.

QUEENS HOUSE *Oct^r* 14*th* 1768.

LORD CHATHAM—The Duke of Grafton communicated to Me Yesterday Your desire of Resigning the Privy Seal on account of the continuation of Your ill State of Health ; as You entered upon that Employment in August 1766. at my own Requisition I think I have a right to insist on Your remaining in my Service ; for I with pleasure look forward to the time of, Your recovery when I may have Your assistance in resisting the torrent of Factions this Country so much labours under, this thought is the more frequent in my mind as the Lord Chancellor & the Duke of Grafton take every opportunity to declare warmly to Me their desire of seeing that. Therefore I again repeat it You must not think of retiring but of doing that that may be most conducive to Your health, & to my seeing You take a public Share in my Affairs ;

Draft, endorsed by the King.

No. 670—*Lord Chatham to the King.*

Printed. Chatham Corres. III. 343.

HAYES *Octob^r y^e* 14*th* 1768.

SIR—Penetrated with the high honour of Your Majesty's gracious Commands, my Affliction is infinite to be constrained by absolute necessity from Illness, to lay myself again at your Majesty's feet for compassion. my Health is so broken, that I feel all Chance of recovery will be entirely procluded by my continuing to hold the Privy Seal, totally disabled, as I still am from assisting in your Majesty's Councils. Under this load of unhappiness, I will not despair of your Majesty's pardon, while I again Supplicate on my knees your Majesty's Mercy, and most humbly implore your Majesty's Royal permission to resign that high Office.

Shou'd it please God to restore me to Health, every Moment of my Life will be at your Majesty's devotion, in the mean time, the most gracious thought your Majesty deigns to express of my recovery is my best Consolation.

I am, Sir, With all Submission and profound Veneration Your Majesty's Most dutifull and Devoted Servant

CHATHAM.

No. 671—*The King to the Duke of Grafton.*

RICHMOND LODGE *Oct^r* 14*^{th}* 1768.

DUKE OF GRAFTON—Tho by the Copy of the letter I have received from the Earl of Chatham, You will see he persists in the desire of Resigning the Privy Seal, yet I think myself amply repayed the having wrote to Him, as it contains an open avowal that his Illness is alone the cause of his retiring, this will even remove any difficulties the Lord Chancellor might otherwise have seen in his own situation ; I think therefore a Copy of this ought to be sent to him. I suppose Lord Shelburne will resign as soon as He knows what has happened ; to prevent all jealousies would it not be right to have Lord Chancellor here at the fixing on a Lord Privy Seal, & also Lieut. Gen. Conway, tho I mean entirely to decide according to what You may think will most strengthen Your hands ; if You have not time to call here tomorrow or Sunday ; I shall be ready on the shortest notice to come to talk this over with You in Town.

Draft.

No. 672—*Lord North to the King.*

[14 *November,* 1768.]

Lord North has the honour of inclosing to his Majesty a List of the Gentlemen who spoke today in the house upon the subject of Mr Wilkes's petition. Sr J. Mawbey presented it, & moved to have it lie upon the table. He was seconded by Mr Sawbridge :

Ld Strange moved that a copy of the Records of the proceedings against him in the King's Bench should be laid before the house. The Debate consisted of little more than a dispute which of the two questions should be first put ; It was rather a conversation than a debate, & ended about five o'clock in a resolution. " That " the petition do lay upon the table, & that the proper officer " do lay before the House a Copy of the Records of the proceed- " ings against John Wilkes Esqre in the court of Kings Bench." There was no division.

Endorsed by the King.

Enclosure.

Sr Jos: Mawbey seconded by Mr Sawbridge—Mr Cavendish was up also to second him.

Ld Strange	Phipps	Mr Dowdeswell
Beckford	Mr Calcraft	Mr Dyson
Sawbridge	Ld Howe	Mr Cornwall
Lyttelton	Ld North	Mr Blackstone.

No. 673—*The Duke of Grafton to the King.*

GROSVENOR SQUARE *Nov^r* 29th
1768.

The Duke of Grafton, relying on His Majesty's Gracious Condescension, presumes to mention that there are but three Lords to make a Board at the Treasury, from the Illness of Messrs Campbell & Jenkinson, & that the Duke of Grafton will not be able to return from thence till past two o'clock. It was the Duke of Grafton's Design to have called on Lord Northington from thence, in hopes of putting forward an Idea of his on the Subject of the American Parturbators of the Peace, & indeed, if it is practicable, the only one Measure of any Efficacy, on which the Duke of Grafton has any hopes of bringing his Majesty's Servants to one mind upon. His Duty & Devotion to his Majesty's Services, occasions the Duke of Grafton to lay this Information before His Majesty, particularly as the latter Part of his employment this morning is on a Business pressing & most necessary to his Majesty's Affairs. The Duke of Grafton makes bold to mention that he dines at the Lord Chancellor & shall be ready to obey his Majesty's Commands any hour of the Evening or tomorrow morning that the King shall please to order his attendance, humbly imploring his Majesty's Pardon for what he has thought the good of the King's Service made it necessary for him to state.

No. 674—*The King to the Duke of Grafton.*

QUEEN'S HOUSE *Nov*^r 29th 1769.

DUKE OF GRAFTON—Though I shall see You this day at St James's I think it right not to defer till then the acquainting You with the contents of a dispatch that arrived late last night from Lord Townshend, the House of Commons by a division of 94 to 71. have thrown out the Short money Bill which was one of the two transmitted from hence as the cause for calling a Parliament ; to which they have added a resolution that the Bill was rejected because it had not taken its rise in the House of Commons. These proceedings are unparallelled since the passing of Poyning's Law, except in 1692. when the House of Commons determined the question in the same manner ; Lord Sydney then Lord Lieutenant prorogued the Parliament of his own accord for Six months, and entered a Protest in the House of Lords of Ireland, His conduct was approved of by King William, and that Parliament was never reassembled. In 1761 the same question was agitated, but the D. of Leinster, Lord Shannon, and the Speaker supporting Government it was thrown out by 147. to 37. though on this occasion they have taken the contrary side.

I am of opinion that the instance of King William ought to be implicitedly followed and that a Cabinet ough[t] in the course of this day to be held that suitable directions may be sent to the Lord Lieutenant.

If in the end this should make His removal expedient I must point out to You how much Your own honour as well as mine requires that his Successor should be a man of at least a blameless Character, therefore I must desire You will not give any encouragement to Lord Sandwich who is as well known in Ireland as here ; besides it is not Your interest that men Should be confirmed in the opinion that favours are only to be acquired by one quarter ; Your old friends would be disgusted at this and might be less hearty on this side of the Water.

Draft, endorsed by the King.

No. 675—*Lord North to the King.*

[? *November,* 1768.]

Lord North has the honour of informing his Majesty that Mr Martin the banker having proposed a motion to the house to this Effect " That John Wilkes Esq: tho he is convicted of a " seditious Libel is intitled to Priviledge." Several alterations were made to it till it came out in this form " That John Wilkes " Esq: tho he is convicted of a malignant, seditious & scandalous " Libel, & of three other impious & obscene Libels, & stands " committed to the King's Bench Prison by virtue of two " judgements in the Court of King's Bench for the said offences, " is intitled, by Privilege of Parliament, to be discharged from " this imprisonment for the said offences " This Question so amended passed in the negative. An attempt was made to prevent the alteration by moving the order of the Day. We approved it, & carried it upon the division by a considerable majority.

Noes	165.
Ayes.	71

Downing Street.   *Monday Even.*

Enclosure No. 1.

For	*Against*
Mr Martin	Lord North.
Serj^t Glyn	Mr Grenville.
Mr Beckford	Attorney General.
Sir George Saville	Mr Dyson.
Sir William Meredith	Sir Gilbert Elliot.

For	*Against*
Sir Jo. Mawbey	Mr Conway.
Mr Ja^s Townshend	Lieut. Col. Lutterell.
Lieut. Col. Barre	Mr Shelley.
Mr Dowdeswell	Mr Rigby.
Mr Montagu	Mr Cowper.
Mr Cornwall	Mr Thos Pitt.
Mr Burke	Mr Stanley.
Lord George Cavendish	Mr Blackiston.

In the King's handwriting.

Enclosure No. 2.

Mr Martin	for	Col^o Barre	for
Lord North	ag^st	Mr Shelley.	ag^st
Mr Grenville	—	Mr Dowdeswell	for
Serj^t Glyn	for	Mr Montagu	for
Att: Genl	ag^st	Mr Rigby	ag^st
Mr Beckford	for	Mr Cooper	ag^st
S^r G: Saville	for	Mr Cornwall	for
Mr Dyson	ag^st	Mr Burke	for
Sr Wm Meredith	for		
S^r J: Mawby	for	Ld G. Cavendish	for
Sr Gilb^t Elliot	ag^st	Mr T. Pitt.	
Mr Conway.	ag^st	Mr Stanley.	
Mr Ja^s Townshend	for	Mr Blakistone.	
Col^o Lutterell.	ag^st		

The four Last spoke upon subsequent questions. L^d G:
Cavendish on one side The other three on the other.

No. 676—*The Duke of Grafton to the King.*

HOUSE OF LORDS ½ *past* 6 P.M.
15^*th* *Dec^r* 1768.

The Duke of Grafton presumes to acquaint his Majesty that
the Address was agreed to with so little Opposition, that he
would have difficulty to describe it ; so also that the second
Evidence has confirmed Mr Wilkes to be the Author of the
Libels.

No. 677—*The Duke of Grafton to the King.*

GROSVENOR SQUARE *Dec^r* 20th 1768

$\frac{m}{10}$ *past* 7 P.M.

The Duke of Grafton presumes to acquaint his Majesty that by the Acceptance from Mr Dyson of the Board of Treasury, a Seat at that of the Board of Trade will become vacant, & that it may be of Consequence to the Successor to have his Writ moved before the Holydays. Lord Lisburne was appri'zed of his Majesty's favourable Intentions previously to the Junction of the Duke of Bedford's friends to the Administration ; the Duke of Grafton humbly submits to his Majesty's Determination whether the present is not a proper occasion to reward a Zeal which the Disappointment of that time did not alter, & whether it would be agreable to the King that those offices should be filled up at the Lime tomorrow.

No. 678—*The King to Lord Weymouth.*

LORD WEYMOUTH—The real regard I have for You would have enclined me with pleasure to have advanced Mr Thyne on the present occasion, had not I found that his not taking an active part in debates would have hurt those that stand forward in the House of Commons, and know Your Zeal for my Service would not make You wish what could in the least be detrimental to it.

Draft.

No. 679—*Lord Harcourt to the King.*

SIRE—Your Majesty having graciously extended your hand to relieve a once unfortunate portion of your subjects, will I hope permit them, Sire, to raise up theirs to your Majesty, in humble & heart felt acknowlegement for that happy change in their situation, which they owe to your royal munificence, & of which, both themselves and their families, cannot but retain to the end of their lives, the most grateful & most dutiful remembrance.

Your Majesty having already humanely condescended to cast your eye over the regulations, lately introduced, with your Majesty's approbation, into the Gaol at Oxford ; I presume, Sire, to submit to your inspection the enclosed account of the manner in which your Majesty's ample donation has been disposed of ; but some farther particulars which could not properly be inserted in that account being contained in a letter from Mr Willoughby to me, I have taken the liberty of sending it by Lady Harcourt, & in case your Majesty should be pleased to look at it, she will, if permitted, lay it at your feet. Will your Majesty think me too presumptious if I add, that I am persuaded nothing less than the indefatigable zeal & activity of that intelligent Magistrate, aided by the confidence his character inspires, could have settled claims so complicated, or have reconciled such jarring interests ?

I am Sire Your Majesty's most dutiful subject   HARCOURT.

see # 167, i. 206

No. 680—*The Duke of Grafton to the King.*

GROS^R SQUARE *Oct^r* 17th 1768.

The Duke of Grafton presumes to inclose to his Majesty the answer, which he has received from the Lord Chancellor, the Tenure of which does not calm the Duke of Grafton's Apprehensions on the bad Effect this unfortunate Circumstance may bring on the present Administration ; of which the Duke of Grafton dare not form a Conjecture till the Lord Chancellor has taken his Part ; and he humbly begs Leave to assure his Majesty that no Pains nor Argument shall be wanting that the Duke of Grafton's Mind can suggest to persuade his Lordship to save the Public from the Confusion that his Retreat will occasion.

The Duke of Grafton thinks it his Duty to add that the Earl of Northington is in Town full of those Sentiments of Duty & Zeal with which the Duke of Grafton has ever seen his Lordship : he more particularly rejoyces at this Circumstance, as his Lordship's Advice to the Lord Chancellor will have & must carry the greatest Weight. His Majesty will also have by this means near his Royal Person a Subject devoted to his Service, & able to give the justest Advice at so embarassing a Moment.

No. 681—*The King to the Duke of Grafton.*

RICHMOND LODGE Oc^t 17th 1768.

$\dfrac{m}{15.}$ p^t 6 P.M.

DUKE OF GRAFTON—I should not deal with the frankness
I mean on all occasions to shew You, if I concealed that I augur
less favourably from the enclosed letter of the Lord Chancellor
than from the one You shewed Me on Saturday ; but the arrival
of the Earl of Northington is so fortunate that I trust His weight
will be of great use in calming Lord Camden's mind for I know
his Zeal is ever to be depended on when my Service is concerned ;
I should think Your acquainting Lord Granby with what has
happened would be very advisable, for dislike of some now in my
Service, makes him open to what ill intentioned Persons may
suggest & it is easier for You whom He vallues to prevent that,
than perhaps remove it if once credited by him ; the attachment
You show on this occasion will ever be thoroughly remembered
by Me, I would say more, but You are such an Enemy to flattery
that commendation when within the bounds of truth is not
agreable to You.

No. 682—*Lord Hertford to the King.*

S^R—Your Majesty will I trust excuse the liberty I take in
offering my humble opinion upon a subject where You have had
the goodness to treat me with so much confidence & condescention. Your Majesty I flatter myself knows me enough to be
persuaded it is not offered from presumption or with a desire to
interfere in any degree with your Majesty's choice of judgment,
gratitude and attachment to You S^r are the leading principles
of my political sentiments & I wish to communicate what I may
by chance learn for your service with no other view than that
your Majesty should apply it as You think proper.

Your Majesty has been pleased to acquaint me with two
resignations that might probably or at least possibly happen
before the meeting of Parliament & by a conversation, I have

since had with the Duke of Grafton I find the one of them which may be important in it's consequences is confirmed.

It is upon this intelligence & upon hearing the Duke's sentiments and the Steps He has already taken in consequence of Lord Chatham's resignation that I beg leave to repeat to your Majesty what I suggested this morning to his Grace, the importance of sending immediately to Lord Granby in order that his mind may be early impressed with proper sentiments for your Majesty's service at this time. The Duke has not sent to him & yet I find He thinks that Lord Granby's opinion may have great weight in determining Lord Chancellor's.

I have strong reasons for thinking Lord Granby will be affected by Lord Chatham's resignation, & it may be very material if your Majesty thinks his voice Important to convince him early that it has been so far Lord Chatham's own act unprovoked by any design on the part of the Ministry that your Majesty was graciously pleased to condescend to ask that It might not take effect. I did not recollect to mention this matter when I had the honor of seeing your Majesty, nor did I propose to have given You the trouble of receiving a letter upon it if I had not discovered from the Duke of Grafton's conversation that it is well worth attention ; I therefore submit it to your Majesty's judgment wishing at the same time that the Duke of Grafton may not think I suspect him of want of proper attention by knowing that I have thought it expedient to communicate my ideas to your Majesty.

I beg pardon for taking this liberty, your Majesty may be assured it is done with the purest intentions for your honor & service to which from duty obligations & inclination I profess the most unfeigned attachment being S^r your Majesty's Most faithful and devoted humble Servant HERTFORD.

LONDON
Octr 17th 1768.

No. 683—*Lord Hillsborough to the King.*

TWICKENHAM, 17th Octr 1768
late at night.

SIR—I have learned with great dissatisfaction the Event that has happened, & as I think I forsee it will produce great confusion in your Majesty's Government, I think it my Duty upon this occasion to lose no time in repeating to your Majesty, that no circumstance or scituation can ever make the least alteration in my firm & dutyfull attachement to your Majesty's Service. I hope, if conferring the Office your Majesty has honoured me with upon any other Person, can facilitate or accomodate, that you will be pleased to do it without hesitation, it will make me happy to be by any means servicable to your Majesty, & I beg leave humbly to assure you, that my Devotion to your Majesty will ever be equal whether in or out of Office. Forgive me, Sir, if I venture to mention my poor opinion, that some plan is absolutely necessary to be immediately concerted & firmly & instantly executed, & at present I can only look for such a one from your Majesty's own Wisdom & Fortitude ; the Prospect is at present very black, & threatens, unless timely prevented, a scene at least very unpleasant if not distressfull to your Majesty, This Idea afflicts me, & makes me most ardently wish that I could do more for your Majesty's Service than my Powers enable me, for it is not possible for any Subject your Majesty has to entertain stronger sentiments of the most respectfull & gratefull Duty towards Your Majesty than I do.

I am Sir Your Majesty's Most Dutyfull Subject & Servant

HILLSBOROUGH.

No. 684—*The King to Lord Hillsborough.*

RICHMOND LODGE *Oc^t* 18th 1768.

LORD HILLSBOROUGH—I have just received Your letter which is an additional proof of that Duty & Attachment I have before experienced from You ; the Post You hold cannot be in hands more to my satisfaction as well as to the credit of my Service ; as to my Fortitude it shall not be diminished, but on the contrary as disagreable events arise is ever encreased as I have no View but the Prosperity of My Kingdoms I trust with some care the ill consequences of the late ill timed Resignation may be staved off ; the Duke of Grafton behaves as He ough[t] & by the attention of the *common friend* that disposition may be encouraged, the

two that require most to be proved are the Lord Chancellor &
Lord North, the latter of whom with great abilities & good In-
tentions is easily disturbed ; When I see You on Friday I hope
I shall be able by that time to shew You a better Scene than
Your Zeal for my Service has at present painted in Your
mind.

Draft.

No. 685—*Lord Hertford to the King.*

S^R—As your Majesty seems desirous of knowing whether I
was perfectly satisfied with the Duke of Grafton's conversation I
think it my duty to inform You that every sentiment which his
Grace expressed was full of zeal and regard for your Majesty's
present and future interest ; I have never seen the Duke more
open or speak with less reserve, nor could I be better satisfied
than I was with all He said to me except in one single instance
which though communicated to me under an injunction of
absolute Secrecy may yet with the strictest honor be told to your
Majesty ; the Duke said in the course of this conversation that it
would be impossible for Him to remain in his present situation if
Lord Campden resigned the great seal, but He said & I am sure He
spoke with sincerity & with his inclination that He would do every
thing in his power to prevent it ; The reason He gave for secrecy
was a good one though such as does not hold against your Majesty's
receiving this private information from me, that if any Idea was
entertained of the present Sistem being likely to dissolve that
the house of Commons would be afloat & every Man would run
to every Shop that was open to receive political Customers ;
The same reasoning will be very strong against his Grace's
quitting even under that Event which I hope will not happen,
& perhaps when urged by your Majesty & strongly enforced by
your service might Still have sufficient weight to persuade the
Duke to lead that Parliament of which He has had the choice &
therefore to be supposed that He has a prevailing influence into
such measures & upon such a sistem as may protect your Majesty's
honor & interest from violence the artifice of Party & every kind
of disgrace. My Brother comes to town this evening upon the
Duke of Grafton's summons & I propose attending him to his

Grace's this afternoon by appointment, happy in any & every instance where I can prove in the smallest degree the true and respectful attachment with which I have the honor to profess myself S^r your Majesty's Most dutiful and most faithfuly humble Servant   HERTFORD.

LONDON
Octr 18th 1768.

No. 686—*The Duke of Grafton to the King.*

GROV^R SQUARE *Octr 19th 1768.*

$\dfrac{m}{20}$ *past* 11. P.M.

The Duke of Grafton, in obedience to his Majesty's Commands, presumes to acquaint his Majesty that from the Conversation of the Lord Chancellor this evening he has more Reason to hope that his Lordship will not desire to quit the Seal ; altho' His Lordship would not decide upon it till farther Reflection. The Duke of Grafton does not dare form a conjecture, how deep that Event would strike on the whole Ministry, if it should unfortunately take Place.

No. 687—*Lord North to the King.*

[8 *November,* 1768.]

Lord North has the honour of laying before his Majesty the names of the Gentlemen who spoke in the debate of today.

Ld Henley moved the address.

Mr Stanley seconded it.

Mr Dowdeswell proposed an amendment by leaving out the words " *To present our most dutiful thanks to his Majesty, for having taken such steps as he judged necessary, for supporting the constitution, & for represing that spirit of Faction & Disobedience, which, in the chief Town of one of his Majesty's Colonies appears to have proceeded even to Acts of violence in direct defiance of all legal authority.*" & by inserting other words which, he contended, were less preclusive of the opinion of Parliament on the measures of Administration.

For the amendment spoke afterwards.

Mr Burke.
Mr Beckford.
Mr Townsend son of Mr Charles Townsend.
Mr Cornwall.
Sr George Saville.
& Mr Barre & Sr Charles Saunders.

Against the amendment Spoke

Ld Clare.
Ld Barrington.
Mr Onslow.
Mr Rigby—Lord Beauchamp.
Mr Solicitor General, Mr Sutton.
Sr Edward Hawke, Mr Aug: Hervey & Lord North.
Mr Grenville & Mr Wedderburn found fault with some measures of Governments but disapproved of the Amendment.

The Address, as first drawn up, pass'd without a division ; The Debate lasted till twelve o'clock.

Endorsed by the King, Nov. 8th 1768.

No. 688—*Lord North to the King.*

Lord North has the honour of informing his Majesty that he has just received a letter from an East India Proprietor with the following account of today's proceedings at the General Court.

"The India Court is up without concluding any thing : "Various Accounts are called for, & the Court are to take them "into consideration on Friday next."

Ld North's correspondent promises to call upon him to-morrow morning with further particulars of this day's trans-action in Leaden-hall Street.

DOWNING STREET *Wednesday Jan*: 4 [1769].

Endorsed by the King.

No. 689—*Lord North to the King.*

Lord North has the honour of informing his Majesty that the General Court have come to a resolution (by a majority of 69 votes against 56) to ballot on Friday next for a Motion to agree with the proposition of the Directors.

The Debate was carried on with much more temper & coolness than on the Wednesday before.

DOWNING STREET.   *Jan.* 6*th* [1769].

No. 690—*Memorandum in the King's handwriting.*

Minority

1st. Jany 16th 1769

2d. Jany 25th

1. 2. Abdy Sir Ant.
   2. Allanson Charles
1. 2. Allen Benjamin.
1. 2. Astley Sir Edward.
1. 2. Aubrey John.
1.   Baker William.
1. 2. Barre Isaac.
1. 2. Barrow Charles.
1. 2. Beauclerk Aubrey
1. 2. Belasyse Lord
1. 2. Bertie Peregrine.
1. 2. Bethel Hugh.
1. 2. Blacket Sir Walter
   2. Blackett Sir Edward.
   2. Bridgeman Sir Henry
1. 2. Brett Sir Piercy
1. 2. Brickdale Mathew
1.   Bridges Sir Brook
1. 2. Buller John Junior.
1. 2. Burke Edmund.
1. 2. Burke William

1. 2. Byng George.
1. 2. Calcraft Lt Col Thomas
1. 2. Calcraft John.
1. 2. Calvert Nicholson.
1. 2. Carnac John.
1. 2. Cavendish Lord George
1. 2. Cavendish Lord Fred.
1. 2. Cavendish Lord John.
1. 2. Cavendish Henry
1. 2. Cholmley Nath.
1. 2. Clarke Godfrey Bagnal.
1. 2. Clavering Sir Thomas
1. 2. Clayton Sir Robert
   2. Clive Lord.
1. 2. Clive George
1. 2. Codrington Sir William
1. 2. Colebrook Sir George.
1. 2. Cornwall Charles
1. 2. Coventry Thomas.
1. 2. Coke Hippesley.
1. 2. Crosby Brass.

1. 2. Damer Hon. John.
1. 2. Damer Hon. George.
1. 2. Danvers Sir Charles
1. 2. Dawkins Henry.
1. 2. Dempster George.
1. 2. Delawal George
1. 2. Donegal Earl.
1. 2. Dowdeswell R^t H. Will.
1.   Downe Ld. Viscount
   2. Drake William Senr
   2. Drake William Junr
   2. Dummer Thomas.
1. 2. Dunning John.
   2. Featherstonhaugh   Sir Math.
   2. Fife Earl of.
   2. Finch Savile.
1. 2. Fitzmaurice Hon Tho.
1. 2. Fletcher Sir Robert
1. 2. Fletcher Henry.
   2. Foley Thomas.
1.   Foley Thomas Junr
   2. Frankland Sir Tho.
   2. Frankland William
   2. Freeman Thomas
1. 2. Fuller Richard
   2. Garth Charles
1. 2. Glyn John.
1. 2. Goddard William.
   2. Gordon William.
1. 2. Granby Marquis of.
   2. Graves William.
1. 2. Gregory Robert.
1. 2. Grenville George
1.   Grenville Henry
1.   Grey Hon. Booth
1. 2. Griffin Sir John.
1. 2. Grosvenor Thomas.
1. 2. Hampden Thomas.
1.   Hamilton Lord Arch.

1. 2. Hamilton William Gerard
   2. Hanbury John.
1. 2. Harbord Harbord.
1. 2. Hay Thomas.
   2. Hobart Robert.
1. 2. Hobart George.
   2. Hope John
1. 2. Honywood Philip
1. 2. Hotham Beautmont.
1. 2. Howard Hon. Tho.
   2. Howard George.
1. 2. Hunt George.
1. 2. Hussey William.
   2. Jennings Philip
1. 2. Irwin John
   2. Johnstone George
   2. Keck Anthony Jarves.
1. 2. Keppel Hon. Aug.
1. 2. Keppel. Hon. William.
1. 2. Ladbroke Sir Robert
   2. Lambton M. John
1.   Laroche James.
   2. Lascelles Edwin.
1. 2. Lascelles Daniel
1. 2. Lascelles Edward.
   2. Legh Peter
   2. Lethuillier Benjamin
1. 2. Ludlow Earl of.
   2. Luther John
   2. Mackworth Herbert
   2. Manners John.
1. 2. Manners George
1. 2. Martin Joseph
   2. Marsham Hon. Charles
1. 2. Mauger Joshua.
1. 2. Mawbey Sir Joseph.
1. 2. Meredith Sir William
1. 2. Milles Richard.
1.   Molesworth Sir John.
1. 2. Molyneux Thomas.

1. 2. Montague Frederick.	2. Plumtree John.
2. Murray James.	1. 2. Popham Edward
1. 2. Musgrave George.	2. Powlett George
1. 2. Norris John.	1. 2. Pownal Thomas.
2. Osbaldeston Ivan. Wen.	2. Pratt Robert
2. Page Francis.	1. 2. Pryce Chase.
1. 2. Parker John	2. Pulteney William
1. 2. Pennant Richard	1. Radcliffe John.
2. Percy Earl.	2. Ridley Sir Mathew
1. 2. Phipps Capt	2. Ridley Mathew.
1. 2. Pitt Thomas	2. Rous Sir John.
1. 2. Plumer William	1. 2. Rushout John

No. 691—*Lord Hertford to the King.*

Lord Hertford thinks it his duty to answer the letter with which He is honored from the King by saying that his wishes and instructions have been expressed in the fullest manner to his Sons and Mr Coleman in regard to Mr Wilkes's case and expulsion : With respect to his Brother He is very sorry that any opinion has been given by Him different to his Majesty's own wishes and Judgment even in Council or at a private Meeting, but he shall be still more unhappy if his Brother thinks it necessary to adhere to that opinion in the house of Commons ; Lord Hertford is totally ignorant of what passed at the meeting alluded to except in having heard that Lord Granby Sr Edward Hawke and Mr Conway were then in opinion against expulsion, but having never heard under what circumstances Mr Conway's opinion was then given, He has always entertained hopes that when it was brought into Parliament with his Majesty's approbation, Mr Conway would be furnished with reasons from the more general voice of the Ministry and Mr Wilkes's unvaried behaviour to agree with the King's Servants, and Lord Hertford is well assured that his brother has gone into the house of Commons without any prejudice upon his mind favorable to Mr Wilkes and desirous of being convinced that the reason is right & that He may be able to support it with his opinion.

GROSVENOR STREET
Jan^{ry} 27th 1769

No. 692—*Lord Hertford to the King.*

Lord Hertford flatters himself that his zeal for the King's service will not betray him into any improper liberty or presumption ; He has had the honor of being admitted two days together into the King's Closet & therefore does not think it becomes him to be again so soon a Sollicitor for that favor. At the same time He is unwilling from what his Majesty has been pleased to say to Him of his Brothers publick conduct & that anything materially relative to it which may be carried in some shape to the King should not be represented to his Majesty in its true light ; He therefore ventures by this means to inform his Majesty that Mr Conway has been acquainted by one of the Gentlemen who was substituted to attend it that a meeting had been appointed last night at Lord North's relative to the measures to be pursued in the house of Commons to which He had not been invited : This together with the coldness He had lately experienced in matters of that sort made Him suspect that his future conduct with respect to Mr Wilkes was determined & concluded for Him, & Mr Conway's observation upon it was that it was unjust after what he had so lately declared in publick to the contrary to suppose He had any leaning or partiality to that Gentleman.

That his past with respect to future measures relative to him was not taken, that if He differed with his Majesty's servants It could only be from the fullest conviction in his own mind that They were mistaken in judgment ; but that to suppose him in the mean time averse to what might be thought right or proposed for the interest of Government was doing Him an injury, as He was incapable of being influenced by popularity or the fear of a Mob and could be led by nothing but by conscientious opinion if He thought himself at last obliged to differ in sentiment with his Majesty's Ministers. Lord Hertford wishes from the sincerest regard to his Majesty's interests, that whilst his Brother's services may be thought essential to promote them that his Majesty's Ministers would condescend to communicate with him in such matters as are to be brought before the house of Commons ; Mr Conway's Nature is generous and grateful & It would be doing him injustice to suppose any faction or unworthy principle would ever lead Him to make an improper return for confidence placed in him & some confidence and communication is necessary to prevent difference of opinion amongst Men who are most inclined to agree. Mr Conway is not sensible of having differed with his Majesty's Ministers in the house of Commons except as to the mode of proceeding which probably might have been avoided by timely & proper communication, His inclinations & best wishes are most sincere-devoted to the King's service and if none of the different Persons who at present form his Majesty's Councils are disposed to remove Mr Conway from them, Lord Hertford submits it with the greatest deference to his Majesty's judgment whether any declared diffidence and distrust may not more naturally tend to a difference than a union & agreement of opinion.

GROSVENOR STREET
Jan^{ry} 27th 1769.

No. 693—*The King to Lord Hertford.*

Lord Hertford, cannot be surprised at Mr Conway's not being invited to the meeting that was to have been held last night at Lord North's, as the General had at the one wherein it was discussed before the Holidays whether Mr Wilkes should be expelled not approved of that measure, consequently could not chuse to give his opinion as to the mode of best affecting that He did not think an eligible measure; I cannot suspect that so unfair a motive as the love of Popularity guides him on this occasion, tho I lament in this instance not having his cordial Support in the House of Commons; I trust Lord Hertford has directed His Sons to Support the Measure, for I should be sorry that any one could say that in a measure Whereon almost my Crown depends, His Family should not have taken an active part.

$\frac{m.}{35}$ *Pt* 5 P.M. *Jan^{ry} 27th* 1769.

Draft.

No. 694—*The King to Lord North.*

Printed. Donne I. 4.

QUEENS HOUSE *Jan^y* 28th 1769.

$$\frac{m}{35.} \; p^t \; 9. \; \text{A.M.}$$

LORD NORTH—Nothing could afford Me greater pleasure than Your account of the great majority the last night, I attribute this principaly to the ability shewn by You both in planning the Measure & in the Execution of it ; I should be glad if You could call here any time convenient to You before dinner, that I may more fully learn what has passed.

No. 695—*The King to Lord North.*

Printed. Donne I. 5.

QUEENS HOUSE *Feb^y* 2^d 1769.

$$\frac{m}{27} \; p^t \; 11 \; \text{A.M.}$$

LORD NORTH—It gives Me great pleasure, that You have so far got through the fatiguing business & do not doubt but that this Day will finally end it, at the same time I cannot help expressing my uneasiness least You should suffer by so very close an attendance.

No. 696—*Lord North to the King.*

[2 *February,* 1769.]

Lord North has the honour of acquainting his Majesty that the House sat till past three o'clock this morning in debate upon a question moved by the Attorney General, upon which Sr George Saville put the previous question. The original Motion was. " That the introduction to the Copy of a Letter addressed to Daniel Ponton Esq: Chairman to the Quarter Sessions at Lambeth & dated St James's, the 17th April 1768 contained in a certain paper intitled, The St James's Chronicle, or the British Evening Post, from Thursday Decr 8. to Saturday Decr 10. 1768.

printed by Henry Baldwin at the Britannia printing office N⁰ 108.
Fleet Street, of which Introduction Mr Wilkes has at the Bar of
this House confessed himself to be the Auther, & Publisher, is
an insolent, scandalous, & seditious Libel, tending to inflame &
stir up the minds of his Majesty's Subjects to Sedition, & to
a total subversion of all good order & legal government." The
Speakers for this motion were. The Attorney General, Ld Clare,
Mr Stanley, Ld Palmerston, Mr Ellis, Mr Cooper, Genl Conway,
Mr Thos Pitt, Sr Fletcher Norton, Mr Dyson, Mr Gilbert, M^r
Rigby, & Ld North.

The Speakers for postponing it by the Previous question were,
Sr George Saville, Mr Dowdeswell, Mr Cornwall, Dr Blackstone,
Sr John Griffin, Serg^t Glyn, Mr Burke, Mr Barre. Mr Cavendish,
Mr Ongley, Sr Jos. Mawbey, Mr Townshend, Mr Fuller, & M^r
Beckford, & Mr Grenville.

The Division was.

Ayes. 239.

No^s 136.

Enclosure.

Mr Symmonds.	Dr Blackstone.
Mr Smith	Mr Scudamore
Mr Herbert	Mr Tempest
Mr Stepney	Mr Masham
5 Mr Keck.	25 Mr Gordon
Sr Chas Danvers	Mr Hanbury
Lord Clive	Mr Buller Jun.
Mr Clive	Sr Thos Clavering.
Captn Clive	Sr W. Blackett.
10 Mr Carnac	30 Mr Scawen
Genl A'court	Mr Fellows.
Sr Edwd Deering	Mr Harbord.
Mr Forrester	Mr Hunt.
Mr Fuller	Mr Cornwall.
15 Ld Gallway. 2.	35 Honble J. Townshend
Mr Strachy	R^t Hon. J. Townshend
Col^n Jennings.	Rose Fuller
Sr Brook Bridges	Sr J. Griffin.
Mr Aubrey	
20 Mr Ongley.	40 Mr Baker.

Col^n Barre
Aldm^n Beckford
Ld Belasyse
E. Burke.
45–W. Burke
Mr Byng
Mr Calcraft
Col^n Calcraft
Ld J. Cavendish
50 Ld G. Cavendish
Mr Cavendish
Sr G. Colebrook.
Mr Coke.
Mr Dowdeswell
55 Mr Dummer
Mr Fitzmaurice
Serj^t Glynn
H. Grenville
G. Grenville
60 Mr Hamden
Genl Keppel
Ld Ludlow
Jos. Martin
Mr Mauger
65 Sr Jos. Mawbey
Sr Wm Meredith
Mr Montagu.
Captn Phipps.
Mr Ridley
70–Sr G. Saville
Sr Chas Sanders
Mr Sawbridge
Mr Seymour
Mr Sutton.
75–Trecothick.
Brass Crosby
Mr West
Mr Whitworth
Genl Whitmore
80–Captn Walsingham

Mr Legh
Mr N. Calvert
Mr Clarke.
Mr Clayton Junr
85–Sr Wm Codrington
Mr Boulton
Mr Conolly
Sr Saml Cornish
Mr Curwen.
90–Mr Damer
Mr Damer
Mr Damer
Ld Donegal.
Mr Durant St Ives.
95 Mr Fenwick
Lord Fife.
Mr Foley
Sr Thos Frankland
Mr Frankland.
100–Mr Goddard
Mr Gregory
Mr B. Grey
Wm G. Hamilton
Mr Harris
105–Col^n Hay
Mr Hotham
W. Hussey.
Genl Irwin
Edwd Lascelles
110–Dan. Lascelles
Mr C. Lowndes
Mr Mc Cane
Mr Milles
Mr Murray
115–Mr Musgrave
Mr Pennant
Mr Plumer
Mr Chace Price
Mr Rushout
120–Mr Thompson

Mr Turner	Mr Howard
Sr J. Vincent.	Mr Fletcher
Mr Weddell	Mr Parker $_{\downarrow}$
Ld Wenman.	Mr French
125–Mr Hobart	130 Mr Whately.

No. 697—*The King to Lord North.*

Printed. Donne I. 6.

QUEENS HOUSE *Feb^y* 3^d 1769

$\dfrac{m}{5}\, p^t$ 11 A.M.

LORD NORTH—Nothing could be more honorable for Government than the conclusion of the Debate this Morning and promises a very proper end of this irksome affair this Day ; I cannot help at the same time expressing some surprise at the very inconsistent part of some of those who opposed on this Debate who had supported the day before.

No. 698—*Lord North to the King.*

[3 *February*, 1769.]

Ld North has the honour of informing his Majesty that the Question for expelling Mr Wilkes was carried in the House today by a Majority of 219 to 137. He will have the honour of sending the List of Speakers to his Majesty tomorrow morning. but thinks him bound in justice to inform his Majesty how essentially Ld Barrington contributed to the Success of this business, who with the greatest zeal & readiness upon principles of attachment to his Majesty & his Government, undertook to make the Motion, tho' he might have most justly pleaded many reasons for being excused.

Endorsed by the King.

Enclosure No. 1.

JOURNAL OF THE HOUSE OF COMMONS

VENERIS 3^d *Die February* 1769.

The House proceeded to hear the Matter relating to Mr Wilkes ; And.

A Motion was made the Q^n being put That John Wilkes Esqr A Member of this House, who hath at the Bar of this House confessed himself to be the Author & publisher of what this House has resolved to be an insolent scandalous & seditious Libel & who has been convicted in the Court of Kings Bench of having printed and published a seditious & three obscene & impious Libels & by the Judgment of the said Court has been sentenced to undergo 22 Mo^s imprisonment & is now in Execution under the said Judgment be expelled this House.

The House divided

    Ayes. 219

    Noes   137. It was resolved in the Affirmative

The Commee's of Supply and Ways & Means deferred til Friday next

The Report from the Commee on the American papers is to be received on Wednesday next

               Adj^d till To morrow.

Enclosure No. 2.

LIST OF SPEAKERS.

For the Expulsion.		Against the Expulsion.
Ld Barrington.	Moved	Mr Thos Townshend. Jun:^{r}
Mr Rigby	Seconded.	Mr Cavendish.
Dr Blackstone		Mr Cornwall
Ld J. Campbell.		L^d J: Cavendish.
Mr Dyson.		Ald:^{n} Beckford.
Serj^t Nares		Mr Grenville
Sir Gilb^t Elliot.		Col: Barre.
Ld Palmerston		Mr Dowdeswell
Mr Ellis		Mr Burke
Att^y General		Mr Mackworth.
Ld North		Mr Thos Pitt
Mr Shelley		Mr Sutton.
Sr John Glynne.		

No. 699—*Lord North to the King.*

[4 *February*, 1769.]

Lord North has the honour of informing his Majesty that after a long debate yesterday, upon a question proposed by Dr Blackstone, Mr Grenville offer'd several amendments ; which amendments having likewise been amended, The House between two & three in the morning, came to the inclosed resolutions.

The Speakers were for Dr Blackstone's Motion. Dr Blackstone, Mr Paine Mr Wedderburn Ld North, Sr Fletcher Norton, Attorney General, Mr Thurlow; Sr John Glynne. Against it Mr Beckford Sr Jos. Mawbey, Mr Townshend Junr Mr Dowdeswell, Mr Paine, Serj^t Glyn. Mr Mackworth, Mr Cornwall, Sr George Saville, Mr Barre.

No. 700—*Lord North to the King.*

[9 *February*, 1769.]

Lord North has the honour of informing his Majesty, that the Agreement between the Treasury & the Directors of the E. I. Company was carried today at the India House by 290 to 250. He begs pardon for having omitted last night to send an Account of the Division in the H^s of Commons upon the question of agreeing with the Lords in the American Resolutions and Address. The Concurrence was carried by a great Majority. 169. against 69. He has inclosed a List of the Members who spoke for & against Agreeing with the Lords.

No. 701—*Lord Hillsborough to the King.*

HANOVER SQUARE 15th *Febry* 1769.

SIR—As Your Majesty may wish to consider the Measures I proposed to the Cabinet on Monday night, before Your Majesty sees the Ministers to-day, I have presumed to enclose a copy of them for Your Majesty's perusal. The determination of them is deferred to a future Cabinet, and as they are certainly of the highest consequence I humbly think very properly, provided the delay be not so great as to render them, if resolved upon, ineffectual & improper I shall be quite satisfied if a Cabinet may

be held & a final resolution come to on Saturday next; I can
delay by means of the Agent, the presenting the New York
Petitions to Parliament 'till next Week but not longer; these
must bring on the whole consideration of the State of America,
& if Administration is not prepared & resolved with regard to
their measures, all will be confusion, & Your Majesty's Servants
make a figure I shall be sorry to see. The Lords of the Cabinet,
except Lord Chancellor & General Conway, I rather think approve
the Measures, but none expressed themselves explicitly. The
Duke of Grafton still entertains doubts with regard to the
Alteration of the Council of Massachusetts Bay, which I am very
sorry for as I think its absolutely necessary to the restoration
& establishment of Civil Government in that Province, & however
those disposed to clamour, may endeavour to represent that
Measure, I am almost convinced it will be generally approved
at Home, & be popular in the Colony. I most humbly request
Your Majesty's Forgiveness for this Presumption, & flatter
myself that if any part of my Ideas are honoured with Your
Majesty's Approbation you will be graciously pleased to
recommend a speedy determination with regard to them.

I have the Honour to be with the most entire Devotion &
most profound Respect Sir Your Majesty's Most Dityfull Subject
and Servant   HILLSBOROUGH.

Enclosure.

MEASURES PROPOSED BY LORD HILLSBOROUGH
TO THE CABINET.

That a Bill be brought into Parliament to vest the Appointment of the Council of Massachusets Bay in the Crown, in the same
manner and under the same Regulations as in the Royal
Governments.

That it be enacted and declared in the same Bill that the
passing or entering upon the Journal of the House of Representatives of said Province, any Note, Resolution or Order,
by which the Power and Authority of Parliament To make
Laws and Statutes of sufficient Force and Validity to bind the
said Province in all Cases whatsoever, are denied or drawn into
question shall be ipso facto an avoidance and forfeiture of the
Charter, granted for the Government of said Province.

To recommend to His Majesty the conferring the Dignity of a Baronet upon Governor Bernard, and that he be directed to avail himself of His Leave of Absence to return to this Kingdom for a limited Time, to Report the State of the Province to His Majesty—The Government in the mean time to be administered by Lieu^t Govr Hutchinson.

That the Instruction given to Govr Bernard to hold the next General Court at Salem or Cambridge, be so explained as to leave the Governor at liberty to use his discretion according to the Circumstances of the Town of Boston.

That General Gage be directed to take into consideration the State of Boston, & Massachusets Bay, and in case he shall be of Opinion that it is unnecessary to continue so large a Body of Troops in that Province as is now there, that it be recommended to him, to send back to Nova Scotia so soon as the Season will permit such part of the Troops as was drawn from thence, and also that so soon as the Circumstances of America will allow of it he do restore the regular course of Rotation of the Army which was to have taken place next Spring.

NEW YORK.

That the Four Councillors who voted for the Prorogation be removed.

That the Papers received from Sir Henry Moore, be laid before Parliament, and an Address moved, that the Governor be instructed to call up the Assembly in Council, and in their presence to make and enter his Protest, in His Majesty's Name, against the Resolution of the Assembly, and to call for the Journals of the Assembly, and erase the said Resolutions, or to bring a Bill into Parliament to make the mover or seconder of such Questions, the Speaker, Chairman, or other Person who puts them, and the Clerk or other Person who enter them upon the Journal, incur a premunire, or disability to serve in any Office.

To direct the Governor of Georgia and South Carolina to call their Assemblies, with proper exhortations in their Speeches.

To move the Repeal of Mr Townshend's last Revenue Act, which is expressly said in the Preamble to be intended to raise a Revenue for the support of the Civil Establishment of the Colonies, with respect to Virginia and the West India Islands where Provision has already been amply made for that Service, and to declare that it shall remain in force with regard to the other Colonies no longer than untill each shall have made such permanent Provision for its own Establishment as His Majesty shall approve in Council.

That the Mutiny Act be so altered and amended as to direct that the Troops be billetted and quartered in public Houses, and furnished with the same necessaries and at the same rate as in England—and in case the public Houses are not sufficient to accommodate them, then in private Houses, unless the Colony build Barracks or hire Houses at the place to which the Troops are ordered for their reception, in which case the Troops shall be quartered in such Barracks or hired Houses, provided that proper Security be given that the Colony will defray the Expence of such Articles as are now required to be furnished to Troops in Barracks or hired Houses.

And in case the proper civil Officers should refuse or neglect to quarter and billet the Troops as the Act directs, they shall be liable to Penalties, and the Act shall direct and require the Governor to appoint Commissaries who shall be authorized by such Appointment to billet and quarter the Troops as aforesaid.

Provided always that the said Act shall continue no longer in force in any Colony, than untill such Colony shall have passed an Act for quartering and billetting of Soldiers to be approved and confirmed by His Majesty in Council.

No. 701A—*Memorandum by the King.*

[*February*, 1769.]

The vesting in the Crown the Appointment of the Council of Massachusets Bay may from a continuance of their conduct become necessary ; but till then ought to be avoided as the altering Charters is at all times an odious measure.

The Second Proposition is of so strong a nature that it rather seems calculated to increase the unhappy feudes that subsist than to asswage them.

Any mark of favour shewn to Governor Barnard is not only proper but judicious as it will teach the Americans that a due obedience to the Legal Authority of the Mother Country, is the means of obtaining rewards.

His coming home is the best method of attaining a thorough insight into the present state of that Country.

The leaving him latitude as to the holding the next general Court at Salem or Cambridge is very proper ; as also to Major General Gage with regard to the troops to be left at Boston, those to return to Halifax, and the restoring the Rotation of the Troops.

The dissolving the Commission of the Peace in the Province of Massachusets seems much called for at this time, as the Governor cannot remove any of the Justices without the consent of the Council tho He can appoint additional ones.

NEW YORK.

The removing the four Councellors who voted for the Prorogation is very right.

The laying the Papers from Sir John Moore before Parliament and the Address proposed seem not much objectionable.

The directing the Governors in general when they meet the Assemblies to hold a moderate yet firm language is highly proper, tho they ought to be instructed to avoid as much as possible giving occasion to the Assemblies again coming on the Apple of Discord.

The conduct of the Virginians was so offensive the last Spring that the altering the Revenue Act in their favour and in that of the West India Islands this Session would not be proper ; tho any hint that could be given that those Colonies which submit to that Law and make proper Establishments for the Governors and other Services expressed in the aforesaid Act, may another Year be exempted from every Article of it except the Tea Duty.

No. 702—*The Duke of Grafton to the King.*

HOUSE OF LORDS *March* 2^d 1769.

$\frac{m}{50}$ *past* 5 P.M.

The Duke of Grafton presumes to acquaint His Majesty that the Address moved by the Duke of Athole & seconded by Lord Egmont was carried after Debate by a Majority of 73 to 18.

The Speakers were

D. of Athole	—	P
Ld Egmont	—	P

Ld Rockingham	C
Ld Temple	C
Ld Lyttleton —	C
D. of Grafton	P
Ld Temple —	C
Ld Weymouth	P
Ld Hillsborough	P
Ld Suffolk —	C
Ld Gower —	P
Ld Suffolk —	C
Ld Sandwich —	P
Ld Dartmouth —	C

No. 703—*The Duke of Grafton to the King.*

ARLINGTON STREET. *March* 5th
1769 ¼ *past* 11 A.M.

The Duke of Grafton presumes to mention a few of the Persons in the Minority the other Day, which it seemed to be his Majesty's Pleasure to know before the Drawing Room to day.

Ld Bellasyse.
All the Clives.
Mr Calcraft.
Sr T. Clavering.
M^d Conolly.
Ld Donegall
All the Damers
Ld Downe
Sr Thos Franckland
Sr M^u Fetherstonough
Ld Fife
All the Foleys
Mr Grosvenor
Mr Greville
Mr Harbord
Col Hay
Mr Noel Hill.

M. Gen: Irwin
Lord Ludlow
the Lascelles.
Mr Montagu
Mr Murray
Mr T^s Pitt.
Mr Pulteney
Mr Rushout
Sr M^w Ridley
Ld Geo. Sackville.
Mr Seymour
Mr Thos Townshend
Ld Thomond
Ld Verney
Mr Cecil Wray
Ld Wenman
Capt Walsingham
the Yorkes.

No. 704—*Lord North to the King.*

[8 *March*, 1769.]

Lord North has the honour of inclosing to his Majesty a Copy of the motion made by Mr Burke to-day in the H^s of Commons. He was supported by Mr Cornwall, Mr Dowdeswell & Ld George Cavendish : Mr Hawke, Sr Jos: Mawbey, & Sr Francis Vincent said a few words likewise on the same side. The Speakers against the Motion were. The Att^y Genl Sr Fletcher Norton, Mr Onslow of Guilford, Col: Jennings, Mr Grenville, Ld Barrington, Mr Harley, Sr Thos Clavering & Ld North. The Motion was rejected by a great Majority.

Ayes. 39
Noes. 245.

No. 705—*Lord North to the King.*

[9 *March*, 1769.]

Lord North has the honour of sending to his Majesty a more correct List of the Speakers in the debate of yesterday, than he was able to send last night.

For Mr. Burke's Motion.	Against the Motion.
Mr Burke.	Attorney General
Sr John Molesworth	Col: Jennings
Mr Cornwall	Col: Onslow.
Mr Dowdeswell.	Sr Fletcher Norton
Col: Barre	Mr Grenville
Sr Francis Vincent.	Ld North
Ld George Cavendish	Ld Barrington.
Sr Joseph Mawbey.	Mr Harley.
Mr Hawke.	Ld Howe.
	Sr Thos Clavering.

No. 706—*The King to Lord North.*

Printed. Donne I. 8.

QUEENS HOUSE *March* 31st 1769

$$\frac{m}{46} \, p^t \; 3 \text{ P.M.}$$

LORD NORTH—I have this instant heard that the Grand Jury have refused to find Bills against any of the Persons concerned in the Audacious Tumult at S[t] James's on the 22[d] Altho Sir Alexander Gilmour and one of the Justices swore to the two Men that had struck them in the execution of their Offices. This seems so extraordinary that I hope You will inquire into it & send Me a full account of what has passed.

No. 707—*The King to Lord North.*

Printed. Donne I. 8.

QUEEN'S HOUSE, *March* 31st 1769.

$$\frac{m}{20}. \, p^t \; 11 \text{ P.M.}$$

LORD NORTH—The short state of the Bills preferred this day which I have just received from You, manifest the factious & partial conduct of the Grand Jury : if there is no means by Law to quell Riots, & if Juries forget they are on their oath to be guided by fact not faction ; this constitution must be overthrown, & anarchy (the most terrible of all evils) must ensue ; it therefore behoves every honest man with vigour to stand forth and by such methods as may seem most effectual to give elasticity to the springs of Government ; I am ready to take any forward path that the present crisis may require & I trust that every Man not absorbed in Faction will now firmly unite to crush this Party that aim at the very vitals of all Government ; as to Your Zeal & firmness I know I can thoroughly rely on them.

No. 708—*The Duke of Grafton to the King.*

ARLINGTON STREET *April* 14th 1769

$\frac{m}{40}$ *past* 6 P.M.

The Duke of Grafton presumes to acquaint his Majesty that, in his humble opinion the Business of the Day, from its Nature, can not fail to be closed to night. He has yet heard no Account from thence, where the Debate must take its Turn so much from Circumstances that will start during the Course of it.

No. 709—*The King to Lord Rochford.*

QUEENS HOUSE *April* 16th 1769.

$\frac{m}{20}$ p^t 10 A.M.

LORD ROCHFORD—Tho' thoroughly satisfied that You Will have every meeting at the London Tavern & at Mile End watched ; yet having seen in the Papers of Yesterday that the Freeholders of Middlesex are summoned to meet at the latter place to morrow ; I think it right to mention how material it is that a proper person be sent there not only to give the earliest intelligence of the Resolutions taken there, as also of those who are the most active in the framing of them. I cannot conclude without a fresh expressing my conviction that if firmness be now shewn this affair will soon vanish into smoke, but if this is omitted no one can answer to what lengths Faction may not go.

Draft, endorsed by the King.

No. 710—*Lord North to the King.*

Lord North has the honour of transmitting to his Majesty a List of the Members of the H^s of Commons, who spoke yesterday upon the Motion to declare that Mr Luttrell ought to have been return'd for Middlesex.

The Debate lasted till after two o'clock this morning.

Ayes. 197.

No's 143.

Enclosure.

Speakers Ap. the 15th.

For the Motion.	*Against the Motion.*
Mr Onslow.	Mr Beckford.
Sr Alex: Gilmour.	Mr Thos Townshend Junr
Mr Payne.	Mr Cornwall.
Mr Jenkinson	Sergeant Glynn.
Attorney General	Mr Aubrey.
Sr Fletcher Norton	Mr Townsend
Mr Stephen Fox.	Mr Burke.
Ld North	Mr Grenville.
Mr Dyson.	Sr W. Meredith.
Mr Thurlow	Capt: Phipps
Col: Onslow.	
Mr Stanley.	

No. 711—*The King to Lord North.*

Printed.　Donne I. 9.

QUEENS HOUSE *April* 16th 1769.

$\frac{m}{27.}\ p^{t}$ 11. A.M.

LORD NORTH—The House of Commons having in so spirited a manner felt what they owe to their own privileges as well as to the good order of this Country and Metropolis, gives me great satisfaction, and must greatly tend to destroy that outrageous licentiousness that has been so successfully raised by wicked and disappointed Men; but whilst I commend this, I cannot omit expressing my thorough conviction that this was chiefly owing to the Spirit and good conduct you have Shewn during the whole of this unpleasant business.

Two drafts.

No. 712—*Lord Hillsborough to the King.*

WHITEHALL 17th *April* 1769. 8 P.M.

SIRE—Mr Bradshaw has sent me the Letter I have the honour to enclose to your Majesty, which I take the Liberty to do as I believe it contains very exact Information, and I presume to request Your Majesty will be pleased to return it to me Mr Bradshaw having desired me to send it back to him when I have read it, that he may enclose it to the Duke of Grafton tonight.

I saw Mr Bradshaw this morning at the House of Commons after I had the honour of my Audience of Your Majesty, and he told me of Lord North's low spirits, & that he had last night a long conversation with him, the Result of which was that His Lordship would certainly continue to bear the unpleasant Scituation he is in, rather than be the Cause of a general change in Your Majesty's Administration I thought it my Duty to mention this conversation to Your Majesty, as I think it makes my Lord's continuance in his office indubitable. From Your Majesty's Most Dutyfull & Devoted Subject & Servant

HILLSBOROUGH.

No. 713—*The question concerning* Litterary Property *determined by the Court of King's Bench on the* 20*th April* 1769. *in the cause between Millar and Taylor.*

[In the King's handwriting.]

Mr Justice Willes thinks in this particular case that the Author's title depends upon the two following Questions

1. Whether the Copy of a Book or litterary Composition belongs to the Author by the Common Law.

2. Whether the Common Law Right of Authors to the Copies of their own Works is taken away by 8. Anne c. 19.

Till 1640. the Crown exercised an unlimited Authority over the Press ; which was enforc'd by the summary powers of Search, Confiscation and Imprisonment, given to the Stationers Company, all over the Realm and Dominions thereunto belonging, and by the Supreme Jurisdiction of the Star Chamber, without the least Obstruction from Westminster Hall or the Parliament, in any Instance.

The Licentiousness of Libels induced the two Houses during the troubles to make an Ordinance prohibiting Printing unless the Book was first licenced, and entered in the Register of the

Stationers Company ; Copy Rights in their Opinion then could only stand upon the Common Law ; both Houses take it for granted.

The Ordinance therefore prohibits Printing without the consent of the owner, or importing on pain of forfeiting the same to the Owner or Owners of the Copies of the said Book ; which necessarily supposes the Property to exist, it is nugatory if there was no Owner ; and at that time an Owner could only exist by Common Law.

In 1649 the long Parliament made an Ordinance which forbids printing any Book legally granted, or any Book entered without the consent of the Owner, on pain of forfeiture.

In 1662. the Act 13. and 14. Car. II Cap. 2. prohibits the printing any book unless first entered an^d licensed in the Register of the Stationers Company ; it also prohibits printing without the consent of the Owner, on pain of forfeiting the book and 6^s 8^d each Copy, half to the King, and half to the Owner ; to be sued for by the Owner within Six Months.

The Act supposes an Ownership at Common Law, and the Right itself is particularly recognized in the latter part of the third Section of the Act.

The Licensing Act of Car. II. was continued by several Acts of Parliament, but expired 9th May 1679. 31. Car II. it was revived by 1. Jac. II. Cap. 7. and continued by 4. Will. and Mar. cap. 24. and finally expired in 1694.

For five years successively, attempts were made for a new Licensing Act ; such a Bill once passed the House of Lords ; but the attempts miscarried, upon Constitutional objections to a Licenser.

By 8. Ann. Cap. 19. for Securing the Property of Copies of Books to the rightful Owners ;

Upon the whole he thinks that there is a Common Law-Right of an Author to his Copy ; that is not taken away by the 8th Anne.

Mr Justice Aston is of opinion that the great question is a general one " How the Common Law stands, independent of the Statute of 8. Ann. Cap. 19. in respect to an Author's sole right to the Copy of his literary Productions ; which for great[er] perspicuity is divided into 1. Whether an Author's property in his own literary composition is such as will intitle him at Common Law to the sole right of multiplying the copies of it ; 2. If the first is admitted Whether the Copy-Right by his own publication of the Work, is necessarily given away, and his consent to such gift implied by operation of Law, manifestly against his Will, and contrary to the Finding of the Jury ; and 3^{tio} Whether this Right is taken away from Him, or restrained by the Statute of Queen Anne."

Mr Justice Aston concludes that every principle of Reason, natural Justice, Morality, and Common Law ; on the Evidence of the long received opinion of this property appearing in antient proceedings and in Law cases ; on the clear sense of the Legislature ; and the opinions of the greatest Lawyers of their time in the Court of Chancery since that Statute ; the Right of An Author to the Copy of his works appears to be well founded.

Mr Justice Yates was of a different Opinion from the two Judges who had spoken before him ; he said the general Question for the determination of the Court is, Whether after a voluntary and general publication of an Author's works by himself, or by his authority, the Author has a sole and perpetual property in that Work ; so as to give him a right to confine every subsequent publication to himself and his Assigns forever. He ends with the words of the Act of Parliament 8. Ann. Cap. 19. that the Author or Purchaser of the Copy, shall have the sole Right for the particular term which the Statute has granted and limited, but no longer : and consequently, that the Plaintiff, who claims a perpetual and unbounded Monopoly, has no legal Right to recover.

Lord Mansfield after referring to the two first arguments without actually repeating them, and desiring that it might be understood as if he had spoken the substance of them, and fully adopted them, gave some additional reasons why he was of opinion that the Author has a Copy right by Common Law.

It may seem presumptuous after mentioning the opinions of such able Judges to venture at deciding which opinion seems most agreeable to common sense ; yet although I am so clear that every man has a right to his own labour, yet when an Author publishes to the World his works, he must rest satisfied with the sale of it as His reward, unless he obtains a patent which gives him an exclusive right for a certain number of years.

No. 714—*The Duke of Grafton to the King.*

ARLINGTON STREET *April* 27*th* 1769
6 *o'clock* P.M.

The Duke of Grafton presumes to acquaint his Majesty that
the Militia Bill is ordered to be committed by 52 ag^t 29.

The Speakers were

Ld Sandys	C	Ld Suffolk C	
Ld Egmont	C	Ld Denbigh P	
D of Bedford	P.	D. of Bolton C	
Ld Egmont	C	Ld Holdernesse P.	
D. of Grafton	P.		

No. 715—*The Duke of Grafton to the King.*

ARLINGTON STREET *May* 9*th* 1769
$\dfrac{m}{7}$ *past* 10 A.M.

The Duke of Grafton in obeying to his Majesty's Commands
has the honor of acquainting his Majesty that the necessary
orders are already given excepting only what regards Mr Fitz
Roy Scudamore whose Reelection is not yet settled.

No. 716—*The King to Lord North.*

Printed. Donne I. 9.

QUEEN'S HOUSE *May* 9*th* 1769.
$\dfrac{m}{38}$ *p^t* 10. A.M.

LORD NORTH—I received early this morning Your Account
of the very honorable issue of Yesterday's Debate, and have this
instant received the list of the Speakers ; the House of Commons
has with becoming Dignity Supported their own Privileges
without which they cannot subsist, it is now my Duty with
Firmness to see the Laws obeyed, which I trust will by degrees
restore good order without which no state can flourish.

No. 717—*The Duke of Grafton to the King.*

GROSVENOR SQUARE *May* 10th

$\frac{m}{25}$ *past* 5 P.M.

The Duke of Grafton is honored with his Majesty's Commands, which he will take care punctually to obey. If he may be allowed to express his opinion on the determination of the Day for the Report of the Comittee of Councils, the Reasons for deferring it till Wednesday next are the best advised.

No. 718

RETURN OF FIREWORKS FOR RICHMOND 19th May 1769

First Division

1 Battery of Marrons
2 Dozen half Pound Rockets, two at a time
1 Regulated Piece of three Mutations
6 Air Balloons
1 Horizontal and Vertical Wheel, representing a Globe
2 Planks of Pots des Brins

Second Division

2 Dozen half Pound Rockets, two at a time
1 Vertical Wheel with White and Azure fire in the Center
12 Tourbillons   Large Brilliant
5 Small Pieces of two Mutations
6 Air Balloons
1 Horizontal and Vertical Brilliant Wheel
2 Planks of Pots des Brins

Third Division

2 Dozen one Pound Rockets, two at a time
1 Regulated Guillochi
6 Pots des Saucissons with brillant Gerbs
1 Horizontal Brilliant Isf
6 Air Balloons.

1 Brilliant Piece, concisting of six Fruitonis with a Vertical
  Wheel in the Center
2 Planks of Pots des Brins

Fourth Division

2 Dozen one Pound Rockets two at a time
1 Regulated Piece with a fixt Sun
1 Flight consisting of four Dozen Rockets
1 Regulated Piece G R with a Glory
6 Air Balloons
1 Regulated Piece of four Mutations
1 Illuminated Piece of two Mutations
1 Flight consisting of 16 Dozen Rockets

THOMAS DESAGULIERS
Chief Firemaster to His Majesty.

No. 719—*John Grant to the Duke of Grafton.*

MY LORD DUKE—Yesterday I had another Dose given me,
which greatly discompos'd me for the day ; and such frequency,
must destroy the parts acted on. And tho' I impute it principally to a fault in the King, Your Grace is also blamable, by
being still in the Ministry and having had a hand in what
involv'd me into those troubles, from which I might with ease
have been preserv'd. And I do request, that my Letter of
yesterday be presented to the King, to the end that I may be
instantly reliev'd, or brought to condign punishment. And if
your Grace has the dregs of honour without probity, your Grace
will not trifle a minute on so interesting a Matter to a human
Being, compounded of the same Materials, and fabricated by
the same power, that constituted his Grace the Duke of Grafton.
I am, My Lord Duk Your Grace's devoted humble Servant
INº GRANT, Journeyman Weaver

N.B. Everybody endued with the right powers and faculties
of the rational mind, will condemn every man of you.

Nº 9.
SKINNER STREET
WITHOUT BISHOPSGATE
May 26. 1769.

No. 720—*John Grant to the Duke of Grafton.*

Let human wretchedness now take its place,
Among the pastimes, that divert your Grace.

MY LORD DUKE—Yesterday again, I had another Dose tipt
me, in a little broth in a dirty Cookshop, in Long Alley Moor-
fields; and it happen'd that I had no money in my pocket,
but told them that I shou'd pay them tomorrow; but now, as
that was the case, damn them if ever they have a farthing of
the Groat while they live.

I am My Lord Duke Your Grace's devoted humble Servant
                    INº GRANT, Journeyman Weaver.
    Nº 9.
SKINNER STREET
WITHOUT BISHOPSGATE
    May 27. 1769.

No. 721—*Lord Winchilsea to the King.*

May 30 1769.

Sᴿ—It is with the utmost Respect deference & Duty to your
Majesty that I presume once more to mention Dʳ Denings
name to you   The most gracious manner in which your Majesty
received my former application's in his favour encourages me
For in the first instance when the Duke of Newcastle put in
Dʳ Caryl to Canterbury I must not forget your great condescension & favour to me in not consenting to it until I had had the
honour of an audience with your Majesty & then Your Majesty
told me what I never had heard before that Windsor was much
better than Canterbury & that Dʳ Dening Should have the first
Canonry of Windsor that should be vacant   When the Second
prebend of Canterbury fell which Your Majesty was graciously
pleased to bestow upon Dʳ Dening   If I did not misunderstand
your Majesty totally I flattered myself that your Majestys
Intentions were still the same & that when the Event should
happen of a Vacancy he might hope to be translated to Windsor
The ill state of my health prevents all possibility of my paying
my duty to your Majesty which I hope will excuse my pre-

sumption in taking the liberty of sending this letter to Your Majesty Tho at the same time I beg leave to assure Your Majesty What Ever determination You Shall be pleased to give to this affair it shall be acquiesced under with the Utmost Submission by Your Majesty Most Dutiful & Loyal Subject & Servant

WINCHILSEA.

No. 722—*Transit of Venus* 3ᵈ *of June* 1769.

The Passage of Venus over the Sun's Disk will happen on the third of June 1769.

Morally speaking, None now living will see the same Phoenomenon again, which will only happen again in 1874, and again 2004.

At Richmond.

It is to be presumed that the Planet Venus will be seen compleatly entered as a black Spot on the Top of the Sun's Disk, at about 23 Minutes and a Half Past Seven in the Evening.

Whence if the Weather is favorable the Observation may last distinct for about One Hour and two Thirds of an Hour, till Sun-Set.

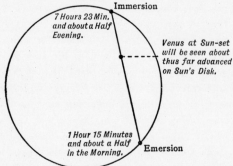

Immersion

7 Hours 23 Min, and about a Half Evening.

Venus at Sun-set will be seen about thus far advanced on Sun's Disk.

1 Hour 15 Minutes and about a Half in the Morning.

Emersion

Whereby Venus will take up about 5 Hours & 52 Minutes in Passing thro' that Line of the Sun's Disk, could We in that Place vizᵗ Richmond see the whole Transit of Venus.

The most desirable Position on this Earth for an Observation of this Transit of Venus over the Sun's Disk would undoubtedly be such as could see the Planet's first Appearance, Progress over the Sun's Disk and Disappearance after the Planet's Passage over the Sun's apparent flat Surface, namely its Immersion on the Disk, Continuance over it, and Emersion out of it.

Some of the Islands in the South Sea would be very favorable for that Purpose.

Within our Northern Frigid Zone, for Example, where the Sun does not set but continues above the Horizon, Observations might be taken to great Purpose.

No. 723—*The Duke of Grafton to the King.*

TREASURY CHAMBERS
June 15th 1769

$\frac{m}{10}$ *past* 12 P.M.

The Duke of Grafton presumes to acquaint his Majesty, that on a Visit to the Archbishop this morning, he collected from his Grace that on the whole the Bishop of St Davids, with all Duty, would rather wish to wait for a future Instance of his Majesty's favor, rather than to go to the Bishoprick of St Asaph. His Grace thinks that the offer of that See to the Bishop of Lincoln may very much affect by gratitude his Lordship, who is most likely to decline it; which if he should do, the Bishop of Landaff by being translated to it, would give the King the opportunity of conferring the Deanry of Winchester on Dr Ogle.

The necessity of writing by this night's Post causes the Duke of Grafton to crave humbly to know his Majesty's Pleasure, particularly as being to attend this morning at Doctors Commons prevents him from paying his Court to day to their Majesties at St James's unless he should receive his Majesty's Commands to the Contrary.

No. 724—*The King to the Crown Equerry, Hanover.*

RICHMOND *ce* 20*me Juin* 1769.

MON GRAND ECUYER—J'ai eu une maladie epedemique entre mes attellages Noir, ainsi il faut que Vous m'envoyes quatres Jeunes Chevaux pour les completer, ils doivtent etre

Draft, unfinished.

No. 725—*The King to the Chief Minister, Hanover.*

RICHMOND *ce* 4me *Juliet* 1769.

MON PREMIER MINISTRE—Je Suis très content de votre plan de la repartition des departmens dans Mon Ministere Electorale ; Mais comme Mr de Hacke n'a pas encore publiquement demandé d'être dispenser de vaguer a la Police et aux affaires des Villes, Je' remet cela jusqu' a Son retour en Allemagne, et Mr de Behr ne manquera pas de lui supplier pendant son Absence ; J'ai aussi choisi que Mr de Behr eut le departement du Hartz. comme je souhait de donner toute sorte de relief au College Supreme de Justice à Celle, j'ai nommé Mr de Wenksterz Ministre, mais de la même maniere que Ce feu Mr de Wrisberg. J'ai avec plaisir fait le present que Vous nommé pour batir le Nouvelle Bibliotheke a Göttingen sachant la part que Vous prenéz a tout cequi regarde cette utile institution.

Draft.

No. 726—*Monsieur de Marenholtz to the King.*

SIRE—Pour obeir sans aucun délait, aux ordres de Votre Maj'té, j'ai choisi tout de suite quatre cheveaux entié, et tout ce qu'il i a eu de melieur, en qualite requise, parmi les attellage de ce poil, je prend la liberté de les marquer sur leincluse, et en i agoutent unne liste de ceux qui restent ici, votre Maj'té aura la grace de rémarquer qu'il a ette tout a fait ein possible, de choisir autrement, et d'éviter ; d'agouter aux nombre des quatres deux que le Département des Ecuries a troque avec Charar du Pais. J'espere toute foi que Votre Maj'té trouvera cette récrue asse bonne, et comme Je suppose, qu'elle souhaite leurs arivée aussitot que possible, je les ferai partir le 12 du courent avec un coché attendu, et son aide par la voix ordinaire dé l'holende, qui est a tout égard la plus sure et la moins coulteuse.

Je supplie du reste votre Maj'té, de conserver en bonne grace un vieux serviteure, dévoué avec le Zèle, le plus ardent, pour le Service de son Maitre, et qui a l'honneur d'être avec les sentimens einviolable, du plus profond respect.

Sire de votre Majté le très humble très obeissent très Soumi Serviteur et Sujet   L DE MARENHOLTZ.

A HANNOVRE
le 6ᵈ Juliet
1769.

No. 727—*Form of Commission.*

[In the King's handwriting.]

[*July*, 1769.]

GEORGE THE THIRD by the Grace of God, King of Great Britain, France and Ireland, Defender of the Faith, &c. To Our Trusty and Wellbeloved

Greeting, We do, by these Presents, Constitute and Appoint You to be

You are therefore carefully and diligently to discharge the Duty

You are to observe and follow such orders and Directions from Time to Time as You shall receive

Given at Our Court at St. James's the   day of July of 69, in the Ninth Year of Our Reign.

No. 728—*Hereditary Prince of Brunswick to the King.*

SIRE—Je hésiterois de parlér à Votre Majesté d'une affaire, de la quelle dépend une partie de mon bonheur. Si je n'avois tant de motifs d'être persuadé de Ses graces inestimables, et si en m'ouvrant à Elle, et à Elle seul sur ce sujet, je ne me sentois entierement exemt de toute vue d'intérêt, ou d'ambition mal entendue.

J'avoue, Sire, qu'en osant Vous faire l'offre de mes services dans Vos Trouppes Allemandes, sans autre condition que celle d'y faire exécutér Vos ordres, mon intention est de cherchér à convaincre Votre Majesté, de mon zéle, de mon attachement, et du désir que j'ai de meritér par quelqu'endroit les bienfaits dont Elle m'honore déja, et je m'adresse directement à Votre Majesté parceque la Grace qu'Elle m'accordera redoublera de prix à mes yeux m'étant accordée par Vôtre propre mouvement Sire. La liaison intime qui existe entre les vrais intérêts de nôtre maison, de ceux de Votre Majesté comme Electeur, rend nôtre position telle, que je ne scaurois me figurér un cas, ou ces intérêts pourraient être séparées, c'est là, Sire, le principe d'aprés le quel je me suis proposé déterminement d'agir dans tout le cours de ma vie, ce fera la base de mes démarches, et c'est d'aprés les reflexions les plus mures sur cet objet que je prends la liberté de Vous demandér, Sire, cette nouvelle preuve de Vos bontées, et de Vôtre confiance ; En me vouant au serviçe de Votre Majesté c'est declarér de la maniére la plus positive que nôtre maison ne conait d'autres intérêts que ceux qui sonts conformes aux vues de Votre Majesté. Les malheurs que nôtre famille vient essuier dans le pais de Brandebourg, et dont les traces ne s'effaceronts pas de sitot met entre la maison de Brandebourg, et la nôtre une barriére qui de longtems ne pouva être lever ; Jugéz, Sire, si je ne dois pas desirér ardament que nôtre famille trouve en Vôtre Majesté cet appui respectable qui nous devient de jour en jour plus nécessaire, et je m'estimerois trop heureux, si j'etais l'Instrument destiné à cimentér irrévocablement cette union entre les deux branches de la maison. L'Europe doit à Vos sages mesures Sire, le calme dont Elle jouit, mais Vôtre Majesté conoit trop la vicissitude des affaires de ce monde, Elle scait trop à quel point la Cour de Versaille cherit les maximes artifiçieuses que l'ambition suggere, Elle ne scauroit doutér de la facilite que la france a d'entreprendre sur l'Electorat d'Hanover, cette heureuse Paix, l'ouvrage de Vôtre bienfaisance, Sire, peut avoir son terme, je suis bien eloigné de croire cette epoque prochaine, et bien plus eloigné encor de la désirér, mais il seroit douloureux pour moi, Sire, le cas du Guerre existant de voir la défense de ma patrie rémise aux soins d'un étrangér il ne serait moins hasardeux pour moi, d'être chargé d'un commandement au començement de la Guerre aprés avoir passé l'intervalle de la Paix, dans un loisir qui m'auroit eloigné de tout ce qui pourroit me mêttre a même de conaitre à fond l'Etat des Trouppes, la Capaçité des offiçiérs et sur tout les intentions de Vôtre Majesté, dont je me ferois une Loi de ne jamais m'ecartér. Les Trouppes Allemandes de Vôtre Majesté, jointes à un Corps de 8 à $\frac{10}{m}$ homes des Trouppes de Bronsvic, que je considererois allors come les Sienes propres, feronts constament le fond essentiel de toutte Armée Alliée, de sorte que l'avantage d'entrér aprésent au Serviçe de Vôtre Majesté, fixe mon sort de la façon du monde

la plus satisfaisante, en me destinant à la defense de ma Patrie,
et en me fournissant l'occasion de m'y preparer, et d'en faire
mon unique Étude. La confiance entiére que j'ai dans les bontés
de Votre Maj: me fait prendre la liberté de Lui parler à cœur
ouvert, sur tout ce qui peut être relatif à la graçe que je Lui
demande, je serais au désespoire si ma demande pouvoit influér
d'une façon désagreable, sur la position de M^r le Maréchal de
Spoerken, je réconnois les talents de ce digne vieillard, sur le
quel je ne puis pretendre à d'autres avantage que l'activité que
produit la différence d'age ; je scai que Mr: le Marechal de
Spoerke s'est occupé d'idées de rétraitte peu aprés la fin de la
Guerre, Vôtre Majesté se l'est attaché dépuis ce tems par de
nouvelles Graces j'ignore coment il pense actuellement, si Vous
daigniez, Sire, le faire sonder à ce sujet peut-être fourniroit il
lui même des moiëns propres à levér les difficultés, je ne forme
aucune demande qui vise au pécuniaire, mon emplaçement
n'occasionera aucun changement ni parmis les Gouvernements
de Ses places, ni parmis les propriataires actuelles des Régiments,
je souscrirai de mon coté à touttes les conditions que Vôtre
Majesté dictera, mon objet unique est d'etre plaçé dans une
position, qui me mêtte en même de La servir, mais de La servir
avec afficaçe : Je ne formerai point d'établissement permanent
à Hanover pour y demeurér avec ma famille, plusiers raisons
S'y opposent, mon intention serait d'y prendre une maison
uniquement destinée pour y habitér lorsque mon dévoir m'ap-
pellera à Hanover, et durant le tems des exerciçes. Ces
détailles dans les quelles j'ai osés entrér Vous prouveronts, Sire,
combien je desire de réçévoire une réponse favorable de la part
de Vôtre Majesté, si elle l'est, une obéissance entiére à Ses
volontés sera la premiére soin que je m'imposerai ; Elle daignera
se rappellér que j'ai passé une partie de ma jeunesse en servant
dans Ses Armées que la Graçe que je demande actuellement à
dépuis longtems fait l'objet cheri de mes désirs, et que j'ai même
osé m'en flatter pour un moment. J'ai sondé Sire les intentions
de mon Pere sur la démarche que je fais, je me suis assuré qu'il
seroit charmé si elle pouvoit réussir, je ne Lui ai cependant fait
aucune ouverture dans les formes, c'est pourquoi j'ose suppliér
Vôtre Majesté de me garder le Sécrêt sur le demande que j'ai
osé lui faire ; je me jette entiérement entre Vos bras Sire, Vos
bontées passées me donent les espérançes les plus flatteuses

pour l'avenir, si Votre Majeste m'accorde la Grace que je Lui
demande, je Lui suis acquis pour le reste de ma Vie, je n'aurais
d'autres intérêts à coeur que les Siens, Ses intérêts se trouveronts
si intimements liés aux nôtres qu'ils ne formeronts qu'une masse
comune dont la direction sera entre les mains de Vôtre Majesté.
C'est avec le plus humble, et la plus soumise dévotion que J'ai
l'honneur d'etre

Sire De Vôtre Majesté le plus humb: plus obeis et plus
soumis serviteur   CHARLES prince.

ANTOINETTENRUH, *ce* 28 *de Juil*:
1769.

No. 729—*Sir R. M. Keith to Lord Rochford.*

Nº 13.   DRESDEN *August* 3ᵈ 1769.

MY LORD—I take the opportunity of Mʳ De Vismes return to
England to send Your Lordship a State of the saxon Revenues
and Expences of Government, which was given to me by a person
not only well informed, but anxious to afford me the most
authentic Lights. I have not attempted to explain the Nature
of the different Taxes, as it would have been encroaching upon
your Lordship's time and that it can be only material to know
the gross Sums of the Receipt and Expence. There may be
some errors in both, but I am persuaded upon the Whole the
Computations are tollerably exact.

In the approaching Diet some new Plan will probably be laid
down to augment the Revenue, particularly in regard to Nº 6. in
the *Caisse Generale de Guerre* that Tax having proved detrimental
to Trade, at the same time that it produces less than was at
first expected.

The Savings to be made in all the Articles of Expence,
(exclusive of the three first, and tenth,) will produce a considerable Sum, and, it is hoped, enable the Sovereign to maintain
the present Army without having recourse to any foreign Sub-
sidies whatever. I have likewise enclosed a State of the Army,
which is almost complete and in very good Order.

I will not presume to give a Character of Count Sacken upon
so short an Acquaintance, and with so few Opportunities of
knowing his true Sentiments. I have found him ever profuse of

1 Rail Battery of Marrons
2 Illuminated double Spiralis
6 Air Ballons
1 Illuminated Horizontal Wheel with a Globe
2 Planks of Pots de Brins
1 Regulated Transparent Piece
1 Illuminated Decoration
1 Flight consisting of 16 dozen of Rockets

THOMAS DESAGULIERS
Chief Firemaster to His Majesty.

No. 732—*Monsieur Messier to Doctor Bevis.*

MONSIEUR—J'ai découvert le 8 de ce Mois (Aout) vers les 11 heures du Soir, une novelle Cométe, qui paroisoit sous le ventre de la Constellation du Belier.   Les Nuits suivantes le Ciel a ete entierement couvert, et je n'ai pu la revoir que la Nuit dernière entre des Intervales de Nuage, J'en ai dètermine la position, ce matin 15 a minuit et demi elle avoit d'ascension droite 38° 35′ 2″ et de declinaison 11° 49′ 32″ Boreale, Son mouvement se fait suivant l'ordre des Signes en s'approchant de l'Equateur, on la voyoit aisement a la vue simple avec une Queue dense de Six degrez.   Son mouvement est tre lent, elle ne parcoure pas 4 min : en 24 heures en ascension droite, et beaucoup moins en declinaison.
Je nai pas le tems actuellement de vous en dire d'avantage.
Lisé ma Lettre je vous prie a la Societé Royale.
J'ai l'honeur d'être avec beaucoup de Respect, Monsieur, Votre très humble et très obeissant Serviteur   MESSIER.

PARIS, COLLEGE ROYALE—
DE FRANCE 15 *Aout*. 1769.

Mons. le Docteur Bevis a Londre

No. 733—*Hereditary Prince of Brunswick to the King.*

SIRE—Il n'est guere possible d'exprimér a Vôtre Majesté combien je suis touché, et remplis de réconaissance de la facon

gracieuse et ouverte, avec la quelle Elle a daigné àgir a mon
égard: Vôtre Majesté sera persuadé par ma preçédente de tout
ce qu'il y avait d'entéressant pour moi dans la proposition que
J'ai osé Lui faire, et combien il importait d'etre instruit des
sentiments de Vôtre Majesté sur ce point. Come je n'ai point
eu le moment present, prinçipalement en vue, mais les événements
futures, et que j'ai considéré la totalité des affaires de cette
partie de l'Allemagne, j'ose assurér trés humblement à Vôtre
Majesté que je me serois soumis aveuglement à la façon coment
Elle auroit trouvé bon de m'emploiér y'attachant une idée de
Gloire de portér les armes pour Vôtre Majesté préférablement à
tout autre Prince : mais come les Volontés de Vôtre Majesté
fonts tous jours Loix pour moi, j'y suis entiérement resigné, dans
l'esperance flatteuse qu'Elle daignera Se persuadér de mon Zele,
et de mon attachment respectueux a Sa trés haute Persone et
à Ses intérêts. Il ne me reste qu'a désirér que Vôtre Majesté
daigne se souvenir dans l'occasion du plus soumis de Ses serviteurs,
qui n'aura toutte sa vie d'autre ambition que de vous prouvér
Sire—son profond respect, et son admiration.

C'est avec la devotion la plus soumise que j'ai l'honeur d'être,
Sire, De Vôtre Majesté le plus humble plus obes st plus Sou serviteur
CHARLES.

BRONSVIC *ce* 27 *Aout*
1769.

No. 734—*Dr. J. Bevis to Mr. J. Kirby.*

DEAR SIR—Since I saw the Comet for the last time this day
sennet in the morning, I have been drawing the Representation
of its several appearances from first to last on one Piece of
paper ; which, as it is more than a yard long, I cannot send
you by the Post, but will do it some other way. I am now
constructing its Orbit, and I find it will be in the Perihelion tomorrow night Octob. 1st when it will be more than thirty times
nearer to the Sun than our Earth is. We cannot see it any more
above our horizon, but it must be very conspicuous to our
Astronomers gone to the South Sea. I am sure it is not any
one of those we have upon Record. M. Messier thinks himself
not a little honoured by two Monarchs ; for, besides His Majesty
having been pleas'd to demand a sight of his Letter to me, the

King of Prussia has wrote one with his own hand on his first Discovery of the Comet.

I am with much regard, Dear Sir, your affectionate humble Servt J. BEVIS.

Septemb. 30th 1769.

Enclosure.

		H	′	″		
Sunday Augt 27.	Comet's Right Ascension .	12..44..5.	0	1		
	Comet's Declination		14..21..45			

	H			
Lambda in the Bull Right Ascension . . .	12..45..27.	0		
Declination		12..32..45		

Mon^y
Augt 28

                                         ′ ″

The Comet had moved in Right Ascension   8..37
North Declination . . . . .   38..20.

By the End of this Week a Scheme of the Path of this Comet, taken from its Curve Line may be compleated.

No. 735—*Lord Bute to the King.*

SIR—As the state of my health renders it necessary for me to try once more the effect of a Warm Climate during the winter months, & the Season forcing me to depart immediately, I presume to trouble your Majesty with these few lines, relative to the questions that may be agitated in Parliament, concerning the Civil List Expenditure ; of the Summs issued during the year I had the honor to serve in the Treasury ; some were for Secret Service, others for Special Services ; which last were regularly delivr'd into Your Majestys Hands ; & were dispos'd of by your Self ; there was besides a Sum of £25000 issued on the tenth of december under the name of Secret Service, that I had the Honor to carry to Your Majesty, in the same manner that I had done those before, that were issued for Your Special Service.

As it may become necessary to state these Matters in Parliament, I humbly beg to know your Majestys pleasure upon it.

I have the honor to be with Inviolable attachment, Sir, Your Majestys most dutiful Servant and Subject   BUTE.

Nov: 4ᵗʰ 1769.

No. 736—*The King to Sir Joseph Yorke.*

QUEEN'S HOUSE *Decʳ* 15ᵗʰ 1769.

SIR JOSEPH YORKE—The experience I have of Your Zeal for my Service and of Your knowledge of the sentiments of the principal persons of the Republic, has occasioned my directing Baron Behr to enquire of You what conduct the United Provinces are most likely to adopt in case the clouds that seem daily to thicken should produce a new War, for if I form a plan of defence as Elector it must in great measure arise, from the hopes of assistance from so natural Ally as the Dutch.

I shall be desirous of hearing from You in consequence of this, and of learning how far the influence of the Prince of Orange gains ground, and whether Prince Lewis still retains [the] weight he had with that Prince.

as this is as yet only an Electoral concern You will send Your letter through the Channel of the German Resident.

Draft, endorsed by the King.

No. 737—*The King to Lord North.*

LORD NORTH—I wish to see You about eight this Evening.

QUEEN HOUSE
Decʳ 20ᵗʰ 1769
$\frac{m}{40}$ p^t 4. P.M.

No. 738—*Sir Joseph Yorke to the King.*

SIRE—Baron Behr deliver'd to me on Tuesday last the 19th Inst at night, Your Majesty's most gracious Letter of the 15th Instant, & I only beg leave to introduce what I have to say in answer, with assuring Your Majesty that your Service is my bounden Duty & my greatest honour, & your Secret my Most Sacred Deposit.

Your Majesty is pleased to ask me, " What Conduct the " United Provinces are most likely to adopt in case the " Clouds that seem to thicken daily, should produce a new " War ? "

To answer this Question it will be necessary to make some observations, &c.

First, the States tasted so much the Sweets of their last fortuitous Neutrality (for it was owing to accident & not at all to their own Conduct) that could they be assured of enjoying the same quiet & reaping the same profit, they would look on to a certain degree with unconcern upon the ruin or at least the diminution of Strength of all around them.   They felt however that their Situation was not exempt from danger, & Marshal Contades's Strong Box exposed too many Secrets relative to them to leave them room to doubt of the Malevolence of France, so that the Most Neutral Members of the States declared to me at that time, that at the Peace they would take their Measures so as not to be caught unawares another time.   Since that the Stadtholder has reached his Majority & the interior situation has undergone some alteration ; what was before look'd upon solely as the Means of preserving the independancy of the State, is now mix'd with a jealousy of the Stadholder's power & ambition, to which an increase of their force might add strength or give a temptation.   In this Sentiment I mean particularly to mark out Amsterdam, whose influence in the Province of Holland which domineers the rest is known to all who are acquainted with this Government.   The Stadholder however when maintaining a good Cause, & supported by his friends & those of his system from without, may always find sufficient strength to stem the Torrent of that Town by the other Provinces.   As this is supposed to be the Case we are to look for the Sentiments of the Prince of Orange first, & then the method he takes to have them adopted by others. Of this I have seen two examples within the space of three Years, the first in the Embassy of the Marquis d' Havrincour, when France affected to take Umbrage at a report of an augmentation of the Republick's Troops, & had order'd her Embassador to represent against it. The Prince plainly told the Embassador, with the acquiescence of the States, that the Republick was free, & having no Evil intentions against any other Power, was equally at liberty with other Sovereigns to make Such interior dispositions as she judged proper. The Second was within these few Weeks, when the Reports from England threatened an approaching rupture with France, upon which the Prince of Orange was strongly alarm'd & immediately sent to the Regency of Amsterdam to tell them of the Danger, & to repeat to them how necessary it was to think of the security of the Republick which was exposed to the first shock & unable to resist it. Amsterdam answer'd to satisfaction, that they desired Peace & wish'd to preserve it, but that they were of opinion with the Prince that in case those Accounts were confirmed, Measures should be taken for the Defence of the Country, notwithstanding two Provinces, Those of Zealand & Friseland were not upon a Par with the others, & pretended an inability to furnish their contingents. The apparent contradiction or relaxation in the next accounts threw us all back into our Antient Channel, & a new alarm must arise a little better supported, to keep up that spirit which the first impression occasions.

The conclusion I would draw from what goes before, is that the Prince of Orange's sentiments are elevated enough, not to permit him to be contented with an Unarm'd Neutrality ; That he really is attach'd to your Majesty & to England ; & that he knows & feels that this Country with his family at the head of it are objects of dislike in France ; That it is in all their Minds to take Measures of Security, whenever the probability of a Rupture Manifests itself, because the danger is too great to risk with an extensive Frontier from the Sea to the Rhine, to be defended with an Army little more than sufficient to Garrison the Towns as they ought to be, when the Enemy's Point is unknown. An Active Part must not however be expected from this Country at the first out-set, if not attacked ; that must be managed by the Prince of Orange by degrees, & to enable him to compass it, a real Confidence must be placed in him, so that by timely & important Intelligence he may know his danger to justify him in Measures of precaution, and means of acquiring strength & security be open'd at the same time, so as to enable him to combat others with Success.

This brings me naturally to the Second Part of Your Majesty's Letter, in which you are pleased to say that " A Plan " of Defence as Elector must in a great measure arise from the " hopes of assistance from so Natural an Ally as the Dutch ".

I cannot but agree with Your Majesty's Sentiments that the *Hopes* of assistance from Holland, must naturally strengthen any Electoral Plan of Defence, but you will forgive me for adding with Zeal & Deference, that it appears to me that it must be from the Private Manifestation of that Plan of Defence, in consequence of a well confirmed danger, that *those Hopes* must spring ; because single & uninformed, & in idea unaided too, the Republick runs a risk of waiting to take its Measures till it is too late, & only fight or Capitulate *Pro Aris & Focis*.

To make myself more clearly understood—The Prince of Orange does not mean an unarmed Neutrality, nor does the Country in general, tho' Many are afraid of the Consequences of Arming ; if England is attack'd they will be frighten'd, & tho' jealous of our Power & our Vivacity would feel the possibility of their suffering in the same Cause ; at such a time, or with the certain intelligence of such a Danger, the Electoral Plan would be very likely to be catch'd at with eagerness, & the Prince of Orange could not but feel his happiness to have such an Ally at hand, whose assistance would not depend upon the Caprice of Continental or Anti-continental Ideas, or upon the prejudice of Parties, who in an Island have time to deliberate with less risk, than those who are in the Jaws of the Enemy. If by *assistance* Your Majesty means a Pecuniary one, I am afraid that would come as heavily without a thorough conviction of the Danger, as it would be lavish & if that Danger was at the Door, Your Majesty's experience of such Governments as this, will Corroborate what I say, of the difficulty there is to bring about expensive Measures of precaution, tho' frequently in the End the Most œconomical.

Your Majesty's next Question may be answer'd briefly, " How " far the Prince of Orange gains ground ".

The Prince's influence is great, but it will certainly increase in Action, as he then becomes the Center upon which every thing turns, his Foreign Connexions & his home Dependance become more extensive ; I see with pleasure that he shews daily more Judgement, Temper, & firmness ; his Bodily health is confirmed, & tho' he never went quite so far with me, I know from the Persons he has let it drop to, that he would not be sorry to Serve, & when he talks of serving Your Majesty may be assured he has no other Idea but of serving against France.

After having said all this there remains one principal Article to be consider'd, which arises from Your Majesty's last Question, viz : " Whether Prince Lewis still retains the Weight he had with that Prince ? "

To this I must answer in the affirmative, for he has taken such effectual care to keep every body at a distance who could influence him in matters of importance, that the Prince thro' habit, respect, & gratitude consults him in everything of Conse-quence ; I see therefore no possibility at present of putting him out of the question in a Deliberation of this importance, as thro' whatever channel it is conducted it will finally revert to him ; But if he opposes the Prince's Bent when he is Shewn a reasonable Security, against an imminent Danger, he must, in my humble opinion, follow or lose his influence. It is natural to ask, why he should oppose a Plan calculated for the Safety of the Repub-lick & the honour of His friend & Pupil ? openly he could not because he approves & avows our Principles, but Collateral & Personal Motives would make him unwilling to embark. His health & strength are no longer equal to the fatigues of War, he would not chuse to leave the Prince to others who must of Course supplant him, & his particular jealousy of his own family would operate more than anything, as he would apprehend their appearing upon the Stage & eclipsing him. As he could never avow however Such Motives, he must look for them in malicious reflecions upon all around him, & in the supposed interior situation of England, with the danger to which the Prince would be exposed by being in the Breach. This is my Idea abridged founded in observation ; but I won't at the same time say he may not be got the better of, especially if he happens to be flatterr'd with being amongst the first in the Secret, & when Your Majesty's Commands & the publick Safety requires it, I am ready to embark in the Discussion, for if he cannot be left out, one must try to take him along, & at the worst I shall be at least able to form a judgement how far He & the Country are to be depended upon.

Before I conclude this Letter, already I am afraid too long, I must take the liberty just to mention the Connexion between the Prince of Orange & the King of Prussia by the Marriage with the latter's Niece. That alliance has brought on a Correspondence between those Princes, & tho' the Stadtholder has no desire to follow his Unkle's advice implicitly, & fancy's himself extremely on his guard, which is increased even too far perhaps by Prince Lewis, from the same principle which actuates his conduct every where, yet Your Majesty will be sensible that such a Correspondence with such a Monarch opens the Door to many Suggestions & Insinuations, the effect of which is not always to be answer'd for ; it will therefore be necessary to take that point into consideration whenever Your Majesty determines to go further, that whoever has the honor to execute your orders may be able to answer such questions as may be put to him relative to His Prussian Majesty, & the hopes or doubts there may be concerning him. To be sure at this Moment, France & Prussia are very ill together, & the Russian alliance won't admit of a reconciliation ; I am too ignorant of H.P.M's system to know how far he would go in behalf of his Nephew & the Republick, but I have reason to believe that what he preaches to the Stadtholder is an armed Neutrality.

I wish I may have been happy enough to satisfy Your Majesty with any part of this Letter, I told Baron Behr the substance of what I write who encouraged me to forward it ; Knowing Your Majesty's indulgence I shall wait your further orders before I presume to take any step, & should be too happy if my Zeal could supply my other Defects when I mean to testify my unbounded attachment & Veneration, with which as I am bound I shall Ever remain, Sire, Your Majesty's Most faithful, Devoted, & Dutiful Subject & Servant   JOSEPH YORKE.

P.S.—The Princess of Orange is just in the Critical Moment of her distemper, Consequently we are not at our ease, however no bad Symptom yet Manifests itself, it must be decided by next Post.

HAGUE. *Dec^r* 22^d 1769.

No. 739—*Memoranda as to the Knights of the Garter.*

[In the King's handwriting.]

[1769.]

1. Sovereign . . .	1. P. of Wales.
	2. D. of Glocester.
	3. D. of Cumberland.
7. D of Kingston	
8. D of Bedford	8. D of Newcastle.
9. D of Montagu.	9 D of Northumberland.
10. E. of Hertford.	10. M. of Rockingham
11. E. of Temple	11. E. of Bute
12. E of Halifax	12. E of Albemarle
13. D. of Marlborough.	13. D of Grafton.

1761.

1. Sovereign . . .	1. late D. of Cumberland.
	2. late D. of York.
	3. D. of Glocester
5. late D. of Newcastle	5. D of Rutland.
	6. D. of Kingston.
7. Duke of Leeds	
8. D. of Newcastle	
9. late D. of Devonshire	9. late E of Winchelsea
10. D. of Cumberland	10. E of Hertford
11. late E of Waldegrave	11. M^s of Rockingham
13. E of Temple	13. E of Bute

1761.	1. Duke of Glocester	. . .	The late King.
	2. Earl of Bute	. . . .	Duke of Portland.
1764.	3. Duke of Mecklenburgh	. .	Earl of Granville
	4. Earl of Halifax . . .	.	Earl of Waldegrave
1765.	5. Prince of Wales . . .	.	Duke of Cumberland
	6. Herd. Prince of Brunswick	.	Duke of Dorset
	7. Earl of Albemarle	. . .	Duke of Devonshire
1767.	8. Duke of Cumberland .	. .	Duke of York
1768.	9. Duke of Marlborough	. .	Duke of Newcastle
1769.	10. Duke of Grafton	. . .	Earl of Winchelsea

KNIGHTS OF THE GARTER ACCORDING TO THE DATE OF
THEIR INSTALLATIONS.

1725.	1. Duke of Rutland.	1731.	2. Earl of Chesterfield
1740.	3. Duke of Kingston.	1742.	4. D. of Saxe Gotha
1744.	5. Land. of Hesse Cassel.	1749.	6. The King.
1749.	7. Duke of Leeds.	1749.	8. Duke of Bedford.
	9ª Prince of Orange.	1752.	10. Duke of Montagu.
1752.	9. Duke of Newcastle.	1757.	12. Earl of Hertford.
1757.	11. Duke of Northumber-	1760.	15. Earl of Temple.
	land.		
	13. Prince Ferdinand.	1761.	17. Earl of Bute.
1760.	14. Marquis of Rocking-	1764.	20. Earl of Halifax.
	ham.		
1761.	16. Duke of Gloucester.	1765.	22. H. Prince of Brunswick
1764.	18. Duke of Mecklen-	1767.	24. Duke of Cumberland.
	burgh.		
1765.	20. Prince of Wales.	1769.	26. Duke of Grafton.
1765.	23. Earl of Albemarle.		
1768.	25. Duke of Marlborough.		

1. Prince William ;	2. Prince Edward ;	3. Prince Ernest ;
		Sec. of State
4. D. of Ancaster ;	5. E. of Pembroke ;	6. E. of Suffolk ;
1st Ld. Admiralty	Governor	Sec. of State
7. E. of Sandwich ;	8. E. of Holdernesse ;	9. E. of Rochford ;
	Gr of State	
10. E. of Dartmouth ;	11. E. of Bristol ;	12. E. of Ashburnham
Ld Lieut. Ireland	Steward	Master Ordinance
13. E. of Harcourt ;	14. E. Talbot	15. Vt Townshend ;
16. Vt Weymouth.		

1. Sovereign.	1. P. of Wales.
Int. D. of Gloucester.	Int. Bp of Osnabourg.
2. D. of Cumberland.	2. Landsgrave of Hesse Cassel.
Int. Pr. William.	Int. Pr. Edward.
3. Pr. Ernest.	3. Pr. of Orange.
Int. Pr. Ferdinand.	Int. D. of Mecklenburgh Strelitz.

4. Pr. Brunswick.		4. D. of Saxe Gotha.
Int. Mar. of Anspach.		Int. D. of Rutland.
5. E. of Chesterfield.		5. D. of Kingston.
Int. D. of Leeds.		Int. D. of Newcastle.
6. D. of Montague.		6. D. of Northumberland.
Int. E. of Hertford.		Int. Mˢ of Rockingham.
7. E. of Temple.		7. E. of Bute.
Int. D. of Marlborough.		Int. D. of Grafton.
8. E. of Gower.		8. Ld. North.
9. E. of Suffolk.		9. E. of Sandwich.
10. E. of Holdernesse.		10. E. of Rochford.
11. E. of Dartmouth.		11. C. of Bristol.
12. E. of Hartcourt.		12. E. of Talbot.
13. Vᵗ Townshend.		13. Vᵗ Weymouth.

1.
2.
3.
4.
5.
6.
7.
8.
9.
10.
Int.

11. E. of Suffolk.		11. E. of Sandwich.
E. of Holdernesse.		E. of Rochford.
12. E. of Dartmouth.		12. E. of Bristol.
Int. E. Harcourt.		E. Talbot.
13. Vᵗ Townshend.		13. Vᵗ Weymouth.

No. 740—*Lord Townshend to Lord Weymouth.*

DUBLIN CASTLE 30. *Decemʳ* 1769.

MY LORD—I transmit herewith, to your Lordship, a Memorial which hath been laid before Me from Major Otho Hamilton and Captain Adam Williamson of the 40ᵗʰ Regiment of Foot, praying for the reasons therein mentioned to be Recommended to His

Majesty for the Brevet Rank of Lieutenant Colonel and Major respectively. And I desire your Lordship will lay the same before His Majesty and Signify to Me His Royal Pleasure thereupon.

I am with great Respect, My Lord, Your Lordship's most obedient humble Servant   TOWNSHEND.

Enclosure No. 1.

To His Excellency George Lord Viscount Townshend, Lord Lieu^t General & General Governor of Ireland &^{ca} &^{ca} &^{ca}

> The Memorial of Major Otho Hamilton & Captain Adam Williamson of the 40th Regiment.

His Majesty by his late regulations having positively Ordered One Field Officer to be constantly resident with each Regiment, has prevented your Memorialist from making any application for leave, and during Twenty five Years Service has been absent only One Year from the Regiment, served the whole War in North America and the West Indies, was wounded at the Siege of Quebec and purchased his Majority in November 1761.

Your Other Memorialist has been upwards of Sixteen Years an Officer Served in North America & the West Indies from the Defeat of General Braddock to the taking the Havana, was twice severely wounded at the Monongahela and Siege of Quebec, and purchased his Company in April 1760.

Your Memorialists beg leave to represent that Lieu^t Colonel Grant being Governor of East Florida, renders it impossible for him ever to Attend the Regiment, and their case in respect to the whole Army is Singular. They Flatter themselves their Characters as Men and Officers will bear the strictest Scrutiny.

Your Memorialists therefore humbly pray that having had the Honour to serve under your Excellency at the taking Quebec, that your Excellency will be pleased to take their Services and case into consideration, and lay their Memorial before His Majesty recommending them for the Brevet Rank of Lieu^t Colonel and Major which Commissions His Majesty was most graciously pleased to Sign for them in 1766, but were afterwards recalled.

Should your Memorialists be so fortunate to succeed, His Majesty's regulations could be complied with & One Field Officer constantly resident with the Regiment.

All which is humbly submitted

OTHO HAMILTON
ADAM WILLIAMSON

CORKE 13*th* *June* 1769.

Ent^d

Enclosure No. 2.

General Williamson to Lord Granby.

MY VERY GOOD LORD—Perswaded of Your Lordships great good will and Goodness towards me and my Son Adam Williamson I take the liberty to mention his Situation in the first place, and then to acquaint Your Lordship of the substance of his letter to me from Dublin in Ireland of the third of this Month. Adam Williamson began his Campaigns in 1755 in America under the Command of General Bradock at the affair at Monongahila in America. he was shot in the thigh and very near loseing his life but escaped with only the cloaths on his back when the Army was totally defeated. he continued to serve in that Country and was with me at the reduction of Louisbourg in 58 ; Quebec in 1759, where he was again shot in the Legg in great Danger of looseing it. was with me at taking Montreal in 1760, and in April that Year I purchased a Company for him in the 40th Regiment. he afterwards went to the West Indies, where he assisted in taking Dominique Martinique and lastly the Havanna which ended ye Warr. he is now with his Regiment in Ireland & the eldest Captⁿ he is near ten Years a Captain, and has the misfortune to have 38 Younger Captains to him whom are now Majors by purchase or otherwise notwithstanding my readiness to asist him all in my power.

by my letter from him the other day I learn that he has preferred a Memorial to Lord Townshend who approv'd of it and promised to send it over to Lord Weymouth.

and now my Lord as I must suppose the substance of the Memorial is the same which I have related to Your Lordship,

& if it is come to Lord Weymouths hands hoping he will be so good to lay it at His Majesties feet ;

Give me leave to pray that Your Lordship will be pleased to speak to His Majesty, in behalf of my only Son who has been so often disappointed notwithstanding his faithfull and assiduous Services.

for any further Character of him I appeal to Sir Jeffrey Amherst, Lord Townshend and General Monckton, with others under whose Command he has Served.

I have the Honor to be with the utmost Gratitude and Respect, My Lord, Your Lordships much Obliged and most Obedient humble Servant GEORGE WILLIAMSON.

22ᵈ November 1769.

No. 741—*Memorial.*

[Apparently emanating from General Paoli.]

[1769 ?]

General de Paoli being admitted to the high honor of a second private audience of your Majesty, by means of the present respectfull Memorial represents to your Majesty's deep penetration the state of the Island of Corsica with regard to the necessary advantageous connexion it might have with the interests of your Majesty's Crown, in case through the influence of Great Britain it were to be delivered from the oppression under which it now Labours, and to be protected in the possession of its Liberty. Corsica is situated in the midst of the Mediterranean Sea distant only a few hours sail from almost the whole coast of Italy, from that of Provence, and not very far from the coast of Africa. It is separated from Sardinia by a narrow pass of the sea of only ten miles, and has large and commodious Gulfs and harbours on every side for the reception of numerous fleets. Hence Corsica might be a check upon the Dutchy of Tuscany, the Republick of Genoa, and the Ecclesiastical State, to hinder them from entring into engagements with the Ennemies and contrary to the interests of Great Britain ; and be at the same time a constant and perpetual security of the faith and amity of the King of Sardinia.

From Corsica Likewise the English would be able to cut off the communication between Spain and France and the two Sicilies; and might easily oblige the Sovereign of these Last States to withdraw himself from the family compact, the greater part of his harbours and chief Cities lying upon the sea coast exposed to the attacks of any small English Squadron. Above all however, the advantages and authority and influence which France proposes to herself in the Mediterranean and throughout all Italy from so considerable an increase of her commerce and naval force, and for which she has spilt so much blood and Lavished away such treasures in the conquest of Corsica, nor scrupled to throw aside all regard to the other Powers, violating the most sacred promises and solemn treaties, and transgressing the rules of war, the Laws of honour, and the rights of humanity, would doubly redound to the advantage of Great Britain, whose glory and effective power must increase in proportion as those, together with the credit, of her natural Ennemy decrease.

Besides capacious and commodious ports for careening and harbouring, the English fleets would find in Corsica abundance of timber for building, sailours and provisions of every kind, without being obliged to seek them from Portugal which may easily change its political maxims and principles; or from Barbary where the Ennemies of Great Britain may through their influence upon those Powers and Governments render them precarious to the English.

Corsica might also furnish seven or eight thousand Men in case of any important expedition or enterprise; and in time of war such a number of Privateers and armed Vessels, as joined with those of Great Britain, would alone and without the interposition of the Royal Navy be sufficient to ruin the french trade in the Mediterranean; a point the more easy as all Vessels sailing to the Levant from the Western Coasts must necessarily make Cape Corse both in going and returning.

The situation of Corsica is Likewise altogether proper to give Great Britain a superior influence to that of France at the Ottoman Ports: because from thence She might with greater ease and conveniency Keep in subjection by means of her fleets the Turkish dominions in the Levant; on which account her alliance would be more courted both by the House of Austria and that of Russia.

If desirous also of extending her influence over the Barbary Powers, Corsica is so well situated for this purpose that the independency of the Island sought the friendship of General de Paoli, without his being obliged to apply to them for theirs with the disbassement [*sic*] of a large sum of money.

All these advantages cannot be had from Minorca, which Great Britain is in actual possession of. The English fleets have there the conveniency of only one port, of which in the beginning of a war their Ennemies by making a sudden descent with fifteen or twenty thousand Men with a few months provisions may easily possess themselves. The whole superiority of the English fleet in such case would not be able to hinder them from effecting their purpose. Corsica on the other hand, its Inhabitants being principally Soldiers, if it were once restored to its Liberty, would become inattackable : whence, besides the advantages already mentioned, it would be the Least burthensom and expensive Ally to Great Britain ; because she would not see herself so frequently necessitated on account of it to sacrifice at the making of a peace her most valuable conquests as She has done on other occasion in order to indemnify the House of Austria and the Republick of Holland for the Losses they have sustained in the Low Countries ; and as it might probably happen with regard to Portugal and the King of Sardinia ; the dominions of both these Potentates being too much exposed to the invasions of the House of Bourbon. These enumerated advantages to be had in time of war, would not be the only ones which Great Britain might draw from Corsica supposing it were free. The Country is by nature fertile, and might become much more under the enjoyment of its Liberty ; whence the exportation of its produce might be very considerable. Corsica has no Manufactures, and those of England would be recieved in preference to any others, which in the present actual State of Corsica would give occasion to the annual exportation of about four hundred thousand pounds sterling. Proportionably more advantageous also would be the situation of Corsica for the commerce of the English Subjects in the Mediterranean, if these last were to make a convenient depository there of the commercial goods of the Levant which would give a mortal blow to the trade of Marseilles. Corsica in short restored to its Liberty and united in interest with Great Britain, would be the properest place to counteract the designs and ambitious views of the House of Bourbon in regard to the Italy ; to turn the scale of commerce to the disadvantage of France in the Mediterranean ; dry up the principal sources from whence she thinks to increase her Marine and Naval power ; and render the influence of Great Britain superior and without competition even in the Mediterranean.

All these reflections are of such a nature that your Majesty deigning to submit them to your Royal consideration cannot but acknowledge the essential relation and advantageous connexion which the situation and Liberty of Corsica may have with the interests of Great Britain ; so as to induce your Majesty to employ the most efficacious means both of negociation and force to rescue that Island of the hands of its Invaders and restore it to the enjoyment of its Liberty.

This necessary expedient would be also an act of Justice on the part of your Majesty ; not so much in regard to the breach of faith committed against the Corsicans in the act of invading their Country ; as the aretefices used by the Court of France in order to decieve in this affair the Powers of Europe ; and particularly the Guarantees of the treaty of Aquisgrana ; The invasion of Corsica being a direct violation of the articles and faith of that treaty ; meant to authorise in Europe the right of force, and to take away every sacred foundation whereon is built the security of States and Nations ; which must necessarily from this example be in perpetual apprehension of whoever may have the power and will of making conquests.

If however other motives besides these alledged may interest the magnanimous disposition of your Majesty in favour of the People of Corsica, there are those of humanity and of your Majesty's innate compassion, moved and excited by the sight of the most unjust oppression and cruel treatment which the Corsicans now suffer ; and which induce them to turn to the Throne of Great Britain all their hopes both of safety and Liberty ; which would be the more dear to them, as it would place them in a situation to show to all future Ages their most respectfull gratitude ; their fidelity and Zeal, and their most obsequious attachment to your Majesty's sacred Person and the interests of your Crown.

No. 742—*The King to Lord North.*

Printed. Donne I. 10.

QUEEN'S HOUSE *Jany 7th* 1770.

$\frac{m}{5} p^t$ 8. P.M.

LORD NORTH—I am so desirous that every man in my service that can with propriety take part in the Debate on Tuesday, should speak, that I desire You will very strongly press Sir Gilbert Elliott and any others that have not taken in the last Session so forward a part as their abilities make them capable of, and I have no objection to Your adding that I have particularly directed You to speak to them on this occasion.

Draft.

No. 743—*Lord North to the King.*

Lord North has, in obedience to his Majesty's order, appointed the three Commissioners to attend at court tomorrow with the Great Seal. He has just received the inclosed letter from Lord Mansfield which he has the honour of inclosing, as an additional proof of the worthy & disinterested character of Lord Chief Justice Wilmot. Lord North has seen the Attorney General, who accepts the Common pleas, but seems very desirous of some mark of favour to his Son. He will, with his Majesty's permission mention this business to his Majesty, when he sees him tomorrow.

DOWNING STREET. *Jan.* 22. [1770] 12 *o'clock.*

No. 744—*The King to Lord North.*

LORD NORTH—I am desirous of seeing You this Evening at Seven.

QUEEN'S HOUSE
Jan. 22^d 1770.

$\frac{m}{13} p^t$ 7. P.M.

No. 745—*The King to Lord North.*

Printed. Donne I. 11.

QUEEN'S HOUSE *Jan.* 23^d 1770.

$\frac{m}{40}$ p^t 10. A.M.

LORD NORTH—After Seeing you last night I saw Lord Weymouth who by My Direction will wait on You with Lord Gower this morning to press You in the strongest Manner to accept the Office of first Commissioner of the Treasury My own mind is more and more strengthened with the rightness of the measure that would prevent every other observation, You must easily see that if You do not accept I have no Peer at present in my Service that I could consent to place in the Duke of Grafton's employment, whatever You may think do not take any decision unless it is the one of instantly accepting without a further conversation with Me. And as to the other arrangements You may hear what others think but keep Your own opinion till I have seen You.

No. 746—*The King to Lord North.*

LORD NORTH—I am desirous of seeing You either at seven this Evening or Eleven tomorrow morning.

QUEEN'S HOUSE
Jany 28th 1770
$\frac{m}{10}$ p^t 5 PM.

No. 747—*The King to Lord North.*

Printed. Donne I. 12.

QUEENS HOUSE *Jan*^{y} 29th 1770.

$\frac{m}{30}$ p^t 9. A.M.

LORD NORTH—I hope You will either this morning or after the Debate in the House of Commons see Lieutenant General Conway for I know how much he is pleased at little marks of attention, and that by placing some confidence in Him You may rely on his warm support. I wish by a line to be informed how You found Lord Mansfield last night, and whether You had any conversation with Lord Chief Justice Wilmot.

No. 748—*The King to Lord North.*

QUEENS HOUSE *Jan^y* 29th 1770.

$\dfrac{m}{10}$ *pt* 10. A.M.

LORD NORTH—I shall be careful not to arrive at the House of Lords till half hour past one. You will inform the House of Commons that the Papers relative to the Custom House Duties in America shall be laid before them.

No. 749—*Lord North to the King.*

[? *January*, 1770.]

Lord North has the honour of informing his Majesty that he was engaged all day yesterday in negociations concerning the accomodation with Spain, which he has the satisfaction to think is in a prosperous way. This prevented him from informing his Majesty that Sr Sidney Smith has declined the seals on account of age. He will pay his respects at St James's today at three o'clock.

No. 750—*Lord North to the King.*

Lord North has the honour of informing his Majesty, that he has not yet been able to see Lord Chief Justice Wilmot. He has had some conversation with Mr Conway this morning, & with Ld Mansfield yesterday in the House of Lords. He is appointed to call upon his Lordship again at eight o'clock this evening in Bloomsbury Square.

Tuesday, Jan. 30th [1770].

No. 751.

SPEAKERS UPON MR DOWDESWELL'S QUESTION.

[31 *January*, 1770.]

Pro.	Con.
Mr Dowdeswell.	Mr Jenkinson.
Mr Pulteney.	Mr Harley.
Mr Dempster.	Mr Stanley.
Mr Burke.	Mr Dyson.
Mr Johnston.	Att^y General.
	Mr Thos Walpole.

Mr Gregory.

upon the subject in general without speaking directly pro or Con.

In Lord North's handwriting.

No. 752—*The King to Lord North.*

Printed. Donne I. 13.

QUEEN'S HOUSE *Feb^y* 1st 1770.

LORD NORTH—I am greatly rejoiced at the conclusion of the Debate a Majority of 40. at this particular crisis considering it is upon the old ground that has been at least ten times before the House is a very favorable auspice on Your taking the lead in Administration. Believe Me a little spirit will soon restore a degree of order in my Service, I am glad to find Sir Gilbert Elliot has again Spoke.

No. 753—*The King to Lord North.*

Printed. Donne I. 13.

QUEEN'S HOUSE *Feb.* 1st 1770.

$$\frac{m}{35} \, p^t \, 5. \text{ P.M.}$$

LORD NORTH—In consequence of my acquainting the Duke of Grafton with the propriety of Colonel Fitzroy's now deciding whether he chooses to accept the office of Vice Chamberlain, the Colonel has been with Me and has in the hansomest manner declined ; You will therefore loose no time in sounding Mr Robinson.

No. 754—*The King to Lord North.*

Printed. Donne I. 14.

QUEEN'S HOUSE *Feb^y* 12th 1770

$$\frac{m}{28}\ p^t\ 10.\ \text{P.M.}$$

LORD NORTH—As the question proposed by Mr Dowdeswell was well calculated to catch many persons I think it has been rejected by a very handsome Majority.

No. 755—*Lord North to the King.*

Lord North has the honour of informing his Majesty that an Express is arrived from Ireland bringing the Lord Lieutenant's desire that Corn may be excepted out of the Embargo. It seems that so much Grain was planted in Ireland upon the encouragement of the Bounty granted last year that it is now a drug.

In the North of Ireland, Wheat sells from 20 Sh: to 28^{Sh} a quarter, In Dublin from 30 to 31 Sh:. Lord North is of opinion that no harm will arise from gratifying the Irish in this particular as the object of the Embargo was certainly flesh-meat. The Irish will, however, find to their great sorrow, that their wheat will bear no great price even after the Alteration of the Proclamation : Corn is at present cheap all over Europe.

DOWNING STREET. *Monday Feb^y* 12 [1770 ?].

No. 756—*The King to Lord North.*

Printed.   Donne I. 14.

QUEEN'S HOUSE. *Feb^y* 16th 1770.

$\frac{m}{48}$ *pt* 10. P.M.

LORD NORTH—Your information of what has passed this day in the House of Commons, does not do Opposition great honour ;   I wish to know in what manner Sir Lawrence Dundas has received the answer I authorized You to give him, in consequence of his very unreasonable and unseasonable application. I suppose You do not wish Mr Robinson should vacat his Seat untill the debate of Monday is over.   Lord Weymouth acquainted Me with his intending to wait on You tomorrow previous to the rest of the Company that are to Dine with you, to talk over the Irish affairs,   He proposes saying that as He understands Lord Townshend would dislike resigning the Lord Lieutenancy that He cannot advise the pressing him on that subject, in consequence of that I should think Lord Halifax a very proper person to be appointed Privy Seal ;   I wish You would in general open the intended arrangements to him which will be kindly taken.

No. 757—*Lord North to the King.*

Lord North has the honour of informing his Majesty, that he did not find Mr Dundas in the house of Commons on Thursday last as he expected, but that yesterday he appointed a meeting with him, at Mr Dundas's house in Saville Row & is to see him there at two o'clock today in the forenoon.   All Sr Lawrence's friends were at the house yesterday, & would have voted with us, if there had been any division.

Lord North returns his humble thanks to his Majesty, for giving him notice of Lord Weymouth's intention, & will not fail to communicate to him every thing that is settled respecting the new arrangement.

Saturday morning.
Feb: 17th [1770].

No. 758—*The King to Lord North.*

Printed.   Donne I. 15.

QUEENS HOUSE *Feb^y* 19*^th* 1770.

$$\frac{m}{55} \, p^t \, 2. \text{ P.M.}$$

LORD NORTH—If the House is up as early this Evening as it has been of late, I desire You will direct Mr Robinson to come at any time before half hour past ten ;   if that cannot be I shall send the Key to You in the morning that in case any question should be asked whether He has the possession of it when his writ is moved that it may be answered in the affirmative, and in that case You will appoint him to be with Me at half hour past three.

No. 759—*The King to Lord North.*

Printed.   Donne I. 16.

QUEEN HOUSE *Feb^y* 20*^th* 1770.

$$\frac{m}{40}. \, p^t \, 8. \text{ A.M.}$$

LORD NORTH—The account of the Divisions last night gives Me great pleasure, if You can find time to call here at Seven this Evening, I should be glad to hear some particulars of the Debate.

No. 760—*Lord North to the King.*

[28 *February*, 1770.]

Lord North has the honour of informing his Majesty, that a motion, made by Mr Grenville, for laying before the H^e of Commons an account of the Civil List expences for the year ending the 30th of December 1769. has been this day rejected by a majority of 97.

Yeas   165.

Noes   262.

No. 761—*The King to Lord North.*

Printed. Donne I. 16.

LORD NORTH—The seeing that the Majority constantly encreases gives Me great pleasure.

QUEEN'S HOUSE
Feby 28^*th* 1770

$\dfrac{m}{40}\,p^t$ 9. P.M.

No. 762—*Lord North to the King.*

[5 *March*, 1770.]

Lord North has the honour of informing his Majesty, that upon his having moved for leave to bring in a bill for repealing the duties on Glass, paper, & painter's colours &c Governor Pownall moved to add *And upon Tea.* which amendment was rejected by a majority of 62.

Ayes   142
Noes   204.

———

LIST OF SPEAKERS

Lord North.   Mr Ellis.
Lord Mayor.   Ld Barrington.
Govr Pownall.   Sr William Meredith.
Mr Grenville   Mr Thos Townshend.
Col: Mackay   Col: Barré
Mr Trecothick   Mr Robt Fuller.
Gen:[1] Conway.   Mr Seymour.
                             Mr Wedderburn.

No. 763—*The King to Lord North.*

Printed. Donne I. 17.

QUEEN'S HOUSE *March* 6th 1770.

$$\frac{m}{40} \, p^t \, 4. \text{ P.M.}$$

LORD NORTH—If You are not engaged at the House of Commons I shall be glad to see You about Seven this Evening, when I hope to hear what has passed at Guildhall this day.

No. 764—*Lord North to the King.*

Lord North has the honour of informing his Majesty that, having seen Lord Weymouth last night, & conversed with his Lordship on the subject of yesterday's proceedings in the City. They were both of opinion to submit to his Majesty, whether he would not chuse to open his Levée rather later this morning than usual, that they may be able to wait upon his Majesty before the Levée begins.

Lord North need not trouble his Majesty with an account of the transactions at Guildhall as they are printed at length in the Middlesex journal of last night.

Wednesday March 7th [1770].

Endorsed by the King.

No. 765—*The King to Lord North.*

Printed. Donne I. 17.

QUEEN'S HOUSE *March* 11th 1770.

$$\frac{m}{20} \, p^t \, 4 \text{ P.M.}$$

LORD NORTH—If you can call here between Seven and Eight previous to Your going to Council I shall be glad to hear what precedents You have got ; but if You cannot come I will briefly by this acquaint You that I continue of opinion that an answer must be given to the Remonstrance and that unless the instances are very similar of having directed a certain Number to attend, it will be every way best to receive them on the Throne.

No. 766—*The King to Lord North.*

LORD NORTH—On coming home I found Your note I had waited till half hour past eight when I gave over expecting if the business at Council should be done by Eleven I shall still wish to See [you] for five Minutes.

QUEEN'S HOUSE
March 11*th* 1770

$\frac{m}{25}$ *p*^{t} 10 P.M.

No. 767—*The King to Lord North.*

Printed. Donne I. 18.

QUEEN'S HOUSE *March* 13*th* 1770.

$\frac{m}{17}$ *p*^{t} 6. P.M.

LORD NORTH—As I understand the House of Commons is up I should be glad to see [you] between Seven and Eight with the answer to the Remonstrance.

No. 768—*The King to Lord North.*

Printed. Donne I. 18.

QUEEN'S HOUSE *March* 16*th* 1770.

$\frac{m}{5}$ *p*^{t} 9. A.M.

LORD NORTH—Nothing can be more respectful to Me nor more honourable for themselves than the conduct of the Majority Yesterday of which I will say more when I see You this day ; as there are so many bills ready for my Assent, I yesterday acquainted Lord Mansfield with my intention of going this day to the House of Lords ; least he should not have sent the Speaker word of this, I desire You will not omit it, and I should be glad of seeing You either about twelve or when I return for the House of Lords.

No. 769—*The King to Lord North.*

Printed.   Donne I. 19.

QUEEN'S HOUSE *March* 18th 1770.

$\frac{m}{47}$. *pt* 5. P.M.

LORD NORTH—The intended Resolutions seem very proper and as they do not end with any severity to the Lord Mayor or Sheriffs, will meet with but a feeble opposition for on that depended the union of all the adverse party. People were very anxious to learn at Court this day the plan You propose for tomorrow, in particular Sir Thomas Clavering, who would I find be flattered with some communication from You on this Subject, which his conduct on Thursday seems to deserve.

No. 770—*Lord Barrington to the King.*

CAVENDISH SQUARE *March* 19. 1770.

I have obey'd your Majesty's Commands by notifying Major General Clavering for the Government of Landguard Fort, and I acquainted him with the gracious manner in which your Majesty had been pleased to confer this mark of your royal approbation of his conduct. I venture to send herewith General Claverings Letter to me, as it shews the effusions of a good and grateful heart. He will present himself this day to kiss your Majesty's hand. I believe the Duke of Queensbury will beg an audience to remind you of Gen¹ Douglas on some future occasion.

I also presume to send your Majesty a Letter I have just received from Mr Ellis ; humbly beging I may not be consider'd otherwise therein than as a meer channel of conveyance. General Munster is coming hither I dare say with an application for the 40th Regiment. As it is on the Irish Establishment I need not attend your Majesty's commands this day, in case you chuse to dispose of it. Lord North will I believe humbly mention Sir Robert Hamilton his relation, as one whom he wishes to be provided for. BARRINGTON.

Enclosure.

Mr. Welbore Ellis to Lord Barrington.

P. GARDEN *March* 19. 1770.

MY LORD—Having yesterday heard of the death of Gen[l] Armiger, permit me to state to your Lordship, the case of my friend Co[l] Coote as it has been represented to me, & tho it is not immediately in your department, as I understand the regiment to be at present on the Irish establishment, allow me nevertheless very earnestly to request the favour of you to lay the circumstances of this case before His Majesty—M[rs] Coote inform's me, that Co[l] Coote having applied to the Duke of Grafton either in 1768 or early in 1769 to use his Grace's interest with the King to promise him a regiment His Grace very readily undertook it ; & after some short time informed Co[l] Coote, that he cou'd not have the first or the second regiment which shou'd become vacant, they being already destined, but that he shou'd have the third regiment which shou'd from that time become vacant, & that His Majesty had been pleased so to settle it. The Co[l] had likewise made his application to Lord Granby who had likewise given him the like assurances that His Majesty had assented to this arrangement. The first & the second Regiments which became vacant after this transaction were given to Co[l] Hale & to Co[l] Evelyn, if I be not mistaken, & the next therefore Co[l] Coote had reason to expect. Before he accepted the command to India he waited upon the D. of Grafton to ask whether if he shou'd accept that command it wou'd injure his claim to the next Regiment ; His Grace assured him that it shou'd not. The Co[l] went to India. The D. of Grafton & L[d] Granby resigned ; & soon after these events, Toovey's regiment became vacant. I am not surprised that in the hurry of great affairs, & neither the D. of Grafton or Lord Granby being on the Spot to remind His Majesty, this transaction & engagement with Co[l] Coote escaped his memory & the regiment was given to Co[l] Elphinston.

If this relation be true, & I believe it to be so, I know His Majesty's exactness so well that I am sure that he will be glad to be reminded of this engagement ; at the same time you will do an essential service to a very distinguished Officer & you will most sensibly oblige, My D[r] Lord, Your most obedient & most humble Servant   W[R] ELLIS.

No. 771—*The King to Lord North.*

Printed. Donne I. 20.

QUEEN'S HOUSE *March* 20th 1770

$\frac{m}{48} p^t$ 7. A.M.

LORD NORTH—The more I reflect on the present remonstrance from the Livery, the more I am desirous it should receive an answer, otherwise this bone of contention will never end ; I therefore am thoroughly of opinion that as the Sheriffs (though falsely) have insinuated that it is properly authenticated that the least inconvenience will be the receiving them on the Throne, and that the Sober party cannot be hurt with it when they find the answer is firm which will draw on a joint Address from the two Houses of Parliament, and will enable the Aldermen and Common Council Men who dissented from this strange libel, on my having received it to write a letter to one of my Principal Secretaries of State protesting against it, who may in answer say something civil from Me in return. If this agrees with Your ideas, I hope You will shew the visitors You are to have this morning the necessity of thus ending the affair which will be honourably for them and their worthy friends. As the Council meet at eight I shall expect You at Seven this Evening.

In the Public Advertiser You will find all that passed with the Sheriffs Yesterday.

No. 772—*The King to Lord North.*

Printed. Donne I. 21.

QUEENS HOUSE *March* 28th 1770

$\frac{m}{18} p^t$ 11. A.M.

LORD NORTH—I shall take care that proper directions are given that Mr Morton and Mr Ambler be presented to the Queen tomorrow before the drawing Room that they may be presented to Me just before the drawing Room as Mr Morton sets out on Friday for Wales.

No. 773—*Mr. Harley to Mr. Robinson.*

[? *March*, 1770.]

Mr Harley presents his Compliments to Mr Robinson, on the motion for allowing Mr Wilkes £500 p ann: out of the City Cash there were for the question

Ald^m	4	against the question	
Comm^n	69	Ald^m	12.
Tellers	2	Comm^n	96.
	—		
	75.	Tellers	2.
			—
			110
			75
			—
			35 Majority.

The next motion was that it is the Opinion of this Court that the granting any Annuity to John Wilkes Esqr Alderman of the Ward of Farringdon without, or the paying any of that Gentlemans Debts out of this City's Cash whether contracted in his Mayoralty or not would be an improper application thereof and a most dangerous Precedent if carried

For		Ag^t	
Ald^m	12	Ald^m	4
Comm.	93	Comm.	74
Tellers	2	Tellers	2
	—		—
	107.		80

Majority 27.

The next was that the Petition of John Maberly & others, the Creditors of John Wilkes presented the 23^d of Oct. last be dismissed, carried in the Affirmative without a division.

No. 774—*Lord North to the King.*

[5 *April,* 1770.]

Lord North has the honour of informing his Majesty, that
Sr Edward Astley having made a motion for laying before the
House all the Pensions, Additional Salaries & Reversionary
Grants from the commencement of the present Parliament, the
latter words were alter'd, & the words "*from the commencement
of his Majesty's reign* " inserted in lieu thereof. Mr Rigby then
mov'd for the Orders of the day, & carried his motion after some
debate by 164 voices to 104.

DOWNING STREET. ½ *after nine.*

No. 775—*The King to Lord North.*

Printed. Donne I. 21.

QUEENS HOUSE *April* 5th 1770.

$\frac{m}{5}$ p^t 10. P.M.

LORD NORTH—I cannot help expressing some surprise at
seeing Lieutenant General Conway's name in support of Sir
Edward Astley's motion which is so antiquated an opposition
point, but which no candid man could be supposed to addopt.

No. 776—*Lord North to the King.*

[6 *April,* 1770.]

Lord North thinks himself obliged, in justice to Lieutenant
General Conway, to explain to his Majesty the manner in which
he was induced to vote yesterday in the minority ; He had
opposed the motion, as it was first made, solely upon an objection
taken to the period from whence the account was to commence,
approving it in other respects. The motion was immediately
alter'd, & another commencement given to the account, by
which Mr Conway was engaged to support the minority, in
consequence of his former declaration.

DOWNING STREET. *Friday morn:^g*

No. 777—*The King to Lord North.*

Printed. Donne I. 22.

QUEENS HOUSE *April* 9th 1770.
$\frac{m}{35}$ p^t 9. P.M.

LORD NORTH—I am rather surprised there could be a debate this day on a matter quite in the teeth of a standing order of the House. If You are willing to fill up the vacant employments before the recess You will have a final conversation with me on those arrangements on Wednesday and the Persons may come to St James's on Thursday previous to my going to the House of Lords, and their Seats may be vacated on that day.

No. 778—*The King to Lord North.*

Printed. Donne I. 23.

QUEENS HOUSE *April* 12th 1770.
$\frac{m}{20}$ p^t 11. A.M.

LORD NORTH—I thoroughly approve of the Steps You have taken, and will now write a civil compliment to Lord Weymouth on the impossibility of having given any rise to his Brother on this occasion.

No. 779—*Lord North to the King.*

[20 *April*, 1770.]

Lord North would have paid his duty to his Majesty this morning at St James's, but was prevented by a meeting of the Gentlemen of the Board, & other principal merchants, whom he had appointed, in order to lay before them the plan of the Budget; They all approved of the design, & some were very sanguine of it's success; Others seem to question whether it would do or not. Lord North thinks that there are great hopes of success, & as it is very honourable & useful to the Publick he will, with his Majesty's approbation persist in it. He has not yet seen any reason to alter the plan, since he had the honour of opening it to his Majesty last Wednesday.

Friday morn:ᵍ

No. 780—*The King to Lord North.*

Printed. Donne I. 23.

QUEENS HOUSE *April* 20th 1770.

$$\frac{m}{57} \; p^t \; 6 \; \text{P.M.}$$

LORD NORTH—Your plan for the Finances this Year is so very honorable that it cannot fail of success, I am the more sanguine on this occasion as it shews in a most striking manner the fairness of Government in their dealings with the Stock holders, at the same time that France have in the most base manner deceived those concerned in their Funds.

The more I reflect on the approaching vacancy for Westminster the more I am confirmed that it is not worth while to occasion a tumult in this City by encouraging a Contest unless some man of an independant Character could be prevailed on to stand which I do not expect.

No. 781—*Lord North to the King.*

[23 *April,* 1770.]

Lord North has the honour of informing his Majesty, that he obey'd his Majesty's commands in waiting upon the Duke of Beaufort, & offering him the vacant Vice-Treasurership of Ireland & that his Grace, with many expressions of gratitude, & duty to his Majesty, declined the offer, but express'd his wishes that, if either of the Lieutenancies of Monmouth or Brecknock shires should be ever open'd his pretensions might be consider'd & recommended his friend Mr Stepney for some office, whenever an opportunity should offer of providing for him. Lord North, being in the neighbourhood of Lord

Edgcumbe, sounded his Lordship upon the subject of the Vice-Treasurership, & found him very willing to accept it, if it should be agreable to his Majesty.

Monday six o'clock.

No. 782—*The King to Lord North.*

Printed. Donne I. 24.

QUEENS HOUSE *April* 24th 1770
$$\frac{m}{46} p^t \text{ 6. P.M.}$$

LORD NORTH—The offer of the Vice Treasurership to the Duke of Beaufort will undoubtedly confirm him in his very handsome manner of acting, though he has declined; You will direct Lord Edgcumbe to come and kiss hands on Wednesday, and Sir Edward Hawke may now nominate another Admiral to the command at Plymouth which at the desire of the Duke of Grafton he had deferred doing untill that Lord should obtain some employment.

No. 783—*Lord Barrington to the King.*

CAVENDISH SQUARE *April* 30th 1770.

I was in hopes I had in some degree pacify'd Lord Lorne yesterday after I left your Majesty; but I have had a visit this morning from his Lordship and Lord Frederic Campbell, who came from their Father whom they report to be uneasy to the last degree as well as themselves, at Lord Loudon's having the 3^d Regiment of Guards. I have done every thing in my power to soften, but in vain; and they are gone to Lord Weymouth (to whom my notification of Lord Loudon was addressed) in order thro' him humbly to entreat your Majesty, that you will admit the Duke of Argyll to an audience before you sign Lord Loudoun's Commission. I am very sorry your Majesty is to have any trouble about this matter, but I thought it right to apprise you of it.   BARRINGTON.

Lord Loudoun will present himself to kiss your Majesty's hand next Wednesday.

No. 784—*Lord Shelburne to the King.*

[? *April,* 1770.]

Lord Shelburne presumes to acquaint Your Majesty, that he did not send the Irish Messenger this morning upon a suggestion of Lord Frederick Campbell's that the Mail of this day might bring something new. The Mail is since come in, but has brought no Letters for the Office, nor do Lord Frederick Campbell's Letters bring any thing new or particular, except that most people were gone or going out of Town, and that it would be difficult to find more Members than are necessary to make a House till after the Recess.

Lord Shelburne humbly submits for your Majesty's consideration the Draft to Lord Townsend containing the commands Your Majesty honour'd him with last night, likewise the Draft of an answer to the address of the House of Commons.

No. 785—*Lord North to the King.*

[5 *May,* 1770.]

Lord North has the honour of transmitting to his Majesty the Remonstrance of the City, which does not appear to be quite so violent & offensive in matter & stile as was apprehended.

Lord North imagines that the answer first intended, will be thought rather too stern & rough for the address, & will with his Majesty's permission, prepare another, He is going to North End, where he proposes to stay till Monday, unless his Majesty has any commands for him tomorrow in Town.

Sat^y Even.

No. 786—*The King to Lord North.*

Printed.   Donne I. 25.

QUEENS HOUSE *May* 8th 1771.

$\frac{m}{30} p^t$ M.

LORD NORTH—I thoroughly concurr in the opinion that the words I had proposed might bear an explanation that would be improper ; I think the alteration of the *injury done to my honour* very right, but wish what has been substituted had been more pointed ; I think the offering Mr Wood, the Housekeeper of Whitehall is very right, and if he does not accept it, You are free of him.

No. 787—*Lord North to the King.*

[8 *May*, 1770.]

Lord North has the honour of informing his Majesty,` That Mr Pownall having proposed the inclosed Motion, Ld Barrington moved to adjourn, which, after a pretty long debate, was agreed to without a division.

The Speakers were,

For the motion.	Against the motion.
Mr Pownall,	
Govr Johnstone,	Lord Barrington
Mr Beckford	General Conway.
Mr Barré	
Sr George Saville	

No. 788—*Minutes of the House of Commons.*

Tuesday May 8th, 1770.

Martis   8⁰ die May 1770.

The House in a Commee on the Redemption Bill went thro' with Amendments to be reported to Morrow.

Sr Chas Whitworth reported from the Commee of Ways and Means the Resolutions of Yesterday which were agreed to and a Bill ordered—And also from the Commee of Supply the Resolutions of Yesterday which were agreed to.

A Motion was made & Q^r proposed—That an humble address be presented to his Maty acknowledging with Gratitude that constitutional Communication which his Maty hath Always maintained with his parliament in every Matter which concerns the State ; to return our unfeigned Thanks for that fresh proof which his Maty is pleased to give of that Spirit of his Government by referring to his Parliament and by recommending to us to consider—" The State of his Government in America ".

To assure his Mty that in ready and dutiful Compliance to his Royal Recommendation we have entered into a serious and attentive Consideration of this Matter referred to us.

With the most profound Respect and Deference to represent to his Maty that we find that Misunderstandings and disputes have arisen in almost everyone of his Colonies in America between the Civil Governor and Military Commanders since the Appointment of a Commander in Chief.

That we find in one of his Maty's Provinces the Representatives of his people in the great and general Court assembled have complained That according to the Arrangement of Commands in America There is a Military Power within said province and uncontroulable by the supreme executive power of the Province which they conceive to be (within the limits of the same) the just and full Representative of the supreme executive power of the whole Empire in as full and ample Manner as is the Lord Lieutenant of Ireland or any other his Maty's Lieutenants in the Dominions to the Realm of Great Britain appertaining.

That we are of Opinion that this unhappy State of Doubts & Disputes has long called for some clear and explicit Definition and Adjustment of the respeve powers and Authorities granted to the Governors and Commanders in Chief of his Matys Provinces and Colonies & to the Military Commanders in Chief of his Maty's Forces in North America & doth require some Express directions and Instructions as to the Exercise of said powers.

And therefore most humbly praying his Maty that he will with the Advice of his privy Council be graciously pleased to give his Directions for the Examination of the sev^l Powers and Authorities contained in the respective Commiss^n granted & in the respective Orders and Instructions issued to these several Commanders to the End that all such Commissions Instructions and Orders may be explained corrected and amended in such Cases where in they clash and interfere with each other or contain any powers or Authorities that are not warranted by Law and the Constitution.

Afterwards moved to adjourn
    Q^r put and agreed to   Adj^d till to Morrow.

Copy, endorsed by the King.

No. 789—*Lord North to the King.*

[9 *May*, 1770.]

Lord North has the honour of informing his Majesty, that Mr Burke proposed to the house today eight motions censuring the conduct of the present Administration with respect to the affairs of America. Three of which were negatived, & the previous question put upon five. There was one division

$$\left\{\begin{array}{ll} \text{For M}^r \text{ Burke's motion} & 79. \\ \text{Against it} \quad . \quad . \quad . & 199 \end{array}\right.$$

Lord North has the honour of inclosing to his Majesty the List of Speakers.

Endorsed by the King.

Enclosure.

9th MAY 1770 SPEAKERS ON THE MOTIONS RELATIVE
TO AMERICA MADE BY MR BURKE

For	Against
Mr Burke	Mr Rice
Mr Seymour	Col^e Onslow
Mr Thos Townshend	Lord Clare
Mr Wedderburn	General Mackay
Mr Grenville	Lord North.

Division	Ayes	79.
	Noes	199.

No. 790—*Lord North to the King.*

Lord North has the honour of informing his Majesty, that he has mention'd his Majesty's gracious intention to Mr Rice who accepts of the Office of Treasurer of the Chamber with the highest gratitude, & will avail of his Majesty's permission to kiss hands today at the time his Majesty was pleased to appoint.

Lord North has sent for Lord Greville Mr Northey, & Lord Robert Spencer, to whom, if his Majesty approves of it, He will offer the vacant places at the board of Trade.

DOWNING STREET *Thursday morn^g.*

Endorsed by the King, May 17th, 1770.

No. 791—*The King to Lord North.*

Printed.   Donne I. 25.

LORD NORTH—Mr Pitt having this day resigned his employment as Groom of the Bedchamber, I have directed Lord Bristol to notify Sir George Osborn as his Successor ; there seeming to be some doubts whether Parliament can be prorogued on Thursday, I shall not object to going to the House on Saturday ; I thought it right to send You word of this as it may the better enable You to settle the business of the week.

QUEENS HOUSE
  May 13th 1770
  $\dfrac{m}{51}$ p^t 3. P.M.

No. 792—*The King to Lord North.*

Printed.   Donne I. 26.

LORD NORTH—If you are at liberty this Evening, I wish You would call here at any time most convenient to You.   The Sheriffs of London have just been here, whom I again have refused to see as coming at an improper place, and have said Wednesday is the time for them to bring their message.   I suppose this is another remonstrance if so I think it ought not to have any answer.

QUEEN HOUSE *May* 14th 1770
  $\dfrac{m}{15}$ p^t 7. P.M.

No. 793—*The King to Lord North.*

LORD NORTH—I desire You will call here about half hour past ten, that I may know what has passed with regard to the Remonstrance.

QUEEN HOUSE *May* 15th 1770

$\frac{m}{52}$ p^t 6 P.M.

No. 794—*The King to Lord North.*
Printed. Donne I. 26.

QUEENS HOUSE *May* 17th 1770

$\frac{m}{10}$ p^t 9. P.M.

LORD NORTH—I have no objection to giving the order of the Bath to Lord Catherlough and Sir John Moore tomorrow after the Levée ; I trust Mr Whitehead will have ordered the Ribbons and Badges to be brought and will have Summoned some of the Knights to attend.

No. 795—*Lord North to the King.*

Lord North has the honour of transmitting to his Majesty a fair Copy of the Speech. It has undergone some trifling corrections since yesterday. What passed in the House of Lords did not make it necessary to alter it materially.

DOWNING STREET. *Saturday May* 19. [1770]

No. 796—*The King to Lord North.*

QUEENS HOUSE *May* 19th 1770.

$\frac{m}{6}$ p^t 11. A.M.

LORD NORTH—In reading over the Speech I have a doubt whether the word Let me at the beginning of the last paragraph

is a usual method of speaking from the Throne and whether
I earnestly recommend to You the exerting in Your respective &c.
would not do as well. I wish to hear what You think of this.

No. 797—*The King to Lord North.*

Printed. Donne I. 27.

QUEENS HOUSE *May* 19*th* 1770.

$\frac{m}{56} p^t$ 7 P.M.

LORD NORTH—The Remonstrance of the City of London is
certainly less offensive than it had been reported and therefore
some of the latter words of the proposed answer You shewed Me
must be altered ; but I look on the whole performance of a
nature to call for a Short dry answer referring to the one I have
already given. I should think on Monday Evening You ought
to communicate the Remonstrance and a Sketch of an answer
to the Cabinet.

No. 798—*The King to Lord North.*

QUEENS HOUSE *May* 22*d* 1770.

$\frac{m}{5} p^t$ 4. P.M.

LORD NORTH—I am desirous of seeing You either at Seven
this evening or a little after nine, to know what has passed
concerning the answer to the City Remonstrance.

No. 799—*Lord North to the King.*

[22 *May*, 1770.]

Lord North has the honour of informing his Majesty that in
obedience to his Majesty's commands, he summon'd a meeting
of the Lords of the Cabinet, & takes the liberty of inclosing a
project of an answer to the City Remonstrance drawn up, as
nearly as possible according to what Lord North conceiv'd to be

their idea : As soon as he can have the assistance of a Secretary, he will send Copies round to them & to Lord Mansfield ; He has just sent for a surgeon to let him blood, & hopes that his Majesty will permit him to wait upon him tomorrow morning instead of tonight, but if it is more convenient to his Majesty to see him this evening, will keep himself in readiness to obey his Majesty's commands.

Tuesday Even:ᵍ

Endorsed by the King.

No. 800.

SKETCH OF HIS MAJESTY'S ANSWER TO THE CITY REMONSTRANCE.

I should have been wanting to the Public, as well as to myself, if I had not express'd my dissatisfaction at the late address ; My sentiments upon that subject continue the same ; and I should ill deserve to be consider'd as the Father of my people, if, in the exercise of any of the powers, with which I am intrusted, I should suffer myself to be prevail'd upon by any importunity to adopt a measure inconsistent with the interests, & dangerous to the Constitution of the Kingdom.

Draft, in Lord North's handwriting.

No. 801—*The King to Lord North.*

Printed.   Donne I. 27.

QUEENS HOUSE *May* 22ᵈ 1770.

$\frac{m}{46.}$ *pᵗ* 6. P.M.

LORD NORTH—I am sorry Your cold has not been removed by the change of Air, and that bleeding has been necessary, which I hope will quite remove it ; I would upon no account have You come out this Evening ; I thoroughly approve of the proposed answer to the City, and think You ought immediately to send it to the Cabinet and have their opinion with regard to it; if You are well enough I hope You will be at St James by half hour past twelve tomorrow that I may know if any alteration has been made in the answer.

No. 802—*The King to Lord North.*

Printed. Donne I. 28.

LORD NORTH—I wish to see You about half hour past nine this evening, and that You will bring the words proper for Lord Hertford to give tomorrow to the Remembrancer Expressing my expectation that the Lord Mayor's unexpected Speech last Wednesday be not looked upon as a precedent.

QUEENS HOUSE
May 29th 1770
$\frac{m}{40}$ p^t 2. P.M.

No. 803—*Lord North to the King.*

[? 16 *June*, 1770.]

Lord North has the honour of informing his Majesty, that he waited upon Lord Mansfield on Thursday Evening, & acquainted him, that he had laid before his Majesty, the letter he had received from his Lordship, concerning the vacancy in the King's Bench, occasion'd by the death of Sr Joseph Yates. Lord Mansfield intended to mention the matter to Mr Wallace, as soon as he could see him & was in hopes that Mr Wallace would be persuaded to accept of the vacant seat, but imagin'd that he would desire to consider the proposal for a day or two, before he returns his answer. Lord Mansfield had intended to be at the levée on Friday in order to obtain his Majesty's permission to speak to Mr Wallace upon this subject, but having learnt from Lord North that His Majesty has no objection to Mr Wallace He proposed to continue in court all Friday morning (it being the first day of the Term) & to take another opportunity of paying his respects at St James's.

NORTH END. *Saturday morn^g.*

No. 804—*Lord North to the King.*

[? 16 *June*, 1770.]

Lord North has been with Lord Mansfield since he troubled his Majesty with his last note. Lord Mansfield has acquainted him, that Mr Wallace has this morning sent him a letter, in which he declines the vacant seat in the King's Bench; There is only one other very eminent Special Pleader, whom Lord Mansfield thinks fit to be made a Judge; The gentleman's name is Ashurst; Tho' [he] is not yet one of your Majesty's council, He is an older Barrister than Mr Wallace. Lord Mansfield will, with your Majesty's permission, apply to him; Should he also refuse to accept, There is no other in that walk of the profession, who, I believe, would be recommended upon this occasion, &, in that case, I imagine that Lord Mansfield's opinion would lean to Serjeant Nares or Serjeant Burland. Lord North begs leave to acknowledge, with the utmost gratitude, your Majesty's goodness in approving the Steps he has already taken in this business.

NORTH END. *Saturday Even^g.*

No. 805—*The King to Lord North.*

Printed. Donne I. 30.

LORD NORTH—As Mr Wallace declines the vacant Seat in the King's Bench, I authorize You to enable Lord Mansfield to sound Mr Ashurst; if he declines the preference ought to be given to Serjeant Burland, whom Lord Mansfield thinks superior in tallents to Serjeant Nares particularly as I find the nomination of the latter would be very detrimental to the interest of the Duke of Marlborough, as his influence in Oxford would be much shook by opening that Borough for so many months.

QUEENS HOUSE
June 16th 1770.

No. 806—*The King to Lord North.*

Printed.   Donne I. 30.

QUEENS HOUSE *June* 16*th* 1770
$$\frac{m}{58.}\,p^t\,4.\text{ P.M.}$$

LORD NORTH—The steps You have taken in forwarding the appointment of a Judge on the removal of Sir William Blackstone into the Court of Common Pleas meet with my thorough approbation.

No. 807—*Lord Barrington to the King.*

CAVENDISH SQUARE *June* 27. 1770.

I have humbly presumed to send some Warrants to your Majesty as they are wanted soon : When they are signed I humbly beg that your Majesty will be pleased to order that they shall be sent to the War Office, from whence they will go to me in the Country for Countersigning.

I believe I did not inform your Majesty that another Captain has shot himself, viz Captain Vorloe of the 31st He was Paymaster of the Regiment, and could not make up his accounts. I have not yet received any recommendation of the Succession, which I presume is owing to M Gen¹ Oughton's being in Scotland.   BARRINGTON.

No. 808—*The King to Lord North.*

Printed.   Donne I. 31.

RICHMOND LODGE *July* 8*th* 1770.

LORD NORTH—You will acquaint General Paoli that I shall with pleasure receive him at half hour past Six on Thursday Evening at the Queen's House.

No. 809—*Lord Hertford to the King.*

SIRE—Your Majesty's goodness and compassion will plead my excuse for begging by this means to absent myself from my duty and attendance for some few days.

I have had the misfortune to lose my Daughter Lady Sarah Stewart who is dead in Dublin in the seventh month of her being with Child after struggling some days with an obstinate fever. My intention is to go into the Country till my spirits are relieved & I am better enabled to appear in publick. I have the honor always to profess myself, Sire, Your Majesty's most faithful and most devoted humble serv^t HERTFORD.

GROS^v STREET
July 23^d 1770.

No. 810—*The King to Lord North.*

Printed. Donne I. 31.

RICHMOND LODGE *July* 28th 1770.

LORD NORTH—I return the Warrants, and by this conveyance communicate to You the papers I have received from the Admiralty concerning the great fire that was in Portsmouth Dock Yesterday, which when You have read I desire may be returned to that Office. I hope You will find Your family all well when You join them in Somerset Shire.

No. 811—*The King to Lord Barrington.*

RICHMOND LODGE *Aug^t* 5th 1770.

LORD BARRINGTON—You have done perfectly right in transmitting to me the Minutes of the Court Martial held at Northampton for the trial of Quarter Master Smith, which Sentence I approve of, but am of opinion that he must by some method be got out of the Regiment, a reprimand to Lieutenant Waller should be privately given through the Channel of Lieutenant Colonel Sloper, for his imprudence in [*unfinished*]

No. 812—*The King to Lord North.*

RICHMOND LODGE
Sep^t 5th 1770.

LORD NORTH—As I understand You was prevented coming to S^t. James's this day by not being able to get at Your cloaths, if that should continue to be the case tomorrow, I desire You will call at St James's in Your frock at half hour past twelve.

No. 813—*Lord Rochford to the King.*

BERKELEY SQUARE 8th *Sep^{tr}* 1770.
$\frac{m}{35}$ p^t 11. A.M.

Lord Rochford humbly begs leave to inform your majesty that he was come to London to meet Lord Weymouth by appointment this morning and as it might occasion great suspicion if he went to Richmond today he proposes having the honor to wait on your majesty to morrow between eleven & twelve unless he should be informed that any other hour suited your Majesty better.

No. 814—*Major Robert Rogers to the King.*

May it please Your Majesty
To incline a gracious Ear to the Representation of Your loyal Subject,

Major Robert Rogers, whom one of Your Majesty's Commanders in Chief in North America commissioned such at a critical Moment in the Field, is (he presumes) not more generally distinguished for the Steady Alacrity and Zeal, with which for many successive years he exherted [*sic*] himself against those who were Enemies to Your Crown, than he has been remarked by those to whom the Truth is known for his Sufferings.

Vouchsafe Sir, to be informed ; that that part of Your Service in the late North-American War ; which he was entrusted to conduct, was carried on in the interior or remote Parts ;

where access to the Publick Money not being practicable in the usual Course, he was obliged to incur heavy Debts on the Public Account in his own Name ; which a Reimbursement not having enabled him to discharge, his Family now starves upon his hands and his Liberty is at the Mercy of Creditors.

Yet Sir, does he not complain that Justice has been intentionally withheld, but that he is a Sufferer by it's Delay. Successors in the great Commands, with which Your Majesty is pleased to entrust, do not but with extreme Caution admit into their Public Accounts Disbursements, which in Point of Time ought to have appeared in those of their Predecessors ;—and when the Royal Command did lately interpose in his Behalf by an Order of Reference ; the Referrers, not being acquainted with such Matters, by Misapprehending a Claim of Right to be a Claim of Favor, reported, that they ought not to prescribe to the Bounty of the Crown, and thereby disappointed his Hopes of Relief at the Time.

He means not to derogate from the Honour of any Officer whom Your Majesty is pleased to Employ :—But Errors in Judgment very often carry the Appearance, and fatally to him have had all the Consequences, and Effects of a determined Resolution to oppress ; For not very long after this, and when he was discharging the Duties of a Command in the Indian Department with a punctual Obedience to Order and an Address, of which there was no superior Example, He was in an Instant, without any previous Question or Intimation, divested of his Command, His Person Seized, confined, loaded with galling Fetters, and even near starved upon no certain, or even avowable Cause of Suspicion, unless it might be (which it ought not to have been) on Deposition taken from a Wretch, who has been twice recorded for Perjury, and who fled the Justice of one Province on a Criminal Charge of so detestable an Enormity ; that the Commission of it is almost as seldom heard-of, as the Outrages perpetrated upon his person, during a Confinement so protracted, as to constitute of itself the severest Punishment.

Nevertheless on Trial, the Charges brought against him were totally deserted ; no one Evidence being adduced to substantiate the Imputed Guilt ; and the Court, as it well might, did absolutely Acquit.—Yet was his Imprisonment not discontinued, no Mode of Reparation for his Injuries thought of, and he was to the Inversion of Justice actually dismissed from Employment, and deprived of Bread.—

May these Hardships most gracious King—touch Your Heart with Compassion ; and may Your Royal Commisseration for the Sufferer incline You to relieve his distressed Family, and his own anxious Fears for his Liberty, by commanding the Matter of his unpaid Accounts to be reported, for the Royal Information by Your Majesty's Treasury-Board, which from its amazing Sources of official Reference in all possible Cases seems most competent. And may a Reputation unjustly wounded, the cruel Severity of a long & rigorous Confinement, the Dismission from Employ after the Justest Acquittal and the annexed Testimonials from Your Generals, incline Your Majesty to bestow some Mark of the Royal Favour, and also to Grant the Sufferer an adequate pecuniary Compensation for his loss and Expence on the whole.— ROBERT ROGERS.

Dated Sept^{br} 29th 1770.

Enclosure.
Lord Loudoun to Major Rogers.

LOUDOUN *Novr the* 16th 1769.

SIR—Yours of the 1st I received the 14th. I am extreamly glad you have been acquitted of the Crimes you were accused of.

I can with great Justice testify, that while you Served under my Command in America You always behaved as a good & diligent Officer.

I should have no Objection of recommending You to the Directors of the East India Company, but I have no connection with them, & You may shew them this Letter if it can Serve You, so wishing You Success, I am, Sir, Your most obedient humble Servant LOUDON.

Lieut.-Gen. Abercromby to Major Rogers.

EDINBURGH 28th *Nov^r* 1769.

MAJOR ROGERS—Your Letter of the 3^d Current having missed me at this place and gone a good Way North ward came only to my Hands two Days ago. I have not the honour to be so

well known to any of the Gentlemen in the Direction of the
East India as to take it upon me to Recommend any Person to
their Favor & Protection ; But in Justice to Your Services I
most readily grant the underwritten Certificate & heartily wish
it may contribute to Your Request, & I am, Sir, Your most
humble Servant   JAMES ABERCROMBY.

By Lieut.-Gen^ll James Abercromby.

These are to Certify that Major Robert Rogers during three
Campaigns that I served in North America, commanded a
Body of Rangers and constantly discharged his Duty to my
Satisfaction.   And I further Certify that I look upon him
to be extremely capable to command a Corps of Rangers in
any part of His Majesty's Dominions abroad.   In Testimony
whereof I have Signed Certificate at Edinburgh this 28th day
of Novr 1769 Years.   JAMES ABERCROMBY.

By Sir Jeffery Amherst.

Major Rogers having desired that I would [give] him a
Certificate of his Services while he was under my command
in America, as he is in hopes of obtaining a Commission in the
East India Company's Service, I hereby declare that he commanded a Corps of Rangers and was on many Occasions very
Serviceable and behaved very well on various Duties he was
employed in ; when the Rangers were reduced I appointed him
to the command of an Independent Company which has also
been reduced.   Given under my Hand in London the 21st March
1770—   JEFF. AMHERST.

By Daniel Webb Esqr.

Lieutenant General of His Majesties Armies &C.—
These are to Certify that Major Robert Rogers did command
a Corps of Rangers during the last War in North America and
was sent on various commands and was very serviceable.   part
of which time he was under my Command and with the greatest
Truth I declare, that he was punctual in the Execution of his
Duty and always did it to my Satisfaction.   I verily think him
fit to command a Body of Light Troops in any part of his

Majesty's Dominions.   Given under my Hand this 26th Day of March 1770.   DAN WEBB.

By Colonel W. Amherst.

Major Rogers having applied to me for a Certificate of his Services during the Time that I was Adjutant General in America, I can declare that the Major Commanding a Corps of Rangers was Employ'd in several difficult Enterprizes, which he executed with an uncommon degree of perseverance and with great Spirit.   I do not know a Man who can better lead a Corps of Light Troops to the Effectual Performance of the Services they are generally employed in, than the Major.—

ARGYLL STREET   W. AMHERST.
   March 27th 1770

By Major-General Monckton.

I do hereby Certify that Major Rogers having been sent with a Detachment from Sir Jeffery Amherst into the Department where I commanded in North America, That he executed his Orders with care and dispatch.   And I do further Certify that I always understood that he behaved well on the different Services in which he was Employ'd.   Given under my Hand in London this 28th day of March 1770.—

R. MONCKTON. Majr Genl

Major Rogers having applied to me for my Testimony of his Services in North America during the late War, I can declare, that the Major having been always considered as the Principal Person to Command the Rangers was frequently employed, in that Service in which he ever distinguished himself. March 31st 1770.—   W. HERVEY.

This is to Certify that during the five Years I served as Aide de Camp in North America to General Amherst & Abercromby That I have been upon Parties (alias Scouts) with Major Robert Rogers, and that I know him to be a diligent Active brave Officer.   JAMES ABERCROMBIE Lt Col 22d Regt

PALL MALL COURT
   April 26th 1770.

This is to Certify that during the time I served as Captain and Major in the 55th Regiment of Foot in North America, Major Robert Rogers was under my Command, and that I know him to be a diligent, active, brave Officer.

GEO. WEST, Colo & Captain of Grenadiers
first Regt of Foot Guards.

PARLIAMENT STREET
the 14th March 1770.

This is to Certify, that during the several years I had the honour to Command the Royal Highland or 42d Regt in North America, Capt Robert Rogers behaved himself as a diligent and brave Officer, and for his Services was promoted to the Command of all the Rangers with the Rank of Major in America.

April 24th 1770.   FRANCES GRANT, Coll 63 Regt

This is to Certify that during the Time I commanded the first Highland Battalion or 77th Regt in America, Major Robert Rogers had the Character of an Active brave Officer and did his Duty with Spirit and Alacrity.   EGLINTOUNE, Col. 51. Regt.

ST ALBANS STREET LONDON
30th July. 1770.

I do Certify the above Certificates are true Copies of the Originals now in my Possession, September 29th 1770.—

ROBERT ROGERS.

No. 815—*Lord Rochford to the King.*

Lord Rochford humbly takes the Liberty to inform your Majesty, that Lord Weymouth not coming to Town last night he thought proper to write him a letter a copy of which he has the honor to send your majesty inclosed in order that your majesty may be fully apprised of every step that has been taken, and prepared for what may happen next Wednesday. Lord Rochford takes the liberty humbly to beg your Majesty to keep the inclosed as He is going this instant to set out for the country by your Majesty's permission.

BERKLEY SQUARE 29th *Seper* 1770
7 o clock A.M.

No. 816—*The King to Lord Weymouth.*

RICHMOND LODGE *Sep*^t 30th 1770.
Six o'clock P.M.

LORD WEYMOUTH—I thoroughly approve of the openess and clearness with which You have in the inclosed draught given Your ideas to Lord Hillsborough on the necessity of more exactly defining Your department in case War should arise, least that Secrecy and dispatch on which the Success of War must greatly depend should suffer by extending the business to too many Offices.

Your conduct during the time You have held the Seals makes me desirous this affair should so far be accommodated as to enable You to feel pleasant in Your department ; on the other hand I should be sorry if Lord Hillsborough felt himself agrieved ; I know Your prudence can be relied on and Your wish of no farther encrease of department than what the good of the Service requires which ought alone to decide this affair, I therefore trust when You both coolly discuss this matter that such an expedient will occur as may be satisfactory, I am anxious that this may be previous to my seeing You on Wednesday.

Draft.

No. 817—*Abstract of a letter from Sir John Lindsay at Madras,* 13 *October,* 1770.

[In the King's handwriting.]

At present the Nabob rents this jaghire of the Company for fourteen Lacks of Rupees, which is much above the real value, which he consents to as it would be a great inconvenience to him if in the hands of another, he is consequently threatened, that he shall be turned out before his term is elapsed.

They took possession of the Circars when Nizam Ally Cawn then at War in the Barand Country [*sic*] depended on the revenue of them for the pay of his Army, but by the treaty concluded in 1766 by General Caillaud the Circars were confirmed to them, but on worse Conditions than had formerly been offered by the present and former Subah, as they were to hold them as

Jaghire and assist with troops only, now they were not only
to give assistance when required but also to pay an Annual
Rent. Upon which the Nizam and English marched against
Bangalore. Nizam Ally Cawn and Hyder soon made up their
differences and turned their Arms against the Carnatick, the
Nizam soon quitted his new ally and in 1768 concluded a treaty
with the Nabob and Company by which he gave Hyder's Country
to the Company.

The Nabob took on himself the expence of the War in to
the Enemys Country, provided they gave him the Sole direction
of the Countries to be conquered, to which they formally
consented.

When the Nabob was negociating Peace with the Nizam,
he was told particularly by Ruccum ud Dowla, the Nizam's
Minister that he might also make a very advantageous Peace
with Hyder Ally, but the Government and Council would not
agree to it.

Though the Nabob had at a great expence brought an Army
to the assistance of the Company in 1768 when General Smith
Commanded, which was to be kept in pay for a certain time,
but [sic] he was soon acquainted that they would reduce it
and incorporate the men in their Army, and that though he
might have the direction of the Country, the whole produce
must be delivered into the treasury of the Company. The
peace with Hyder Ally was made without repaying the Nabob
the expence of the War, which had been promised him was a
condition they would not conclude without obtaining, and
brought a charge of ten lacks of Pagodas against him, which
he has refused to pay, and has appealed to the Company.

The Nabob is a man of business, superintends the affairs
of the whole Carnatick himself, his troops seem well disciplined,
He and his family sincerely attached to the English, three of
his Sons of Mans Estate, he has two younger fine boys.

In order to give an idea of the political management of the
Company's Servants, they made peace with Nizam Ally Cawn,
the Subahdar of the Decan in 1768. with a promise of sending
him troops when he should judge it necessary ; the Mahrattas
have made frequent claims for assistance against Hyder Ally ;
and their late treaty with this last obliges them mutually to
assist each other should their respective Countries be attacked.

The Nabob affirms the Subahdar of the Decan, Nizam Ally Cawn, and the Mahrattas are both collecting forces and preparing Artillery; proposals are said to have passed between them, that if the Nizam will assist the Mahrattas in reducing Hyder Ally, they will join him to invade the Carnatick, should this alliance take place Hyder Ally will soon be obliged to make Peace perhaps by a cession of part of his Country, and if the three should join, their power will be superior to that of the Nabob and Company.

As the Mahrattas have wished to be in friendship with the English, and as the concessions of Salsette and Bassine can be obtained of them by the Company; it would be good policy to cultivate them, and they are willing to grant whatever may give security to the Carnatick, and make over Several territories on the Malabar Side to the Company, with the privilege of Sandal Wood, on condition of assistance against Hyder Ally; but the Vacquiel receives no encouragement and the desire of the Company's Servants to yield every alliance for that of Hyder Ally cannot be accounted for. The persevering in a Scheme of conquest will be the ruin of the Company as it makes all the Princes of the Country look on with a jealous eye.

The letters from Bengal mention a most dreadful famine that has swept off Six hundred thousand inhabitants, many reasons are alledged for this severe calamity, particularly the monopoly of Cotton by the Servants of the Company, and the unfair means of raising the price of grain; but I apprehend there are others arising from the very nature of the government in those Provinces, which in the present situation of affairs will be difficult to be removed. The Princes in India look on their whole Country as their Estate, and the Inhabitants as their property; the gains of the husbandmen and labourers after supplying the necessities of their Families belong to the Prince, it is at his expence Villages are rebuilt if destroyed by an Enemy, the Tanks are repaired, seed Supplied for the ground, and Cattle for his people, and even Cloaths and grain are purchased from his Treasury.

General Cootes leaving this country as the President and Council refuse him the authorities he thinks inseperable from Commander in Chief, and the liberty of carrying with him to another Presidency where he is acknowledged, every necessary appendage of his Office, may be very detrimental to the Company's affairs.

No. 818—*Lord Barrington to the King.*

BECKETT *October the* 15*th* 1770.

I am incapable of expressing my grateful Sense of your Majesty's Goodness in admitting among your motives for promoting Major Leland, the good will I bear him. He is indeed my old friend and Acquaintance ; I rejoice in his Success, but I have ventured to postpone the notification your Majesty has directed ; which I hope you will not disapprove when I have stated the motive of that delay.

Major Leland was a very active & zealous officer last war ; but since the Peace, he has marry'd a Sussex Heiress who brought him an Estate & Country Seat : He has a good House in London & by the death of a Relation has succeeded to a fortune in Ireland. I am not certain that he will now make as diligent a field officer as he would have done seven years ago. I shall write to him by this post in a way that will make that matter clear : If I find he may be depended upon in Peace as well as in War, abroad as well as at home I will immediately obey your Majesty's Commands : If not, you will have a good Lieutenant-Colonelcy to bestow on some officer who will execute all the duties of that Station. BARRINGTON.

No. 819—*The King to Lord North.*

Printed.   Donne I. 32.

RICHMOND LODGE *Oct.* 21*st* 1770.

$$\frac{m}{15} p^t 9. \text{ A.M.}$$

LORD NORTH—As I doubt not but You will hear of applications for the Royal Regiment of Horse Guards on the death of the Marquiss of Granby, I think it right to acquaint You that Lieutenant General Conway whilst Secretary of State and again on resigning that Office had the promise that he should succeed to that Corps I shall therefore immediately send to Lord Barrington to make out the notification, and for Major General

Carpenter as his Successor as Colonel of the 4th Regiment of Dragoons, which will vacate the 12th Regiment of Dragoons for Major General Pitt whose meritorious conduct will make his appointment very creditable besides he has long had reason to expect such a mark of my favour.

No. 820—*Duke of Richmond to the King.*

Sire—It is with the most profound Respect that I beg Leave to address Your Majesty.

Lord Holland having informed me, in the Year 1763 of Your Majesty's gracious Promise of honoring me with the Command of the Royal Regiment of Horse Guards Blue upon the Death of Marshal Ligonier, when Your Majesty intended to give the first Regiment of Foot Guards to Lord Granby, I should have thought it my Duty to have applied to Your Majesty on that Event, had I not learned at the same Time of another Disposition's having taken Place whereby the Blues did not then become vacant.

But as I have heard this moment that Lord Granby is deceased, I hope Your Majesty will excuse my taking the Liberty, humbly to renew to Your Majesty the deep Sense I feel of Your Majesty's Goodness, and to express the Ambition I shall have upon all Occasions of serving Your Majesty in any Capacity I may be thought Equal to : but as many Circumstances have happened since the Time of Your Majesty's gracious Message to me by Lord Holland, and as possibly it might be more convenient for Your Majesty's present Arrangements if this Engagement did not subsist, I most humbly presume to beg of Your Majesty, if this should be the Case, to permit me to relinguish this Claim to the Blues which Your Majesty has formerly given me with so much Goodness, and to assure Your Majesty that no Situation, however desirable, can equal the Satisfaction I shall have in proving the Attachment, Respect, and Duty with which I most humbly entreat Your Majesty's Permission to subscribe myself, Sire, Your Majesty's Most Loyal and obedient Subject and Servant   Richmond, Lenox and Aubigny.

Goodwood
october the 21st
1770.

No. 821—*Lord Barrington to the King.*

BECKETT *October the* 22^d 1770.

On receiving last night an Account of poor Lord Granby's death, my first intention was to come immediately to Town, that I might be in the way to obey any commands your Majesty might have concerning the Blues ; but recollecting that when you are pleasd to give any thing immediately away, your Majesty commonly Sends your directions in writing ; I have ventured to follow my original Plan of staying here till next Sunday, if nothing unforeseen requires my earlyer attendance.

I have had an answer from Major Leland, but not quite so explicit as I wish : I shall therefore write to him again, & hear again from him before I venture to make my report to your Majesty.

As I am now writing to your Majesty on official Business, I will humbly presume to return my most dutyful acknowledgments of your great Goodness to Captain Barrington. Indeed Sir I am incapable of expressing my sense of those gracious marks of your Royal favour and approbation, which your Majesty is continually shewing to me and my family. If any thing can equal your Goodness, it is my Gratitude & Devotion.

BARRINGTON.

No. 822—*The King to Lord North.*

Printed.   Donne I. 35.

QUEENS HOUSE *Nov*^{r} 9th 1770.

LORD NORTH—Though the more I reflect on what Lord Mansfield has suggested of the expediency of not assembling the two Houses of Parliament untill the arrival of the Spanish Messenger, the more I am convinced that it would be improper as that Court and that of Versailles would upon it augur that we are resolved at all events to accommodate the present dispute, and consequently would encourage them to raise perhaps so much in their demands as would make War absolutely necessary ; yet I am desirous to hear by a line what he has said on that subject as well as on the appointment of a Chancellor ; and what

has passed between You and the Attorney General; Lord
Weymouth has applied a new in favour of his Cousin Lord
Dysart for the vacancy in the Sixteen, which I thought it would
not be right at this time to refuse, besides he will undoubtedly
prove a constant attender, and when I named the application to
You in the Summer You thought it a very proper one.

No. 823—*Lord North to the King.*

Lord North has the honour of informing his Majesty, that he
is now going to call at Lord Mansfield's in Bloomsbury Square,
& will wait upon his Majesty to apprize him of what shall have
past at such hour as his Majesty will be pleased to appoint.

The Attorney General will not refuse the Seals if offer'd to
him, but will expect at least the same terms as Lord Camden.

DOWNING STREET. *Sat^y morn^g* [10 *November*, 1770].

Endorsed by the King.

No. 824—*The King to Lord North.*

QUEENS HOUSE *Nov^r* 10^*th* 1770.

$$\frac{m}{25} p^t 3. \text{ P.M.}$$

LORD NORTH—I am this moment returned from Richmond
and found Your note on my table, I am ready to receive You
now or after Your dinner which ever is most convenient to You
though as we are pressed in time I think the Sooner the better.

No. 825—*Lord North to the King.*

[10 *November*, 1770.]

Lord North will do himself the honour of attending his
Majesty this Evening a little after six o'clock; Being engaged
to dine out, he did not receive his Majesty's letter till 9 o'clock:
He has seen Lord Mansfield & the Attorney General this morning,
& will have the honour of relating to his Majesty what pass'd,
when he pays his respects at the Queen's House: In the mean

while, He thinks it right to inform his Majesty, that Lord
Mansfield has no objection to opening the Session of Parliament
in his present situation.

RUSHINGTON STREET. *5'o'clock.*

No. 826—*The King to Lord North.*

Printed. Donne I. 36.

QUEENS HOUSE *Nov^r* 11th 1770.
Six o'Clock P.M.

LORD NORTH—The Speech and Address of the House of
Commons thoroughly meet with my approbation ; Lord Mansfield has been with Me to explain his conduct and to declare
that as it is now known that a Chancellor is intended to be
appointed he makes no difficulty of acting as Speaker for some
time nay said for a month or two if that could be of any utility.

No. 827—*The King to Lord North.*

Printed. Donne I. 37.

QUEENS HOUSE *Nov^r* 13th 1770.
$\frac{m}{58} p^t$ 10. A.M.

LORD NORTH—I am desirous of knowing what sort of an
attendance You had last night at the Cockpit at the reading of
the Speech and shall expect when the House is up to hear
whether any thing material passes there.

No. 828—*The King to Lord North.*

Printed. Donne I. 37.

QUEENS HOUSE *Nov^r* 13th 1770.
$\frac{m}{25.} p^t$ 7. P.M.

LORD NORTH—Your account that the Address has passed
without any amendment gives me great pleasure as this event
will strike Foreign Courts very much. When I see You to-

morrow I shall be curious to learn on what the Debate chiefly
run as well as on what has passed between You and the Attorney
General.

No. 829—*The Empress of Russia to the King.*

MONSIEUR MON FRERE—La faveur et la justice que les
Souverains doivent au merite m'offrent une Occasion d'écrire
à Votre Majesté, et l'intimité des sentiments qui m'unissent a
Elle y applaudit.   Le Seigneur Fawkener officier dans ses gardes,
qui avec sa permission a fait la campagne comme Volontaire dans
la premiere de mes Armées, s'est comporté avec une distinction
dont je me fais un plaisir d'informer Votre Majesté.   Le
temoignage que Lui rend Mon feld Marechal ne Sauroit être plus
favorable, Soit dans les actions generales, soit dans quelques
emplois particuliers dont il a été charge.   Il s'est conduit en
homme plein d'amour pour la gloire et d'un attachement Zèlé
pour le bien de mon Service.   C'est a ces titres que je le recom-
mande avec confiance aux bontes et a la bienveillance de Son
Souverain, à celles d'un Roi ami Sincere et reconnu de Moi et
de mon Empire.   C'est toujours avec une nouvelle Satisfaction
que j'arrête mes idées sur tous les rapports heureux, qui sub-
sistent entre Nos Personnes et nos Monarchies, et que je reitere
les assurances de L'estime distinguée avec la quelle je suis,
Monsieur Mon frere de Votre Majesté La bonne Soeur et parfaite
Amie   CATERINE.

ST. PETERSBOURG
ce 13 *Novembre*
    1770.

The signature alone is written by the Empress.

No. 830—*The King to Lord North.*

Printed.   Donne I. 38.

QUEENS HOUSE *Nov*[r] 14th 1770.

$\dfrac{m}{55.}$ p^t 5. P.M.

LORD NORTH—The value of the enclosed intelligence from
Paris depends on the confidence reposed there in the authors of

it ; which not being known here we cannot estimate it. As the Treasurer of the Household is out of Town, I am unacquainted what Privy Counsellor is deputed from the House of Commons to know when I will receive them tomorrow. You will therefore direct that he may Report to the House that I will receive them at half hour past two.

No. 831—*The King to Lord North.*

QUEENS HOUSE *Nov^r* 15th 1770.

$\frac{m}{55}$. p^t 9. A.M.

LORD NORTH—Least the load of business that must necessarily take up Your thoughts at the opening the Session of Parliament should have occasioned Your forgetting to prepare an answer to the Address of the House of Commons, I give You this notice that it may be draw up in time.

No. 832—*Lord North to the King.*

Lord North has the honour of informing his Majesty, that the Common Council have voted a bounty of 20 Shillings for every ordinary seaman & 40 Shillings for every able seaman who shall enter aboard the fleet, They have likewise determined upon an address, petition, & remonstrance upon the same matters with the former. The Sheriffs are order'd to go tomorrow to St James's, to know when it will be agreable, to his Majesty to receive it.

DOWNING STREET. *Nov^r* 15. [1770]

No. 833—*The King to Lord North.*

Printed. Donne I. 39.

QUEENS HOUSE *Nov^r* 15th 1770

$\frac{m}{5}$ p^t 11. P.M.

LORD NORTH—The idea of a fresh Address, Remonstrance and Petition is so extremely absurd and considering the time I

may add puerile that it deserves contempt I shall think Wednesday
next a proper time for receiving it ; the answer ought to referr
to what I said the last year and be dry and Short but more of
this when we know the precise words of this performance.   I
have directed Lord Weymouth to call on Lord Northington and
learn whether he is resolved to resign ; I hope You have now
authorized Lord Cornwallis to come to Court if Lord Weymouth
has acquainted Lord Berkley of Stratton that I accept his
resignation.

No. 834—*The King to Lord North.*

Printed.   Donne I. 39.

QUEENS HOUSE *Nov^r* 16*th* 1770. $\frac{m}{5}$ *p^t* 8. AM.

LORD NORTH—The enclosed is an extract I have taken on
reading this morning Mr Justice Foster's Report on the case of
Alexander Broadfoot for the murder of Cornelius Calahan a
Mariner, which contains his general idea of the legality of granting
Impress Warrants ; as this Subject will probably come forward
this day I thought this might not be unpleasing to You.

No. 835—*Lord North to the King.*

Lord North has the honour of informing his Majesty that
Mr Seymour has put off his motion till Monday.   As far as Lord
North can learn, It does not relate to the power of impressing
seamen.   He is much obliged to his Majesty for his extract
from S^r M: Foster's Crown Law, which seems to contain every
thing that can be said on the subject, & is conclusive to the
legality of Pressing.   Lord North thinks there is an opening to
acquire not only Mr Wedderburn, but all Mr Grenville's friends :
He will explain this to his Majesty on Sunday :   He intreats his
Majesty to excuse the writing of this note, as he is almost blind
with a cold in his head, which however, he hopes is now going.

DOWNING STREET. *Nov^r* 16. [1770]

Endorsed by the King.

No. 836—*The King to Lord North.*

Printed.   Donne I. 39.

QUEENS HOUSE *Nov^r* 19^*th* 1770.

$$\frac{m}{10.} \; p^t \; 5. \text{ P.M.}$$

LORD NORTH—If You are not engaged this Evening, I wish You would call here at any time most convenient, as I want to fix up the answer to the Remonstrance of the City of London, and to hear Your opinion on the answer arrived this day from the Court of Spain.

No. 837—*Lord North to the King.*

Lord North has the honour of apprizing his Majesty, that Lord Cornwallis will be at the Levée this morning to kiss his Majesty's hand, upon his appointment to the Office of Constable of the Tower.

Lord North has communicated to the Lords of the Cabinet the intended answer to the Remonstrance of the Common Council, which, with a few alterations they approved. Lord North will wait upon his Majesty with it this morning.

DOWNING STREET *Nov^r* 21. [1770]

Endorsed by the King.

No. 838—*The King to Lord North.*

Printed.   Donne I. 40.

QUEENS HOUSE *Nov^r* 23^*d* 1770

$$\frac{m}{2} \; p^t \; 5. \text{ P.M.}$$

LORD NORTH—I saw Lord Weymouth on his coming from the Spanish Ambassador ; the projet produced this day differed but little from that of Wednesday ; Lord Weymouth has renewed

the demand of the Governor of Buenos Ayres being disavowed
and the Island restored unattended by any discussion on the
night; Prince Masserano said he saw we meant war, but on
going said he would draw up another projet which Lord Weymouth declared he could not accept unless agreable to the demand;
Lord Weymouth wished I would name an Admiral for the
Mediterranean Squadron and give orders for augmenting the
Army the former I thought ought to be proposed first at a
Cabinet Meeting the latter I thought ought to be deferred until
Monday by which time we should know whether the Ambassador
has powers to conclude in a manner suitable to our just demands.

No. 839—*The King to Lord North.*

QUEENS HOUSE *Nov^r* 26th 1770.

$\dfrac{m}{15.}$ p^t 6. P.M.

LORD NORTH—Not having seen You this day, if You are not
particularly engaged I wish You would call here this Evening.

No. 840—*Lord North to the King.*

Lord North received his Majesty's commands by Lord
Barrington. He has likewise had a card from Mr Frances &
has appointed him at eight o'clock this evening. The 40,000
seamen pass'd today without a division in the H^s of Commons.
The H^o of Lords are yet sitting.

The Bill having pass'd for the prohibition of the exportation
of grain, it will be necessary for his Majesty either to go down to
the House tomorrow, or to appoint a Commission to give his
Majesty's assent to it, as the former Bill expires twenty days
from the commencement of the Session. There are no other
bills ready for his Majesty.

DOWNING STREET. *Nov^r* 28. [1770]

Endorsed by the King.

No. 841—*The King to Lord North.*

Printed. Donne I. 41.

QUEENS HOUSE *Nov* 28*th* 1770

$$\frac{m}{35} \, p^t \text{ 7. P.M.}$$

LORD NORTH—I gave directions to Lord Weymouth to give notice that I shall tomorrow pass the Corn Bill at the House of Lords; though I have but little hopes of any change in the conduct of the Court of Spain yet I shall be very anxious to learn what shall pass between You and Mr Frances; therefore if he leaves You by ten I wish You would call on me, if not that You will send Me a line, for every feeling of humanity as well as the knowledge of the distress War must occasion makes me desirous of preventing it if it can be accomplished provided the honour of this Country is preserved.

No. 842—*The King to Lord North.*

QUEEN'S HOUSE *Nov* 29*th* 1770

$$\frac{m}{4.} \, p^t \text{ 7. P.M.}$$

LORD NORTH—I am glad You have been able to end the Debate so early this day I wish You would just by a line acquaint me how You found Lord Suffolk.

No. 843—*Lord Rochford to the King.*

Lord Rochford is too anxious for whatever relates to the present critical situation of affairs, to refrain from laying before your majesty not only what occurrs to him from a slight knowledge of naval affairs but what he has collected, from consulting the most intelligent persons in navy matters, the inclosed paper he apprehends is a true state of the present Conditions of the Navy and there can arise no inconvenience from enquiring into the Truth of it it ought to be done with caution, & it ought particularly to be recommended to the Admiralty to add another Column to their reports, as your majesty would then judge whether the ships were in Condition or not, which Lord Rochford greatly apprehends are not.   Lord Rochford has had a Conversation to day with Mr Wood, who he found outrageous that your majestys Servants would prevent Lord Weymouth, who held, as he said, the pen, from giving the most fatal Blow that could be given to France by attacking them in the East Indies, Lord Rochford Imagines therefore that to morrow at Council that point will be warmly Contended for by Lord Weymouth but he must be overruled in a measure so destructive whilst there is the least glimmering hope of its being accomodated, Ld Rochford will Continue to be watchfull to the minutest event at this Critical period, and will not leave your majesty ignorant one moment of any thing essential that passes.   The inclosed letter was omitted by mistake out of the packet Lord Rochford had the honor to send your majesty this morning.

Berkley square 6th Dec^{br} 1770

$\frac{m}{10}$ p^t 8. a.m.

No. 844—*The King to Lord Rochford.*

Queens House Decr 6th 1770. $\frac{m}{44}$ p^t 10 a.m.

Lord Rochford—As I shall probably not see You alone this day and as the sending for You might occasion suspicion, I choose to take this method of opening my ideas to You on the very important subjects that will be this Evening laid before the Cabinet.   From the moment Lord Weymouth expressed yesterday a wish that Mr Harris might be recalled and that I had from others heard he had at the meeting the night before avoided answering the proper question You had put whether all present were ready to advise the accepting the declaration if containing simply a disavowal of Mr Buccarelli and a restoration of the Island ;   I have seen the above proposal as intended with a view to prevent any accommodation.   I owne I have no expectation the Spaniards will end this affair amicably yet I do not wish they should have it to say that they would have complied provided we had not recalled the Secretary of the Embassy without giving them an opportunity to conform to our uniform demanded [sic]. The opening a new the negociation would be highly improper the delaying his recall not less so ; but the sending him an exact draught of such a Declaration as we can receive with orders to acquaint Mr Grimaldi, that if he does not receive the King of Spain's consent to it without the alteration of an iota, the next day he instantly quit Spain ; Such a measure would enable the Spanish Ambassador to stay and obey any directions he may receive whilst that proposed would of necessity immediately oblige him to quit the Kingdom, and consequently entirely shut the door against concluding this irksome affair as every honest and considerate man must wish.

As to the desire of the East India Company that they may be permitted to order Pondicherri and the French factory at Bengal to be attacked this seems to me highly improper, as the ordering them to collect their Forces and that if a War should be commenced they will soon receive directions to attack those places, which we may within a month send by a Frigate and for fear of accidents a Messenger may also be sent by land. I should be desirous of having an answer to this that I may know Your exact sentiments on these very important questions.

Draft.

No. 845—*Lord Rochford to the King.*

Lord Rochford humbly begs leave to return your majesty his sincere thanks for the Confidence your majesty is pleased to place in him which it shall ever be his endeavours to deserve the continuance of. Lord Rochford is clearly of opinion that Mr Harris ought at all events to acquaint the Spanish ministry that Negociation is at an End here with prince Masserano and that in twenty four hours he will quit the Court of Spain unless our Demand which has been uniform is simply and instantly complied with a measure of this kind cannot hurt Your Majesty's Dignity and any opposition to it can only arise from a wish to see this unlucky affair terminate fatally, Everything that can be urged in support of this opinion shall not be omitted in Council to night but as yet no council is Appointed, it is humbly therefore Submitted to Your Majesty whether it would not be proper for your majesty to insinuate to Lord Weymouth at Court today the necessity of assembling your majesty's servants this Evening. As to the proposal of the East India Company the sending a Frigate a month hence will answer every purpose and that point will certainly be carried, perhaps unanimously, in Cabinet provided by the Ship that is now going orders are sent to the Governor at Madrass to prepare for the Instructions he may receive which there can be no objection to & it tallies entirely with your majestys Views. Ld Rochford takes the liberty to send your majesty copies of Letters that passed between him and Lord Shelburne relative to Falkland Islands & the Manilla Ransom which perhaps your majesty may be curious to Revise at your Leisure and then Your Majesty will have the Goodness to return them to Lord Rochford.

BERKLEY SQUARE *Dec^{br}* 6th 1770

$\frac{m}{5}$ p^t 12 A.M.

No. 846—*The King to Lord Rochford.*

QUEENS HOUSE *Dec^r* 6th 1770. $\frac{m}{5}$ p^t 10. PM.

LORD ROCHFORD—The enclosed paper seems very judicious and ought to be attended to, I therefore would have You make that use of it that may best answer the putting the Naval Preparations into a more expeditious as well as more certain state. The conduct of Mr Wood seems every day more unbecoming his Station ; the East India Warlike preparations cannot be otherways decided upon but in conformity to what I expressed myself to You this morning. I rely on Your acquainting Me with the minutest events that may regard this critical period.

Draft.

Enclosure.
Memorandum.

Reflections on the present state of the Navy and the reasons why the Fleet is not in greater forwardness than it is, and the evil consequences that may arise in case of War if the present management is not changed.

The 7th of Septr eighteen Guardships were ordered by Lord Weymouth to be got in readiness; the 19th of the same month twenty two Ships of the Line more were ordered by Lord Rochford to be put in Commission; we are now informed that these forty Ships are fit for service excepting a deficiency of about 6000 men which may be immediately got by Impressing from Protections and other methods that will be pointed out by the Admiralty, these with the fifteen Ships now lately ordered would make a respectable Fleet and enable us to begin the War, if necessary with success; but it is not the number of Ships nor their being compleatly manned which proves our strength, for if these Ships are deficient in any Respect the disapointment will be equally felt; and it appears by the Ships that were sent to Corke that their bottoms were not clean of course they ran great risk of foundering at Sea, and if the remainder which are now supposed to be ready should turn out to be in the same condition, the most dreadfull consequence may be apprehended from it; it is therefore to be wished that when the Admiralty make a return of the state of the Fleet to the Secretaries of State, that they would add another Column, and mention when each Ship had last its bottom cleaned; then the true state of the Fleet will appear in its exact state; it is to be observed that at Sheerness there is but one Dock, at Portsmouth two at most, at Plymouth four, and if every Ship is put into Dock, the present practice, in order to see the state of her bottom, it would take up an immense time, whereas if all the Ships in Commission had been, and were to be for the future immediately on their being Commissioned, heaved down along side the old Ships of War that are unfit for Service three or four might be dispatched at the same time, this was practised by Admiral Vernon in the West Indies, and might be done here with much greater ease whilst the Ships are only in Ballast and have not taken in their Guns. All these are doubts that have arisen in the breast of the person who makes these reflections, the enquiry into the truth of the assertions can but be attended with the best of consequences, as infinite mischief must arise if there is ground for the Suspicion.

Copy, in the King's handwriting.

No. 847.

SPEAKERS ON SERJ^T GLYNN'S MOTION 6 DEC^R [1770].

For	Against
Serj^t Glynn.	Mr Jenkinson.
Mr Oliver.	Mr Cooper.
Sir J. Mawbey.	Mr Onslow.
Mr Sawbridge.	Lord Clare.
Mr Cornewall.	Mr C. Fox.
Mr T. Townshend.	Mr Herbert.
Mr Phipps.	Sir G. Elliot.
Sir Geo. Savile.	Mr Attorney General.
Mr E. Burke.	Mr Forrester.
Mr Dunning.	Mr Sollicitor General.
Lord Geo. Sackville.	Mr Fitzpatrick.
Mr Ja^s Townshend.	Col^l Onslow.
Colonel Barré.	
Mr Calcraft.	
Mr Wedderburn.	

No. 848—*Lord Rochford to the King.*

Lord Rochford thinks it his Duty to acquaint your majesty of what passed at Council last night; The sending to recall Mr Harris & for him to make the Categorical Demand was proposed and long Debated, but on Lord Weymouths declaring that he would not on any account instruct Mr Harris to renew the Negociation, which he could never be made understand would not be the case if he, Mr Harris, was suffered to ask a Question of Monsr Grimaldi, the Rest of your majestys servants rather than be disunited in this critical situation acquiesced so far, as to resolve to send no messenger at all, from well Considering the affair it was thought it could not be attended with any bad consequence as the final answer must be set out from Spain before the messenger could arrive, it would not be doing Justice to Lord Weymouth not to report that he shewed the greatest temper & moderation, and on being very much pressed by me to say whether he would or would not accept the Conditions if they came at last, his answer was that though contrary to his Opinion Higher demands were not made, yet as he should allwayes when he could possibly, Acquiesce with the majority of the Cabinet that he certainly would recommend accepting them if they came in time. The next thing that was produced was a letter written by Lord Weymouth to the chairman of the East India Company, the latter part of which was so directly opposite to the Ideas of your majestys servants, & besides so confusedly written that it was impossible to suffer it to go in that Shape for it would have empowered the Company, if they had seen any preparations for Defence at pondicherri, to have attacked the French without waiting for the final orders by the Frigate, all the latter part of the letter therefore was left out and as it now stands no mischief can arise, this Ld Weymouth though with great reluctance Consented to Lord Rochford flatters himself this brief account of last nights transaction will meet with your majestys approbation.

BERKLEY SQUARE Decr 8 1770. $\frac{m}{15}$ p^t 9 AM.

No. 849—*Lord Rochford to the King.*

Lord Rochford is greatly ashamed to be so troublesome to your Majesty, but having seen Lord Hillsborough he has desired him to inform your Majesty that he is under the utmost uneasiness even with regard to the first part of the Letter to the East India Company which he thinks full of that sort of Ambiguity that may be made an ill use of he mentioned this frequently in the Cabinet last night but their attention was so taken up with the more exceptional parts, that he could not prevail upon them to consider what he said upon the first part, Lord Rochford does not see this in so Strong a light as Lord Hillsborough does though he thinks the letter had better be more precisely expressed this your Majesty will best Judge of upon reading the Draft.

Dec^{br} 8th 1770

$\frac{m}{5}$ p^t *one* P.M.

No. 850—*Lord Rochford to the King.*

Lord Rochford takes the earliest opportunity to have the honor to inform your Majesty that yesterday he was above two hours with Sr Edward Hawke from whom he received a satisfactory Account of the State of the fleet and particularly that 22 ships of the Line now in Commission, have been not only Docked but are Sheathed the 18 guardships have only received their annual Docking & must of course be put into Dock again next spring Sr Edward approves also of the scheme of an additional Column, & for the future it will be added to all the Admiralty reports, Sr Edward says further that Sr Peter Dennis is gone to hoist his flag at Chatham, Buckle to hoist his at Portsmouth and Spry his at Plymouth, these admirals will give their assistance and press the armaments in those ports, all the builders & surveyors have been threatned to be suspended if they do not give the utmost attention to their Duty, there is great hopes therefore that things will go on well and expeditiously The Impressing from protections cannot take place untill the nights grow Dark which will be in five or six nights hence. Sr Edward begged it might be made known to your Majesty the Impossibility of his attending the house of Commons, but intends if possible having the honor to attend your Majesty to morrow at St James's.

BERKELEY SQUARE 9th Dec^{br} 1770

$\frac{m}{50}$ p^t 9 A.M.

No. 851—*The King to Lord Rochford.*

QUEEN'S HOUSE Decr 9th 1770 $\frac{m}{6}$ p^t 11 A.M.

LORD ROCHFORD—The account of the State of the Fleet given You yesterday by Sir Edward Hawke is very satisfactory ; his good sense made me immagine he would with pleasure order the additional Column to the future reports.

I examined Lord Weymouth's draught to the Chairman of the East India Company with great attention, and though I am of opinion it is not entirely clear, yet I do not think it big with the mischief Lord Hillsborough seems to apprehend, his objecting so much to the want of precision rather surprises me, as it is a fault his Secretary frequently falls into.

Draft, endorsed by the King.

No. 852—*Lord Rochford to the King.*

Lord Rochford thinks it his Duty to lose no time in acquainting your Majesty that yesterday he had a long conversation with Lord Weymouth, who told him he found it Impossible for him to go on contradicted by your Majesty's Servants on five occasions & where his own Department was immediately concerned, he is resolved to mention this to your Majesty to Day, and says he has no objection to my being present, he will do any thing rather than break up administration, but that he would supplicate Your Majesty to find some means of his quitting his employment, his Chief Complaint is that We are in a state of uncertainty and are taking no measure to distress the Enemy, it was in vain represented to him, that we were not prepared as yet for any thing Hostile, he then again proposed recalling Mr Harris, He then begged me to mention this to Lord North, which I did last night, who will have the honor to see your Majesty to day, after Ld Weymouth ; Lord Rochford thinks this a most Critical situation, and only begs leave to assure Your Majesty that his humble services will be ready for any situation that can tend to extricate Government at this moment from this very critical situation, and presumes to offer as his advice that it would be prudent to day to listen only and to take if it shall be found necessary, twenty four hours to consider any proposition that may come from Lord Weymouth, this will give your Majesty time to see afterwards any of your Servants your Majesty from your known wisdom shall think prudent and fit to confide in.

BERKLEY SQUARE 10th *Dec^{br}* 1770

$\frac{m}{10}$ p^t 8 A.M.

No. 853—*The King to Lord Rochford.*

QUEENS HOUSE *Dec^r* 10th 1770

$$\frac{m}{33.} \; p^t \; 8 \text{ P.M.}$$

LORD ROCHFORD—The conduct of Lord Weymouth at this critical moment is rather distressing, I shall think it most prudent to listen to what he shall say and to take a day's consideration ; the only difficulty that occurs to me is how to find an employment for him ; for as to the Seals they cannot cause any inconvenience.

Draft, written on a page of Lord Rochford's
letter of same date.

No. 854—*Lord Rochford to the King.*

Lord Rochford humbly takes the Liberty to inform your Majesty that he has seen Lord Weymouth this morning, and has learnt from him finally that he would accept of any employment that should be fit for him, but have rather have none, he suggested that if Lord Sandwich was made Secretary of State for the Northern Department the post office if given to Mr Thynne would be vacant, and such an employment given to his Brother would be a convincing proof to the World that he Lord Weymouth had not quarrelled with administration, at the same time he would bring into his Brothers Borough a determined friend to Government, Lord North has been informed by me of this arrangement and seems to think it very feasible.

BERKLEY SQUARE *Dec^r* 11th 1770

$$\frac{m}{6} \; p^t \; 2 \text{ P.M.}$$

No. 855—*Lord Rochford to the King.*

Lord Rochfords sole motive in troubling your Majesty is, that he is convinced Lord Weymouth will defer giving up the seals as long as it will suit your Majestys Conveniency, but it strikes Lord Rochford that it will be more adviseable for him to tell Lord Weymouth that he Lord Rochford received your Majestys orders through Lord North with regard to your Majestys wish of his holding the seals a few days longer, as Lord Weymouth will be surprised at your Majestys conveying a message by me and it will come very naturally through Lord North as it was by Lord Weymouths desire that I spoke to him Yesterday, Lord Rochford will therefore take that method this Morning unless he shall receive contrary directions from your Majesty. it is necessary to observe to your Majesty that your Majestys last Note dated last night was not brought to Lord Rochford untill nine o'clock this morning.

BERKLEY SQUARE 12 *Dec^{br}* 1770

$$\frac{m}{55} \, p^t \; 9 \; \text{A.M.}$$

No. 856—*The King to Lord North.*

Printed.   Donne I. 42.

QUEENS HOUSE *Dec^r* 14*^{th}* 1770.

$$\frac{m}{30} \, p^t \; 10 \; \text{P.M.}$$

LORD NORTH—I have just received Your account of Lord George Germain's two motions and the very handsome majority in favour of Government. If You have not as yet intimated to Lord Sandwich my intentions of entrusting him with the Seals of the Northern Department; I wish You would not longer deferr as the manner greatly enhances or diminishes every favour; besides others may insinuate it which might make him imagine that to them he owed His advancement.

No. 857—*Lord North to the King.*

Lord North has the honour of informing his Majesty, that Mr Francis was with him last night & desired to have a conference with Lord Weymouth & him this morning upon the

subject of a letter just received from the D: de Choiseul, Lord
North has sent to Lord Weymouth, & is every minute expecting
his answer.

Lord North will obey his Majesty's command with respect
to Lord Sandwich immediately.

DOWNING STREET *Saturday morn^g* [15 *December*, 1770].

No. 858—*The King to Lord North.*

Printed.   Donne I. 43.

QUEEN'S HOUSE *Dec^r* 15th
1770. $\frac{m}{2}$ p^t 3 P.M.

LORD NORTH—I am extremely desirous of being informed
what Mr Francés has to communicate, and therefore shall be
desirous of seeing You at any convenient time this Evening,
as I am able to hear but by a severe cold in my breast am
prevented from Speaking. I should rather imagine Lord
Weymouth will decline to be one at the conference.

No. 859—*Lord North to the King.*

[15 *December*, 1770.]

Lord North has received a message from Lord Weymouth
declining the Conference with Mr Francés, who has not yet
informed Lord North of the subject of his dispatches ; Lord
North has appointed him tomorrow morning at ten o'clock,
He will have the honour of obeying his Majesty's Commands
at half an hour after seven o'clock this evening, unless his
Majesty would chuse, to defer seeing him till after his conference
with Mr Francis. Ld Sandwich being at Hinchinbroke Lord
North has dispatched a messenger with the intimation of his
Majesty's pleasures.

DOWNING STREET 4' *o'clock.*

No. 860—*The King to Lord North.*

Printed. Donne I. 43.

QUEENS HOUSE *Dec* 17*th* 1770.

$$\frac{m}{33.} \ pt \ 9 \ \text{A.M.}$$

LORD NORTH—I am desirous of hearing whether You have had as yet any answer from Lord Sandwich, if he is in Town and has consented to accept ; I will instantly direct a Council to be Summoned for the Swearing him in this day ; for the affair is thoroughly known, and every delay is disadvantageous, particularly by the total stop now in all material business in the Southern Department ; I shall be glad also to learn when I see You what has passed with Mr Francés though I have no comfortable expectation ; my cold though much abated will prevent my going to St James's this day therefore I shall Expect you Here.

No. 861—*Lord North to the King.*

Lord North received a letter last night from Lord Sandwich by which he learns that his Lordship has received his Majesty's commands with much gratitude, and will obey them with pleasure, He is not yet in Town, but Lord North expects him every moment. Lord North will, with his Majesty's permission, pay his respects at the Queen's House to day at twelve o'clock, He is sorry to say, that he conceives no great hopes from the conversation he had yesterday with Mr Francés.

DOWNING STREET *Monday.* [17 *December*, 1770]

No. 862—*Lord North to the King.*

Lord North has, in obedience to your Majesty's commands, talked with Lord Frederick Campbell upon the subject of Mr Conway.

He is of opinion the proposition itself will not at sight, please his Brother, & that he is not likely to come into it willingly unless it comes immediately from your Majesty. He doubts

likewise very much how acceptable the proposed plan will be
to the present Lord Lieutenant, though he thinks upon the
whole, that the arrangement will be for his advantage. There
has been no difficulty or delay in either of the houses today,
but there has been a duel this morning between Lord George
Germaine & Governor Johnston, I understand that two pistols
were fired on each side, but neither of the parties was hurt,
This Duel was caused by some words that were spoken by Governor
Johnston in the debate on Friday last.

DOWNING STREET *Dec^r* 17. [1770]

No. 863—*The King to Lord North.*

Printed. Donne I. 44.

QUEENS HOUSE *Dec^r* 17*th* 1770.

$$\frac{m}{30} \, p^t \; 10 \; \text{P.M.}$$

LORD NORTH—I made no doubt but Lord Frederick Campbell
would be of opinion that Lieutenant [Gen.] Conway would not
at first sight like the proposition ; but it is asking a little too
much that I shall be the first breaker of unpleasant news ; I am
very ready to take my proper Share [in] the soothing him when
made acquainted with it.

Lord George Germaine permitting so many days to elapse
before he called Governor Johnston to an account for the words
he made use of on Friday does not give much idea of his resolution
but that he has at length been persuaded by his Friends to take
this step.

As You have not mentioned any time for Lord Sandwiches
acceptance, I suppose You have not had time to talk that affair
over with Lord Rochford.

No. 864—*Lord Barrington to the King.*

CAVENDISH SQUARE *Dec^r* 18. 1770.

I am at last able to submit to your Majesty's consideration
a Plan for the appointment of officers to the light Companies ;

and I presume to send it, that as little time as possible may be lost before the notification.

Where officers are out on their Pay so that the youngest Captain is only paid as Lieutenant, the Captain Lieutenant get's the Company, & is succeeded by the eldest Lieutenant: When this is not the case the Captain is taken from the half pay.

One of the new Lieutenants is taken from the half pay, & the other is the eldest Ensign promoted, except in I think two Regiments where the Ensigns are none of them above two years standing. In some Corps there are Lieutenants serving as Ensigns: when that is the case they fill both Lieutenantcies. Your Majesty will see in the last Column by whom the new Ensigns are recommended. All the vacancies of Ensign are not fill'd, because I am got to the End of my list of applications; but I shall soon have more. I think what is now submitted to your Majesty is as exact as possible; infinite pains have been taken to make it so, but if any mistakes should be found, I hope I shall be allow'd to set them right. Some few blanks are left which as yet I am not able to fill entirely to my satisfaction. Two Companies are still vacant; If your Majesty consents to Mr Stanley's request in favour of Mr Isaacson (whose pretensions I inclose) he may have one of them, & I have a very good Captain on half pay for the other. None of the half pay officers submitted to your Majesty's consideration retired *voluntarily*; they were all reduced with their Corps. What promotion there is you will find to be *regimental* & *in succession* without one instance of *favour*.

I shall attend at St James's to morrow to receive your Majesty's directions, which will be every most dutyfully obey'd by me.

BARRINGTON.

No. 865—*Lord North to the King.*

[18 December, 1770.]

Lord North met Lord Rochford, & Lord Sandwich soon after he left his Majesty yesterday morning, & found them of opinion that tomorrow morning at the Levée is the proper time for the arrangement to take place. Mr Thynne will kiss hands at the

Levée, & Ld Sandwich in the closet. If his Majesty approves this resolution, Lord North will inform all the parties concern'd, Mr Thurlow will consent to such an arrangement as may be most useful to his Majestys service without being dishonourable to himself. Lord North intends to employ the remainder of this day in completing the plan of Law appointments, & hopes to succeed to Mr Wedderburn's desire.

No. 866—*The King to Lord North.*

Printed. Donne I. 45.

QUEENS HOUSE *Dec^r* 18th 1770.

$\frac{m}{30.}$ *pt one.* P.M.

LORD NORTH—Tomorrow morning will be a very proper time for the arrangement to take place, you will therefore inform the different persons of it. I am glad Mr Thurlow consents to assist on this occasion, which will satisfy Mr Wedderburne, and You ought therefore to prosecute the Law plan, now you have grounds to go upon. Though I never incline to dejection, I think I do not to the contrary, but am certain that the present arrangement will be of considerable advantage to the stability of Government.

No. 867—*The King to Lord North.*

Printed. Donne I. 46.

QUEENS HOUSE *Dec^r* 19th 1770.

$\frac{m}{43}$ *p^t* 9. A.M.

LORD NORTH—As my Cold is not so abated that I can with safety go to St James's, and that I have rather more fever to day ; I have through Lord Rochford directed that the Privy Council for swearing in Lord Sandwich [*sic*], I have directed Mr Thynne to attend so that my prudence will occasion no inconvenience.

No. 868—*Lord Sandwich to the King.*

[22 *December*, 1770.]

Lord Sandwich takes the liberty to inform His Majesty, that the Earl of Stair cordially & gratefully accepts the honour done him.

Lord Sandwich saw Ld Weymouth immediately after he left St James's, & found him thoroughly sensible of your Majesty's goodness, he thought it must make the same impression on Ld Dysart, and wrote his opinion to him on that head ; your Majesty will receive herewith his Lordship's very extraordinary answer ; which however is of very little consequence, as Ld Weymouth entirely disavows him, & feels himself still under additional obligations, for this last mark of your Majesty's kindness. letters to all the Scotch Peers were dispatched last night from my office, solliciting their votes in behalf of Ld Stair.

Endorsed by the King, Dec. 22nd, 1770.

No. 869—*Lord Sandwich to the King.*

In consequence of Ld Mansfields answer which comes with this, Lord Sandwich will take care that five Cabinet Councellors shall be at St James's to morrow at one o'clock, Unless he recieves any orders from Your Majesty to the contrary.

Lord Sandwich saw Ld Marchmont yesterday, who very readily consented to send his Proxy in favour of Ld Stair.

Dec. 25. 1770.
five minutes past two P:M:

No. 870—*The King to Lord North.*

QUEENS HOUSE *Dec^r* 26th 1770.

$\frac{m}{15}$ *pt* 9. P.M.

LORD NORTH—I cannot refrain from communicating to You an intercepted letter I have received from the Duc de Choisseul to the French Chargé des Affaires at Hamburgh, as it confirms my opinion that we shall not have such offers from the Court of Spain as can enable me to preserve to my Subjects the blessings of Peace.

No. 871—*Lord North to the King.*

Lord North has the honour of returning to his Majesty the
D: of Choiseul's intercepted letter, with his most grateful
acknowledgements for the communication of it. It certainly
gives little hopes of peace, but there is one circumstance which
I can not understand ; The Duke of Choiseul's proposal of a
reserve des droits was sent over to Mr Francés (as he told me)
in a letter dated from Versailles on the 3^d of December ; The
intercepted letter is dated on the 2^d of December, when the
negociation had been broken off upon a proposal of annexing
a Convention to the declaration of Spain, & not from any refusal,
on our part, to allow of a reserve des droits. This consideration
may perhaps make the conduct of the Duke of Choiseul appear
more suspicious & may induce us to believe that France is
determined to find some pretext or other for a war, notwithstanding the very pacifick language that has been held for these two
or three days past by The Comte de Guignes, & Mr Francés :
We must continue preparing, but I can not yet think, that such
a mutual reservation of Rights as I mention'd to your Majesty
this morning, if properly express'd ought to be rejected. If
it preserves peace, it will preserve it without diminution to our
credit ; If it fails, it will put France & Spain intirely in the
wrong, according to their own principles.

DOWNING STREET. *Dec^r* 26. [1770]

No. 872—*The Managers of the Opera to the Lord Chamberlain.*

The Managers of the Opera beg permission to solicit the
Lord Chamberlains protection, and to lay before his Lordship
a real state of the hardships under which they suffer.

They beg leave to represent to his Lordship that it is impossible
for the Receipts of Italian Opera's only to support the necessary
expences.

That the Salaries of the first Singers and Dancers being so
enormous they are at a larger yearly expence than the other
Theatres, and instead of six Nights in a Week have in effect
only one as on the Tuesdays they constantly play to great loss.

That the Subscription Saturday Nights are only twenty five and the few nights after the Subscription scarce worth taking, as the People of fashion are out of town.

That the Kings Theatre was originally a play house under his Majestys immediate protection and that of the Lord Chamberlain and continued such till Mr Collier came into a compromise with the Managers of Drury Lane to suspend giving plays at the Opera House on condition the Managers of Drury Lane engaged not to play on Opera Nights and to allow the Directors of the Opera as a further compensation Two Hundred Pounds a Year: an Agreement which has not been fulfill'd on the side of the Patentees of the other Theatre for many years: on the contrary, they have given the strongest pieces they possibly cou'd at both houses, on Opera Nights, and given both comic and serious English Operas with Italian Music, to the great detriment of the Managers of the Opera.

That the Salary of even one capital Performer at the Opera House, is more than equal to those of three at the Playhouse: tho the latter play six times a Week and the Opera House but twice, and one of those Nights a certain loss.

That his Lordship has been so good in consideration of the impossibility of supporting Operas without some indulgence to allow the Managers two Masquerades but from their being become so common, and given every where, they do not pay the expences, and therefore they have this year been obliged to decline them and have only given one tho' his Lordship was so good to allow them two.

That besides the above disadvantages the Pantheon a new undertaking, establish'd since the present Managers came to the Kings Theatre in the manner it is now carry'd on, is to the utmost degree ruinous to the Opera, as they not only divide the Musical audiences, but by offering the most exorbitant terms to Italian Singers make it almost impossible for the Managers of the Opera to engage any Performers, except at prices which even the utmost success can never enable them to pay. This they can easily do as they are a numerous body fifty persons at least divided amongst whom the salaries are but trifles, and many of whom, being (as we are inform'd) tradesmen find their account in furnishing refreshments, as well for the common nights, as for Masquerades &c.

That the present Managers have embark'd a large Sum in the purchase which must be sunk with perhaps much more, unless his Lordship has the Goodness to grant them an extention of their present licence.

That in the days of Shakespear London contain'd no less than seventeen play houses a circumstance to which we probably owe that immortal writer.

That the present number of Theatres in this Capital being so very inadequate to the amazing encrease of its inhabitants since the act of limitation, the Nobility and Gentry, continually refus'd places, and weary'd out by repeated disappointments have to the great discouragement of dramatic genius, almost left off frequenting the theatres.

That if there are any solid objections to an additional theatre, they cannot affect the Opera House, originally built and licens'd for a play house, and honor'd with the name of the Kings Theatre.

That the present Directors encourag'd by the general wish of the Nobility and Gentry to have plays at a Theatre so conveniently situated, humbly entreat that the licence for the Opera House, now confin'd to Italian performances, may be extended on the intermediate Nights to theatrical entertainments in the English language also.

If a licence for plays is absolutely impossible that his Lordship will be so good to permit English Operas on the intermediate nights, or if that cannot be had, a summer licence in the nature of Mr Foote's patent but on different nights.

If it shou'd be urg'd that the present Managers of Drury Lane and Covent Garden House purchas'd at a great expence, the Managers of the Opera have done the same, and have ever since play'd to loss, whereas the profits of the other theatres, even with a third wou'd be immense : it is also to be considered that the law restraining the number of theatres expressly gives Power to the Lord Chamberlain to licence more at his pleasure, and therefore the purchases of Drury Lane and Covent Garden have been always made under the supposition that more might, and probably wou'd be granted.

Nor was the Act of Limitation intended to limit the number which is still in the Lord Chamberlain's power but to restrain the licentiousness of the theatres : Nor wou'd such an extention

of their licence as the Managers of the Opera humbly solicit,
add to the number of theatres, which wou'd be still the same :
a consideration which has encourag'd them to ask his Lordships
protection.

No. 873—*Considerations on the State of the Stage.*

[1770.]

As an Act of Parliament passed in the Reign of His late
Majesty restricting Theatrical performances, it is proposed to
examine into the Cause, as 'tis not impossible it may be understood to have its rise from a presumption that the Number
existing at that time was prejudicial to Society in general : but
this was not the Case—for its affects are directly contrary, as
can be easily proved from various instances & Reasons—but
prior thereto it is fit to shew whence the restriction took its
rise,—about the year 1738 a Theatre was opened in Goodmans
feilds W^h for some time performed Theatrical Peices unmolested
—their success encouraged a Broken Wit (says Cibber) to collect
a 4th Comp^y in the Hay market ; who soon finding the best
Plays ill performed turned to a bad Acco^t, thought it necessary
to give the Public some extraordinary peices, of such a Specie
that no bad Acting coud Spoil ; and that from their Nature,
shoud, if not draw the attention of the Judicious, at least attract
that of the Million (the Mob) : under this distress he became
Intrepidly abusive and licentious & in several Frank and free
Farces, he pelted his Superiours and seemed to Aim at the
destruction of every Idea of distinction in Mankind, both on the
Heads of Religion, Governm^t, Priests, Ministers & Judges ; all
were leveled by this Draw-cancer in Witt, who Spared neither
Friend nor Foe till at last by his own Poetic Fire (like a second
Erostratus) he consumed his own Stage, by writing up an Act
of Parliament, for the purposes before recited—thus farr *Cibber*
who wrote at the time the Act passed : but it was suspected
that this Adventurer was hired to do this dirty business by the
Patentees, who possibly were apprehensive if some Check was
not given their Emolum^{ts} woud soon decrease. if 'twas so, no
price was too high for the purchase of so invaluable a privilege
—from hence tis Evident 'twas the licentious use & abuse of
the Stage that was the real Cause of the Restraint by w^h only

Two Theatres were from that time permitted, and those under ye immediate Inspection of the Ld Chamberlain, whose licence must give Sanction to every peice before it can appear : this restriction has totally suppressed every abuse nay it has even banished every indelicacy ; so that there is now nothing left that can Shock the Ears of an Audience. The good Effects of this part of the restriction is further Evident as it has been the Cause of rooting out the Indelicacies of Old Authors as well as refining the Modern—the Stage at this day is so Chaste, that it is become a School of Morality—and considering the strong effect theatrical representations have on the Heart where is there so good a Master—no Lecture on Lawless Ambition can ever operate on the Mind with equal power to the Animated Scene of a *Macbeth* ; nor will any sermon on the relative duties sink so deep in the young Heart, as those inculcated by a *Barn-wall* : and it is further to be observed that since frequenting the Theatres has become general, that the manner and Conversations of the people in this kingdom is become more delicate more refined ; for what woud have been received as Wit in 1675 woud in this Age be deemed obscenity.

If in the year 1737 Two Theatres were thought necessary, how inadequate will they appear in 1770—when population is so immensely increased in this Metropolis : tis but to examine those vast Spaces of Ground which from Bond S^{tr} were so lately green fields, and are now Covered with almost Numberless buildings, forming the New Squares and Streets extending even to Mary-Le-Bon, to be Convinced of the vast disproportion there is in the two periods ; and if to this we add that there is in every part of London an increase of Play goers in proportion as 20 is to 1 : since the time the Act passed : should general observation not bring conviction—another Test can be produced amounting to a greater certainty—tis about 20 years since drury Lane House did not contain when full £180—and then but Seldom subject to an overflow : and that every House is at this day generally inaccessable for the greatest part of the Season, though it is enlarged so as to contain £280—and the same observation holds good at the other House, can there want a Stronger proof that 3 Houses now is not more in proportion than *one* was at the period referred to.

That it does not, nor ever has been looked upon as an amusem^t

that Infringes too much upon the time and attention of a Trading People, or as being too expensive to them, is a fact ; the Law was framed to Correct the language not to restrain the frequenters of the Theatre ; nor was any Arguments used upon that occasion that had that tendency—but solely turned upon the Insolence, Malice, Immorality and seditious Calumny which was at this time propogated by Theatric peices : nor did it then pass without a Vigorous opposition ; and leaving in His Majesty an indiscriminate power at any time to extend by his Royal Letters patent this prerogative whenever, he in his Wisdom should think fit to grant such an Indulgence ; within 10 Miles of his usual Residence —Relaxations are necessary, they will they must dissipate ; Men do it now at the Theatre, instead of the Tavern, by this means excess is avoided, the mind improved & domestic society is promoted ; nay tis economy, for tis less expensive to pay for a Place in the Pit or Gallery than a Tavern bill—the Mistress of a familey in this Age has not a less propensity to relax, if so, tis surely better to lead her to an amusem^t that will edify—than to see those Hours spent in Visiting and being Visited, the general apendage to which is the Card Table,—and tis too well known that every Mimicker of Fashion is too well bred to play low : of w^t importance is it then to divert them from a Gameing Table, and lead them to the much more moderate expence of a rational Evenings entertainm^t at the Theatre—Nay so farr is it from being deemed an Amusement prejudicial to the Minds or Interest of a Trading people there is many, the most Consequential Corporations in this Kingdom, have, *as bodies Corporate* applied to parliam^t and obtained Royal Patents for Theatres, thinking such amusem^ts absolutely necessary to keep the Active mind well and soberly employed, by which they continue Industrious ;

As there is at present with all the increase of population with all the Thirst among all ranks of people for this usefull amusem^t no more than 2 Theatres which was only thought Sufficient 33 years ago, thousands are excluded and fly to more expensive and less edifying scenes of Pleasure,—and these have no choice —they attempt to get to a Play—find no Access Night after Night, the House is full ; tis so true that many Women of fashion give up sending for places, many a Tradesmans familey is drove into more dangerous pleasures Admitting there is any truth in the preceeding observations 'tis humbly hoped his

Majesty will graciously condescend to use his prerogative in Granting a 3ᵈ Patent for a Winter Theatre, but shᵈ any doubts arise in respect to the influence it may have upon the propperty of the present Patentees it may with deference be urged, that as to the proprietors of Drury Lane, they have by a Continuation of Royal Indulgence Made princely Fortunes, one of them without Heirs to Inherit ; the other having only an Illegitimate Son— the other Patentees possess by purchase ; but to any argumᵗˢ in their favour, the following observations may tis hoped with Justice be opposed—tis certain they Clear communibus Annis £10,000—for which they have invested a Capital of £60,000— which after deducting the Interest at 5 P Cᵗ leaves them a Clear proffit of £7000 P Ann: with their patent (wᶜʰ being perpetual always retains its value)—so that admitting a 3ᵈ Patent shoud be granted as it cannot be presumed to rival them, no oppressive disadvantages can arise,—let it be admitted some division of proffit shoud be made, it woud not be unjust ; their gain is great—it will bear a Reduction—and if 'tis tried in the Scale of Justice it will not preponderate in their favor—12 P Cᵗ is more than a proffit to the Man of Trade who gives a Credit, and runs the Risk of bad Debts for his Goods—what then may it be called in a Business—where the money is paid dailey ? clear of every Risk—Clear of every deduction—admitting this it allows a drawback upon them—of £3000—leaving them a Clear proffit of about 12 P Cᵗ—but it is by no means certain they coud suffer even that deduction—

This monopoly of Royal Favor ties up even the Hands of Government from extending its influence for we find in History it has been no uncommon thing to reward the faithfull services of distinguished Characters by this Mode of Grant, which Created a new place a Sine Cure well worth the Acceptance of any Govᵗ whose merit wethor in parliamentary or other Capacities intitled them to solicit such marks of favor—being no less then £2000 pʳ Ann: among which were.—Collier Esqʳ MP.

Sʳ Wᵐ Davenant	Mʳ Congreve
Henry Killigrew	Sʳ Jnᵒ Vanbrugh
Sʳ Tho. Skipwith	Sʳ Richᵈ Steel M.P.

who obtained the Grant often in favor of persons who conducted the undertaking paying them the stipulated allowance.

No. 874.

Expence of His Majesty's Household in the year 1770

	£	s.	d.
Bread	805	6	7¾
Wine	3,233	4	9
Beer Ale & Cyder	1,152	16	11
Bristol Water	31	18	0
Spicery	480	1	2¾
Wax Lights	2,181	7	6½
Tallow Lights	839	17	2
Lamps	2,288	8	6
Tea Coffee & Chocolate	321	5	0
Fruit & Confections	680	18	4
Washing Table Linnen	655	19	4
Milk Cream Butter & Cheese	333	6	9¾
Fuel	4,502	4	6¾
Incidental Creditors	1,248	5	6½
Kitchen Creditors	8,261	3	9¾
Maundy Creditor	98	4	4
Richmond Creditors	7,375	11	2
	34,489	19	7¾
Allowances Boardwages Bounties & other Articles paid at the Board of Green Cloth	10,103	1	5¾
Salaries Allowances & Pensions to the Household	22,763	10	6
	67,356	11	7½
Boardwages to the Chambers & Chapels	14,355	9	6
Wages to the Chambers	2,155	4	8
Wages to the Chapels	425	14	7
Stable Salaries	11,463	18	5½
Stable Provisions	3,611	19	3¼
Stable Creditors	448	9	5
	99,817	7	6¼

No. 875—*Memorial.*

[A copy in the King's handwriting.]

[*End of* 1770.]

In case His Majesty should think it adviseable to form any enterprize against Spain. The most important and decisive in my humble opinion would be that upon Ferrol, in the Bay of Biscay. The advantageous situation of this place and the goodness of its Road and Harbour have determined the Spanish Ministry to make it the Rendevouz of their Fleet, and the General Depot for their Marine ; as they can with ease keep a strong Squadron cruizing off Cape Finister, which protects their Coasts, greatly annoys our Trade and by uniting with the Brest Fleet can invade Ireland, and be entirely Masters of the Channel.

I am credibly informed they have there at present near forty Ships of the Line besides Frigates and a prodigious quantity of Naval Stores. So that by destroying this place an end would be put to the Spanish Marine which for many years could not possibly be reestablished.

This place is situated on the left side of a fine Bay about six miles from the Sea is quite open and without any defence towards the land and is but a small Town or rather a Village. The Harbour is an oblong Square Surrounded by a very strong wall towards the Sea on which were one hundred and thirty four embrazures for large Cannon, but in 1767, had none mounted, nor was the wall entirely finished.

The passage leading up to Ferrol is deep and in some places very narrow and runs between two very high mountains ; at the bottom of which are placed several batteries to prevent Ships from going up to Ferrol, which constitutes its whole defence. On the right as you enter is a Battery of about twelve guns situated upon a high hill which hinders Ships from coming to an anchor in the opposite Bay, and is so high that it cannot be destroyed by Ships, but having no defence behind excepting a low thin wall can with ease be taken. About half way up the Channel are situated two Castles one on each side called St. Christopher and St. Martin which are fortified likewise towards the land as marked in the plan and are capable of some defence if attacked by Ships only, but being situated at the bottom of high and steep hills which command them entirely if attacked on that side, they must soon surrender.

The rest of the Batteries are so low that our Ships would soon destroy them and then the Fleet may without any difficulty sail up to Ferrol and come to an anchor in that Road, or on the left hand in a Bay called La gragna where the Spanish Ships generally lay.

The number of men commonly kept there amount to about twelve hundred, but as I am not informed how many there are at present it is impossible to determine how many are required to attack it with well grounded hopes of success. I would therefore humbly propose that a Merchant Ship be immediately sent thither with orders to Consul Banks to inform himself exactly of the number of men in the Province of Gallicia and how many precisely at Ferrol, Corugna, Betancos and the neighbouring Towns; whether any new works have been erected, where, and of what kind; likewise how many Ships rigged, unrigged, or on the Stocks &c.

Upon receiving his report it will be easy to determine the number of men and Ships to be employed on this occasion. As there are no Roads in that Country excepting for small Carts, whose Wheels are about three feet diameter and the axletrees nearly the same, it would be necessary to get some carriages made upon that plan for our field pieces, Howitzers and some few for twenty-four pounders. The axletrees may be made with several holes in them, so that the wheels may be contracted or enlarged as necessity requires.

Though at present it be impossible to determine what forces are required for this enterprize, yet supposing the Enemy have no more than four or five thousand men, we must have between eight and ten thousand which must land in the following manner.

Five thousand must land at the Bay of St. George on the left hand of the mouth of the Channel leading to Ferrol, and instantly take possession of the great hill on their right, then send detachments to take the Batteries on the Shore, and proceed to the hill behind the Castle of St. Christopher and erect Batteries to destroy it, as well as St. Martin on the opposite Shore which is easily done, the Channel being very narrow and the two Castles so low that they cannot bring their Cannon to bear against the Troops placed on the hills. Another considerable

Battery must be erected on the hill behind the Village of La gragna to play upon Ferrol the Shipping, Docks &c. these batteries must consist chiefly of howitzers.

If there are not above two or three thousand Men at Ferrol I would have the division above mentioned consist of Six thousand men of which about one thousand must be sent to attack the Batteries and Castles on the Channel to their Right, and the remainder must march directly to Ferrol, and destroy the Shipping, Stores and Docks as well as the Harbour itself, which is easily done by fixing a Fireship to the Wall which covers it.

There is behind Ferrol a rising ground upon which some Redoutes must be raised (which is soon done) if there are many troops in the neighbourhood in order to protect our people while employed in destroying Ferrol.

The remainder of the Troops must land in two Divisions. A thousand men must be sent to occupy the hill between that branch of the Sea which goes to Corugna and that which leads to Betancos and having taken possession of an old Redoute there, must destroy two or three small batteries placed at the bottom of the Rocks ; this being executed any part of the Fleet may sail into the Bay of Corugna, and if they think proper land a few men upon the hill opposite the Gate which goes into the Country, from whence they may with a few Guns and Howitzers destroy the Town and Shipping.

The last Division of the Troops must sail up the River which goes to Puente d'Eume, and by keeping close to the Shore on the left hand, the boats may land in a fine and extensive sandy Bay, at Redes, there being only one small Battery on the top of the hill which is avoided by keeping close under it.

This Division being landed must send two detachments of four or five hundred men each with two pieces of Cannon ; The one must occupy Puente d'Eume and the other must proceed to Neva both are marked in the Plan. The rest must occupy the great hill on their left and destroy the batteries placed at the bottom to defend the Channel which leads to Ferrol.

If these measures are adopted and punctually executed, it seems impossible to fail in the attempt.

The Success however will greatly depend upon Secrecy. I would therefore humbly recommend that the Officer destined to command on this Expedition should alone have the King's Orders to make the necessary preparations which must not by any means pass through the ordinary forms of Office. No transports must be employed excepting to come after the Fleet (when it has sailed a few days) with Stores, Provisions &c. the Troops must embark on the King's Ships as well as they can, and prefer the good of the service to a few conveniences. They must receive the orders for marching only the day before without mentioning the place they go to.

It would be necessary to have five hundred setts of pick axes, Shovels &c and two Fireships to burn the Docks and destroy the harbour, and four battering Cannon.

When this enterprize is happily executed, a Division of about three thousand men may be sent to St. Andero to destroy the Ships now building there, and the great foundery called la Cava, about four miles off and then the whole may proceed to Carthagena and destroy it ; all which may be executed in two months provided we undertake it before they bring there great bodies of Troops.

The Success of those enterprizes will entirely destroy the Spanish Marine for many years to come, and secure a solid peace which from the conduct of the House of Bourbon we cannot hope to obtain otherwise than by reducing them to the impossibility of breaking it.

No. 876—*Lord Rochford to the King.*

Lord Rochford who has but this minute quitted the foreign ministers takes the earliest opportunity to inform your majesty that the spanish ambassador is under the greatest apprehensions that the Recall of Mr. Harriss will do infinite mischeif and most likely make his court quite untractable, which, he went so far as to own, he beleived would come into our terms, he proposes sending a messenger away to morrow night, and wishes to have a letter for Mr. Harris ordering him, ' though he should have taken leave to defer his departure ' till further orders ; this seems to be a question of so much Importance, that Lord Rochford has sent a messenger to Lord North who is at Lord Hillsborough's at Twickenham to desire their attendance at his

office to morrow morning at eleven o clock, and as Lord Gower
is in Town he can also attend.

BERKLEY SQUARE 3^d Jan^{ry} 1771 $\frac{m}{40}$ past 4 P.M.

No. 877—*The King to Lord North.*

LORD NORTH—I feel Your attention in not coming to me at
so late an hour as four : I shall be glad to see You at Seven this
Evening.

QUEENS HOUSE
Jany 6th 1771.

$\frac{m}{52.}$ p^t 4 P.M.

Draft.

No. 878—*Lord Rochford to the King.*

Lord Rochford has the honor to return your majesty for
your information the Draught to Lord Harcourt, altered agreeably
to your majestys direction, the word *Monday* was put in by
mistake owing to Mr. porten not being able last night to read
my foul draught. Ld. Rochford has further to inform your
majesty that yesterday he had a very long conversation with
Lord Weymouth on the subject of Sr. Edward Hawkes resigning
which he had some suspicion of, Lord Weymouth seemed rather
inclined to beleive the Duke of Grafton would accept, but hinted
that it would be well worth the consideration of your majesty's
servants whether the Duke of Grafton would not be troublesome
in cabinet having been there before in a higher situation, and
as far as I could understand from his conversation which was
uncommonly open, and unreserved, it is my opinion that was
Lord Weymouth in cabinet at this moment and consulted upon
this measure, he would rather be against the Duke of Grafton's
coming in, as this sentiment of Lord Weymouths destroys the
Idea of his imbarking with the Duke of Grafton for the present,
at least, in any discontent, Lord Rochford thought it necessary
your majesty should be early informed of it. Lord Rochford
saw Lord North last night and found him much averse to inviting
the Duke of Grafton to accept, convinced he would not refuse

it, but your majesty is to decide what your pleasure is, and if
Lord Rochford can be of any use in this transaction, he hopes
your majesty is convinced of his readiness as well as zeal in
obeying your Majesty's orders.

St James's 7th Jan^{ry} 1771

$\frac{m}{50}$ past 12 p.m.

No. 879—*The King to Sir Joseph Yorke.*

QUEENS HOUSE *Jan.* 9th 1771.

SIR JOSEPH YORKE—Your letter has in the fullest manner
satisfied the questions upon which I was desirous of information,
and will be very material for my guidance whenever the calamity
of War shall appear indispensably necessary at present the firm
though temperate language that has been held to the French
Court has lowered their tone, and will I flatter myself shew that
they must be less high in their future discussions ; but great
attention must be had to their conduct as they can never be
trusted to and whenever I see any cause of just suspicion shall
through Your channel convey my ideas to the Prince of Orange.
I cannot help expressing my sorrow that the King of Prussia
has any weight with that Prince, as I can never look upon him
as either a sincere friend to this Country or to the United Provinces and as I know He has painted him to the Brunswick
Family in the most unfavourable colours.   I confess my political
Creed is formed on the system of King William, England in
conjunction with the House of Austria and the Republic seems
the most secure barrier against the Family compact, and if
Russia could be added to this, I think the Court of Versailles
would not be in a hurry to commence hostillities ; but this
plan may be difficult to be effected, though I am sure it is the
real interest of the four States.

Draft.

No. 880—*The King to Lord North.*

[11 *Jan.* 1771.]

LORD NORTH—I have seen Lord Sandwich, and thought it
right to acquaint him with Sir Edward Hawkes's intention of

resigning tomorrow, that I had learnt from You that he would willingly preside at that Board, and that knowing His activity I should very readily place him in that department he thoroughly and with pleasure accepts and agrees with Me that He ought to be appointed tomorrow. You ought therefore to lose no time in sounding Lord Suffolk.

$\frac{m}{15}$ pt 4 P.M.

Draft.

No. 881—*Lord Rochford to the King.*

Lord Rochford was prevented to day by Lord Sandwich's presence from throwing himself at your majesty's feet and returning his most unfeigned thanks for the great goodness your majesty was pleased to shew him yesterday in the Note your Majesty did him the honor to send him. After he left your majestys closet to day he saw Lord North and told him he beleived your majesty would give him your orders relative to Mr. Vassall Lord North made no objection to it, and threw out a probability of his coming into Parliament, which as far as Lord Rochford can, shall be carried into Execution, and proposes sending for his Brother to town directly, as any Delay may give rise to applications, and as soon as Lord Rochford learns that your majesty has signified your pleasure to Lord North, which is all that is wanting Lord Rochford will send the warrant for your Majesty's signature.

BERKLEY SQUARE
13th. *Jan*^{ry} 1771
$\frac{m}{5}$ *past* 7 P.M.

No. 882—*The King to Lord North.*

Printed.   Donne I. 49.

LORD NORTH—Not having heard any thing of Lord Suffolk since Friday, I am desirous of hearing whether You have not yet seen him ; a thought has occurred to me if he cannot speak French which is an absolute requisite for one who is to treat with

Foreign Ministers, whether Lord Rochford could not transact the whole department of Foreign affairs, which is the case in every other Court, and then Lord Suffolk might have the home departments which would be composed of all domestick affairs with the addition of Scotland and Ireland ;

QUEEN'S HOUSE
Jan^{ry} 13th 1771.

$\frac{m}{46}$ p^t 7. P.M.

Draft.

No. 883—*Lord North to the King.*

[13 *Jan.* 1771.]

Lord North was last night with Lord Suffolk, and intended to relate to his Majesty today what passed between them, but was detain'd in conversation till his Majesty had left St. James's. Lord Suffolk is to give his final answer tomorrow. Ld. North suggested to him that, if he could not speak french, an arrangement might be made by putting Ld. Hillsborough or Lord Halifax into the Northern department, if it should be agreable to your Majesty, and to them. He said he was a very bad frenchman, but he did not seem to decline the department on that account. Lord North will inform his Majesty of Lord Suffolk's final determination, the instant he hears from him, and will when he sees him again repeat to him the difficulty he will be under if he undertakes the Northern department without being sufficiently ready in the use of French.

DOWNING STREET *Sunday Even^g*

No. 884—*The King to Lord North.*

QUEENS HOUSE *Jan^y* 15th 1771.

$\frac{m}{8}$ p^t 4 PM.

LORD NORTH—I am desirous of seeing [you] about seven this Evening.

Draft.

No. 885—*The King to Lord North.*

Printed. Donne I. 50.

[Lord Halifax's motto was " *Otium cum Dignitate.*"]

Queens House *Jan^y* 16th 1771.
$$\frac{m}{25} p^t \ 10. \ \text{A.M.}$$

Lord North—If Lord Halifax is desirous of the Northern
Seals, I can have no objection to it, though had I been in his
Situation and of his Age I should have preferred his Motto. You
will in consequence acquaint the Secretaries with this, let Lord
Rochford order a Council for swearing in Lord Halifax and Lord
Suffolk and let the Seals of the Privy Seal and of the Northern
Secretary be delivered this day.

Draft.

No. 886—*Lord North to the King.*

[16 *Jan.* 1771.]

Lord North has received the honour of his Majesty's note.
To prevent any mistake He thinks himself obliged to represent
to his Majesty, that Lord Halifax did not appear to him desirous
of changing his office though he certainly does not mean to make
a merit of his compliance. He was ready to accept the seals in
the idea that it would facilitate a serviceable arrangement to his
Majesty's affairs, but Lord North believes that he would quit
the Privy Seal with a degree of reluctance.

Downing Street. *Wednesday morning.*

No. 887—*The King to Lord North.*

Printed. Donne I. 50.

Lord North—To prevent future mistakes in this business
I am willing to give the Northern seals either to Lord Suffolk
or Lord Halifax, the longer delaying the arrangement I think

disgraceful to my service and therefore expect that which ever accepts them it be done this day.

QUEENS HOUSE
Jany 16th 1771
$\frac{m}{58}$ *p^t* 11. A.M.

Draft.

No. 888—*Lord North to the King.*

[16 *Jan.* 1771.]

Lord North has the honour of informing his Majesty, that Lord Halifax will obey his Majesty's commands, if his Majesty should think it for his service to put the Seals of the Northern department into his hands.

Wednesday morn^g

No. 889—*The King to Lord North.*

Printed. Donne I. 51.

LORD NORTH—As Lord Hardwicke has declined accepting the Northern Seals, I desire You will this Evening call on Lord Dartmouth with the same offer which I hope will be early enough for Me to hear His answer to night.

QUEENS HOUSE
Jany 16th 1771.
$\frac{m}{10}$ *pt* 5. P.M.

Draft.

No. 890—*Lord North to the King.*

Lord North has, in obedience to his Majesty's commands, waited upon Lord Dartmouth, who has desired him to express in the strongest terms his sense of his Majesty's goodness to him, but hopes that he may be allow'd a short time to consider of a step which he looks upon as so important to him. Lord North is rather of opinion that he will decline, but can not pretend to judge with any certainty of the event.

DOWNING STREET. *Jan^y*: 16. 11 *o'clock.*

No. 891—*Lord North to the King.*

[16 *Jan.* 1771.]

Lord North has the honour of informing his Majesty, that the House sat till half an hour after nine last night upon a Motion for a Committee to search the Lords Journals, which was rejected by a majority of 21. $\begin{cases} \text{Naes. 48.} \\ \text{Ayes. 27.} \end{cases}$ That Motion must however be carried today or tomorrow, as the Lords seem resolved to exclude the Members of the H^e of Commons together with other strangers.

Lord North call'd upon Lord Rochford after the House was up, and learnt from him, that Lord Weymouth would not be averse to some arrangement which might remove him to another office, but that he is eager to quit his present situation at all events ; As a proof of this, Lord Rochford mention'd that Lord Weymouth had named Lord Hardwicke to him as a very proper person to succeed to the Northern department.

Lord North has the honour to return the paper he received some time ago from his Majesty. He has received his Majesty's note, and will if possible wait upon his Majesty between six, and seven this evening.

No. 892—*The King to Lord North.*

Printed. Donne I. 52.

LORD NORTH—It gives me much pleasure that Lord Dartmouth has desired time to consider whether he will accept of the Seals of Secretary of State as it shews that inclination to my Service that gives me personal satisfaction when it comes from a man of his excellent Character.

QUEENS HOUSE
Jany 17th 1771.

$\frac{m}{3.}$ p^t 9. A.M.

Draft.

P

No. 893—*Lord North to the King.*

[17 *January*, 1771.]

Lord North has had a long conference with Lord Dartmouth this morning, after Dr. North's wedding, in which he took the liberty of communicating to him the note he had the honour of receiving this morning from his Majesty. Lord Dartmouth appear'd extremely sensible of his Majesty's goodness, but begs leave to decline the offer of the Seals for reasons, which Lord North will have the honour of explaining to his Majesty, in conversation, as he can not do justice to Lord Dartmouth's sentiments in the compass of a note. Lord North would intreat the favour of waiting upon his Majesty this evening at the Queen's house, had he not engaged himself to Mr Francés, who has very earnestly desired a conference with him this evening, upon the matters now depending between Gt Britain and Spain. He imagines that his Majesty would rather chuse to postpone hearing the conversation between Lord Dartmouth and Lord North, than to have the visit of Mr Francés defer'd to another day.

No. 894—*Lord Hillsborough to the King.*

Lord Hillsborough who never means to ask a Favour but from Your Majesty immediately, and will always receive any such with a Satisfaction which he cannot express when it flows from Your Majesty's own Goodness to him, Humbly presumes to remind your Majesty of his particular Situation as having no Settlement in England, and that the New Forrest is now vacant by the Death of the Duke of Bedford.

HANOVER SQUARE
17*th. January* 1771. ¼ *past one* P.M.

No. 895—*Lord Rochford to the King.*

Lord Rochford has the honour to inform your Majesty that in his Conference with the french ambassador this morning, he

told Lord Rochford that there certainly would be war unless
the recall of Mr Harris was repaired by the Nomination of another
ambassador, Mr Frances afterwards softened the proposition
and said if we would send and order Mr Harris to return and
Communicate it ministerially to prince Masserano, that then
he Mr Frances would tell us the last proposal of the court of
spain, and that everything might absolutely be settled, before
the 22d.   Frances is to see Lord North to night.

St James's 17 *Jan*^{ry} 1771. $\dfrac{m}{15}$ *past* 3 P.M.

No. 896—*The King to Lord North.*

Printed.   Donne I. 163.

Queens House   *Jan*^{y} 17th 1771.

$\dfrac{m}{55}$ p^t 4 P.M.

Lord North—I am sorry Lord Dartmouth declines the
offer that has been made to him, Your shewing him my note
was very proper as it contained nothing but my sentiments
with regard to him ; I wish You could call here previous to
seeing Mr Francés or that You would see him so early as to
call here still within reasonable hour I mean by that ten this
Evening.

By a note I have received from Lord Rochford I know what
Mr Francés has to propose to You it is that orders may^t be immediately sent to Mr Harris to return to Madrid upon which the
Spanish Ambassador will communicate his fresh instructions,
if this is not complied with he is to threaten War ; I could not
help assuring Lord Rochford that I thought this a very absurd
proposition for that as the Secretary is recalled we ought to
know whether we shall have such terms as we can accept for
otherways we shall be tomorrow ordering him to return and in
less than two days perhaps a new directing him to come home.

No. 897—*The King to Lord North.*

LORD NORTH—As the Chief Justice is an Invalid, an earlier hour May be agreable to him, You will therefore appoint him at a little after Seven this Evening.

QUEENS HOUSE

Jany 21st 1771. $\frac{m}{25}$ p^t 4 P.M.

Draft.

No. 898—*The King to Lord North.*

Printed.   Donne I. 53.

LORD NORTH—Least I should not have clearly enough this day fixed it with [you] that Mr. Justice Bathurst is tomorrow to receive the Great Seal I write now that there may be no mistake ; You will therefore order him and the other two Commissioners to attend with the Seal.

QUEEN'S HOUSE *Jan^y* 22^d 1771. $\frac{m}{20}$ p^t 10. P.M.

Draft.

No. 899—*Lord Mansfield to Lord* [*North*].

MY LORD—I have seen L^d Ch: J. Wilmot and now write, in his presence. His Office does not exceed 3000$^£$ a y^r. I reasoned by mistake from the value of my own. What I mentioned would be monstrous, an Imposition upon the King, and a very bad Precedent. He begs only to have 1200$^£$ a y^r if it is 1500$^£$ or 2000$^£$ it will be very handsome. He has read the above, is strongly of that opinion, and insists upon my writing to y^r Lo^p immediately. It is very honorable in him, but I think He is right. I had no Idea that my Office was in value so much superiour to his. The King will see what it is to have to do with Men of honour. It imports his Majesty not to make a bad Precedent. We shall all want to resign. I am extremely glad he happened to call upon me, I should have been the author of bad advice without meaning it. I beg you would communicate this to his Majesty and say that L^d Ch. J. Wilmot has read it.

I am with the greatest Respect Y^r Lo^{ps} most ob : : hu : Sev^t.

MANSFIELD,

No. 900—*The King to Lord North.*

Printed. Donne I. 53.

[Lord Chief Justice Wilmot's successor was Sir William de Grey, afterwards Lord Walsingham. Wilmot's pension was fixed at £2400 a year.]

LORD NORTH—If any thing was wanting to confirm my opinion of the Worth and disinterestedness of Lord Chief Justice Wilmot His noble conduct upon this occasion must establish it ; as that was not the case it only adds to my sorrow at loosing a man of so much honour ; which is a little contrasted by what You mention of his intended Successor. I am clear that the pension ought to be £2,000. per annum.

QUEENS HOUSE

Jan^{ry} **23**^{r} **1771.** $\frac{m}{43}$ p^t 8 A.M.

Draft.

No. 901—*The King to Lord North.*

Printed. Donne I. 54.

QUEENS HOUSE *Jan*^{y} 28th 1771.

$\frac{m}{30}$ p^t 6. P.M.

LORD NORTH—As the only proper candidates for the Vice Chamberlain's, were Lord Hinchinbrooke and Lord Garlies, I have decided in favour of the former, and have acquainted Lord Sandwich that I shall appoint his Son as Soon as it may suit the County Court. I have had much conversation on the Fleet with Lord Howe whom I find in opinion a great Enemy to Guard ships on the late plan, and wishing to see whenever the Peace establishment is adopted a Fleet of ten or twelve Ships of the line fully manned as a greater Security and more easily put into motion. I merely mention this that You may be apprised of both sides of the question before it is the subject of deliberation.

Draft.

No. 902—*The King to Lord North.*

Printed. Donne I. 54.

QUEENS HOUSE *Feb*^{y} 1st 1771.

LORD NORTH—I have learnt from Lord Talbot that the Mr. Watts who is recommended by the Archbishop of Canterbury and the Bishop of London, for the Pulpit at the Temple, is the person I immagined he is one of my Chaplains a man of great abilities and from my knowledge of him an excellent Preacher, I therefore consent to his appointment which You will direct to be prepared.

Draft.

No. 903—*Lord North to the King.*

[The " late negotiations " are those with Spain concerning the Falkland Islands.]

[4 *February,* 1771.]

Lord North has the honour of informing his Majesty, that after the papers were read which were presented today to the house, Mr Seymour made a motion to address his Majesty, to inform the house, if there had been any interference of the court of France in the late negociation, and to acquaint them with all transactions relative to the said interference, if there has been any. a debate ensued, which lasted till eight o'clock when the motion was negatived.

Ayes   57.

Noes   173.

SEYMOUR PLACE ½ *after eight.*

No. 904—*The King to Lord North.*

Printed. Donne I. 55.

QUEENS HOUSE *Feb*^{y} 4th 1771.

$$\frac{m}{23.} \ p^t \ 9. \text{ P.M.}$$

LORD NORTH—After the very open communication that has this day made to Parliament of the entire transaction on the dispute with Spain, Mr. Seymour's motion has no appearance of candour, and cannot consequently do honour to the Supporters of it, but be advantageous to Administration as it shewed so great a Majority in their favour.

Draft.

No. 905—*Lord Harcourt to the King.*

PARIS *February the 5th*, 1771.

SIR—I take the Liberty of sending your Majesty A Catalogue of the Count de Guiche's Pictures, which are to be sold by Auction next Month. If your Majesty should be inclinable to purchase any of them, you will be pleased to honour me with your Commands.

If another Blue Ruband should become Vacant, while I have the Honor to be employed in this Country : I hope My Absense might rather plead in My Behalf, than be a Disadvantage to any little Claim, which I might have to your Majesty's Favour.

It has been the Object of my Life to deserve well of your Majesty, and to be worthy of some distinguishing Mark of your Favour. And however desirable such a Distinction might have been at Other Times, it becomes far more Valuable to me in My present situation, as it would enable me to serve your Majesty with more Weight and Credit : Foreign Ministers are more or less considered in the Courts, where they reside in Proportion the Favour and Countenance which their Respective Princes shew them. of all the Courts in Europe, Versailles is the Court, where the greatest Attention is paid to those Appearances.

I have avoided importuning your Majesty for Places of Emolument, for of them there are few I ever aspired to, and perhaps still fewer I may be fit for. The little Ambition that I have left in the Decline of Life, has been directed towards more honourable Pursuits, the Garter has been the chief Object of my wishes. If they should not succeed, I shall have the Misfortune to think that I must have forfeited your Majesty's good Opinion, which will lessen me in the Esteem of honest Men, and greatly affect me in every Respect except in the inviolate Attatchment with which I shall ever remain, Sir, Your Majesty's Most faithfull and Devoted Servant   HARCOURT.

No. 906—*The King to Lord North.*

$\dfrac{m}{13.}$ *pt* 8. P.M.

LORD NORTH—As I learnt on Friday from Lord Sandwich that the appointing His Son Vice Chamberlain tomorrow will be the day that will suit best the County Court I desire You will in my name intimate to Lord Grantham that his resigning the Key as soon as the Levee is over tomorrow will be the properest time. I have just heard how things have passed in the House of Lords this day, and am not of opinion that the total silence of the Members of the Cabinet except Lord Rochford was either advantageous or shewed that zeal for my Service that my conduct towards them gives me a right to expect.

Draft.

No. 907—*The King to Lord North.*

Printed. Donne I. 55.

[This refers to an attempt to repeal a clause in the *Nullum Tempus* Act, giving parties twelve months in which to sue, notwithstanding the Act; of which clause Sir James Lowther had taken advantage. The attempt, after some vicissitudes in the Commons, finally failed.]

LORD NORTH—What has passed this day in the House of Commons is fresh proof that truth, justice and even honour are constantly to be given up whenever they relate to Sir James Lowther; though this cannot please You yet it does no ways regard Administration.

QUEENS HOUSE *Feb*^{y} 11th 1771. $\dfrac{m}{35}$ p^t 9 PM.

Draft.

No. 908—*Charles Hotham to the King.*

SIR—Your Majesty's time is so precious, that I think by this method of laying myself at Your Feet to ask a Favour, I shall give less Interruption to it than if I had presumed to take that Liberty in person. And as every mark of Goodness You have been graciously pleased to bestow upon me has been the immediate Act of Your Majesty Yourself, I am ambitious of increasing, if possible, the Gratitude I feel towards Your Majesty already.

There are now several Vacancies in the Order of the Bath. An Honour one of my Ancestors enjoyed in the time of King Edward the second. And if Your Majesty should think me worthy of Reviving that Distinction in my Family, so ostensible a Proof of Your Royal Favour and approbation would make me extremely happy, particularly at this time, as I should then have the honour of being Installed with one of Your own Royal Family.

I do not presume to urge one Word to induce Your Majesty to comply with this my most humble Request. If You shall be pleased to do so, I shall owe it, as I do every thing, solely to Your Indulgence ; not to any Merit of mine. I can pretend to none, and shall only say, that as a Soldier, I hope my Conduct has been such as not to disgrace the Order, that as a Gentleman I shall not degrade it, but that my having the Honour of being Your Majesty's Servant, will give credit to it.

I have the honour to be with the most profound veneration and Respect, Sir, Your Majesty's Most Dutiful & Obedient Most faithful, Obliged And Devoted Humble Servant and Subject

CHA: HOTHAM.

February the 12*th* 1771.

No. 909—*Lord North to the King.*

[13 *Feb.* 1771.]

[Mr. Whitehead was Secretary and Registrar of the Order of the Bath.]

· Lord North has the honour of informing his Majesty, that he has received a letter from Mr. Whitehead, by which he learns that he can not have the things ready for the investiture of Mr. Payne this morning, but has written to Mr. Payne to propose Monday next, if it is agreable to his Majesty.

Lord North received a letter last night from General Montagu desiring that Lord North would mention his name to his Majesty for the other vacant ribband. Should his Majesty approve of him, He may receive the investiture on Monday at the same time with Mr. Payne.

Lord North has, in obediance to his Majesty's commands, appointed General Paoli to wait upon his Majesty at the Queen's House this Evening at seven o'clock.

DOWNING STREET. *Wednesday morn.*

No. 910—*The King to Lord North.*

Printed.   Donne I. 56.

LORD NORTH—I perfectly approve of Monday next for investing Mr. Payne with the order of the Bath, You may acquaint Lieutenant General Montague that will at the same time have the other vacant Ribband and You will apprise Mr. Whitehead of both.

ST. JAMES'S *Feb.* 13*th* 1771 $\frac{m}{15}$ p^t M.

Draft.

No. 911—*The King to Lord North.*

Printed.   Donne I. 57.

[The " great majority " was of 271 against 157 in favour of the address approving of the Spanish Declaration concerning the seizure of the Falkland Islands.]

LORD NORTH—The great majority yesterday is very creditable for administration, the seeing Colonel Burgoyne's name on the side of the Minority appears so extraordinary that I almost immagine that is a mistake, and that Nicholson Calvert being put on the Majority is also erroneous.

QUEEN'S HOUSE *Feb.* 14*th* 1771. $\frac{m}{50}$ p^t 11. A.M.

No. 912—*Lord North to the King.*

[Sir William Meredith's Bill was the attempt already alluded to (No. 907) to repeal a clause of the *Nullum Tempus* Act.]

[20 *Feb.* 1771.]

Lord North is sorry to inform his Majesty, that Sr William Meredith's Bill was committed today by a Majority but not by so great a majority as gave leave to bring in the bill.

Ayes — 155.

Naes — 140.

Majority   15.

20th. February 1771.   Speakers on the Motion for the
Committment of Sr Wm. Meredith's Bill.

For	Against
S^r Wm. Meredith	Sir Wm. Bagot
Si^r Cecil Wray	Rose Fuller
Mr Phipps	Mr Harris
Mr Burke	Mr Ellis
Sir George Savile	Lord Beauchamp
Mr Wallace	Mr Sol^r General
Mr Dunning	Lord North
Lord G: Cavendish	Lord Clare
	Mr C: Fox

No. 913—*The King to Lord North.*

Printed.   Donne I. 57.

[The " affair of the printers " arose out of a complaint by Colonel George
Onslow of misrepresentation by printers of speeches made in the House of
Commons. The business was so foolishly mismanaged that it led to a
conflict of jurisdiction between the House and the City of London, to
riotous proceedings in London, and, incidentally, to the re-establishment
for the moment of the political power of John Wilkes. The House of
Commons was heavily defeated, and a death-blow was dealt to the old
tyranny of Parliament.]

QUEENS HOUSE *Feb*^y 21st 1771.

$$\frac{m}{40} \; p^t \; 8. \; \text{A.M.}$$

LORD NORTH—I am sorry so very arbitrary a measure as the
Duke of Portland's dispute could be ordered to be committed
though glad the majority is lessened as it may be a means of
throwing [it] out before it comes to the House of Lords.

I have very much considered the affair of the Printers that
is now coming before the House, I do in the strongest manner
recommend that every caution may be used to prevent its becoming a serious affair ; if You are of opinion that any Alderman
will take the unjustifiable part You hinted at Yesterday, why

may not the Messenger be made to understand that on summoning them he could not find them ; it is highly necessary that this strange and lawless method of publishing Debates in the Papers should be put a stop to ; but is not the House of Lords as a Court of Record the best Court to bring such miscreants before, as it can fine as well as imprison ; and as the Lords have broader shoulders to support any schism that this salutary measure may occasion in the minds of the vulgar.

Draft.

No. 914—*Lord North to the King.*

[? 20 *Feb.* 1771.]

Lord North has the honour of informing his Majesty, that a Motion, for taking the printers into custody on account of their contempt of the house for not appearing according to the order of the house, was carried today by a great majority.

Ayes — 160
Noes — 17.
———
143.

26th February 1771.

Persons who divided ag^t the Printer being taken into Custody

Mr Dowdeswell	Sir Robt Bernard
Sir George Saville	Mr Chas Turner
Mr Dunning	Mr Burke
Mr Cornewall	Mr Wm Burke
Mr Barre	Mr R^d Whitworth
Mr Standert	Mr Sawbridge. Teller
Sir Piercy Brett	Mr Oliver
Sir Robt Clayton	Mr Townsend. Teller
Mr Mauguer	Mr Nathaniel Bailey

No. 915—*The King to Lord North.*

Printed.　Donne I. 58.

[The papers referred to concerned the Spanish Declaration respecting the seizure of the Falkland Islands.]

QUEENS HOUSE *Feb*^{y} 26th 1771.

$$\frac{m}{10.}\ p^t\ 7.\ \text{P.M.}$$

LORD NORTH—There being so many of the Principal persons of the Opposition in the Minority this day and yet the number amounting only to 19. appears rather extraordinary ; I flatter myself that if this affair is conducted with that circumspection that I am certain You will think it deserves, the ill consequences will not ensue which I in the beginning very much feared.　The papers that are to be sent to the House of Commons in pursuance to the Address that has past in the House of Commons this day, I judge to be in consequence of Mr. Pownall's motion.

Draft.

No. 916—*27th February* 1771.

Speakers on Sir William Meredith's Motion for the Speaker to leave the Chair to go into the Committee on the Nullum Tempus.

For	Against
Sir Wm Meredith	Mr Dyson
Mr Phipps	Mr Gascoigne
Mr Dowdeswell	Mr Ambler
Mr Seymour	Mr Ste: Fox
Mr Cornewall	Mr Vane
Sir Wm Meredith	Sir Wm Bagot
Mr Thos Townshend	Serj^t Leigh
Mr R^d Sutton	Mr C: Fox
Mr Sawbridge	Lord Beauchamp

Ayes — 154.

Noes — 164

Majority — 10.

No. 917—*The King to Lord North.*

Printed. Donne I. 59.

[Adolphus Frederick, King of Sweden, died suddenly on the evening of the 12th of February in the twentieth year of his reign.]

QUEENS HOUSE *Feb^y* 28*th* 1771.

$\frac{m}{42.}$ *p^t* 7. P.M.

LORD NORTH—Though I think You could not mistake my sentiments this day on the new Scene that arises by the sudden death of the King of Sweden, I choose shortly again to sketch them. It has ever occurred to Me that the gaining the Court of Sweden is no real object of this Country, for if after a considerable expence that is effected it will be impossible to keep her Friendship unless a Subsidy is granted for that power cannot subsist without foreign money. Besides as there is no publick mode of obtaining the money that is expended in that corruption it must be taken from my Civil List consequently new Debts incurred and when I apply to Parliament for relieving Me, an odium cast on myself and ministry as if the money had been expended in bribing Parliament. I therefore think we ought only to feed the Opposition to France, that that Crown may carry no essential points, and may be drove to spend much greater sums to little purpose.

Draft.

No. 918—*Lord North to the King.*

[4 *March*, 1771.]

Lord North has the honour of informing his Majesty, that the Rev^d: Mr Scot has intimated to him through Mr Robinson, that he chuses to decline the living of Worplesden in expectation of succeeding to the living of Simondesburn in Northumberland of which he had some hopes given him about a year ago. Lord North intended to have mentioned this circumstance to his Majesty if he [had] been time enough for court, but being too late he spake of it to Lord Rochford, who proposes to recommend Mr Thomas Fountayne to his Majesty for Worplesden. Lord

North is obliged in justice to say that he believes the living can not be bestow'd on a more deserving man.

DOWNING STREET *Monday*. ½ p^t *four*.

No. 919—*The King to Lord North.*

Printed. Donne I. 60.

QUEENS HOUSE *March 4th.* 1771.
$$\frac{m}{55} \; p^t \; 5. \; \text{P.M.}$$

LORD NORTH—Mr. Scot chusing to decline the Living of Worplesden I very readily consent to Mr. Fountayne's obtaining it, and that the former may wait for the living of Simondsburn in Northumberland, You will therefore direct the Warrant to be prepared.

Draft.

No. 920—*Lord North to the King.*

[5 *March,* 1771.]

Lord North has the honour of informing his Majesty, that the Address, after a long debate which lasted till after an hour after two in the morning, was carried by a majority of 118.

Ayes — 275.

Noes — 157.

_____

Majority — 118.

DOWNING STREET ½ p^t 3.

No. 921—*The King to Lord North.*

Printed. Donne I. 61.

LORD NORTH—I am not surprised that Mr. Pownall's absurd motion could not produce a very long debate ; indeed it is a convincing proof that the author of it is not calculated to make a figure in foreign affairs.

QUEEN'S HOUSE *March 5th* 1771.
$$\frac{m}{5} \; p^t \; 8. \; \text{P.M.}$$

No. 922—*Lord Townshend to* [*Lord North* ?].

[Copy in the King's handwriting.]

DUBLIN CASTLE 6*th March* 1771.

Private and
Confidential.

MY LORD—On receipt of Your Lordship's private and confidential letter of the 18th past, inclosing a plan which has been approved of by His Majesty for adding a Tenth Company to each Regiment in the Irish Army ; I directed an Estimate to be prepared, stating the number of the Infantry now upon the Irish Establishment, and the numbers which will stand upon it according to the New plan, and specifying as well the additional charge which will be created by it upon the Establishment as the immediate saving of half pay which will be made by the appointment of the new Officers mostly from that Establishment, as also the provision to be made for the Serjeants who are to remain Seconded on their respective Regiments, and inclosed I send Your Lordship a copy of the Estimate which has been prepared and laid before me accordingly.

By this paper Your Lordship will find that upon the military Establishment there will be an addition of 81. Officers 81. Corporals and 54. private men, and a reduction of 189. Serjeants and 216 Drummers, leaving the Infantry 189. less in number than the present Establishment.

That an annual saving will be made by Great Britain by the promotion of the Officers who remain seconded on Irish Regiments amounting to £2,859–3–4. British Money.

That there will appear to be an additional Charge of £3,531–7–6. remaining on the Irish Establishment.

That there will be a saving of half pay on the Irish Establishment amounting to the annual Sum of £2,101–15–10. for the Officers who will be provided for in the Regiments serving in Ireland, and of £836–9–2. for the Officers to be removed from the Irish half pay to service in the five Regiments which are paid by Ireland now on Foreign duty.

And that there will be provided for by the King's letter (their being no contingent fund here for that purpose) to make good the difference between the pay of 189. private men and 189. Serjeants, or so many of them as are to be retained, which for the whole number would amount to the Sum of £2,874–7–6.

And that upon the whole according to the above totals, the present annual Additional Expence is calculated to amount to the Sum of £3,467–10–0.

With respect to the Communication of this measure to Parliament, I must take the liberty of informing Your Lordship, that upon the settlement of the present subsisting Establishment of the Army for this Kingdom, greater objection was made to the mode than to the number of which it was proposed the Army should consist, and that in the Debates in Parliament upon the late augmentation, it was very strongly urged that altho the number fixed upon might be proper, if not necessary, it might be formed upon a plan of better Oeconomy, by reducing some of the Regiments, to save the heavy charge of Officers, and by augmentating the Remainder with Private men, and this opinion seemed to be so general Altho the whole plan was adopted, that I should be very apprehensive the present scheme would not be approved of altho it might not be rejected. however as the additional expense thereof upon the whole appears to be very inconsiderable, if His Majesty shall judge it necessary for the general good of his Service to be carried into execution in this Kingdom, I should rather consider it as a measure not of sufficient consequence in point of Expence to be communicated to Parliament, but to be effected by his Majesty's letter during the interval of Parliament.

As by this plan provision will at once be made for all the Officers who remain Seconded on the Regiments of Infantry on the Irish Establishment, I need not trouble Your Lordship with a particular answer to Your letter of the 8th past inclosing a Copy of one from Lord Barrington to Your Lordship that it was my full intention before I received Your said letter to recommend those Officers as vacancies should happen from time to time in their respective Corps, except their absenting themselves without leave or some very extraordinary case should prevent it.

I am with very great respect, My Lord, Your Lordships Most obedient humble Servant   (Signed) TOWNSHEND.

No. 923—*Lord Rochford to the King.*

Lord Rochford has the honor to acquaint your Majesty that he found Mr Francois very moderate but insisting on the same point with the ambassadors and to morrow night Lord Rochford will be having a meeting of your Majesty's Servants to see what is possible to be done. The inclosed private letter from Lord Townshend Lord Rochford humbly apprehends will answer your Majesty's wishes.

SECRETARYS OFFICE ST JAMES'S

6 *March* 1771 $\frac{m}{50}$ p^t 3 PM.

No. 924—*Lord Rochford to the King.*

Lord Rochford having received late last night the inclosed letter from the Chancellor with one from the Chancellor in Ireland takes the liberty to send it for your majestys perusal before he returns it to Lord Appsley, as Lord Townshends letters mention nothing of this Riot.

BERKLEY SQUARE

7th *March* 1771 $\frac{m}{5}$ p^t 9 AM.

No. 925—*Lord North to the King.*

Lord North has the honour of informing his Majesty, that Mr Dowdeswell's motion today was for leave to bring in a Bill to settle doubts concerning the right of Juries in trying libels ; this Motion was no sooner seconded by Sr George Saville, than it was opposed warmly by other gentlemen in the Opposition. The Friends of Government sat still, and let them debate it amongst themselves ; the debate lasted, nevertheless, till past ten o'clock, when the House divided upon a motion of Mr Phipps, to adjourn.

Yeas — 218.

Noes — 72.

Enclosure.

7th March 1771   Speakers on Mr Dowdeswell's Motion

For it	Against it
Mr Dowdeswell	Mr Ja^s Grenville
Sir George Saville	Mr Phipps moved to adjourn
Mr Coxe	Mr A. Paulett
Mr Calcraft	Mr Graves
Mr Thos Townshend	Mr Field
Mr Dunning	Mr Aubrey
Mr Barre	Mr Mackworth
Mr Cornwall	Sr Wm Meredith
Mr E: Burke	Genl Conway
Lord John Cavendish	Mr Popham

Question of Adjournment put.

Ayes — 218.
Noes — 72

Majority — 146

No. 926—*The King to Lord North.*

Printed.   Donne I. 62.

QUEENS HOUSE *March* 8th 1771.

$\dfrac{m}{30.}$ p^t 8. A.M.

LORD NORTH—I sincerely rejoice at the very good conclusion of yesterday's debate, and at nothing more than the wisdom of leaving the opposition as they were divided in their sentiments the whole altercation; besides if Gentlemen can let their reason guide them to differ with their friends on what they might deem a popular question, it is to be hoped they will by this be encouraged to hold on future occasions the same propriety of conduct.

Draft.

No. 927—*The King to Lord North.*

Printed.　Donne I. 62.

LORD NORTH—I heard this day that Mr. Vivian Professor of Modern languages at the University of Oxford is dead ; You ought to apply to the Chancellor of the University that a Man of sufficient abilities may be proposed for my approbation for filling that Office.

QUEENS HOUSE
　March 8th 1771.
$\frac{m}{20}$ p^t 5. PM.

Draft.

No. 928—*The King to Lord North.*

Printed.　Donne I. 63.

QUEEN'S HOUSE *March* 10th 1771.
$\frac{m}{40}$ p^t AM.

LORD NORTH—Your account of Admiral Pye's having yesterday carried the Election at Rochester by so great a Majority gives me much pleasure.　I have also received Your acknowledgement of the note I sent You desiring You to consult the Chancellor of Oxford as to the properest person for the vacant Professorship, because I think those offices having been instituted for promoting Learning in the Universities, ought not to be given by favour, but according to merit.

Draft.

No. 929—*Lord Halifax to the King.*

GROSVENOR STREET
Wednesday Afternoon
March y[e] 13th 1771.

Lord Halifax's Indisposition of Health not having permitted him to wait on his Majesty today, he thinks it his Duty to take this Method of acquainting his Majesty, that Lord Chancellor cannot attend the Recorder's Report on Friday without Inconvenience to his Court, but can conveniently attend on Monday, in Case his Majesty shall be pleased to receive the Recorder's Report on that Day.

No. 930—*The King to Lord North.*

Printed. Donne I. 63.

[The minority divided the House of Commons twenty or thirty times by various methods in order to avert the arrest of the peccant printers. See No. 913.]

QUEENS HOUSE *March* 13th 1771.

$$\frac{m}{50.} \ p^t \ 5. \ \text{P.M.}$$

LORD NORTH—I apprehend the majority must have been much fatigued at being detained till five this morning ; but the litigiousness of the minority cannot give them any weight, on the contrary must offend every moderate man.

No. 931—*Lord North to the King.*

[15 *March*, 1771.]

Lord North has received the honour of his Majesty's commands. As he has not yet heard from Lord Dartmouth, He takes it for granted, that Lord Dartmouth will attend at the Recorder's report today. He returns his most grateful acknowledgements to his Majesty for his goodness, but begs leave to aprise his Majesty, that he should esteem it no inconvenience to him to officiate at the report, if Lord Dartmouth were out of the way.

BUSHY PARK. *Friday morn^g*

No. 932—*Lord Hertford to the King.*

SIRE—Permit me when I return the paper inclosed herewith to accompany it with my best acknowledgements for the confidence and favor shewn me by the communication of it. The person who drew the List for Lord Townshend has been misinformed himself or meant to mislead in Stating therin what relates to me, and I should be willing in candour to ascribe it to the first and most justifiable cause, if the expression wherein Mr Price is named did not seem discoloured with ill intention.

I am farr from wishing to assume any power I have not and it is in truth not from any jealousy of that sort that I observe the word only introduced into that sentence unnecessarily either to him or me except in that view ; and I am unfortunately and against my wishes the rather obliged to adopt this opinion because it is not true in fact that Mr Price voted against the Castle interest : I have a letter from him from his Country house wherein He acquaints me that He has not been in Dublin and begs me to excuse his attendance in Parl^t as well on account of the badness of his circumstances and the inability He is under of living in Dublin, as the danger to which He should leave his family and property exposed from the threats He has received from a set of people whom your Majesty must have heard of who call themselves hearts of Steel that do mischief or are disposed to do it to all those Gentlemen who resist such lawless proceedings. Mr Price has added and he speaks with truth that He has been neglectfully and disrespectfully treated by Lord Townshend and has no reason to expect any favor from him, but that being chosen by me into Parliament He would take no part against Gov^t.

This letter as a proof of my openess and sincerity towards his Excellency I sent some time ago to Lord Drogheda desiring He would communicate it to Lord Townshend.

Mr Dobbs is chosen for a popular borough in which both Lord Donegall and I have interest, Lord Donegall's was exerted very strongly against Mr Dobbs and mine supported him. The contest was a troublesome and expensive one, Mr Dobbs was returned but there was ground for a petition. It has been threatened by Lord Donegall and still hangs over him which may make the Gentleman more cautious not to give offence of any kind, at the same time that He owes much to the popular part of his Constituents.

Sr John Parnell was made a Baronet by my recommendation to your Majesty when I was in the government of Ireland, but

I believe that alone without any other reason will not be thought in common observation or experience a very sufficient reason for supposing him under my influence.

Sr William Parsons I barely know by sight, have no connection of any sort with him and the writers might as justly have ascribed to me the management of the whole house of Commons. Thus stand the different Persons marked in the list as in relation with me ; how far my influence in any or either of the cases can be supposed to operate I submit to your Majesty's judgment. I am very farr from being an ill wisher to Lord Townshend's government though He must have mistakenly supposed me such to act as he has done and when he betrays that disposition the minds of all such Persons as He supposes in any degree influenced by my wishes or sentiments will be more disinclined to his gov^t.

This cannot in justice be ascribed to me as I have gratified neither passion nor prejudice in encouraging it, and if it is a mistake of Lord Townshend's I am more entitled to indulgence than censure from the World.

With respect to your Majesty and English government I suppose there is not a Man in Ireland in or out of the sphere of my connection who thinks me worth a thought that does not know my sentiments. Your Majesty placed me in a situation where I had necessarily opposition and occasion to shew them in a publick character ; In a private light I have never concealed them for they are in every view founded in principle in my mind and as such I have always expressed them.

In regard to You Sire I will be bold enough to say there cannot exist a doubt : my professions of personal attachment have been uniform and to the utmost of my power and ability my conduct very sincerely corresponds with those professions ; I do not live in connection with any of the professed Parties in the state and have therefore no title to expect a very flattering picture of my behaviour from any such Politicians ; I shall only expect in justice that the features when heightened may bear some resemblance and I am persuaded that the truth and zeal with which I am from gratitude actuated for the honor the ease and security of your Maj^{stys} person and government will never leave it such a caricature that I should have reason to fear.

I am ashamed to leave your Majesty with such a detail ;

my motive is to stand fairly in your opinion where it is my
ambition to deserve it by acting honestly and uniformly.

In this view I hope for your excuse with liberty to subscribe
myself Sire your Majesty's most faithful and most devoted
humble servant   HERTFORD.

GROS^R STREET,
   March 16^{*th*} 1771.

No. 933—*The King to Lord North.*

Printed.   Donne I. 64.

[This letter marks the progress of the affair of the printers.   Charles
Jenkinson is the future Lord Liverpool and father of the Prime Minister.]

QUEENS HOUSE *March* 17^{*th*} 1771.

LORD NORTH—Though I have sent Lord Hillsborough to
You with my opinion, that as the Lord Mayor having presumed
to dispute the privilege of the House of Commons ordering
Printers to be brought to the bar ; and even to issue a warrant
for committing the Messenger of the House to the Compter for
attempting to obey this order, the authority of the House is
totally anihilated unless it in an exemplary manner shews its
rights are not unpunished to be infringed. I am therefore
clearly of opinion that the Lord Mayor and Alderman Oliver
ought to be committed to the Tower, and then a Secret Committee may be appointed to examine farther into the affair ;
it will be necessary to consider if they refuse to obey how they
are to be forced ; I wish You would send Jenkinson to Lord
Mansfield to bring You his opinion as to the best mode of effecting
this, and that You would send for the same purpose to the
Chancellor ; as things are come to this pass there is no means
of retracting the honour of the Commons must be Supported.

Draft.

No. 934—*The King to Lord North.*

QUEENS HOUSE *March* 17^{*th*} 1771.

LORD NORTH—Though I sent Lord Hillsborough to You
with my opinion, that as the Lord Mayor has presumed to set

the privilege of the House of Commons of ordering Printers to be brought to the bar at nought, and even to issue a Warant for committing the Messenger to the Compter for executing the duty of his Office ; the authority of the House of Commons is totally anihilated if it is not in an exemplary manner supported tomorrow, by instantly committing the Lord Mayor and Alderman Oliver to the Tower ; as to Wilkes he is below the notice of the House ; then a Secret Committee or any other mode of examining farther into the affair is open for the Wisdom of the House ; I wish You would send Jenkinson to Lord Mansfield for his opinion as to the manner of enforcing the Commitment if these people should continue to disobey ; a message of the same kind to the Chancellor might also be right ; You know very well I was averse to meddling with the Printers, but now there is no retracting the honour of the Commons must be Supported.

Draft, endorsed by the King.

A fair copy in the King's handwriting.

No. 935—*The King to Lord North.*

Printed. Donne I. 65.

[The Lord Mayor, Brass Crosby, had defied the authority of the House of Commons ; and the majority had resolved that he should attend in his place on the morrow to answer for his conduct. He came in his coach, and made a triumphal procession to and from the City.]

QUEENS HOUSE *March* 19*th* 1771.

$$\frac{m}{3.} \; p^t \; 9. \; \text{A.M.}$$

LORD NORTH—The conduct of the majority seems to have been of that firm and dignified kind, which becomes those that are on right ground ; I am not surprised that the whole House except Alderman Sawbridge, Alderman Oliver, and Sir Joseph Mawbey joined in condemning the conduct of the Lord Mayor, and in asserting the privilege of the House, which if not in an exemplary manner supported on this occasion must anihilate the House of Commons and thus put an end to the most excellent form of Government which has been established in this Kingdom ; go on with resolution and this affair will be happily concluded ; it occurs to me that the mode of conducting the Lord Mayor ought to be well considered that no rescue may ensue ; might not the conducting him by Water be the most private manner.

No. 936—*Lord North to the King.*

[19 *March*, 1771.]

[Alderman Oliver, who, like the Lord Mayor, was a member of the House, had joined him in defying the authority of the Commons.]

Lord North has the honour of informing his Majesty, that when the House of Commons had come to one preliminary resolution upon the late Breach of Privilege, the Lord Mayor complain'd of his health, and desired leave to retire. After his departure the House came to two other resolutions and then proceeded to the case of Mr Oliver, whom they committed to the Tower about three o'clock this morning. There were three divisions.

| Ayes. 272. | Noes. 214. | Ayes. 170. |
| Noes. 90. | Ayes. 97. | Noes. 38. |

Lord North will send the List of Speakers about noon.

Tuesday morning 50 min: p^t 3.

No. 937—*Lord North to the King.*

[19 *March*, 1771.]

Lord North has the honour of informing his Majesty, that, the Lord Mayor not attending, an order was made for his attendance tomorrow, if his health will permit : an adjournment of the debate was moved, and that motion amended : there was a division upon the amendment, which was carried by a great majority for the friends of the main question. Nobody pretended to defend the Lord Mayor, except Alderman Sawbridge, Alderman Oliver, and Sr Joseph Mawbey. The rest of the House join'd in condemning the Lord Mayor, and asserting the privilege of the House.

The division upon the amendment was as follows.

Ayes — 80
Noes — 267

No. 938—*The King to Lord North.*

Printed. Donne I. 66.

QUEENS HOUSE *March* 20th 1771.

$\frac{m}{55}$ p^t 9. A.M.

LORD NORTH—I am sorry the business of committing the Lord Mayor could not be concluded last night, for every delay in a breach of privilege of so enormous a kind, seems to indicate to the bystander, a less attachment in the House of Commons to its own authority, than every well wisher can desire, besides whatever time is given to the Lord Mayor, is in reality allowing consultation and plans of disturbance to the Factions. I owne I could have wished that Wilkes had not been ordered before the House; for he must be in a jail the next term if not given new life by some punishment inflicted on him, which will bring him new Supplies; and I do not doubt he will hold such a language that will oblige some notice to be taken of him.

Draft.

No. 939—*The King to Lord North.*

Printed. Donne I. 67.

QUEENS HOUSE *March* 21st. 1771.

$\frac{m}{57}$. p^t 8. AM.

LORD NORTH—Your account of yesterday's debate has given me great pleasure, as it seems to have been guided with dignity and with attention to the Privileges of the House; the apparent intention of not examining Wilkes meets thoroughly with my opinion and this unpleasant affair seems now to promise an issue that will tend to restore due authority to the injured privileges of Parliament.

Draft.

No. 940—*Memorandum by Sir John Lindsay.*

[Copy in the King's handwriting.]

Sir John Lindsay Madras Oct. 13th 1770.   Rd March 21st 1771.

The Governor and Council declined giving me any assistance in delivering their Majesties letters to the Nabob [of Arcot] with the Ceremony usual in that Country.   I then applied to General Coote, who agreed with me in opinion but added " I am not acknowledged as Commander in Chief " and consequently he could not give any directions.   I therefore waited on the Nabob and settled the reception in as becoming a manner as could be under the present circumstances.

Though not intending to announce my Plenepotentiary Powers to the Governor and Council on my first Arrival, yet as I found they intended to assist Hyder Ally in his War against the Marattas : I acquainted the President with this and that the great object of my mission was to endeavour to maintain Peace in India agreable to the express Stipulation of the 11th Article of the Treaty of Paris.

On my writing in the King's name for an account of the rise and progress of the late unfortunate War with Hyder Ally and Nizam Ally Cawn, and the transactions of the Company's Servants with the Nabob since the Definitive Treaty, they refused complying with it.

Their expressing great apprehensions of a War with the Marattas, and the precarious situation of the Carnatick, made me apply to the Governor and Council in the politest terms, begging to know the Political State of the Country, and to offer the assistance of His Majesty's name, and the sanction of his authority if they thought it could be of use in negociating Treaties, or could contribute in effecting a permanent Peace, but they have totally refused to cooperate with me.

I then applied to the Nabob, and after having given him all proper assurances of His Majesty's firm resolution of keeping the promises made by his late Royal Grandfather on the 21st of February 1760, when he declared to the Nabob his invariable resolution of continuing firm to all his Allies in every part of the World, and that should it appear that the distressed situation to which his Country was reduced, had been occasioned by the intrigues of any of His Majestys Subjects, he might depend on His Royal protection and friendly assistance, as soon as he should be informed of the real state of the hardships which he labours under in that respect. I therefore applied to him for a full and succinct account of all his Transactions with the Company since the Treaty of Paris, and as exact an account as possible of the causes of the rise and progress of the late destructive war with Hyder Ally and Nizam Ally Cawn ; that His Majesty might be enabled to redress past evils as much as possible, and that measures may be taken to prevent the like for the future.

In answer to this His Highness was pleased to express himself in terms full of gratitude for these distinguishing marks of His Majestys friendship and these repeated assurances of His Royal protection to himself and Family. At first he seemed willing to give every light in his power ; but by threats and insinuations of the insufficiency of the authority by which I acted, he soon became afraid to enter on the Subject ; but since I have fully opened my Commission to him, he has been open, free, confidential and I think sincere.

The first cause of the War with Nizam Ally Cawn was the Companys Troops seizing on the Circars in consequence of a Phirmaund from the Emperor of Indostan, without the permission of Nizam Ally Cawn the Subahdar of the Decan who was their immediate superior—That the Treaty the Companys Servants concluded with the Nizam, in which they promised him assistance when required, and of which the reduction of Bangalore then in possession of Hyder Ally appeared afterwards to be an object though not specified.—And by which the Nabob was obliged to give him five lacks of Rupees, which enabled him to pay his Army, (at that time ready to mutiny) and march from Hyderabad. —Their joining him with troops, which gave him consequence and strength enough to oblige the Polligars to pay their tribute, without which he could not have prosecuted his march, were the causes of the first War with Hyder Ally. And when Nizam found it necessary to make a separate Peace and gave up the Circars to the Company for a certain consideration ; he at that time gave them Sanceds for the Davannee of the Mysore Country then in the possession of Hyder Ally ; this made him once more fall on the Carnatick and ravage it with fire and Sword even to the Gates of Madrass.

The transactions of the Nabob, the Company and other Country powers are as follows. The Nabob's friendship for the English commenced very early, of which he gave proofs when he marched an army to relieve Madrass during his Father's life, after which at the desire of Mr. Hinde he marched again and forced the French to raise the Siege of St. Davids. Mr. Hinde had engaged to pay the expence of his Troops on the arrival of the Europe Ships ; but this amounting to near fifty lacks of Rupees he gave up, to gain the friendship of the English. He chearfully took the expence of the Siege of Madrass in 1759. upon himself, as it was the Residence of his friends ; but the Presidency charged him with the Siege of Pondicherry ; to which he acquiesed on condition of having the Stores that might be taken in the place. The Governor and Council chose to keep the Stores ; but allowed him one lack, seven thousand three hundred and Seventy Pagodas in account for them ; this however was disapproved of by the Directors, and was ordered to be placed again to his account ; he paid the whole expence amounting to two lacks, forty thousand, three hundred and eighty Six Pagodas.

They obliged him to take the Government of Madura and Trenevelly [sic] from his brother Mahomed Mafoose Cawn, and to give it Esouph Cawn ; one whom he highly disapproved. This man was employed in reducing him and paid the whole expence of the War ; that with the unpaid Revenues during the time Esouph Cawn had possession of the Country, he computes at near two crore of rupees.

The Company's Servants contrary to express Articles of agreement interfered in the civil government of his Country, by meddling with, and giving countenance to several of his people, particularly the Zemindars of Travencourt [sic] and Tanjore, and obliged him to make concessions which hurt his revenues and prejudiced his Country.

The expence of the Sieges of Madrass, Pondicherry &c. being

placed to the Nabob's account, he by this means owed a very considerable sum of money to the Company ; to pay which by an agreement of the 11th. July 1760. he was to give twenty eight Lacks of rupees annually till the debt should be discharged, and three lacks of rupees besides, for the expence of the Garrison of Trichanopoly ; and if they would allow him troops to collect his Tribute due to him from his Polligars &c. he engaged to pay them off in a year. Deductions were also to be made out of the annual payment in case any misfortune should happen to his Country, from the War or otherwise ; but contrary to this agreement they demanded fifty lacks of rupees in one year which his Country could not afford to pay. This obliged him to borrow money of individuals, which laid the foundations of his debt to private Creditors. The annual or what they call the running expences paid by the Nabob to the Company for the defence of the Carnatick was encreased to three Lacks of pagodas, then to four lacks ; to which at last they added two lacks more which they called extraordinary expences ; and in time of War they demand what they pleased. They have even charged him with three lacks, two thousand, one hundred and two pagodas, at a time without his knowledge, and his representations have been without effect ; they did not give him the Troops for collecting the tribute from the Polligars, and instead of allowing deductions for the destruction of his Country by a ruinous War, every new Governor encreases the ballance.

After the reduction of Pondicherry, the Governor and Council wanted some districts round Madrass to which he consented, and on his sending them certain conditions to sign, they refused doing that adding that he owed his whole Country to the Company, that *it was theirs to give his to receive*, this was after the Peace was concluded.

No. 941—*Lord North to the King.*

[25 *March*, 1771.]

Lord North has the honour of informing his Majesty, that the Lord Mayor attended in his place, and made his defence, but having desired that the City's Charters might be sent for, and that Counsel might be heard, a debate began during which he complain'd he was extremely ill, and desir'd the farther consideration of his business might be put off till this day seven-night. We consented to defer it till Friday when he was order'd to attend, if his health would permit. Oliver and Wilkes will attend at the same time. The Lord Mayor being withdrawn, We enter'd into two or three other debates, in the course of which we had two questions, which we carried by great majorities. The Clerk of the Lord Mayor is to attend tomorrow with the Book containing the minutes of the recognizances, that we may expunge the recognizance enter'd into by our messenger, and direct all proceedings at Law against him to be quash'd. a Debate is expected upon that subject, as well as upon a question for allowing Counsel to the Lord Mayor.

The first division was
Ayes — 79.
Noes — 202.
 ———

The second was
Ayes — 188.
Noes — 56.
 ———

No. 942—*The Nabob of Arcot to Sir Eyre Coote.*

To Major General, Sir Eyre Coote Knight of the Bath [*here follow three lines of names and letters*]—Nabob of ARCOT & THE CARNATIC presents his Compts.

I have had the Happiness to receive two Letters, which you was so good to write to me ; one from Bombay of the 21 November 1770, another from Bupora of the 18 January 1771, and rejoiced exceedingly in receiving such agreeable Accounts of your Health and Welfare.

I have a most perfect Sense of your Goodness and Attention to me, and beg you will accept my best Acknowledgements for the singular Instance you have given me in sending so particular Accounts of the State of Affairs on the other Side of India and the Designs which were forming against the Carnatick.

The Marattas have at length succeeded in doing what the English Army should have done before—they after hovering a considerable time about the place to which Hyder had retired found at last an Opportunity of bringing him forth to an Engagement near Seringapatam, the Capital of the Mysore Country, in which he was so severely handled by the Marattas, whose Numbers were much inferior to his, that a large part of his Army was cut to pieces, many of his General Officers were taken prisoners and he himself escaped on Horseback by Night with the utmost Difficulty. His whole Army was plundered by the Marattas.

Manderow, the Chief of the Marattas deputed to me and the Governor and Council, Manderow Sadashoo, one of his privy Councillors, a Man of a very respectable Character to sollicit our Assistance, or at least a Continuation of our Friendship upon the Terms which were sent and approved of a long Time before with which you are well acquainted. He still waits for an Answer with the greatest patience altho the Marattas have thus succeeded against Hyder without our Assistance.—You have been told what will be the Consequences of these Measures and may expect to hear of them very soon.

Notwithstanding the Governor and Council became Guaranters for the due Observance of the Treaty of 1762 between me and the Rajah of Tanjore, which was settled and ratified without my Desire, they have suffered the Rajah to raise Disturbances in the Southern Countries, without attempting in the least to quell them; and notwithstanding I have represented to the Governor and Council that the Rajah has done so without Reason, without my privity or Consent, and against my Inclination, for I wish to preserve continually perfect Tranquillity in my Country yet he is suffered to oppress the Great and little Marawar and others, who at the Siege of Madura, by the great Assistance they brought to me, gave the strongest proofs of their Attachment and of their Readiness to support my Government. These people have received Assurances from myself General Lawrence and Colonel Monson that so long as they behaved dutifully to me they should be protected against all their Enemies.

It is much to be regretted that Chundah's family was not delivered into the Custody of my people as they might have lived together in Quiet and Satisfaction—they are now dispersed and connected with different Powers and Rajahs and have been the Cause of many Troubles which have happened in my Country.

The very high Honor, confered upon me, by his most gracious Majesty my steady friend and Ally, to whom I owe the greatest Obligations, in appointing me to represent his most sacred person in investing you and Sir John Lindsay with the Honorable and Military Order of the Bath : has manifested to all the powers of India the very strong and invariable friendship which subsists between me and the English Nations and has made my own Happiness complete. I feel the greatest Satisfaction in performing the Ceremony, to which nothing was wanting but your presence that you might receive from my Hands this Mark of Favor which was designed for you by your Royal Master. I shall keep the Ensigns of the Order, until I hear whether you intend to stay in your native Country or to come abroad again, as you proposed.

I am obliged by your recommendation of Captain Johnstone to me—I am sensible of his Merit. He delivered your letter to me very faithfully.

I have not the least Doubt that you have signified to the British Parliament and to the Company my respects and Gratitude for their Attention to me and my Affairs.

I earnestly desire you will express to his Majesty in the most respectful Terms the very warm Sentiments of Gratitude with which I am inspired by so distinguishing a Mark of his Royal Favor and Friendship.

Captain Dent who is charged with Sr John Lindsays Dispatches to the Ministry has promised to deliver this letter to You.

I always pray for your Health and Welfare.—

What can I say more ?

MADRAS
26 *March* 1771.

No. 943—*The King to Lord North.*

Printed. Donne I. 68.

QUEENS HOUSE *March* 26th 1771.

$\frac{m}{20}$. p^t 9. A.M.

LORD NORTH—Considering the new indecent method of protracting the business of Parliament, I am rather surprised You could advance so far last night, and the great majoritys on each question will shew the House means to protect its privileges, without which it must soon degenerate and in lieu of the bulwark of Liberty become contemptible.

Draft.

No. 944—*Petition of Jeremiah Sisson.*

To the Kings Most Sacred Majesty.

The Humble Memorial of Jeremiah Sisson.

That your Majesty of your great goodness, caused me to be employed to make an Equatorial instrument for a fixed price, and I through my great Zeal for your Majesty did make it on the Noblest construction possible where wood and brass are connected, that it might Excell all that I ever made, or perhaps ever may, which stood me in more than the Agreed price which your Majesty of your great goodness was pleased to cause me to be paid what it stood me in more than what agreed.

The same Misfortune has befall me tho' in a much greater degree in the Grand Mural Arc I made for your Majesty, the new Principle of making both sides alike, to preserve both a Ballance and to strenghting it's figure took me near double the time in framing than what I thought of, as your Majesty has Experienced the tediousness of it's making. While I was about it, it made me quite Meloncholly not knowing when it would be finished, and the thought of having it stand me in more than what I agreed for the making hurt me greatly in my mind, to think that I am so great a Sufferer by making it at the fixed price ; the sum I find it stands me in more than the agreedment is £150 which I acquainted Dr. Demaimbrey as soon as it was fixed up ; which said sum I hope your Majesty of your wonted goodness will be pleased to Consider my prayer in a proper light and not to lett me be so great a Sufferer ; If this memorial should not be properly wrote I hope your Majesty will be pleased to pardon it, as it from a want of Words to express my self in so delicate a manner as should to your Majesty.

I ever remain one of our Majesty's Most Dutyfull and Loyal Subject   Jeremiah Sisson.

March 26. 1771.

No. 945—*House of Commons.*

27th March 1771.

Speakers.

[On a motion that the Lord Mayor be committed to the Tower.]

For	Against
Mr Sol^r General	Mr Baker
Mr Curzon	Mr Martin
Lord North	Serj^t Glynn
Mr Ellis	Mr Burke
Sr Robt Fletcher	Mr Aldⁿ Townsend
Lord Strange	Mr Wm Burke
Mr Attorney General	Sr Wm Meredith
Ld Hinchingbrooke	Sr George Saville
Lord Advocate	Mr Barre
Mr Jolliffe	Mr Cornewall
Mr Ongley	Mr Pownal
Mr De Grey	Mr Seymour
Mr Mackworth	Mr Trecothick
Sr H: Houghton	Mr Hart
Mr Stanley	Lord Mayor
Sr Edwd Blackett	Col Jennings
Mr Dyson	Mr Phipps
	Mr H. Cavendish
	Mr R: Whitworth
	Sr Cecil Wreay
	Sr Jos: Mawbey
	Mr Calcraft
	Mr Pulteney

Ayes — 202
Noes — 39

163 Majority.

No. 946—*The King to Lord North.*

Printed. Donne I. 68.

[Lord North had been in peril of his life from the mob on the previous day.]

QUEENS HOUSE *March* 28*th* 1771.

LORD NORTH—The conclusion of the Debate and division has proved very honorable for the House of Commons and I trust a due firmness will subdue the violence that has been encouraged by men of some property, who dare not avow it ; I rejoice much at Your having got without farther insult home ; and hope You will come to St James's when I return from the House of Lords this day ; I would upon no account pass the Bills otherwise than in person at a moment like this ; believe me the spirit You shewd yesterday will prevent its being often called upon, they now know You are not to be allarmed and therefore will not dare to again attempt what must revolt every man that has any regard to Law or even to humanity.

Draft.

No. 947—*The King to Lord North.*

Printed. Donne I. 70.

QUEENS HOUSE *April* 10*th* 1771.
$\frac{m}{30} p^t$ 10 PM.

LORD NORTH—I am glad to find the debate this day has not been so teazing as has been usually the case on the opening the Budget. I hope to hear from You tomorrow what ideas seem to occur in the Secret Committee.

Draft.

No. 948—*Lord North to the King.*

[Young Allen had been killed in a riot at St. George's Fields at the time of the election of John Wilkes for Middlesex.]

[25 *April*, 1771.]

Lord North has the honour of informing his Majesty, that Serjeant Glyn presented to the H^s of Commons today a petition from Mr Allen, the father of young Allen, who was killed on the 10th of May 1768. complaining of that fact, and of several others, by which he said that he had been prevented from obtaining justice : a debate ensued which lasted till near eleven o'clock, upon the question. Whether the petition should be brought up ? It was carried in the negative

Ayes   33.

Naes.   158.

Lord North has the honour of inclosing the List of Speakers.

For the Question	Ag^t
Mr. Serj^t Glyn.	Lord North.
Sir Geo. Savill.	Colonel Onslow.
Mr. Dowdeswell.	Mr. Charles Fox.
Sir Wm Meredith.	Lord Barrington.
Mr. Burke.	Sir George Osborn.
Mr. Thos Townshend.	Mr. Wood.
Mr. Cornwall.	
Sir Jos. Mawbey.	
Mr. Alderman Townsend.	

No. 949—*The King to Lord North.*

Printed. Donne I. 70.

QUEENS HOUSE *April* 26th 1771.

LORD NORTH—I am sorry You was detained so late last night with so fruitless an affair as Allen's petition and I am sorry any man could have the face to harangue on so inviduous an affair ;

every man that ventures into a riot whether a party or Spectator
is liable to be killed that the unhappy Young man was of the
former can be but little doubted.

Draft.

No. 950—*Lord North to the King.*

[? *April*, 1771.]

Lord North has the honour of informing his Majesty, that
the Examination of the Witnesses at the House of Commons
today lasted till near ten o'clock, when a debate ensued upon a
motion to order the attendance of General Murray on Monday
next, which ended a few minutes before eleven by the following
division.

Ayes	36.
Noes.	90.

No. 951—*The King to Lord North.*

Printed.   Donne I. 71.

[Alderman Sawbridge brought forward annually a motion to shorten the
duration of Parliaments. Mr. Cornwall's motion on the Lottery Bill was to
forbid any member to subscribe for more than twenty tickets; the whole
number being generally absorbed by the friends of Government before
the public had a chance of subscribing. This was nothing new.]

QUEENS HOUSE *April* 26th 1771.

$\frac{m}{13}$. *pt* 11. PM.

LORD NORTH—The motion of Mr Sawbridge was in its nature
so absurd and so detrimental to Trade that I am surprised he
could find so many Supporters, and Mr Cornwall's so indecent to
his brother members that it cannot raise him in their opinion ;
though I am not conscious of having much gall in my composition
I cannot help thinking that the uniform conduct of this dis-
jointed opposition is a medley of absurdities which tends to
nothing less than encouraging a contempt of the Laws and of
that Subordination that alone can preserve Liberty of which
they pretend to be the Guardians.

No. 952—*The King to Lord North.*

Printed. Donne I. 72.

RICHMOND LODGE *May* 7*th* 1771.

$$\frac{m}{15} p^t \text{ 2. P.M.}$$

LORD NORTH—I thoroughly approve of the Speech as it contains very exactly my way of thinking ; I am as well pleased with the wording of it, except a doubt whether *My Good Brother the King of Spain* would not be more agreable to the usual method of Speaking from the Throne than *His Catholick Majesty* ; if You would enquire of Mr. Dyson who is so thorough a Master of form this can easily be solved. I shall immediately order every thing for my going to the House of Lords tomorrow, which I prefer to Thursday ; and on Sunday authorised Lord Rochford to Summon the Cabinet for tomorrow morning in case the business should then be ready.

Draft.

No. 953—*Lord North to the King.*

[8 *May*, 1771.]

Lord North has the honour of sending to his Majesty a Copy of the Speech which has undergone a few alterations since yesterday. Lord North sent Mr Robinson to consult Mr Dyson about the expression of *His Catholic Majesty.* Mr Dyson was entirely of opinion that the usual and regular expression was *My Good Brother the* King of Spain, but thought that in the part of the Speech where the other words stood, that expression might carry the appearance either of an unbecoming irony, or of too much complaisance. He did not much like the words, *His Catholic Majesty*, and proposed leaving them both out, and using these words, *The Satisfaction made me for the Injury I received* : But Lord North is afraid that that manner of speaking will be thought too flat and general. He has, however, in compliance with Mr Dyson alter'd *the injury done to my honour* into *the injury I had received*, being of opinion with him, that an Injury done to the Honour of a Prince, marks an offence of so high a nature as would perhaps, be thought to require a more ample satisfaction than has been obtain'd.

Lord North must go down to the House early this morning to make a House, and to put the Speaker into the chair, and would, therefore, desire his Majesty to excuse his attendance at St James's. If, however, his Majesty has the least reason to require his presence, he will not fail to attend.

Lord North will, with his Majesty's permission, offer Mr Manners's place to Mr Wood, as his Majesty seem'd desirous of providing for the latter. His writ, in that case, may be moved this morning.

Wednesday morn^g

No. 954—*The King to Lord North.*

Printed. Donne I. 72.

RICHMOND LODGE *May* 11th 1771.

LORD NORTH—I have just received Your recommendation of the Revd Mr Speke, a Relation of Lady North's for the Living of Curry Mallet in Somerset Shire, for whom I with the greatest pleasure desire You will direct the presentation to be prepared.

Draft.

No. 955—*The King of Sweden to the Princess of Brunswick.*

[Copy in George III.'s handwriting.]

A STRALSUND *ce* 12. *de Mai* 1771.

MADAME MA SOEUR ET COUSINE—Vous m'avés inspiré une si grande confiance par votre caractere franc et honnete que je ne balance pas de m'adresser à Votre Altesse Royale pour une chose qui me tient fort au coeur. Je ne vous ai pas caché ma facon de penser en general, et vous savés par consequent que je ne pretend pas etre un champion de l'Angletere ; mais V.A.R. sait aussi que je n'ai aucune raison, encore moins aucune envie de me brouiller avec cette Couronne, dont j'estime infiniment le Monarque et dont je ne crois pas d'ailleurs que les interets soyent opposés a ceux de la Suede, cependant le Ministre d'Angletere à Stockholm se conduit comme si j'étois l'ennemi juré et déclaré de Son Maitre, il est a la tête de tous les factieux qui déclament contre l'administration, il les encourage par ses largesses et par ses conseils, et sans meme respecter la decense du caractere dont il est revetu, il paroit ouvertement dans leurs assemblees dont il augmente la Chaleur par les déclamations les plus propres a ranimer la populace qui les compose. Je laisse à Votre Altesse Royale Elle meme a juger si ce sont la les fonctions d'un Ministre public, residant a une Cour etrangere si en tout cela le Sr Goodrike agit comme j'en suis persuadé, contre les intentions du Roi son Maitre, je vous prie instament de m'en defaire, tachés de me procurer a sa place M. Woodword que j'ai connu a Hamburg, c'est un homme doux et pacifique, il ne me fera pas la guerre en Suede quand je ne demande pas mieux que de vivre en paix avec La Grande Bretagne. Mon Ministre a Londres ne se melera certainement jamais des affaires qui agitent la nation aux dedans d'elle meme. Mais si je me croyois permis d'y prendre quelque part surement ce ne seroit pas contre le Roi que je me declarerois ; V.A.R. sait mieux que personne ce que je pense sur ce sujet. Pourquoi faut il donc que je sois l'object des cabales du Ministre Brittanique à Stockholm, il y à a cela si peu de justice que je m'attends que les choses seront changée si V.A.R. veut bien se donner la peine d'y mettre la main, Elle connoit les voyes propres et j'abandone tout à la sagesse, etant a jamais avec le plus inviolable attachement Madame Ma Soeur et Cousine de Votre Altesse Royale Le bon Frere et Cousin   GUSTAVE.

No. 956—*Lord Hardwicke to the King.*

[Thomas Carte, the historian (*d.* 1754), left his papers to his widow, and she in her turn left them to her second husband, Nicholas Jernegan, who obtained large sums for granting the use of them to Lord Hardwicke and others, and eventually sold them to the Bodleian.]

ST JAMES'S SQUARE *May the* 13th 1771.

SIR—Lord Rochford being out of Town, I most humbly beg leave, to transmit to your Majestys own Hands, the enclosed Extracts from Mr Carte's MSS, wch are no improper Supplement to the Papers wch your Majesty has already condescended to cast an Eye upon.

When Sir ! You have excused this great Liberty, wch I have presumed to take, I have only to desire, that the Papers may be returned to Me, without passing thro' any other Channel but your own, or My Lord Rochford's, as Mr Jernegan is extremely Jealous, least They should be communicated without his Privity, —or to speak Truth, without his having the Benefit of Them,— and I have engaged my Word, to be very Cautious in that Particular.

I am, Sir, with the greatest Respect Your Majesty's most dutiful, & most obedient Subject & Servant   HARDWICKE.

No. 957—*The King to Lord North.*

Printed.   Donne I. 73.

QUEENS HOUSE *June* 7th 1771.

LORD NORTH—The sincere regard I have for You makes me though much hurt at the certain loss of so amiable a man as Lord Halifax, yet with pleasure acquaint You that whenever I shall receive the account of his death, I shall immediately appoint You Ranger of Bushy Park as I am resolved to make out none of those Grants but during pleasure, and have done so in the cases of my Brothers. I am certain You will very willingly accept it on that footing which from the conduct You uniformly hold must be a tenure of a permanent kind. I cannot conclude without assuring You that every opportunity of shewing You the sincere regard I have for You is giving Me the greatest pleasure   GEORGE R.

Draft.

No. 958—*The King to Lord North.*

[*June*, 1771.]

LORD NORTH—I sincerely rejoice at Lord Suffolk's having now consented to accept ; I am desirous of seeing you for five minutes that the time of acceptance to the different offices may be now settled which would be a shorter mode of fixing it than by letter.

$\frac{m}{30}$ p^t 9. P.M.

No. 959—*The King to Lord North.*

Printed.　Donne I. 74.

[Lord Halifax died on the 6th of June.　Lord Suffolk succeeded him as Secretary of State for the Northern Department, vacating the office of Lord Privy Seal.]

QUEENS HOUSE *June* 9*th* 1771.

LORD NORTH—As I find Lord Halifax is dead, You will I hope have prepared everything for Lord Suffolk's being on Wednesday Succeeded either by the Duke of Grafton or Lord Weymouth ; You will also direct the Warrant to be prepared for appointing You Ranger of Bushy Park, and cannot help adding the pleasure I feel on bestowing on You what You seem so much to desire ; I have ordered on Wednesday Sevenight a Chapter of the Garter when my Second Son is to have that order, and the next vacancy whether of a Subject or a foreign Prince I mean to bequeath this Order on You, which I shall do with the greater pleasure as I never have had any intimation from You that it is an honour You are in the least ambitious of.

Draft.

No. 960—*Lord North to the King.*

[10 *June*, 1771.]

Lord North has received his Majesty's most gracious letter, and can not think of going to bed till he has express'd, in the strongest and most grateful manner, his lively sense of the great and undeserved marks of Royal Favour, which his Majesty's letter contains. The very distinguish'd honour, of which his Majesty has been so good as to give him hopes, without any solicitation on his part, is as much beyond Lord North's expectation, as his merit : Desirous, ambitious, as he has always been, of every distinction, which might declare to the world, his Majesty's gracious approbation of his conduct, he never yet presumed to solicit the garter ; wishing to see it always disposed of in the manner the most conducive to his Majesty's honour and interest, and fearful, least his Majesty's favourable disposition towards him might prove an obstruction to either. He can not now be sorry, that he never troubled his Majesty with such an application, since his Majesty's goodness has open'd to him the flattering prospect of receiving this eminent distinction from his Majesty's unsolicited choice.

The peculiar convenience of Bushy park to Lord North made him, perhaps, request the Rangership of it with too much eagerness, but he did it in confidence, that his Majesty would freely declare, if he had destined it, in his intention, to any other person.

Upon the maturest consideration, Lord North is of opinion that it will be advisable for his Majesty, to make the first offer of the Privy Seal to the Duke of Grafton, and will, with His Majesty's permission, write to his Grace, upon the subject, as well as to the other Lords of the Cabinet to inform them of his Majesty's intention.

The poor services, and dutiful attachment of Lord North have been due to his Majesty long ago : For these late instances of his Majesty's goodness, He can not make any other return, than his most sincere and most grateful acknowledgements.

HENDON 10. *clock Monday morn.*

No. 961—*The King to Lord North.*

Printed.   Donne I. 75.

[The Duke referred to is the Duke of Grafton.]

LORD NORTH—You have done extremely well in writing to the Lords usually consulted and also to the Duke he being as I was told yesterday at Newmarket his answer cannot be received untill tomorrow, but should he decline Lord Weymouth being in Town in either case the Privy Seal may be appointed on Wednesday ; I am much pleased with the manner in which You have received my unasked intimation of Conferring the next vacant Garter ; I should not be surprised if it should happen in a few weeks, as the next Brother to the Duke of Gotha died the last of May, that event may by what I have learnt very likely release him from the weak state he is now reduced to.

QUEEN'S HOUSE
June 10th 1771.

$\frac{n_v}{15}$ p^t 2. P.M.

No. 962—*Lord North to the King.*

[10 *June*, 1771.]

SIR—The time of night at which I received your Majesty's most gracious letter, and the confusion into which I was thrown by the great, and unmerited marks of your Majesty's kindness towards me, made me, I am afraid, return your Majesty a most strange, perplexed, and unintelligible answer ; I do not remember exactly what I wrote, but this I am sure of, that, if my letter did not express the strongest attachment and zeal for your Majesty, as well as the warmest gratitude for your Majesty's repeated favours, and for your most gracious manner of conferring them, It did not convey a true picture of the real sentiments of my mind.

Upon revising your Majesty's note, I have thought myself authorized to write to the Duke of Grafton and the other Lords of the Cabinet, without waiting for any further orders from your Majesty. I hope your Majesty will not disapprove what I have done. It is, and ever will be one of the first objects of my life, to deserve your Majesty's approbation, and to shew myself, upon all occasions, Sir, your Majesty's most obliged, most dutiful and most humble subject and servant   NORTH.

No. 963—*Lord Harcourt to the King.*

Monday Morning June 11*th* [1771].

SIR—I take the Liberty of sending your Majesty the Remarks which Col: Blaquier made upon such of the French Corps, as he had an opportunity of seeing, and some observations which he made upon that Service ; which seem to be judicious. I must however beg Leave to observe, that had they been intended for your Majesty's Perusal, they would have appeared in a better Form and Dress. They were designed only to gratify My Curiosity, and at the same time to convince me that he had not mispent his Time, or made a bad use of the Letters of Recommendation, which I had procured for him, and which enabled him to take a more Minute View of the several Parts of that Service, than foreign Officers in general are able to do.

If these Remarks afford your Majesty one moments Amusement, I shall have no Reason to be uneasy for having presumed to put them into your Hands. I beg leave to assure your Majesty of my most inviolable Attachment and am, Sir, Your Majesty's Most faithfull Dutyfull Servant   HARCOURT.

No. 964—*The King to Lord North.*

Printed. Donne I. 75.

LORD NORTH—Nothing can be more handsome than the Duke of Grafton's manner of accepting the Privy Seal, which convinces Me that He would have been hurt if it had not been offered to him ; I must bear testimony that He ever thought the confidential Cabinet too numerous and that on Lord Bristol's getting the Privy Seal he therefore desired it might be stipulated that He should not be of those Meetings ; and as He thinks the same in his own case I cannot see any reason for Summoning him of Ministerial Questions except when they regard some affair to be debated in the House of Lords ; on other occasions if his advice is asked he will undoubtedly give it privately. You will give Lord Suffolk notice to bring the Privy Seal.

QUEENS HOUSE

June 11th 1771. $\frac{m}{43}$ p^t 7 PM.

Addressed and sealed by the King.

No. 965—*The King to Lord North.*

Printed. Donne I. 76.

LORD NORTH—I am pleased with the attention of sending to me the Poll for Sheriffs, as the two Senior Aldermen appear now to have a fair prospect of Succeeding, I trust no zeal will be wanting that their Success may be as brilliant as possible, the more so as it will unveil what has certainly been all along the fact, that Wilkes has been in his various struggles supported by a small though desperate part of the Livery, whilst the Sober and major part of that body have from fear kept aloof.

QUEENS HOUSE
June 26th 1771.

$\frac{m}{35}$. p^t 11. P.M.

No. 966—*The King to Lord North.*

[*June,* 1771?]

LORD NORTH—The Poll this day is undoubtedly very unpleasant, but that ought to make every friend to order and good government use every means to bring a handsome number tomorrow in favour of Mr. Plumbe.

m/30 *p^t* 5 P.M.

No. 967—*The King to Lord North.*

[*June,* 1771?]

LORD NORTH—The Opinion of yesterday was so full that Mr. Plumbe would make so good a figure this day that I am not a little mortified at the State of the Poll ; I hope the Quakers will be called upon and every other Engine used that can bring the two Aldermen so near as with decency to demand a Scrutiny, which I trust will place them at the head of the real Poll of the Livery.

m/35 *p^t* 7 P.M.

No. 968—*Lord Rochford to the King.*

Lord Rochford has had the honor of receiving your Majestys Commands but previous to them he had already taken every possible precaution by ordering the Justices and peace officers to be particularly attentive to their Duty, he will not fail conferring with Lord Hertford, and General Harvey, and has reason to beleive from what he has heard that everything will go on much quieter than is expected but the truest security is to be upon ones guard. Lord Rochford has further to inform your majesty that he has seen to day a particular friend from the city, who is well acquainted with the designs of the Faction, and he says that your majestys receiveing them graciously will be the truest means to disapoint them, and that if your Majesty's answer can be worded so, as to let the city, as a Corporation, see that your majesty is ready to redress any real grievance but to pay no regard to the remonstrances of a misled Faction, that such an answer will have a good effect for the informer says, Wilkes hopes the city will be ill received, and from that he has expectations of getting a pension from them of £600 a year, and of getting Crosby continued Mayor, as soon as ever Lord Rochford can get a Copy of the Remonstrance, he will draw up an answer for your Majesty's approbation and send a Copy of it to Lord North.

BERKLEY SQUARE 7th July 1771

$\frac{m}{15}$ past 7 P.M.

No. 969.

To His Most Gracious Majesty George the Third, King of Great Brittain, France & Ireland &c. &c. &c.

most humble Memorial & Petition of C. L. and C. R. in the name of the German colonists of Rowan County North Carolina in America.

ut intus

May it please the KING's most excellent MAJESTY

The memorial of Christopher Layrle, and of Christopher Rantelman, of second Creek, in Rowan County, in the province of N. Carolina. America most humbly sheweth

That your memorialists being recommended by your Majesty's Governor of the said province, and their Application validated by the great seal thereof and moreover, (as appears by proper vouchers,) being of your Majesty's German subjects in North America, moreover, being recommend'd (as appears by instruments annexed) by the Right reverend the BP of London, and by the Society for the propagation of the Gospel, to raise a sum of mony to build a Church for your Majesty's said German Lutheran Subjects, for the worship of Almighty GOD ; and also

for building a School, & for the maintenance of a minister, and
of a School master for your Majesty's said German Lutheran
Subjects of North Carolina, and Your Majesty will be pleased to
permit your memorialists to affirm, that in the said County of
Rowan, within a space of twenty miles, there are settled more
than two thousand German Families, who are annually increasing,
being a fruitful people, besides an addition of emigrants continually coming, and YOUR MAJESTY's said humble memorialists
have the honour to be recommended upon this Ac^{ct} to your
ROYAL Favour, by your Majesty's Secretary of State for American
Affairs the right Honourable the Lord Hillsborough—
WHEREFORE, in the name of your MAJESTY's faithful German
Subjects in the said County of Rowan N. Carolina, we most
humbly crave Your royal benevolence, and also that your
MAJESTY would grant a brief under your MAJESTY's royal letter
patent, to collect the charitable alms of your MAJESTY's loving
Subjects for this purpose, to build a Church, and School, and for
the maintenance of a godly painful and learned minister and
School master, and your humble memorialists, in the name of
your MAJESTY's faithful German Subjects, as in Duty bound,
and wishing all blessings to descend on your royal MOTHER, your
CONSORT and your POSTERITY, shall as in duty bound for ever
pray YOUR MAJESTY's humble memorialists and petitioners

CHRISTOPHER LAYRLE.

CHRISTOPHER RANTELMAN.

Enclosure.

Copy.

At a General Meeting of the Society for the Propagating of
the Gospel in Foreign Parts. Held in Dean's Yard Westminster
on Friday July 19th : 1771. A petition with a Testimonial thereunto annexed by his Excellency Governor Tryon, from the
German Settlers on Second Creek in Rowan County. North
Carolina having been laid before the Board,

The Society did approve the pious and useful design therein
contained, and declared, that in case the proposed subscription
shall meet with success & such a sum be raised as shall afford a
reasonable prospect of establishing a fund adequate to the
permanent support of a Minister & Schoolmaster in the said

settlement. They will contribute to such a fund and give such encouragement thereto as corresponds with their ability & the nature of their institution

By order of the Society

D BURTON Sec^ry

Recommended

HILLSBOROUGH Ric: London.

ABINGDON STREET
WESTMINSTER
July 19. 1771.

No. 970—*The King to Lord Sandwich.*

RICHMOND LODGE
August 3^d 1771.

LORD SANDWICH—The enclosed Memorial comes from the Son of an old Servant of my Mother's, He bore a good character when a Surgeon on board the Fleet ; He is a worthy Man ; and She seems to interest Herself in his favour but as I am totally ignorant of the propriety of this application I have only promised to transmit it to You.

Draft.

No. 971—*Lord Barrington to the King.*

CAVENDISH SQUARE *Aug^t* 13. 1771.

On reconsideration Lord Sandwich hopes the Marines may be able to work at the Fortifications of Portsmouth on Mondays, and has wrote to direct it, if it can be done.

Among the Warrants left with your Majesty last Friday, are some for changing the Quarters of the Guards, which I find will soon be wanted. BARRINGTON.

Since writing the above I have had a Letter from Genl Harvey at Portsmouth, proposing that the Invalids (who he thinks sufficiently able) should do this duty, which will be so order'd, if the Admiralty either cannot furnish Marines or wish to be excused from doing it—at all events the duty will be done.

No. 972—*The Duc d'Aiguillon to Lord Harcourt.*

Á COMPIEGNE *le* 23. *aout* 1771.

MONSIEUR—J'ai vu avec une extreme Surprise dans la Gazette de france l'indécence avec laquelle les redacteurs y ont inseré un article sur madame la comptesse de Waldergrave, qu'ils ont vraisemblablement puisé dans les nouvelles publiques d'angleterre. Nous devions d'autant moins nous attendre á cette etourderie de leur part que nous avions même pris les précautions necessaires pour empêcher qu'à l'exemple des gazettiers etrangers, ils ne s'avisassent de faire usage de particularités qui pouvoient interesser des personnes considerables.

Sur le compte, Monsieur, que j'en ai rendu au roi, sa M^{té} m'a ordonné de congedier les auteurs de cette feuille periodique et de leur en substituer d'autres plus instruits des égards qui sont dus à la naissance et au rang de ceux dont ils ont occasion de parler dans leur ouvrage.

J'ai l'honneur de vous informer, Monsieur, de cette resolution du roi, par laquelle V^{re} Ex^{ce} jugera du mécontentement de sa M^{té} et de son attention à donner à la cour de Londres, sans attendre aucune requisition de sa part, la satisfaction qu'elle pourroit desirer en cette occasion.

J'ai l'honneur d'etre avec un sincère attachement, Monsieur, de V^{re} Ex^{ce} le trés humble et trés obeissant Serviteur

LE DUC D'AIGUILLON.

a Son ex^{ce} M. le Cte d'Harcourt.

No. 973—*A Paper of Information concerning the French Possessions abroad, endorsed,*

Received from Lord Harcourt, 30 August, 1771.

ISLES DE FRANCE.

1771.

1 Gouverneur General	.	.	.	. 100,000 ⎫	103,000
Secretaire		.	.	. 3,000 ⎭	
1 Intendant General	.	.	.	. 70,000 ⎫	73,000
Secretaire	.	.	.	. 3,000 ⎭	

1 Commandant General		24,000
2 Lieutenants du Roy, 1 a L'Isle de France l'autre a ⎫ Bourbon . . . . . à. 10,000 ⎭		20,000
2 Major Idem . . . . à. 6,000 ⎱		
2 Commissaires Ordonnateurs . à. 6,000 ⎰		24,000
2 Premiers Generaux . . . . à. 6,000		12,000
14 Commissaires . . . . à. 4,000		56,000
2 Greffiers a 2000. 2 Notaires Idem, et 4 Huissiers a 1000		12,000
15 Pretres a 1200. et 6 Peres Lazarites, à 500 . .		21,000
4 Apotecaires. 2 a 2000. et 2. a 1500. et deux æconomes a 1800		11,600
Employes, sous Commissaires, Tresoriers &cᵃ &cᵃ .		55,000

Etat Major du 2 Regiments de 2000. Hommes Chacun—

1 Colonel . . . . . 16,000 ⎫		
2 Lieutenant Colonels . . . 16,000 ⎪		
2 Majors . . . . . 12,000 ⎬		63,200
4 Aides Majors . . . 12,000 ⎪		
4 Sous Aides Majors . . 7,200 ⎭		
40 Capitaines . a 3000		120,000
40 Lieutenants . a 2400		96,000
40 Enseigns . a 1800		72,000
4000 bas Officiers. Soldats &cᵃ		600,000

Etat D'Artillerie

1 Commandant . . . . 10,000 ⎫		
1 Major . . . . . 8,000 ⎪		23,000
1 Aide Major . . . . 3,000 ⎬		
1 Sous Aide Major . . . 2,000 ⎭		
6 Capitaines. a 3,600.—6 Lieutenants a 3,000. et 6 Sous Lieuᵗˢ : a 2,400		54,000
300 Hommes d'artillerie, et de Genie . . .		70,000
200 Ouvriers divers. a 800		160,000
Architects et Arpenteurs		20,000

Capitaine des Ports, Lieuᵗˢ : Pilotes, Constructeurs
    Officiers, Mariniers, Matelots, Entretiens du Port,
    Cabotage de 4 Petits Vaisseaux, et des Batteaux
		170,000

Poudre, Bals, et Fusils		400,000

Bleds, Ris, Mahys, Magnoa, Legumes, et Bois . .	1,000,000
Entretiens des Batimens Civiles	150,000
Vetement pour 200. Noirs	36,000

Hopital de L'Isle de France . . .	200,000	
Idem L'Isle de Bourbon . . .	100,000	306,000
Isle Rodrigues	6,000	

Armements, Gages, et Nourriture d'Equipages de 2. Flutes de 1200. Tonneaux	300,000
4000. Barriques de Vins, de Bourdeaux . . .	400,000
4000. Tiercons d'Eaux de Vie at 100 . . .	400,000

	4,875,800

Pondicherry.

1 Commandant General, subordonné à celui des Isles de France	40,000
Un Lieu[t] du Roy	10,000
1 Commissaire, Ordonnateur, President au Conseil Superieur, subordonne au Lieutenant General .	12,000
1 Procureur du Roy	6,000
7 Conseilliers . a 4000	28,000
1 Greffier a 2000. 1 Notaire a 2000. 1 Huissier a 1000 .	5,000
2 Chirurgiens. a 3000.—1. a 2000.—1 Apothecaire a 2000. 1 Æconome a 1800	8,800
4 Pretres. a 1500	6,000
10 Emploies, Contracteurs, Tresoriers, Imprimeurs et Commis	24,000

Etat Major.

1 Colonel	8000	
1 Major	6000	18,800
1 Aide Major	3000	
1 Sous Aide Major	1800	
9 Capitaines . . . . à	3000	
9 Lieut[ts] . . . . . à	2400	64,800
9 Sous Lieut[ts] . . . . . à	1800	
600. bas Officiers, Soldats avec Augmentation de Paye, pour les bas Officiers d'artillerie, et du Genie		120,000

1200. Sepoys, Capitaines, Officiers, tout compris .	250,000
Cabotage et depense des Rades	30,000
Hopital	50,000
Entretiens des Batimens	50,000
Depense des Pions, Couriers et Gardiens . . .	12,000
Effets et Ammunitions pour Envoyer d'Europe .	100,000

Mahá

Gratification au Commandant	4,000
1 Sous Commissaire	2,400
2 Commis	3,000
1 Chirurgien	2,000
1 Aumonier	1,500
Hopital	6,000
Entretiens des Batimens	6,000
Pions, Couriers, et depenses des Rivieres . . .	6,000

Karikal

Gratification au Commandant	4,000
Sous Commissaire, Emploie, Chirurgiens, Aumonier, } Hopital, Entretiens des Pions, Batimens &c^a }	24,000

Assanoon

1 Sous Commissaire	3,000 }	
Pions pour garder les Loges &c^a . .	3,000 }	6,000

Mazulipatam.

1 Sous Commissaire	3,000 }	
Pions pour garder les Loges &c^a . .	3,000 }	6,000

Chandernagore.

1 Commandant	20,000
1 Commissaire	6,000
3 Emploies	5,000
2 Pretres. a 1500	3,000
1 Chirurgien	2,000

Hopital	12,000
Capitaine du Port, Pilots, Bateaux et Navigation du Gange	25,000
Reparations des Batimens, Pions, et Couriers . .	3,000
1 Sous Commissaire a Cazimbazard, avec Entretien de la Loge	6,000
1 Idem. à Iongdis	6,000
1 Idem. à Patua	6,000
1 Idem. à Dosa	6,000
1 Idem. à Balacar	6,000
1 Idem. à Bassara	6,000
1 Idem. à Surata	6,000

> N:B: To the above List of Troops, must
> be added Those, sent off last
> February, and March.

No. 974—*Travelling Route.*

August.—[1771]

Tuesday	13th.	Embarked
	29th.	Lisbon.
September	3d.	Left Lisbon.
	7th.	Gibraltar.
	13th.	Left Gibraltar.
	21st.	Minorca.
	23d.	Left Minorca.
	27th.	Genoa.
October	2d.	Left Genoa. went to Alexandria.
	3d.	Turin.
	4th.	Turin.
	7th.	Left Turin. went to Ambroise.
	8th.	Noualles.
	9th.	Modene.
	10th.	Aiguebelles.
	11th.	Chambery.
	12th.	Tour du Pin.
	13th.	Lyons.
	15th.	Left Lyons. to Macon.
	16th.	Chaigny.

17th.   Langres.
18th.   Joinville.
19th.   Rheims.
21st.   Left Rheims. went to St Quintin.
22d.   Douay.
23d.   Bethune.
24th.   Calais.
26th.   London.

No. 975—*Lord Sandwich to the King.*

[? *September*, 1771.]
ADMIRALTY *Friday* ½ *past four.*

Lord Sandwich has the honour to inform your Majesty that Sir Hugh Palliser and he have been this morning with Ld North, and that he hopes that they have settled the method of conveying the General and Judges to India in a Ship to be hired for that purpose ; according to the plan in the enclosed paper.

Lord Sandwich allso sends a paper containing a sketch of what is to be seen to morrow in Deptford Yard ; to which may be added the dextrous method of baking sea biscuit, which your Majesty could not see at Portsmouth as the bakehouse was in the middle of the town.

Your Majesty will have the goodness to excuse the writing of the latter paper; as it was necessary that it should be in S^r: H: Pallissers own hand for the sake of secrecy.

No. 976—*Lord North to the King.*

[11 *or* 18 *September*, 1771.]

Lord North has the honour of requesting his Majesty's permission to pay a visit to Lord Guilford at Waldershare for a few days. He proposes, if his Majesty has no commands for him in London, to set out immediately after the Lévee, in hopes of arriving at his journey's end this Evening. If it is not inconvenient to his Majesty, he will request the honour of being admitted into the closet this morning before the Lévee.

Mr Louis Bagot proposes, with his Majesty's leave, to kiss hands this morning for the Canonry of Christ Church, which his Majesty has been so good as to declare his intention of conferring upon him. Sr William and the rest of the family have declared to Lord North the grateful sense they have of his Majesty's goodness to them upon this occasion.

DOWNING STREET. *Wednesday morn^g*

No. 977—*A Short State of Saxony.*

[In the handwriting of the King.]

It is far from being in the flourishing State it was in at the close of King Augustus II. of Poland, arising from Mal Administration, fluctuating Councils, and measures which have brought the Country into Wars and their terrible consequences; which cannot be retrieved in less than fifty years, and should the Elector be persuaded by France to depart from a System of Neutrality, the Sufferings of his Subjects and his own personal difficulties must be of longer duration.

The Court.

The Court is composed of

1. The first Marshal.
2. The Great Chambellan.
3. The Master of the Horse.
4. The Great Forrester.
5. The Great Master of the Household.
6. The Great Cup Bearer.
7. The Great Master of the Wardrobe.
8. The Captain of the Swiss Guards.
9. The Marshal of the Court.
10. The Marshal of the House-hold.

As these employments are lucrative and agreable they are much sought after, and have many Subordinate Officers.

Privy Council.

Whatever regards Justice, Polity, Commerce, new arrangements of Finances, Ecclesiastical and Feudal Affairs, as well what relates to the Empire, as connected with other German Courts, belongs to the Privy Council, which in several points, most especially Religious Matters, may give Law to the Elector by Virtue of the Constitution, and in consequence of the Reversalia signed by Augustus II. when he abjured Lutheranism to qualify himself for the Crown of Poland.

The Members of this Council are styled Excellencies, there are twenty Six of them, but only six have the right of Session with deliberative and decisive Voice namely

1.	Count Stubenberg	4.	Baron Fritch
2.	Ponikau	5.	Wurmb
3.	Stammer	6.	Baron Gutschmidt.

This Council has Privy Referendaries who propound the affairs to be discussed in Council, besides Secretaries, Registers &c.

General Affairs are carried before the Cabinet Council com- posed of the three Secretaries of State who have also the titles of Excellency. *Cabinet Council.*

1. Secretary for foreign Affairs Count Sacken.

2. Secretary for Domestick Affairs Baron Ende.

3. Secretary of War, which has been vacant since the death of Count Belgrade, appointed by the Administrator whose Governor he had been, this nomination gave disgust as he was a Roman Catholick.

The detail of Administration belongs either to particular Colleges, or to Committees appointed by the Prince, who are obliged to conform themselves to known Ordinances, or to the particular Instructions they receive from the Elector and his Council. *Colleges.*

The Elector has other Ministers called Counsellors of Con- ference, whom he consults on matters of doubt, or when dissatis- fied with the opinions of the Secretaries of State, among these are several Roman Catholicks, and Father Hartz his Confessor has no small sway on such Occasions. *Coun- sellors of Confer- ence.*

Justice is administered by the Council of Regency, by the Tribunals depending on the same, by the Bailifs, and by the Proprietors of Fiefs. *Justice.*

The Saxons have their own peculiar Laws with a mixture of the Roman and Common Law according to the Institutions of which they ought to proceed, yet Justice is said to be ill adminis- tered though Chancellor Schönberg boasts of the Simplicity of the Saxon Laws which he says are without Exceptions.

There are so many formalities, quirks, appeals, revision of appeals, and the revision of revisions that greatly delay Law suits, and a Criminal though clearly convicted if he has money to feed the Law may spin out his fate for some Years; the

Butcher who ravished and murdered a beautiful Young Woman above two years ago in a Solitary place by the Elbe not far from Dresden is a proof of this, as he is neither cleared, nor punished for that execrable Deed.

Polity.

The part of Government termed Polity has not been well instituted, and much less fairly and incorruptly administered; for excepting some regulations of Commerce there are scarce any Establishments of publick Utility. In the whole Electorate there are but two Workhouses, one at Leipsig the other at Waltheim, No Foundling or Lying in Hospital; nay if a poor unmarried person is found pregnant, the Magistrates in Towns, and Bailifs in the Country oblige Her to pay a fine of Seven Dollars, called Straffe Gelt, and lie twenty four hours in Prison. This rigour drives many to destroy the Child they bare, which crime is more common in the Electorate than in many Countries four times as extensive.

The poorer sort of Saxons feel much the want of Charitable establishments, from the Scarcity of grain, and the inability of the Elector to pay off the Salaries and Pensions of his Court, which have caused the greatest Calamity, but the opulent are not very forward to grant any relief; hence the Foreign Ministers are much importuned; Mr. Keith has shewn great humanity to the distressed.

Finances.

The Finances are wretched administered, whether owing to the disorder they were thrown into by the prodigality of Count Brühl in the late King of Poland's Reign, that it is impracticable to reduce them to method and regularity, or whether the persons employed find it their interest to leave the confusion, or to the incapacity of the Directors, it is certain the Elector does not draw the resources that his Country could afford, even with a moderate Administration. The Activity and Industry of the Subjects offer real advantages to the Sovereign; but the extorsions of those Employed, turn into hidden Channels what should be for the advantage of the State.

In no European Country are Employments so multiplied, and the Salaries annexed to them so high as in Saxony. The Elector possesses fine Domains, but there is not a proper ballance between his Revenue and Expences, the former not answering by some hundred thousands of Dollars.

The Debts are heavy as they amount to forty Millions of

Dollars, the interest of which absorbs a great part of the Revenue ;
besides many and great Appanages paid by the Elector to his
Family, and a number of pensions to many undeserving persons.

The Chamber of Finances regulates

1. The Electoral Domains.
2. Rivers and Forests.
3. The Tythes of the produce of Mines.
4. The Exclusive Sale of Salt.
5. The Porcellaine fabrick at Meissen.
6. The Game.
7. Post Office.
8. The Toll and other Such Duties.
9. The Provincial Excise and the Duty called Import.
10. The Mint.
11. The Stamp Office.
12. The principal part of the Revenues of Lusace.
13. The Income from Mersebourg, Zeitz and Weissenfels.

The Chancery of War receives

1. The Rations and Portions allotted the Army.
2. All sort of Grain accorded to D°.
3. The dues of Vassallage.
4. The Contributions of Schwartzbourg &c.
5. The Military Contributions from Lusace.

The College of Excise regulates and collects the General Excise.

The Steur College receives

1. The Land Steur
2. The Schock Steur
3. The Quatember Steur
4. The Drink Steur
5. The Capitation or Poll Tax
6. partly the Flesh Steur.

The Military Affairs belong to the Secretary of War, the
Field Marshal Chevalier de Saxe, and the Chancery of War under
the direction of the Elector.

When the late Administrator gave up the Reins of Government, He left an Army of near 32,000 Men, but this was above
the finance of the State ; the different Corps now Subsist, but
are greatly reduced ; The Corps are

Infantry. One Regiment of Grenadier Foot Guards.

twelve Regiments of Infantry.

One Corps of Artillery divided into Town and Field Brigades.

One Corps of Invalids.

Cavalry. One Regiment of Life Guards.

One Dᵒ of Carabiniers

One Dᵒ of Curassiers.

Four Dᵒ of Light Dragoons.

One Corps of Cadets.

One Dᵒ of Ingineers with a Military School, besides the Swiss Guards, and an independent Company at Warsaw, as a Guard to the Saxon Palace.

The Saxon Army consists of 25,372. Men ; the Uniform White for the Infantry and Cavalry, Red for the Dragoons, and Green for the Artillery and Ingineers.

Fortresses. The Fortresses in Saxony are few and such as can be of little defence to the Country.

Konigstein where State Prisoners are confined, Torgau, and Wittemberg.

Arsenal. The Arsenal of Dresden is well provided with Field pieces, but not with heavy Artillery, the Carriages provided by the late Administrator from being made of green wood are not fit for use.

Except one Foundery there is not a Military forge in the whole Electorate.

Population. The Population amounts to 1,600,000. persons the frequent emigrations must gradually decrease this number.

Soil. The Soil is rich and well cultivated, and the People very industrious, and cultivate most Arts of Necessity or Luxury.

The Inland Trade is much diminished through a Scarcity of Species.

The Foreign Trade is much cramped by the prohibition of Saxon Manufactures in the Austrian and Prussian Dominions, and by the negligence in repairing the Roads. Count Boltza a Rich Banker much in credit at Court has proposed many plans for remeding this but as yet without effect.

However the Ballance of Trade is about 400,000. Dollars in favour of Saxony.

Endorsed by the King, Taken from a paper delivered by Mr. O'Carroll. Jan. 7. 1771.

The form of Government gives the Elector a very considerable Form of Government.
share of power ; but in many instances the Assembly of the
States decide, particularly in the Leying new Taxes, to which
their consent is absolutely necessary. The Diet or Assembly of
the States is composed of a certain body of Nobility, Clergy, and
Deputies sent from particular Towns.

The right of sitting in this Assembly is determined for the The Diet.
Nobility by proving a Pedigree of Sixteen Quarters, and having
an Estate in Land called a Rittergut independent of any Baliage.
The Clergy who have a right to sit in the Diet are the Deputies of
the two Universities of Leipsig and Wittemburgh, and are chosen
among the Doctors of Divinity. The Chapter of Merseburgh,
Naumburgh, Zeits, and Meissen, send Deputies to the Diet, and
these are elected from among the Cannons, for those Dignitaries
retain their Antient Privileges though the above mentioned
Chapters have been Secularised. The Deputies sent from the
Towns to the Diet are fixed upon and elected by a Majority of
Voices among the Burgomasters.

The rights and privileges of the States are founded rather Privileges of the States.
upon Custom than established Laws, and on that account frequent
disputes arise between the Elector and the States. He is obliged
to call an Assembly of the States at the end of the Term for which
the Diet granted the last Taxes, which is generally limited to
three or six Years ; the Diet of 1763. and that of 1766. granted
the Taxes for three years only, but that of 1769. for six years, so
that there will not be another Diet till 1775.

As soon as the States are assembled they begin by forming Committees.
two Committees, the one called Der Engern Ausschus, the other
Der Weitern Ausschus. All matters of business pass by these
Committees before they are represented to the Plenum of the
Nobility and Deputies of the Towns, called Allgemeine Ritter-
schaft, der Stadten. The Elector by one of His Ministers of the
Privy Council acquaints them with the general Sum of his
demands to be charged upon the Country, leaving it to the
consideration of the Diet to determine and fix upon the least
burthensome manner of levying the required money ; but before
the States grant these Supplies they present to the Elector a List
of the Griefs and Complaints they have against the conduct of the
Court relative to the interior Government ; if the Elector returns
a favourable answer to their complaints, then they easily grant

the Sums He demands, otherways there sometimes happens a violent opposition in the Assembly of the States.

Foreign Affairs.

The States have no pretentions to interfere in foreign affairs, that branch as well as what relates to the Court is at the absolute direction of the Elector, and also the distribution of his own particular Finances, of which the principal branches are the Balliages and the Lands assigned to him, the Waters and Forests, and the produce of what is called Les Droits relaliens.

Privy Council.

All affairs relating to Justice, Police, Commerce, new arrangements of the Finances, all Ecclesiastical and Feudal concerns as well as those relating to the Empire appear finally before the Privy Council (called Das Geistliche Consilium) which in several points, but particularly in matters of Religion may give Law to the Elector in virtue of the Constitution, and of the Reversalia signed by Augustus II. when He abjured Lutheranism to qualify himself for the Crown of Poland. The business is brought before the Privy Council by privy referendaries (called Geheimste referendarii) and when discussed, decided by the majority of Votes. The Elector presides in person; the Members have the Title of Excellency and are twenty Six in number, of whom five only (as per margin) have a decisive voice, and they are distinguished by the name of Ministre de Conference, or Conference Ministri.

Count Stuben- bergh, Baron Stammer, Baron Fritsch, Baron Wurmb, Baron Gut- schmidt.

Cabinet Council.

Since the death of the old Count Brühl there has been no Prime Minister in Saxony, the affairs he directed alone are now under the inspection of another Council called the Cabinet, composed of three Secretaries of State who have also the title of Excellency.

Count Sacken. Baron Ende. Vacant.

1. A Secretary of State for foreign Affairs

2. A Secretary of State for the Finances and domestick Affairs.

3. A Secretary of State for the War Department.

This last Employment has been vacant ever since the death of Count Bellgrade a Savoyard Nobleman who enjoyed it but a short time, having obtained it from Prince Xavier at the close of his Administration; he had been that Prince's Governor; his nomination gave great disgust on account of his being a foreigner and a Roman Catholick. All military affairs are now transacted by a Council of War.

Besides the two above Councils the Elector has for his private Coun-
information other Ministers called Counsellors of Conference, sellors of
distinct from the Ministers of Conference ; with these He usually ence.
deliberates before he decides on any opinions represented by the
Secretaries of State. Among these Counsellors of Conference are
several Roman Catholicks ; and Father Hartz a Jesuit, the
Electors Confessor, who has much influence.

The other parts of Government are directed by different
Councils called Colleges, which are obliged to conform them-
selves to the particular Instructions they receive from the
Elector and His Privy Council ; of these the chief are the
Regency, the Council of War, the Ecclesiastical Council, and
that of the Finances.

The Regency (called die Regierung) in which the Chancellor Regency
presides, is at the same time a Court of Justice, Equity, and or Law
Police. Other Tribunals, Bailiffs, and Proprietors of Fiefs Council.
depend upon the Regency. The Saxons have their own Municipal
Laws with a mixture of the Roman and Canon Law, according
to the Institutions of which they ought to proceed, but Justice is
ill administered, and very tedius ; there is now a Law Suit
laying before the Council of Appeals between the Families of
Rheder and Schulenbergh which has been depending above 136
years. A criminal though clearly convicted of Murder and the
most atrocious Crimes may spin out his miserable fate for several
years by appealing from one Court to another, and by procuring
delays, if he has money to bribe and pay.

The Police is ill regulated, there are but two Work Houses in Police.
the Electorate the one at Leipzig, the other at Waltheim, no
foundling, no Lying in Hospital ; the want of Bread the last
Summer at Dresden is a strong proof of the bad Police, for the
Directors of the Police and the Magistrates permitted such a
considerable Exportation of Corn this year to Ratisbon, Munich,
and different parts of Germany, that bread rose to thrice the price
of the year before, and so scarce that the Populace oppressed with
Hunger surrounded the Bakers Shops, and an Insurrection was
daily expected in the Town untill a supply of Corn was obtained
from Magdeburgh.

The Commission of Police at Dresden is composed of two
persons from the Council of Regency, one from the Chamber of
Finances, one Military, and two Magistrates. Many of these

having different Interests and Principles loose their Time in disputing while the Public Suffers.

Army. The Military Affairs are regulated by a Council of War the President of which is Major General Fleming. The Feldt Marshal Chevalier de Saxe a natural Son of Augustus II. King of Poland is the oldest Officer in the Service and has a general command over all the Military Arrangements. When the Elector took the Reins of Government into his own hands the Army amounted to 30,000. men ; but this being more than the distressed Finances of the Country can support, it has by two reduction been brought down to about 23,700. Men.

The different Corps are as follow

Infantry. One Regiment of Foot Guards, all Grenadiers
twelve Regiments of Infantry called Feldt Regiment

Cavalry. One Regiment of Horse guards
One Regiment of Carabineers
Six Regiments of Curassiers
four Regiments of Light Dragoons.

Separate Corps. One Corps of Artillery
One Corps of Ingineers with a Military School
One Company of Swiss Halbardiers at the Palace of Dresden.
One Independent Company at Warsaw to Guard the Palais de Saxe
One Corps of Invalids
One Corps of Cadets

Uniforms. The Uniforms of the Infantry and Cavalry are White of the Dragoons Red, of the Artillery Green.

Fortresses. The Fortresses are, Königstein, which is thought to be impregnable; it is the Chief State Prison, Torgau, and Wittenburgh.

Arsenal. The Arsenal at Dresden has been well provided with Artillery since the Peace of Hubertsburgh in 1763.

Finances. The Finances of Saxony are certainly in a miserable condition, owing to the prodigal Reign of the late King of Poland, and the enormous Expenses occasioned by the last War ; though the Elector possesses very fine Domains, and the Industry of the Subject offers every substantial Advantages to the Sovereign, yet there certainly is not a proper Ballance between his Revenue and Expences.

Revenue. The Revenue as collected at present does not far exceed Six

Millions of Dollars. The Expences of Government amount to some hundred thousand of Dollars above that Sum, so that the Debt annually encreases.

The Debts are very heavy on the Country as they amount to forty millions of Dollars, the Interest of which is very considerable. The many and great Appanages the Elector pays to the different Branches of the Electoral Family, and a number of private Pensions absorb a considerable part of His Revenue.

The Revenue is composed of four principal Classes   Revenue.
1. The Chamber of Finances.
2. The Council of War.
3. The College of Excise.
4. The Steur College.

The Chamber of Finances regulates   Chamber
1. The Electoral Domains.   of
2. The Rivers and Forests.   Finances.
3. The Tythes of the Produce of the Mines.
4. The exclusive sale of Salt.
5. The China Fabrik at Meissen.
6. The Game.
7. The Toll and Road Duties.
8. The Revenues of Lusatia.
9. The Income from Marseburgh, Leitz, and Weissenfels.
10. The Mint.
11. The Stamp Office.
12. The Post Office.

The Council of War regulates   Council
1. The Rations and Portions allotted to the Army.   of War.
2. The Dues of Vassalage.
3. The Contributions of the Houses of Swartzburgh, Rudostat and Tonderhausen.
4. The Military Contributions from Lusace.

The College of Excise regulates all the Affairs relating to the College of general Excise in Saxony, and imposes a Tax upon all Provisions Excise. brought into each Town, which is paid according to the established Tariffe.

The Steur College regulates   Steur
1. The Land Steur.   College.
2. The Schock Steur.

3. The Quatember Steur.
4. The Beer or Trank Steur.
5. The Meat or Fleisch Steur.
6. The Capitation or Pole Tax. Personen Steur.
7. The Voluntary Gift of the Nobility.

The Land Steur is at 14. Tennings per Schock. The Schock Steur is at 44. Tennings per Schock. The Quatember Steur so called because collected four times in the year ; it is a personal arbitrary tax imposed in every Municipal Jurisdiction or Seigneurie according to the power it may be thought each Inhabitant has of contributing his Share

The Beer Steur is a tax of one Dollar and a half upon every Ton of Beer containing four Barrells.

The Meat Steur is a Tax of a Tenning upon each pound of meat, so that 288. pounds of meat pay a Dollar.

Capitation.

The capitation or Poll Tax is imposed rather according to the Rank and Quality of the person, than to their Income or Power of paying it.

Don Gratuit.

The Voluntary Gift of the Nobility is very uncertain ; but at each Diet or Assembly of the States, the Nobles allways grant something to the Elector and Electress. This arises from an antient Custom in Germany that every Military Fief should furnish one, two, or three armed men and Horses for the defence of the Country, or that the Possessors of those fiefs should make a gift in lieu.

All these different Taxes are granted, abolished, encreased, or decreased by the States when in Diet assembled according to the Exigency of the Times.

Debts.

The Debts are arranged under three Classes

1. The Debts of the Steur, for which the Assembly of the States is allways responsible.
2. The Debts of the Excise.
3. The Debts of the Court.

28.Millions.

The Debts of the Steur amount to 28. millions of Dollars at 3. per C^t.

6.Millions.

The Debts of the Excise amount to more than 6. millions of Dollars at 3. per Cent.

6.Millions.

The Debts of the Court to 6. millions of Dollars some at $3\frac{1}{2}$.

40.Millions. some at 4. and some at 5. per Cent.

The Money borrowed at Hanover upon the Balliages of Tangerhausen was at 3½. per Cent.

The Money borrowed in Holland during the War (for which the Elector's Jewels were pawned as a Security) is at 4. per Cent.

The different Sums borrowed at Genoa for fitting out and payment of the Troops are at 5. per Cent.

Saxony is very far from being at present in the flourishing condition it was at the Close of the Reign of Augustus II. The principal causes of its decay are to be attributed to the fluctuating Councils and Political connections which brought on the Desolation it met with the last War ; should the Elector depart from the System of Neutrality which His Ministers loudly profess, the sufferings of His Subjects as well as the difficulties he himself labours under must in all probability be of long duration. But if the administrating part of this Government proves active and diligent, the advantageous situation, the richness of the Soil and the uncommon industry of the Inhabitants will afford infinite ressources to recover all the losses and detriment this Country has sustained.

Saxony with all the Electoral Territories contains near four *Produce.* thousand miles Square, is well inhabited, and Susceptible of all most every sort of produce the Earth can afford. The Circle of the Mountains near Freybergh contain very precious Mines of Silver and Copper ; many of the other Mountains bear Vines sufficient for the consumption of the Lower Inhabitants. Thuringia and the Bishopricks of Merseburgh, Naumbourgh, Wurtzen and Feitf have very rich Grass Lands ; and the Circles of Meissen and Leipzig near the Center of the Elector's Dominions are composed of a rich and fertile Soil abounding with the finest Corn.

Dresden is situated on a fine navigable River by which all their Merchandizes can be transported to Hamburgh and from thence embarked for different Countries.

The Electors Dominions contain 326. Towns, near 6,000. *Popula-* Villages and Hamlets, and the Population of the whole Country *tion.* (although greatly diminished) now amounts to 1,500,000 Souls of which Dresden contains 69,000. in the year 1700 they reckoned that these dominions contained 500,000 Men more.

The Entry of Charles XII. into Saxony in 1705. was the first Check to the Population of this Country, but the dissipating Reign of Augustus II. and the last Wars have occasioned much poverty and distress, which consequently allways tend to diminish the number of Inhabitants. The Diet immediately after the Peace of Hubertsburgh proposed in 1763. several Plans to remedy this Evil ; but soon after an unfortunate mistake in the management of the Saxon Commerce became highly prejudicial to the encrease of Population, for the decrease of Commerce must allways contribute to the decrease of Inhabitants.

Industry. In point of Industry the Saxons excell most Nations, and there can scarce be named any Art of Luxury or necessity that they do not know. Their China and Linnen Manufactures are justly celebrated. There is an Institution called the Oeconomical Deputation to which Agriculture and Industry have great obligations ; but the prodigy of Industry is to be seen at Herrenhuth, and Establishment formed by Moravians in Upper Lusace, where they have formed an Assemblage of all Arts, Fabricks, and Manufactures. They send their youth to learn fine Workmanship in England, then return to Herrenhuth and furnish the adjacent Countries with every kind of handicraft productions.

The most considerable manufactures are

Manufacture.
1. The Linnen in Upper Lusace, the most famous of which is the Damask Table Linnen made at Zittaw.
2. The China at Meissen.
3. The Cotton Stuffs, but particularly the Fustian and Bazin in the Circle of the Mountains.
4. The Cloth at Goerlitz and several other Towns.
5. The Camelots, Baracans, Serges, and other Silk and Woolen mixed Stuffs made in the Circle of Voigtland, and Neustadt.
6. The Laces and Blondes made in the Circle of the Mountains, to which may be added the Embroydery in Muslin made at Dresden and Leipzig.
7. The refining of Allumn, Vitriol, Kubold and other Fossils in the Circle of the Mountains.
8. The Fabricks in Wood and Straw.
9. The Armory of Sahla, which supplies half of Germany, and exports considerably to the Indies.

Mines. The Mines in the Circle of the Mountains contribute much to the prosperity of the Manufactures, by furnishing so many of the necessary Ingredients of Minerals and Fossils ; so much Silver is not produced as in the last Century ; but the Copper and Tin are not diminished. The general produce of all the Mines may amount to near 1,000,000. of Dollars. The Elector has a right to a tenth part of the neat produce of them every Year. The richest and most considerable Mines are near Freybergh, where the general Direction of all the other Mines is held ; the produce of the Mines and Manufactures are the basis of the Saxon Commerce.

Untill 1765. the Commerce was very considerable, as the Exportation to all the Neighbouring States was free ; but in that year an absolute prohibition was issued forbidding the Entry of Several Austrian and Prussian Manufactures, though the same Merchandizes were permitted from England, France, and Holland. But this ill judged step drove those Courts to prohibiting all Saxon Manufactures, and to establishing fabricks in opposition to them. <i>Com- merce.</i>

The Inland Trade is much diminished through a scarcity of Species, great part of the Sums that used to be employed in Domestick Traffick has within these seven or eight years in rebuilding a great part of Dresden reduced to a heap of Rubbish by the Prussian Bombardment.

The Foreign Commerce is greatly cramped by the Prohibition of their Selling Goods in the Austrian and Prussian Dominions ; but [also] by the exorbitant Duties laid upon all kind of Merchandizes passing to and from Saxony through the Prussian Territories, whether by the Elbe or through Silesian and Poland which branch of Commerce was formerly very lucrative.

The Ballance of Trade in favour of Saxony does not amount to 400,000 Dollars about £70,000 ; the fairs of Leipsig dwindle every year, and the large Sums annually sent out of the Country for interest of the Debts does not promise a reestablishment of the Saxon Finances.

Government from mistaken notions instead of encouraging the Manufactures and promoting Trade, have taken steps which greatly check Industry ; among others a Tax called Land Accise [sic] very prejudicial to the Interior Commerce. The States proved the last Diet that a piece of Camelot made at Voigtland in the Electors Dominions, before it could be sold at Dresden paid 9½. per Cent to that Tax, whilst the same kind of Stuff brought from other Countries paid only 8½. per Cent.

If Trade had been understood in Saxony it must have greatly

flourished, for besides exporting home made manufactures, the Commerce of Passage must have occasioned a very advantageous circulation of Species.

The Articles Saxony is obliged to import for Her own use are

1. Fine Cloths from Britain, France and Holland.
2. Velvets and Silks from the Indies, Italy and France.
3. Toys and many Merchandizes of Luxury from France.
4. Spices, Herrings and Dry Cod from Holland.
5. Furs from Russia and different Countries.
6. Sugar, Coffee, Cotton, Indigo, Cochenille, and many Medicinal Drugs from the Indies.
7. Persians and Cottons from the East Indies.
8. Wines from France, Franconia, the Rhine and Moselle.

Leipzig is the deposite of all Merchandizes that either come in or go out of Saxony ; but the trade and profits are greatly diminished. The other Towns are in a miserable Situation, allmost ruined by the heavy Contributions demanded by the Elector the last War, and the Breweries which were their great Support having lost great part of their business by the general Stop of Trade. The Towns near the Elbe are allmost ruined by the diminution of the passage of that River, arising from the many Tolls which are become so severe that it does not answer to pay the Duties upon the Several Articles of Trade.

The Soil of Saxony is so good and the Industry of the People so great, that with a strict Oeconomy it would again flourish.

Appanages annually paid by the Elector to the different Branches of the Electoral Family

To the Electress Dowager . . . . 130.000. Dollars
To Prince Xavier formerly Administrator . 80.000.
To Prince Charles . . . . . 50.000.
To Prince Albert . . . . . . 50.000.
To the Elector of Triers . . . . 50.000.
To the three Princesses, Christine, Elizabeth,
and Cunegunda . . . . . 40.000.

_____

400.000.

The Elector also maintains three Younger brothers and two Sisters who have no fixed Appanages, untill the next meeting of the States in 1775.

A GENERAL VIEW OF THE FINANCES OF SAXONY

RECEIPT OF THE DIFFERENT CASES

	Dollars
1. The Steur receives	
The Land Steur	150,000.
The Meat Steur	30,000.
The Beer Steur	250,000.
The Quatember	882,000.
The Tenings	696,000.
The Poll tax	200,000.
	2,208 000.
2. The General Excise receives	580,000.
3. The Chamber of Domaines	2,500,000.
4. The Military Chest receives.	
Rations, Portions, and Magazines	600,000.
The Assessments on the Bishopricks of Mersebourgh, and Naumbourgh	84,000.
The Contributions of Lusace	112,000.
Do from Swartsbourgh	11,334.
The Duty on Mills	150,000.
For Horses furnished by the Vassals	72,000.
	1,029,334.
Total Receipt	6,317,334.

DISBURSEMENT OF GOVERNMENT

	Dollars
1. The Funds for paying off the Interest and Debt of the Steur	1,100,000.
2. Do of the Chamber of Domaines	300,000.
3. The Interest of the particular Debts of the Court	300,000.
4. The Establishment of the Court	600,000.
5. The Appanages of the Electoral Family	400,000.
6. The maintainance of the Army together with the Military Extraordinaries and Pensions	2,400,000.
7. The Civil Salaries and Pensions	650,000.
8. The payment of Ministers at Foreign Courts	120,000.
9. The Electors Chapel &c.	50,000.
10. The Stables and Studs of Horses	100,000.
11. Game and Expense of la Chasse	40,000.
12. Buildings	100,000.
13. Private Expences of their Electoral Highnesses	100,000.
14. Extraordinary Expenses	400,000.
Total Expences	6,660,000.
Total Receipt	6,317,000.
Balance against Government	343,000.

Since the above was drawn up there has been a reduction made in the Army which is said to amount to 300,000. Doll. consequently the present Expences are diminished to Dollars . . . 6,360,000. and the Army to 20,500. Men.

Endorsed by the King, State of Saxony from Mr. Osborne's dispatches, Sept. 13th 1771.

No. 978—*Lord Sandwich to the King.*

MYSTLEY *Sept*: 20. 1771

Lord Sandwich begs to receive Your Majesty's final commands about the Launch of the Grafton at Deptford, which must be on Wednesday next the 25ᵗʰ: instant.

Lord Sandwich has communicated your Majesties intention of being present on that occasion to no one but the Secretary of the Admiralty, and the Comptroller of the Navy which could not be avoided, on account of orders to be given for the necessary preparations, the latter was desired to put down his thoughts, as to what would be proper upon this occasion, and which are here enclosed : but as it is very possible your Majesty may not approve of the whole or of any part of this plan ; Lord Sandwich begs to know whither he might attend at Richmond any hour on Sunday morning to recieve your commands, for which purpose he will not fail to be in town to morrow evening.

Your Majesty I think mentioned your intention of walking over the Dock Yard, but it is to be feared that the crowd would be particularly great, as the Launch of a Man of War is a holiday for the whole neighbourhood, and attended at all times by a great concourse of people ; and the shutting the gates and keeping the populace at a distance, would possibly occasion complaint and disturbance

No. 979—*Memorandum by the King.*

On the Visitation of the Dock Yards in 1771.

At Chatham the Ardent 64. Guns proved a total decay her Timber and Plank almost universally rotted ; She was built at Hull in 1764. never at Sea, her prime cost about £23,000. the repairs now ordered estimated at £17,000. this is owing to her being built of Green Timber.

The Exeter 64. Guns built in 1763 having received damage by driving on Shore from her moorings soon after her Launch, will probably when Docked be found unfit for Service untill Repaired.

Guns

Formidable . . . . 90. ⎫
Prince George . . . 90. ⎬ Building on the Stocks
Sterling Castle . . . 64. ⎪
Roebuck . . . . 44. ⎭

Ardent . . . . 64. ⎫ Repairing in Docks
Medway . . . . 60. ⎭

Jersey . . . . 60. fitted for an Hospital Ship
St. Florentine . . . 60. intended for a Breakwater
                                at Sheerness.
Enterprise . . . . 44. ordered to be broke up.

At Sheerness

Bristol . . . . 50. Building on a Slip.
Unicorn . . . . 28. ⎫ Repairing in the Docks.
Racehorse . . . Sloop. ⎭

At Portsmouth

Ludlow Castle . . . 44. ordered to be broke up.
Princess Royal . . . 90. ⎫
Berwick . . . . 74. ⎬ Building
Lyon . . . . 60. ⎪
Falcon . . . Sloop ⎭
Sandwich . . . . 90. ⎫
Superb . . . . 74. ⎬ repairing in Docks
Chatham . . . . 50. ⎭
Savage ⎫
Diligence ⎬ . . . . Sloops repairing at the Jetty
                                heads

At Plymouth

Conqueror . . . . 74. ⎫
Monmouth . . . . 64. ⎬ Building
Nonsuch . . . . 64. ⎭
Burford . . . . 70. ⎫
Bienfaisant . . . . 64. ⎬ Repairing in Docks
Belle Isle . . . . 64. ⎭
Southampton . . . 32. Repairing on a Slip.

At Deptford

Grafton . . . . 74. ⎫
Cumberland . . . . 74. ⎬ Building
Culloden . . . . 74. ⎭

Richmond .   .   .   . 32. Repairing in a Dock
Royal Charlotte Yacht .   .   Repairing on a Slip.

At Woolwich

Bedford .   .   .   . 74.⎫
Defiance .   .   .   . 64. ⎬Building
Ruby .   .   .   .   . 64.⎭
Lark .   .   .   .   . 32.⎫
Ferret .   .   .   Sloop⎬Repairing in Docks

In 1771.

The Number of Men belonging to
     Chatham Dock Yard .   .   .   . 1603.
     exclusive of the Ordinary .   .   . 366.

The Number of Men belonging to
     Sheerness Dock Yard .   .   .   . 456.
     exclusive of the Ordinary .   .   . 216.

The Number of Men belonging to
     Portsmouth Dock Yard⎫
     including the Ordinary ⎬   .   .   . 2,709.

The Number of Men belonging to
     Plymouth Dock Yard ⎫
     including the Ordinary⎬   .   .   . 2,313.

The Number of Men belonging to
     Deptford Dock Yard   ⎫
     including the Ordinary ⎬ .   .   . 1,066.

The Number of Men belonging to
     Woolwich Dock Yard ⎫
     including the Ordinary ⎬ .   .   . 840.

No. 980—*The King to Lord North.*

Printed. Donne I. 76.

[Nash was the Lord Mayor elect. The poll was for the shrievalty of the
city of London, which was greatly coveted by Wilkes.]

LORD NORTH—I sincerely rejoice at the prospect of Mr
Nash's Success ; if the same zeal is shewn the rest of the Poll ;

will greatly tend to restore the tranquility of this greatest Trading City in the World ; but if riot is to continue must soon become despicable

RICHMOND LODGE
Sept. 30*th*. 1771
$\frac{m}{30}$. p^t 4 PM.

No. 981—*The King to Lord North.*

Printed. Donne I. 77.

RICHMOND LODGE
October 1*st* 1771. $\frac{m}{38}$ p^t 9. P.M.

LORD NORTH—I am much pleased at Your attention in transmitting the prosperous situation of Affairs in the City ; I wish Nash and Halifax had joined from the first as it would have prevented any of the factions being returned this Year to the Court of Aldermen and would have been the fullest disavowal of the Strange conduct held of late by the Livery.

No. 982—*Lord Rochford to the King.*

Lord Rochford received last night the inclosed dispatch by a messenger from paris and has the honor to submit it to your majesty as a first thought, whether it would not be proper for him, to make known to the Duke D'aiguillon, who seems hurt at the Idea of our desiring to have Mr de Guignes here, that we have not the least predilection for that minister, but that all we desired was not to have mr de Breteuil, if your majesty approves of this Idea, it shall be conveyed privately to paris when the messenger returns.

BERKLEY SQUARE *oct* 2*d* 1771 $\frac{m}{50}$ *past* 7 A.M.

On the back the King has scribbled some calculations of expenses for building.

No. 983—*The Hanoverian Finance Minister to the King.*

ALLERGNÄDIGSTER CÖNIG, CHURFÜRST UND HERR—nach-
folget mit dem heute abzugehenden relationen, der Etat von
der Closter (?) und Universität Casse, so nach Eure Majestät
mir ehemals ertheilten gnädigsten Anweisung über das Cassen-
wesen, in Tabellen gefasst ist und da aus den Einkünften des
? Pädagogen noch etwas jährig übrigbleibet, so habe ich
allerunterthänigst dafür gehalten, dass mit Eurer Majestät
gnädigsten Genehmigung, davon dreihundertst jährlich,
Aushülfen für die Universität Goettingen angewandt werden
können, worüber gleichfalls die jetzige allerunterthänigste
relation angeht. und beharre ich in tiefster Unterwürfigkeit und
in Hannover, den 5ten October 1771.

(Signed) *illegible.*

No. 984—*The King to Field Marshal Wangenheim* (?).

RICHMOND *d.* 8*ten Oct.* 1771.

MEIN FELDT MARSCHAL—Ich habe nicht wollen Eurer beiden
Memoriale der Lieutenants von der Garde die vor den jetzigen
Tit. Captain Lieutenant von Hacke stunden durch einen Rescript
zu accusiren, weil darin gesetzet war dass grosse vergehen welches
diese Lieutenants im ersten Feuer gewagt zu refusiren ihre
gehörige Dienste zu leisten ; aber weil Ihr es dieselben öffentlich
vergeben, auch versprochen die Memorials hierüber zu senden
hofte ich dass bey Euch kein zorn überblieb, den neuerlichen
vorschlag vom Lieutenant von Ledebar zum Capitain Lieutenant
in der Garde, scheinet zu zeigen dass dieses noch nicht vergessen
ist ; ich recommandir aufs ernstlichste, diese junge Leute wieder
freundschaftlich anzusehen, und auch zu denken wenn es nicht
möglich ist sie wieder so zu ermuntern dass die einigkeit beim
Regiment erhalten werden welches zum Dienste höchstnötig ist.
Ich kenne Euren guten Hertzen und habe desswegen so offen-
hertzig geschrieben.

Draft.

No. 985—*The King to* (?).

RICHMOND *d.* 8ten *Oct.*
1771.

MEIN GEHEIMTER RATH UND CAMMER PRESIDENT—Ich habe
Euren Brief vom 10ten Sept. richtig erhalten, aber nicht können
viele Plätze lesen ; vom Zustande des Osnabrückschen bin ich
sehr zufrieden, und von die [*sic*] angedachte Pachtung des
abgedrockenten Landes ins Diepholzscher. Der schlechte
Zustand der Unterthan durch die schlechte Witterung muss
bestmöglichst geholfen werden. Ich bin sehr verwundert von
Euren vorschlag den Gothaischen Cammer Junker von Lenthe
zum Cammer Rath weil Ihr auch alle gelegenheit geäussert
keinen jungen menschen bey diesem Collegio einzuziehen ; seine
Jugend würde genug sein mich es abschlagen zu machen, aber
dass er nicht die gehörige Studia hat ist unverantwortlich ; ich
bin Eurer bester Freund und darum wünsche dass dieses unbe-
kannt bliebe indem würde sehen wie unschicklich dieser vorschlag
ist, und würde Euch beschuldigen vor verwandte zu sorgen
anstatt zu denken an was meinem Dienste gemäss ist [*sic*].

[*Unfinished Draft.*]

No. 986—*Observation on the Reports and Minutes of M*^{r}——

   M :—— [*by Captain Guy Carleton.*]

[22 *October*, 1771.]

[Captain Guy Carleton is the future Commander-in-Chief in Canada,
later Lord Dorchester.]

These reports point out a scheme for the attack of Portsmouth
Dock-yard by a Coup-de-main, for this purpose a body of troops
is to land on the Coast of Sussex or Hampshire : The minutes
contain his thoughts for the defence of the same : And tho' upon
the whole, his notions appear to me as intelligent as can be
expected from most Officers of his service and rank in the Army,
yet I think they fall short of that experience and ripeness of

Judgement, necessary for such critical operations : the defence
is the most deficient of the two.

To give an attack of this sort a probability of success, Secrecy
and Dispatch are essentially requisite, I will therefore for the
present suppose a rapidity in the Enimy's motions never to be
exceeded in practice ; let His transports, unexpected, with ten
thousand men appear off Selsea harbour, which, as I shall shew
hereafter, is so near St Helens as an Officer who knows the
Country will venture to approach : The alarm then must be
given by this numerous fleet, the people will naturally fly, and a
few officers who may preserve their senses amidst the first panic
terrors, should conduct every man able to carry arms, directly
to Portsmouth, where I presume Arms, amunition and Intrenching tools may be found in great abundance. I will suppose the
Enemy's motions so rapid that the Officer who commands at
Portsmouth has not assembled numbers sufficient to attempt the
defence of the lines at Portsea bridge, without imminent danger
of being forced, and cut off from the town and dock-yard ; for
unless this be his situation, not to attempt the defence of the
whole Island, would be an unpardonable Error ; I will further
suppose he has not time to cover the Dock-yard wall by an
intrenched Camp ; His first care then should be, to distribute the
people able to carry arms, among the troops or companies He
may find under his command ; to station every One at the post
he is to defend ; to seize and fortify the Chapel, and other strong
houses a little before the Dock-yard-wall ; all other houses within
a thousand yards should be leveled to the ground, and every thing
combustible destroyed ; proper Crews appointed to patrole and
prevent fire within the Dock-yard and Artillery and Store-yard ;
others to erect Stages or Galleries for the musketry to fire over
the top of the wall, and thro loop-holes six feet from the ground ;
Loop-holes should also be pierced a foot above the pavement,
and a slight trench made within, that the troops may more
conveniently fire thro' : that part of the town which flanks these
walls and houses on the right, should be crowded with Cannon ;
two hulks drawn up the Creeks, to flank them on the left, well
stored with amunition, especially grape-shott. Let the Enemy
who appeared off Selsea escape all the dangers of that situation,
and the difficulties of the port, let Him land all his troops safe,
the same day, and march them five and twenty miles, thro an

unknown and difficult country, and arrive within sight of the
Dock-yard the second ; He ought to find this object of his
expedition secured as above ; an attack by a Coup-de-main
could then, only be attended with destruction and defeat, no
officer in his senses would attempt it in that state of defence.
The first great point is to acquire numbers, for without hands
no great work can be speedily performed, the Dragoons therefore,
who may be quartered near those parts, should compel all the
men to go to Portsmouth, and to intimidate by violence, if nothing
less can avail.   The second, no less essential to the preservation
of that great magazine, is, that the Commander be an officer of
knowledge and experience ; in himself determined and calm,
who by his own example, and by clear and judicious orders, shall
quickly draw the mob from their distracted state, into good order
and confidence ; for should He, who must direct all, be infected
by the terrors and confusion of the multitude, these great deposits
of Naval and Artillery stores may be lost, and should the latter
furnish where withal, and the Enimy procure subsistance for his
troops, the Town itself may be carried in eight, or ten days ;
tis a mistake to fancy ten thousand men, cannot preserve the
town and Island, and render the port, at least useless to us,
unless they are masters of the Sea ; in that situation they might
sooner be reduced by famine, than force.

The mouth of Chichester harbour is within three leagues of
St. Helens, and within sight of the Kings Ships at Spithead ;
besides, it is a tide harbour, to be entered only when the water is
high ; a fleet necessary to transport ten thousand men could not
expect to get all in the first, nor the second tide, the remainder
must lye off at the mercy of the Ships of War, one of these that
could get off the harbour's mouth might prevent their entrance
and defeat the expedition ; the harbour itself, when over the
bar, is very inconvenient for many ships, the greatest part must
be left on the mud by the ebb, before they could get up to the
Emsworth ; the landing tedious for the troops ; so that should
they imprudently push for this place, and succeed beyond
imagination, the delay must be greater than I have supposed
above.

Hayling bay is nearer still to St. Helens, the troops might
here get ashore with more ease, but, the Ships of War out of the
way, 'tis a very improper place for offensive measures, a few

peasants the first ebb might render the only road to the main impassible, a few troops might confine them there a considerable time, perhaps oblige them to return to their Ships.

Thorney island has united the difficulties of both, they are proper situations for a retreat, from the land forces.

Selsea also is an improper place to land, but I had a desire to bring them as near as might be with common sense, the more clearly to prove, that nothing less than the folly of the Officer who commands can draw on us that great misfortune ; not but I think, that, even in profound peace, some attention should be paid, in the distribution of the troops, to that great place of Arms ; and the Officers, who command corps within reach of it, or near the coast, instructed how to act in such situations, and both they and their officers should acquire a knowledge of the country, and report in writing what might be done in different cases, was this only to instruct them in their profession and Duty at large, and that the abilities of every one might be well known.

Should the Enemy bring Cannon, nothing less than an intrenched camp can cover the Dock-yard ; unless the Covert-way of the works proposed, with its Lunetts be finished, and I should think a redoubt in the mud on the left necessary ; for the hulks become untenable, when batteries are erected against them. Operations with cannon draw more into length and afford opportunities to distress an Enemy in his provisions, should He appear in this shape, all that might subsist His troops within, or near the island must be removed or destroyed, and all that may afford them cover or fuel, should be set in flames ; in either case all horses, and every sort of live cattle should be drove off, all bridges on, or near his road broken down, and if time will permit, many rows of wells or pitts, five or six feet deep should be sunk in the Creek before the lines, these will retain the water on the Ebb : I must suppose we cannot leave an Enimy, in the lines or open batteries, Cannon and stores to attack ourselves.

The difficult passes mentioned in the Report and minutes are tollerably accurate, but tis far from probable, even was the country more difficult, that any considerable number of troops could be collected, so as effectually to check His motions ; notwithstanding, whatever they may be, they should diligently attend Him night and day ; and, to gain time, They should put on an Appearance of acting offensively, while they cautiously avoid any thing more serious than a Skirmish, unless with great advantages indeed, and almost a certainty of success, for to gain time is certain Victory.

I have confined my observations to the main object of Mr. M: s report and minutes ; the project, just hinted, of three different descents, cannot have in view a flying expedition only ; it indicates a design to fix the Seat of war in this country : to say anything useful on this important matter requires reflections of a higher, and more extensive nature.   G. C.

Endorsed, Rec^d. 22 October, 1771.

No. 987—*The King to Lord North.*

LORD NORTH—I have this instant received Your note wherein You mention having a matter of importance which ought to be immediately communicated to Me ; if it is not inconvenient to You I should be glad You would come here directly, as the expression makes me anxious to be acquainted with the contents You are possessed of.

RICHMOND LODGE

Novr. 4th. 1771. $\frac{m}{13}$ p^t 6. PM.

No. 988—*The Hanoverian Finance Minister* (?) *to the King.*

HANNOVER, *den* 5ten *November* 1771.

ALLER durchlauchtigster Grossmächtigster König, ALLER-GNÄDIGSTER KÖNIG, CHURFÜRST UND HERR—Nach Eurer Majestät höchstem Befehl werde ich nunmehr morgen zu der Besprechung nach dem Harz [?] und zu den Landesgerichten in den Goettingschen und Grubenhagischen abreisen.   Mir geht [?] sehr nahe, dass hinselbst die Geld-bedürfnisse zu dem erforderlichen Korn Ankauf veranlasst zu versuchen, Geld zu 4 pro cento aufzunehmen, welches ich gerne abzuwenden gesucht und einige andere Mittel vorgeschlagen habe ; die meisten sind aber dagegen gewesen und musste ich sehen, dassolches nicht von den allernachtheiligsten Folgen für Eure Majestät sein möge. Da ich selbst glaube, dass die Unterthanen sich an den meisten Orten, wo die Uebungs [. . . ?] nicht gewesen sind, eben so gut durch einen sorgfältigen Haushalt und wenn verreist, durch die Dienste guter Zufuhr bethätigen werden, sich aber so gut helfen können, als durch die Hülfe von der Cammer. Inzwischen gönne ich meinem Vaterlande und Eurer Majestät alles guthe ; nur drückt mich, dass die schlimme Veränderung des Zinsfusses 3 zu 4 pro cento den Kredit der Cammer nicht verbessern sondern verschlimmern werde, und dass zu besorgen sei, dass 700/m die bereits zu 3 pro cento reduciert sind, gleichfalls werden zu 4 pro cento hinauf gebracht werden, worüber ich gerne alles mögliche für Eure Majestät Interesse anwenden werde, welches ich jedoch bei meinem geringen Vertrauen hinselbst durch nichts zu erhalten weiss als durch Eure Majestät gnädigste Gesinnung zu welcher ich mich einzig und allein in tiefster Unterwürfigkeit überlasse und in aller Demuth liefere,

Eurer Majestät allerunterthänigster und gehorsamster Knecht

(Signed) [(?) *illegible.*]

Die Route von meiner
Reise geht allerun-
thänigst hierbei.

REISE ROUTE.

WochenTage	Datum	Meilen	
November.			
Mittwoch den	6	4	Brügen
Donnerstag	7	7	Cinbeck, Northeim, Osterrode
Freitag	8	,,	Land Gericht darselbst auch über Westerhoffe
Sonnabend	9	2	Nach Clausthal
Sontag	10	,,	Ruhetag zum Clausthal
Montag	11	,,	
Dienstag	12	,,	
Mittwoch	13	,,	Fünf Tage zur Berg Rechnung
Donnerstag	14	,,	
Frietag	15	,,	
Sonnabend	16	3	Nach Elbingerode

Sontag	17	3	Ruhetag
Montag	18	,,	Landgericht Elbingerode
Dienstag	19	4	Nach Schartzfels

WochenTage	Datum	Meilen	
November			
Mittwoch	20	1	Landgericht darselbst, Abends nach Hertzberg
Donnerstag	21	,,	Landgericht darselbst
Freitag	22	1	Nach Caltenberg Landgericht darselbst auch über Brunstein
Sonnabend	23	1	Nach Wibbrechthausen
Sontag	24	,,	Ruhetag darselbst
Montag	25	1½	Nach Harste
Dienstag	26	1	Landgericht darselbst und nach Goettingen
Mittwoch	27		Stille Lager zu Goettingen
Donnerstag	28	1	Nach Niedeck Landgericht darselbst auch über Rudolfshausen
Freytag	29	1	Nach Friedland Landgericht auch über Brackenburg und Rheinhausen
Sonnabend	30	2	Nach Münden.

December.			
Sontag	1		Ruhetag
Montag	2		Landgericht zu Münden
Dienstag	3	3	Nach Uslar
Mittwoch	4		Landgericht zu Uslar auch über Nienover und Lauenhoerde
Donnerstag	5	2	Nach Möhringen
Freytag	6		Landgericht zu Möhringen auch über Hardeysen Abends nach Rothenkirchen 1 Meil
Sonnabend	7		Landgericht zu Rothenkirchen auch über Saltzderhelden
Sontag	8	1½	Ruhetag Abends nach Ehrichsburg
Montag	9		Landgericht zu Ehrichsburg
Dienstag	10		Nach Hannover Gmünd.

No. 989—*The King to the Master of the Horse, Hanover.*

11 *Nov.* 1771.

MON GRAND ECUYER ET CHAMBELLON—Je prend ma plume pour Vous temoigner mon contentement de la manière que Vous Vous êtes aquités de mes ordres en conduisant ma Soeur La Reine de Danemark par Mes Etats : en meme tems Je ne veut pas ometre de Vous annoncer que J'entend de toute part un si grand Eloge de mes Atellages de Cheveaux Noirs que dans une Couple d'années je propose de faire amener d'Hannovre deux Attellages de cette couleur, ainsi Vous ne pouver pas trop accroitre cette race, au contraire Je n'aime pas les Chevaux de Poille de Souris ainsi j'aimerai de les changer l'attellage de cette couleur a Hannovre pour un autre de Noir   G.R.

No. 990—*Memorandum by Captain Guy Carleton.*

Secret.

[15 *November*, 1771.]

The probability of an intended invasion, its practicableness, the dangers that must ensue, the means of guarding against them.

The only difficulty France has to fear, in carrying a plan of invasion into execution, arises from our superior fleet ; could her transport pass the seas unmolested, our land forces, were they much more numerous than at present, could not guard our extensive coasts, nor prevent an enimy's getting ashore : great as the obstruction of our navy may be, tis more than probable france will attempt to invade this country the opening of the next war, as the least difficult plan for weakening that power, so formidable to her in the last ; by experience she must now feel, what good sense ought to have dictated, that, our Austrian alliance disolved, and the armies and arcenals of that, and of every other great power removed to a considerable distance, from her frontiers, when she no longer has any thing to fear for her own country, the most judicious way of carrying on a war with Great Britain, is to establish the seat of war in England.

With her numerous land forces, she must for ever [go] on every distant war, offensive or defensive, across long seas, while we are masters of those seas, with such disadvantages as in the end will prove ruinous to her commerce, and, perhaps, strip her of all her settlements. None of her colonies are of sufficient strength to defend themselves, but require her powerful assistance ; she cannot strongly reinforce them all on an appearance of war ; a bad climate must remain their chief defence against a well calculated expedition. Should she attempt any thing more than to spread an alarm and sweep off some plunder, a considerable force must be sent out, these must be kept together and protected by ships of war ; should they be fortunate, and escape our Squadrons, they may overrun some of our colonies, but they cannot long possess them, nor can the blow prove very hurtful to us : I except the East Indies, which is under peculiar circumstances, and Canada, where the natives are strong, and entirely in the french interest. Should france get out force to conquer the first, the immediate loss to us, and profits to her would be very considerable ; an expedition to dispossess her would be attended with great expence, the immence distance will expose the forces to sickness and other casualties not uncommon to such armaments, the unavoidable delay must give the enimy time to fortify himself, to gain the natives, and encrease his strength by their assistance, possession of the Isles of Bourbon lessen all those difficulties to france. The regaining Canada would, tho not lucrative, prove very advantageous to her ; she will thereby instantly acquire so strong a footing on the continent of N: America, that it would cost much treasure, and loss of time to drive her out ; if left neglected, their own natural strength, envigorated by the french form of government, together with their influence over the savages, would again enable them to carry the war into our colonies, if they should not find out a new system of politicks more pernicious to Great Britain. These are the only distant conquests she can expect to maintain any considerable time, after she is in possession ; the rest are scarcely worth the expence and hazards of an expedition, under so many disadvantages ; for these reasons I think it more than probable, that whatever attempts france may make to alarm and divert our force, her chief object will be to establish the seat of war in England ; where with less difficulty and more expedition, she may transport her land forces, with all necessary supplies, in great numbers, where she strikes the first blow at the root of all our power, by which the whole Empire may at once become enervated, and incapable of succouring its different parts.

The plan for carrying their schemes into execution, I should apprehend to be as follows ; on the appearance of a war, a large body of troops will march to the coasts of the channel and bay of Biscay, the latter attended by ships of war for distant expeditions ; Squadrons of the Kings ships will be sent to observe them : I suppose enough remain to be masters of the channel, for should france with her allies be able to dispute this sea, the difficulty of crossing lessens, or entirely disappears : but whatever superiority we may have, winds arise in the winter which force our ships to seek shelter at home, their retreat is to Plymouth, Portsmouth, and the Downs ; a South East wind, if I have been well informed, will confine our ships in their retreats, at the same time will carry the french transports in twelve hours to the coast of Kent and Sussex, from all their ports between Dunkirk and Cherbourg both included : from Arundel to Hythe, near eighty miles in length, the coast is clear of every thing dangerous to navigation, with very small exceptions ; where the chalk-cliffs stand close to the sea they are seen at a great distance, by steering a little to the East or West they approach a bold shore, and a commodious beach for landing troops.   Forty thousand old troops may be appointed for this service, divided into five seperate Corps, of eight thousand each ; to assemble after their landing at Hythe, Rye, Brighthelmstone, Shoreham and Arundel ; the transports will have orders to put the troops a shore, as near their respective places of rendivous, as the winds will permit, without loosing time by too great precision : the field artillery will sail with the troops, but the battering train with the intrenching tools will be landed at Hythe, and Arundel. The success of this first attempt, together with the strength and situation of our forces, must determine the Enimy's further conduct : should his passage prove successful, and we have no considerable force to check his progress, the Hythe division will march to Maidstone, to Chatham, attack those lines, and then Sherness ; by which every thing to the East of the Medway is cut off, he becomes master of a fertile country for the subsistance of his troops, and of Ports, the most contiguous to france, equally convenient for receiving succors, or for a retreat. The Arundel corps will march to attack Portsmouth. The remaining divisions of Rye, Brighthelmstone, and Shoreham will march in two days to Tunbridge, to E: Grinsted, and to Gilford: if the two former divisions require no assistance, these will march in two more, that from Gilford to the three bridges of Kingston, Kew, and Putney; that from E: Grinsted to the three bridges of Westminster, Black-friars, and London; they will assume the appearance of intending to force the passage, when in reallity they only mean to cover the operations of the Tunbridge Corps, which will march at the same time to Southwark, endeavour to set in flames all ships below bridge, destroy all the timber yards, with all naval and artillery stores down to Deptford, to Woolwich, and as low as the Medway. Purfleet may be the enterprize of a Partizan. When the business near the Borough is secured, the divisions opposite the bridges, if necessary, may fall back to Petersfield, and cover the siege of Portsmouth : The Enimys situation will then stand thus, fourteen thousand men behind the Medway, two thousand at Rye; this town they will fortify and make a place of Arms : eight thousand for the siege of Portsmouth, fourteen thousand the covering army; two thousand at Arundel, as guard for the artillery stores, and to forward them to the siege : when they are masters of the lines of Portsea bridge, fourteen thousand will be sufficient to defend these lines, and carry on the siege, provided they have laid in stores enough and provisions for the troops; the remaining ten thousand will be at liberty to co-operate with the Medway army.

The foregoing plan contains nothing more difficult nor dangerous than has often been undertaken with judgement, and executed with success; I have pointed out the evils we are exposed to, that a remidy more easily may be procured. The passage of the Channel is not impossible to the french; we have no fortified towns in his way; we have no army, or one so small little can be expected from it, yet Chatham, Woolwich, Deptford, London are but four days march from the Coast, Portsmouth and Plymouth are close upon it : as the law now stands, our only resource is in the Militia, but whatever Gentlemen may say in the heat of debate, I cannot persuade myself there is one, who, in his cool senses, would not shrink at the Idea, that the fate of this Country was to be decided in a battle, on one side the old troops of france, on the other an army called together in haste, composed chiefly of militia. To render our danger still more evident, we have but to muster all the forces in great Britain, and scetch out a general disposition for them : without attempting great accuracy, our whole force in Regular troops, after deducting the necessary guard, for the safety of the Royal family, will not I believe amount to ten thousand men rank and file, beside the artillery (the Marines I suppose with the fleet) of those ten thousand, two thousand may be Cavalry : the Militia, supposing all embodied agreable to those laws, under thirty one thousand, total under forty one thousand, of which three fourths are Militia. Scotland requires some of those troops, so will the North of England, ten thousand for these two corps, Plymouth six thousand, Portsmouth four thousand, Chatham one thousand ; there remains for the Main army, under twenty thousand men, of which five thousand may be regulars, without any further resource in case of misfortune, except what depends on the whim, and caprice of a mob ; it therefore seems to me indispensably necessary for our own safety, either that the regular troops be more numerous in time of peace, or that the King be empowered, in all imminent dangers of invasion, to draft the Militia, in order to augment His regular forces to such numbers, as may be judged requisite for the preservation of the State, further that each County be obliged to form Militia of a second class, equal in numbers to those of the first, and enrolled in the same manner, solely for the purpose of immediately compleating them, therefore they will neither require arms, cloathing, nor pay. these laws once in force, when the public safety is in danger, the army may immediately be augmented to seven, or eight hundred men a battallion, from that to twelve, or fourteen hundred men a Regim^t, divided into two Batt^{ns}, and so on ; these may be quickly formed by the Officers, who of course will be all at their posts, as it will be no longer necessary to disperse them about the country with parties, to beat up for voluntiers, when an Enimy is upon the coast. The Militia may then in greater numbers be thrown into the lines for the protection of the Dockyards, especially into those of Plymouth, which is at too great a distance to be combined with the operations near London and as more left to it self, requires a greater strength. After ye lines of Plymouth, Portsmouth, and Chatham, are sufficiently provided

for, and the troops appointed for the North of England, and for
Scotland ; while we remain uncertain of the Enimy's intentions,
I think the right of the Main army should encamp near Gilford,
the left near Maidstone, and the center in different camps on the
down above Dorken, Reygate, Godstone, and Riverhead, where
all the great roads from the coast between Portsmouth and Rye,
pass in their way to London. A flying camp should be formed
in Essex to protect the north side of the river, and a bridge of
boats thrown over for a more speedy communication of the
troops in Kent and Essex. The light infantry and some Dragoons
may be sent to the coast, but as an Enimy does not always act
as we think he ought, I should not advise the advancing the
main army too low down, before we are certain of His motions,
least by landing in an unexpected part, we become forced to
make a precipitate return, with loss of time, always precious on
such occasions. I would post the Militia chiefly behind the
intrenchments, as it cannot be expected from those troops, however brave they may be, that they should move in line, in
presence of an Enimy, with so much order, as those who have no
other profession. It may be worth observing, that as in peace
we preserve but the frame in which an Army is to be formed for
war, and that it is possible we may be much pressed for time, it
becomes necessary we should adopt that system of training,
which will most expeditiously perfect our recruits or drafts, in
their exercise and discipline ; and particularly that both Regulars
and Militia be made excellent marks men ; this is the most
difficult, the most essential part of exercise, without which all
infantry become nerveless, yet 'tis the most neglected by all the
Armies in Europe. The light Infantry should be very active
men, and practiced to move with great celerity ; they should be
trained up in the Partizan war, that of the Savages I think the
most formidable : they might also be taught to mix with the
Cavalry ; this country in general is so much enclosed, the latter
will seldom be able to approach an Enimy, without assistance
from the Infantry. After all, when we have formed and disciplined an Army, and selected our best troops to compose it, it
may not be a miss to consider, that the Enimy may and ought
to have the best troops of france to oppose us, without a recruit
or aukward man, that when we come to a decisive battle, France
hazards those troops, so does England, but England hazards

besides, her Empire of the Seas, and the desolation of her whole
Country ; common sense therefore requires we should not
precipitate an event, generally very uncertain, where we have so
much to loose, and the Enimy so much to gain : the plan of an
able Officer therefore should be to take such strong Encampments
as will not allow the Enimy to attack him without great disadvantages ; but he must also know how to change his position,
so as still to cover those important places, whatever movements
the Enimy may make to turn his camp ; and endeavour to ruin
him by degrees without risking the fate of this country on the
cast of one die for the hopes of gathering the brilliant splendors
of a great Victory, this caution should have no timidity, but be
the result of a strong judgement and firm mind, equally quallified
to descern when circumstances change and of assuming a different
conduct when it is required by good sense.　　GUY CARLETON.

Endorsed, Rec^d from Mr Carleton 15 Nov. 1771, 11 o'clock
A.M. J(ohn) R(obinson).

No. 991—*The King to Lord North.*

QUEENS HOUSE *Nov^r* 15th 1771.

$\frac{m}{46} p^t$ 7. PM.

LORD NORTH—I am desirous of seeing You this Evening.

No. 992—*M. Mühl to the King.*

A VIENNE. *ce* 6. *de Dec.* 1771.

SIRE—Je profite, Sire, de nouveau d'une occasion sure, pour
presenter à Votre Majeste plusieurs pieces, dont j'ai trouve moyen,
de me mettre en possession, et qui m'ont paru digne d'attention.

1º. L'instruction du nouvel exercice de Cavallerie, telle
qu'elle a eté donnée avant le camp de Münkendorff près de Cazem-
bourg.

2º. Un suplement contenant le detail de tous les manœuvres
y executés devant Leurs M^tes Imp^les, avec 37. plans y apartenant.

3º. Un cahier de remarques faites par le Marechal dans les

campemens, sur L'Infanterie, et nommément Les defauts, qu'il lui a trouves.

4º. Le detail de tous les depots militaires, contenant leurs noms, les Regimens respectif assignés sur chacun, et le repertoire de tout ce qui s'y trouvoit respectivement à la fin de l'année passée.

5º. Le tableau Special du Revenu d'Etat du Banat.

6º. La liste des magazin et depots de blé, erigés en Hongrie et Moravie pour l'Armée, et qui dans la derniere disette ont du faire les envois à la Boheme, Lesquels doivent etre remplacés a cette heure.

Je dois remarquer à cette occasion, que l'on a averé par les Regitres des Douanes, qu'il est sorti de la Hongrie dans l'année courante 3. Millions de boisseaux, et que cependant il est constaté dans les autres Provinces, qu'elles n'ont recu de ce Royaume que $\frac{1200}{m}$. Cest excedant exorbitant de $\frac{1800}{m}$ est allé probablement à l'etranger, et donne maintenant lieu à des recherches tres soigneuses et severe. Toutefois, outre les abus, qui peuvent s'y etre glissés, on ne peut ignorer, que le General Stahremberg a ouvertement fourni du blé de meme que des armes blanches aux Turcs, ainsi que le General Wallis a vendu 30. Canons aux Confederes.

Je suis avec un Zele, et un Respet des plus achévés, Sire, De Votre Majeste, le très humble, très obeissant, et très soumis,

MÜHL.

Je joins encore tres humblement

7º. Le tableau de la population, et des possessions dans Le Banat.

Enclosure.

HAUPT MAGAZINE.
    Temesvar
    Peterwardein
    Ofen
    Comorren

DEPOTS.
    Sanczowa an der Donau
    An der Donau zwichen Neusass u. Fusack

Zu einem Dorf Boukin an der Donau
Im Barzenher Comitat.
Effek
Carlstadt
Sihark an der Sau
Fraiha an der Sau
Brod an der Sau
Gradisca
Weissaburg Ofen
Neuerlich au Arad gegen den Banat u. zu Curhau

MAEHREN.
Iglau
Brünn
Olmütz.

No. 993—*The Rev. Mr. Farish to* (?).

Copy.

CARLISLE *December* 15*th* 1771.

DEAR SIR—You would see, in the papers, several Accounts of a travelling Moss amongst us ; and would naturally expect some Account from me of so extraordinary a phenomenon. This You should have had, if I could either have relied upon the Stories I heard of it, which I soon found I could not do ; or had had an Opportunity of seeing it sooner Myself. The Mischief it has done in Mr Graham's Estate is very considerable : it has laid waste not less, I suppose, than a thousand Acres of the finest Land in the Country ; but considered only as a natural Appearance, is neither without Example, nor difficult to account for.

Solway-Moss is situate upon the top of a pretty high Hill : what might pass, I suppose, for one at least in Surry, though not in Cumberland. It lies about a Mile N.W. of Longtown ; is between 2 and 3 Miles in length, and half as much in Breadth. The interior part of the Hill seems to have been Nothing, but a vast Collection of Mud, so much diluted with the Water of the Springs dispersed in several parts of it, as to have a considerable Degree of fluidity. It had always even in the driest Summers, so much of a Quagmire, that it was hardly safe for any thing heavier than a Sportsman and his Gun. In the time of Henry VIII. a considerable part of a Scotch Army under the

Command of Oliver Sinclair, perished in it : and I have heard, that the Skeleton of a Trooper and his Horse in compleat Armour, were found by some peat-diggers not many Years ago.

Hitherto the Shell of more Solid Earth in which this fluid Mass was inclosed had been sufficient to resist the pressure : but it's force with it's fluidity, having been considerably augmented by the late excessive rains, it forced a passage at the Eastern Extremity on which side it had probably been weakened by digging peats.

Having once made a Breach, it soon enlarged it, and poured a Deluge of Mud into a Valley, which runs along the bottom of the Hill. This Valley is near 200 Yards broad and near 40 deep. At the bottom of it ran a Brook, which being now choked, has formed a lake. The torrent of Mud having filled the Valley was now at liberty to spread over a fine plain, which extends near a Mile to the Banks of the Esk.

As this Calamity happened at Midnight, the people of the Villages on the plain, as You may imagine were thrown into great Consternation : nor could, till Day-light, conjecture what had happened. Some were alarmed by the uncommon Noise the torrent made in it's progress : others, not till it had entered their Houses ; nay some, I was assured not till they felt it in their Beds. No lives, however, were lost, I mean human lives : for a great many Cattle that were housed were suffocated. The Case of a Cow belonging to Mr Graham of the Lake deserves mention. She was the only one of 8. in the same Cow House, that was saved ; after having stood 60 Hours up to the Neck in Mud and Water. When She was taken out she had an Appetite for food ; but Water she would not taste nor even look at it without horror : She had almost the Symptoms of a real hydrophobia. I hear She is now reconciled to Water ; and is likely to recover.

The Villages which I have mentioned upon the plain, are not so large as Villages commonly are. They consist in General of one Farm House, and a few Cottages annexed to it. Of these Villages one or two have entirely disappeared : of Others only the Thatch is visible ; and all of them to the Number of 13 or 14. are rendered uninhabitable. The greatest part of the plain on which they stood, was laid out in fine Inclosures ; the Hedges of which though 8 or 9 feet high, are now totally invisible, except in those parts where the Innundation has but just reached.

In the mean time, the Moss itself, which was before a level plain, on the top of a Hill is now a Valley ; along the bottom of which runs, with considerable rapidity, a Stream of black Liquid peat Earth. The Surface of the Hill gradually subsides ; as the Mud which supported it, is discharged ; and appears all over broken into Fragments, which are in some places so irregularly thrown together, as to resemble an heap of ruins. Some of these Fragments falling into the Stream and floating down with it, are dispersed over the plain, which appears spotted with them, like the Skin of a Leopard : only that the Ground is black, and the Spots are brown ; the Heath and other Vegetables they produce, still remaining upon them.

The Innundation is still proceeding farther and farther, without any Signs of being exhausted ; and is now advanced almost to the Banks of the Esk. As this River runs with a rapid Current it is to be hoped, that it may carry off a great Quantity of the Mud : especially, if the Winter-rains should raise it so much, as to overflow it's Banks : but after all an immense Quantity must remain, which it will require Ages to remove.

No. 994—*The King to Lord North.*

QUEENS HOUSE *Dec^r* 29*^th* 1771.

$\frac{m}{8}$. *pt.* 9 PM.

LORD NORTH—A Messenger is just arrived from Lieutenant Colonel Blaquiere with a note He has received unsigned from the Duke d'Aiguillon, who seems much allarmed at the idea of a Fort erected by us on the River St. John in the Gulph of Darien ; I do not recollect that any such establishment has been directed from hence, so that I am at a loss to understand what he alludes to.

There is also arrived a Messenger from the Lord Lieutenant with the account that He has passed the Money Bill, that in consequence of it Mr Clements has pressed that a loan for 100,000£. may be immediately made ; that doubts having arisen whether this can properly be done untill the Second Money Bill is passed ; the Chancellor and Mr Malone Chairman of the Committee of Supply have given it as their opinions that it may be

done ; he has sent into the Country for those of the Prime
Serjeant, the Attorney and Sollicitor General which when received
he will also transmit, and wishes to have directions on the subject
from Hence ; He adds a Postscript that He Supposes the Money
Bill will not be decided upon here, till he sends the Report of the
three last mentioned Lawyers.

No. 995—*Lord North to the King.*

Lord North has received the honour of his Majesty's commands. He is pretty positive, that during the course of the last
four years, no settlement has been directed from hence, which
can possibly answer the description of that, which is mention'd
by the Duke d'Aiguillon : If there is any Fort building upon the
river St John, He imagines it must be the work of the settlers on
the Musquito Shore : He is the more confirm'd in this conjecture
by the situation of the River St John, which does not fall into the
bay we usually call the Gulf of Darien, but issues out of the Lake
of Nicaragua and holding an eastern course to the Sea forms the
southern boundary of the Musquito Shore : The Settlers there,
having establish'd themselves originally without the assistance,
concurrence, or even knowledge of Great Britain, and living
under no regular System of Government, have very little connexion or correspondence with Europe and may certainly make
new establishments in different parts of that country long before
we are inform'd of them. The cause of the present alarm is,
probably, some picket or blockhouse erected by the Musquito
settlers for their convenience or defence which has been magnified
into a Fort built at the expence of Great Britain. The English
settlements in those quarters are an old matter of complaint, but
they have now subsisted considerably above a hundred years,
and it is to be hoped that Spain will not chuse to pick a quarrel
with Great Britain upon that subject at this time of day. Lord
North believes that Mr Blaquiere may very safely be told, that
no orders are gone from hence to build any Fort on the River
St John, and that we are here totally unacquainted with the
subject of the Duke d'Aiguillon's alarm. Lord North will, with
his Majesty's permission, write to Lord Hillsborough to-morrow
to enquire whether he has, either from the Governor of Jamaica,

or from the Agent at the Musquito Shore, received any account of this transaction.

Lord North can have no doubt but that the opinion of the Ld Chancellor of Ireland and Mr Malone on the subject of the Irish Loan-bill is right, but, as the money-bill is return'd, the question seems of no great importance in the present moment, and the heavy arrears on the Civil Establishment of Ireland call loudly for the Loan.

DOWNING STREET. *Sunday night.* ½ p^t. 11. *Dec^r.* 29. 1771.

No. 996—*Stanier Porten* (?) *to the King.*

[Possibly a fragment.]

Porten was much embarassed when he first read Colonel Blaquiere's Letter, and much more when he could not immediately obey Your Majesty's Orders. he could not meet with any one last night to give them any lights, but it is his first care this morning to procure some Informations, that he may have the Honour of sending them to Your Majesty.

ST JAMES'S PLACE

30 *Dec^r* 1771 $\frac{m}{30}$ *past* 8. AM.

No. 997—(?) *to the King.*

It does not appear that Your Majesty's Subjects have had any Settlement in the Gulph of Darien except at Caledonia Point, which has been abandoned by them for above half a Century.

Captain Spier reports that the English sometimes trade as far southward as Carpenter's River about seventy miles South of St John's River, but have no Settlement there, and that their most southern Settlement on the Mosquito shoar is at Bluefield's River about one hundred miles to the North of St John's River. he adds, that there are many English dispersed about on the Mosquito Coast but scarce any in the Inland parts ; that on the River St John there is only one Fort belonging to the Spaniards called Fort St John at the Entrance into the Lake of Nicaragua,

but he believes the Mosquito Indians never had any kind of Fort
on their side the River St John, nor any Canon.

St James's
30 *Dec^r* 1771.

No. 998—*The King to Lord North.*

Printed.   Donne I. 78.

Queens House *Jan.* 2^d 1772.

$$\frac{m}{10} \; p^t \; 10. \text{ a.m.}$$

Lord North—I return the letters You left with Me yesterday;
Sir Jeffry Amherst's is coutched in civil terms, but not without
that commendation of his own Services, which though very great
would not be lessened if he left the appreciating them to others ;
Lieut: General Conway having very handsomely quited the
Seals and having at that time had hopes of the Blues, cannot be
looked upon as forgetting Sir Jeffry ; the third Regiment of
Guards has ever been held by a Scotch Man, therefore this
instance also is without foundation.

Mr. Allen's is only an additional proof of that aversion to
English Government and of that avowed profligacy that the
Gentlemen of that Country seem to despise masking with the
name of conscience, and must sooner or later oblige this Country
Seriously to consider whether the uniting it to this Crown would
not be the only means of making both Islands flourish.   Lord
Townshend's idea of a pension to Lord Shannon when the Session
is over, seems absurd, to let him do all the mischief He can whilst
his assistance could be of use, and then reward him when his
good wishes can avail nothing ; but if He would during the
Sessions come forward that might be worth admitting, provided
the Lord Lieutenant would cut off other Pensions to satisfy his
demand, for additional pensions must not be granted.

The enclosed is the memorial I mentioned yesterday if it can
be of any use to Your family I shall rejoice at it, if not I desire it
may be looked on as my desire of being of service to them.

No. 999—*Lord North to the King.*

Lord North has received his Majesty's commands with the deepest sentiments of gratitude for his Majesty's goodness and kind intentions to him and his family. He will have the honour of paying his respects to his Majesty tomorrow after the Lévee. In the mean while, He is desired by Lord Suffolk, who is so ill by the gout in his hand that he cannot write, to learn whether it will be agreable to his Majesty that Mr. Harris should kiss his Majesty's hand tomorrow upon his appointment to the Envoyship at Berlin

DOWNING STREET. *Jan.* 2. 1772.

No. 1000—*The King to Lord North.*

Printed. Donne I. 80.

QUEENS HOUSE *Jan.* 2^d 1772.

$\frac{m}{40}$ p^t 6. PM.

LORD NORTH—When I wrote to You this morning I omitted taking notice of Lord Bellamont's declaration that Lieutenant Colonel Luttrel intends to come and resign his Seat for Middlesex; I had heard a week ago a report of it, but thought it was too absurd to give any credit to it ; I do not yet see how he can affect it ; but would insinuate whether Lord Townshend might not receive a private intimation from You not to give him leave to quit his Attendance in Ireland, which will at least postpone what might occasion some noise.

No. 1001—*The King to Lord North.*

Printed. Donne I. 80.

LORD NORTH—My Sister has apprized Me that the Duke of Brunswick has ordered Mr Teronce [de Feronce] to apply to You concerning some of his demands relative to the Last War, which Major Lutterloh has persuaded the Duke You are willing this

Session of Parliament to bring again on the Carpet ; I assured Her it was impossible to enter again into an examination of those affairs ; She said Teronce was of that opinion, and therefore meant to write to You tomorrow hoping to obtain his answer on paper, which he would transmit to Brunswick ; if You write that will end the business, if You give it him verbally he will be ordered to remain here, and will torment You the whole Winter.

QUEENS HOUSE *Jan* 4*th* 1772.

$\frac{m}{8}$ *p*^t 5 PM.

No. 1002—*The King to Lord North.*

Printed. Donne I. 81.

QUEENS HOUSE *Jan.* 6*th* 1772.

$\frac{m}{15}$. *p*^t 5. PM.

LORD NORTH—The sketch of the Speech meets with my approbation, when the Sentences are a little more rounded and that the Foreign Article is added, I doubt not but it will make a very good one.

No. 1003—*The King to Lord North.*

Printed. Donne I. 82.

LORD NORTH—I hope Your cold is better and Should be glad if You could come here, that I may have some conversation with You on the publications against both Houses of Parliament.

QUEENS HOUSE
Jany 25*th* 1772.

$\frac{m}{2}$. *p*^t one PM.

No. 1004—*The King to Lord North.*

Printed. Donne I. 83.

LORD NORTH—There cannot be a greater proof that the Opposition is against Men not Measures than that Sir Charles

Saunders, and Adm. Keppel who have at all times cried out for an Additional Number of Seamen should now it is proposed object to it, which will meet with no kind of approbation from any Quarter and have no other effect but detaining You very uselessly for four Hours.

Jany 29th 1772.

$\frac{m}{14}$ *p^t* 7. PM.

No. 1005—*The King to Lord North.*

[? *Feb.* 1772.]

LORD NORTH—The opening of this Session is very honourable and I trust provided no unexpected fatallity arises that it will prove an easy one, and will enable Administration to propose right measures, and not postpone any from apprehension of difficulties. The Message concerning Marriages in my family ought now to be drawn up; I trust You have prepared an Answer to the Address.

No. 1006—*The King to Lord North.*

Printed. Donne I. 85.

QUEENS HOUSE *Feby 4th* 1772.

$\frac{m}{50}$ *p^t* 8 PM.

LORD NORTH—I am much pleased with the draught of the Message, and with that of the Bill for preventing Marriages in the Royal Family without the previous consent of the Crown, except the Issue of Princesses that have or may be married into Foreign Families ; but am much of opinion that the Addresses of Thanks from the two Houses of Parliament should be Seperate and brought by the usual Messengers, as this though a salutary Measure, is of utility to the Dignity of My Family and not merely of public Advantage, which are the occasions that require the most Solemn Mode of expressing gratitude to the Throne.

No. 1007—*The King to Lord North.*

Printed. Donne I. 86.

QUEENS HOUSE *Feb^y* 5*th* 1772.

$\frac{m}{8}$ *p^t* 5. P.M.

LORD NORTH—In mentioning to the two Secretaries of State that it might be necessary to alter an expression in the Bill for rendering the Consent of the Crown necessary previous to the Solemnization of any Marriage in the Royal Family; this occasioned some conversation on the Bill, which gave rise to the idea that to render the Bill perfect it would be right to add that in case the King should be a Minor then the Regent with the Advice of the Council should have this right of giving consent, otherways a period might happen when the Children of the Crown could as in a late instance enter into improper Alliances. I therefore desire You will have this addition made to the Bill in Words agreable to the Regency Act.

No. 1008—" *Anecdotes of the Court of France by Mr. Ainslie.* "

[Copy in the King's handwriting.]

PARIS *Jan.* 3*d* 1772.

The report of the King's intending to Marry the Princess of Lamballe is without foundation; this was propagated by the Orleans Family, and believed from the assiduity of that Princess's attendance of late at Court, where She passes much of Her time with the Dauphiness and the Countess of Provence.

What encouraged the Orleans family to spread this report was, to hurt the credit of Me du Barry and of the present Ministry, and to persuade the Publick, that the three Young Princes are incapacitated from begetting Children from a natural defect, and that the King marries merely on that Account.

It is certain neither the Dauphin nor the Comte de Provence have consummated their Marriage, yet there is no outward symptoms of incapacity in either of them. The King in speaking about a month ago in Me du Barry's Appartment said; " the

Dauphin is well made and perfectly well formed (*parfaitement bien conformé*) yet has hitherto shewn no desire for Women, nay rather seems to loath them ; as for the Comte de Provence he has both inclination and warmth of constitution, his Youth only prevents him from indulging them. I hope a little time will bring these backward Plants to Perfection."

The disputes among the Ministers run higher than ever, the Chancellor lately looked upon as lost from the junction of all the other Counsellors with the D. d'Aiguillon, not only stands his ground but it is thought the Duke's interest is on the decline ; these two Men are incompatible, and it is generally believed the Duke will be either out of the Ministry by July next, or at least in a more inferiour Department.

Me du Barry is more powerful than ever, Her system seems to be the keeping all the Ministers dependant upon Her.

The Dutchess of Brancas has retired from Court on a dispute of etiquette with the Comte de Provence ; the Dutchess of Valentinois has succeeded as Dame d'honneur ; who is succeeded by the Dutchess of St. Mégrin as Dame d'Atour.

The Marquis de Marigny brother to the late Marquise de Pompadour, is to loose the post of Intendant des Batiments, because not in favour with the present favourite, and it is thought du Barry will succeed him.

The proposed Marriage of the Viscount du Barry (nephew to the Comtesse) with Mlle de Bethune Daughter of the Marquis de Bethune a Lieutenant General occasions a bustle at Court ; the Lady and the rest of Her family are much against the Match, but the Father's ambition makes him listen to the idea. He demands to be made a Mareshal of France, with the reversion of Colonel General de la Cavallerie (which He now enjoys) for his Son a Child of twelve Years of Age, and the Place of premier Ecuyer (formerly held by Mr de Beringham) for his future Son in Law. The Marquis de Castries, Mestre de Camp General, and the Comte de Beuvron Harcourt Commissaire General de la Cavallerie, both threaten to resign if a Child is put over their heads.

The Mesdames were inconsolable when they heard the D. de Choisseul had lost the Colonel General des Suisses at Grisons ; they quarrelled with the Comte de Provence who at first was to have succeeded Him, beleiving that He had engaged the King to distress Choisseul " who already laboured under Misfortunes he noways merited " ; and ordered a door which communicated betwixt their Appartments and those of the Comtesse of Provence to be walled up ; besides they engaged the Dauphin in the quarrel, by representing that the Comte de Provence was too near in Succession to the Crown to be entrusted with a Command He might employ to bad purposes ; the Dauphin insisted on his Brother's declining that Employment, for which reason it was given to the Comte d'Artois ; and they would not be reconciled to the Comte de Provence till he declared he had no share in engaging the King to take it from the D. of Choisseul.

The King is tired of the unsettled State of His Court, His aversion and inapplication to business encrease daily, and his dislike to the Ceremonious life of Versailles, He talks often with rapture of the Sweets of a retired life, and there is great reason to believe He is much disposed to embrace a life of greater retirement. Orders were yesterday given to embellish the Environs of Fontainbleau ; the Palace is also to be repaired and undergo considerable alterations, which occasions a Surmise that the King has thoughts of retiring thither and of abdicating the Crown in favour of the Dauphin, whom He treats of late with remarkable tenderness and deferrence. It is supposed this may take place soon after the Marriage of the Comte d'Artois, which will in all probability be hastened on account of the opinion of the Sterility of the two Eldest Princes.

There are reasons to induce Me du Barry to encourage the King in this disposition

1°. His constitution is much impaired by intemperance has of late altered much for the worse, this must naturally make Her look forward to Her situation in case of the King's death.

2°. If He abdicates She may secure Her fortune by contracting a private Marriage with the King.

3°. Her Situation might be secured at all event by a Treaty with the Dauphin and the other Princes previous to the abdication.

On the contrary if She out lives the King in the Character of His Mistress, She has to apprehend severe treatment under His Successor, from the resentment of the Court and Nation, which would end in Her being stripped of Her Riches and being shut up in a Convent. And if She aims at a Marriage in Her present situation, the Court of Spain, and all the Princes of the Blood Royal as well as the Nation in general would never approve of Her becoming Queen of France, and would oppose with all their might her being divorced from du Barry ; this previous step She seems to have in view from Her intimacy with the Court of Rome and from the Great favour of the Pope's Nuncio.

There are other circumstances which encourage the idea of the King's having thoughts of abdicating, as his sordiness being much encreased of late ; he has a prodigious Sum in Specie, yet continues scraping together, he pays nothing, but not averse to granting orders on the Publick Treasury ; the change of outward behaviour of the Dauphiness and Me du Barry, which till of late was rude and uncivil, though now attentive and polite but cold ; which was brought about by an application to the Court of Vienna at the request of Me du Barry, through the mediation of Count Mercy.

I was yesterday assured of the truth of an anecdote I formerly heard, that after the attempt of Damiens on the King's person, His Majesty was desirous of abdicating in favour of the late Dauphin, but hindered by Me de Pompadour who from motives of self preservation insinuated that the Dauphin was not free from Suspicions relative to that horrid action ; I shall add one more Anecdote ; the King about a Month ago was in Me du Barry's Appartment who was Sick, He was obliged to go out on account of Some Ceremony, on which He with warmth complained of being eternally the Slave of Etiquettes and said He would soon certainly get rid of this subjection, but recollecting that the Physician and another person were in the room added, I will soon retire to Trianon where the Ministers shall attend Me daily for publick business, but none of the People of my Court shall be admitted but when they are sent for.

The Abbé Terrè is still Comtrolleur General des Finances, notwithstanding the publick outcry and the attempts of the D. d'Aiguillon's party to remove him ; indeed He is now very subservient to the Duke, yet as the Finances are in a worse situation than ever, he must either adopt more effectual measures to Support publick Credit, or must loose his place.

France labours under a Debt of 250. Millions Sterling, the nominal interest of which at 5. per Cent forms a new Capital of 12½. Millions yearly as no part of it is paid off. The want of credit is such, that this National Debt or what they call *Les effets Royaux* loose on an average at least 50. per Cent. By the conduct of the French Ministry and the Tenour of the King's Edict of 16th. September last, it appears that it is meant to discredit these National engagements still more, perhaps with a view of reducing them to the lowest pitch suppose 20. per Cent of their original value, and then by an Act of Authority with an appearance of Justice call them all in for the King's Account at the then current price, convert them into new Engagements bearing interest at 4. per Cent ; thus reduce the National Debt to about 50. Millions Sterling, and the interest could be paid regularly without imposing New Taxes, or obstructing the ordinary Expences of Government.

The Dauphiness some days ago was lamenting with some Ladies not having as yet become pregnant, as this would give such satisfaction to the King and the Nation, Me de Noailles said She was very Young and only Married a Short time, and must trust to Providence, the Dauphiness replied Ah Madame il n'y a pas de Providence pour les Dauphines ; it is whispered at Court that the Dauphiness is partial to the Prince de Lambesc Son to Me de Brienne, and would not repine if He was Her Providence.

The Family of the Du Barrys are originally from the neighbourhood of Toulouse ; where they enjoyed an estate of about 150£. Sterling, giving themselves out as related to the family of Barrymore in Ireland. There are Seven of them known at Court.

1. The Comte du Barry (who formerly kept Me du Barry) he placed the Lady at Court, he was married about 25. years ago at Toulouse where his Wife Still lives.

2. Comte Guillaume du Barri Brother to the former and Husband to the Countess ; He was a Captain of Foot retired on a pension of 20£. a year ; He was sent for from Toulouse to marry the Comtesse previous to Her publick presentation at Court, He saw Her once, and that at the Altar, but comes sometimes to Paris, and is now very rich.

3. The Chevalier du Barry another Brother, who was a Captain of Cavalry but now Colonel of the Queen's Regiment, He seldom comes to Court and has no influence.

4. The Viscomte du Barry Son to the first Comte by his Wife that now lives at Toulouse, He is about 24. years old a favourite

at Court, where he constantly lives, has the rank of Colonel and serves in the Chevaux Legers, he is destined for Mlle de Bethune.

5. La Comtesse du Barry the King's Mistress, formerly called Mlle l'Ange.

6. Mlle du Barry (called Mlle Chou) is Sister to the du Barry's was placed by Her Brother at Court, has rendered herself necessary to the Comtesse, the first uses She made of Her influence was to Supplant Her Brother, who now has no correspondence with the Comtesse.

7. Another Mlle du Barry (called la Boiteuse) sister of the above, placed by the Comte to be a check on Mlle Chou, but having no abilities, She has no influence.

No. 1009—*The King to Lord North.*

Printed. Donne I. 81.

LORD NORTH—I have signed the new Commission of Irish Excise and cancelled the former one. I trust I shall hear from You tomorrow the numbers that shall have attended at the Cock Pit this Evening

QUEENS HOUSE
Jany 20th 1772.
$\frac{m}{59}$ p^t one PM.

No. 1010—*The King to Lord North.*

Printed. Donne I. 86.

QUEENS HOUSE

Feby 6th 1772. $\frac{m}{50}$ p^t 5. PM.

LORD NORTH—I have made some enquiry into Sir Gilbert Elliot's request in favour of his Son, who is undoubtedly a very pretty Young Man, and on account of the Father should be glad to place in the Army; but the obtaining at once a Captain Lieutenancy would not only occasion clamour in the Army but disoblige many Peers and Members of Parliament as it could not be done for their Sons ; in short I shall be glad when I can assist Sir Gilbert but that must be in an unexceptionable mode for I will not for any Man do a wrong thing or what is next to it that which opens the door to other unreasonable requests. I have desired Lord Barrington to give You on paper the State of the case that You may satisfy Sir Gilbert of the impossibility of obtaining what he seems to desire ; the Commission of Captain obtained, in an illegal method cannot be a claim to rank at coming in it might in time be a plea for advancement.

No. 1011—*Lord Hertford to the King.*

Lord Hertford has every thing prepared in case of the Princess of Wales's death to submit to his Majesty's pleasure, supposing that the directions given when the late Prince of Wales died will probably in his Majesty's judgment be the properest precedent to follow ; The orders were issued by the privy Council in most of the instances upon that occasion and probably will be pursued by the King's direction in this instance if such an Event should take place, but Lord Hertford will be privately prepared to receive and obey all necessary instructions and commands that the most perfect respect may be shewn agreably to his Majesty's pleasure.

GROS^R STREET,
   Feb^{ry} 7th 1772.

No. 1012—*The King to Lord North.*

Printed. Donne I. 88.

LORD NORTH—I am sorry to acquaint You that My Mother is grown so much worse that I cannot appear at Court this day ; whenever this tragical Scene is ended I shall give You notice of it that I may not from any personal affliction put the least delay to Public business

QUEENS HOUSE
   Feb. 7th 1772.
   $\frac{m}{23}$ *p*^t 11. A.M.

No. 1013—*The King to Lord North.*

Printed.   Donne I. 88.

LORD NORTH—What I yesterday expected has happened My Mother is no More ; I desire You will call here about one.

QUEENS HOUSE
  Feby 8th 1772.

  $\dfrac{m}{5}$ p^t 10. A.M.

No. 1014—*Lord Hertford to the King.*

Lord Hertford has the honor of acquainting his Majesty that the different Workmen have all engaged to be prepared for the interment of the late Princess of Wales on saturday next. Mr. Leackes is of opinion that the Livery Servants have worn their Liveries at all the funerals which he remembers, but whatever his Majesty's pleasure is it will be obeied.

If his Majesty has no objection Lord Hertford will propose to the Dutchess of Richmond to be chief Mourner ; She is the first in rank, and behaved with great propriety in the last roial funeral when there was some difficulty in settling it, and he fears there may be some difficulty in obtaining the proper number upon looking at the list of Ladies of that rank.

GROS^R STREET
  Feb^{ry} 9th 1772.

No. 1015—*The King to Lord North.*

LORD NORTH—I wish You would call here any time most convenient to You, previous to Your going to the House of Commons.

QUEENS HOUSE
  Feby 10th 1772.

  $\dfrac{m}{50}$. p^t 10. A.M.

No. 1016—*Lord Hertford to the King.*

[Lady Beauchamp was the wife of Lord Hertford's son and heir, Viscount Beauchamp. She was only twenty-two years of age.]

SIRE—I have made part of a scene this morning that has almost disabled me from doing even my duty to your Majesty. I could not therefore return an answer from your Majesty to the house of Lords which I would otherways have done.

Poor Lady Beauchamp died to day at four o'Clock more easily than She has lived for many months past.

Inclosed herewith I take the liberty of troubling your Majesty with the answers returned from the Crown for some years past upon such melancoly occasions which I received from Mr Strutt, and to vary the expression a little I had prepared three upon the same sort of plan either of which if any one of them should appear proper in your Majesty's judgment I will beg your Majesty to permit me to transmit to the Lord Steward who I am persuaded will readily upon so sad an occasion return the answer for me if your Majesty is pleased to approve it. I have the honor to be with all possible duty respect and attachment, Sire, your Majesty's most faithful and most devoted humble servant

HERTFORD.

GROS^R STREET.
Feb^{ry} 11th 1772.

No. 1017—*Lord Hertford to the King.*

SIRE—I trust your Majesty will pardon my addressing You once more, I am sensible I have done it very often lately but my circumstances have been such that I could not avoid it and be assured I was doing my duty, a principle which I flatter myself will make it excusable to your Majesty whom I wish to serve and please to the utmost of my power. I am now with regret bound to ask your Majesty's leave to absent myself personally on saturday and that the Vice Chamberlain may officiate for me. My Son has made it his earnest and anxious request that I should not appear in publick till after Lady Beauchamp is buried and as his petition is founded upon the common practice of the world in such cases, I hope your Majesty will not think him blameable or that I would offer any reason but such as I thought your Majesty would approve for avoiding any part of my Duty and particularly where your Majesty's family and feelings were concerned.

Your commands shall be obeied if my judgment is mistaken in this respect; In every other instance within my province nothing has or will be omitted to shew the utmost attention to your Commands and the most perfect respect upon the melancoly occasion. The Lists are very near compleation, when they are entirely so which I expect to night or to morrow morning I will beg leave to transmit them for your Majesty's satisfaction.

I have the honor to be with the truest attachment and respect, Sire, your Majesty's most faithful and most dutiful servant

HERTFORD.

GROS^R STREET
Feb^{ry} 12th 1772.

No. 1018—*Lord Hertford to the King.*

SIRE—I have no doubts but that my Son's personal and unhappy feelings have misled him ; your Majesty's goodness to all your Servants is well known, and no one can be more sensible or more grateful for the many proofs given of it than myself.

Your Majesty will forgive the father and the Son from the principle upon which they were severally misled ; In grief and affliction Men are easily exposed to error, when the passion is strong and reason weak. I shall certainly attend, as You command ; your Majesty's orders are perfectly sufficient to satisfie and direct me and the occasion is too correspondent to the Event felt in my own family not to be easily distinguishable by any part of it from every other publick ceremony. I have the honor to be with constant and perfect attachment, Sire, your Majesty's most faithful and devoted humble servant

HERTFORD.

GROS^R STREET.
Feb^{ry} 12th 1772.

No. 1019.

CEREMONIAL FOR THE INTERMENT OF HER LATE ROYAL HIGHNESS
AUGUSTA PRINCESS DOWAGER OF WALES IN KING HENRY
THE SEVENTH'S CHAPEL AT WESTMINSTER ON SATURDAY
THE 15TH. FEBRUARY 1772.

Knight Marshall's Men with Black Staves.

Servants in Livery

Pages of the Presence
Mr. Finlay   .   .   .   .   Mr. Higgs

Pages of the Backstairs
Mr. Murray   Mr. Nicolai Junr.
Mr. Nicolai Senr.   Mr. Latman.
Mr. Palman

Gentlemen Ushers Quarterly Waiters
Mr. Watts   .   .   .   .   Mr. Ritzo

Pages of Honour
Augustus Maitland Esq. Charles Nassau Thomas Esq.

Physician.
Sir John Pringle

Chaplains

Clerk of the Closet

Equerry
Alexander Maitland Esq.

Clerks of the Household
John Secker Esq.   William Scott Esq.

Secretary
Mr. Kluft

Officers of Arms

Comptroller of Her late Royal Highness's Household Charles Jenkinson Esq.

Treasurer of Her late Royal Highness's Household. Samuel Martin Esq:

An Officer of Arms

Commissioner of Horse Andrew Leslie Esq:

Lord Chamberlain to Her late Royal Highness Lord Boston.

Lord Chamberlain of His Majesty's Household Earl of Hertford.

A Gent: Usher John Parsons.	Clarencieux King of Arms bearing a Coronet on a Black Velvet Cushion	A Gent: Usher Wm. Egerton Esq:
Supporters of the Pall Three Countesses.	The Body,	Supporters of the Pall Three Countesses.

	Carried by .. Yoomen of the	
1.	Guard, covered with a Black	2. Countess of
	Velvet Pall adorned with	Buckinghamshire
3. Countess of	Eight Escutcheons and under	4. Countess of
Harrington	a Canopy of Black Velvet	Waldegrave
5. Countess of	borne by Eight Gentlemen of	6. Countess of
Macclesfield	Her late Royal Highness's	Aylesford
	Household.	

Mr. Child.	Mr. Griffiths
Mr. Russel.	Mr. Midgeley
Mr. Duiel.	Mr. Ward.

A Gentleman Usher J. Beau Waters Esq.	Garter King of Arms	A Gentleman Usher J. Maitland. Esq.

Supporter to the Chief Mourner Dutchess of Bolton.	Chief Mourner Dutchess of Grafton Her Train borne by the Lady of a Baronet Lady Gideon.	Supporter to the Chief Mourner. Dutchess of Queensberry

Assistants to the Chief Mourner Marchionesses or Countesses	Assistants to the Chief Mourner Marchionesses or Countesses
Marchioness Grey	Countess of Pembroke
Countess of Northampton . . .	Countess of Denbigh
Countess of Essex	Countess of Litchfield
Countess of Abington	Countess of Holderness
Countess of Coventry	Countess of Ferrers.

First Gentleman of Her Royal Highness's Privy Chamber
Lieutenant Colonel Lewis Charles Montolieu

Ladies of the Bed Chamber
Lady House   Lady Berkeley

Second Gentleman of Her Royal Highness's Privy Chamber
George Powlett Esq

Maids of Honour

Miss Mostyn	Miss Neville
Miss Vansittart . . .	Miss Evelyn
Miss Egerton	Miss Irby

Bed Chamber Women

Mrs. Clavering . . .	Mrs. Cornewall
Mrs. Granville . . .	Mrs. Egerton
Mrs. Walkinshaw . .	Mrs. Breton

Yeomen of the Guards.

N.B.—Peers, Peeresses, Peers Daughters, and Privy Counsellors
to be marshalled by the Officers of Arms according to their
respective Ranks and Degrees.

No. 1020—*The King to Lord North.*

QUEENS HOUSE *Feb^y* 17*th* 1772.
$$\frac{m}{46}.\ p^t\ 7.\ \text{PM.}$$

LORD NORTH—As Mr. Comtroller did not bring the Address
from the House of Commons this day, I desire You will send the
enclosed answer to Him which may be delivered by Himself if

well enough, if not by the Vice Chamberlain without the Ceremony
of waiting untill my next Levee day.

No. 1021—*Lord Rochford to the King.*

Lord Rochford has the honor in a very great hurry to inform
your Majesty that we very early went into a Committee where
we now are [;] the Marquis of Rockinghams Motion I objected
to and it is still debating if there is a division upon this your
Majesty shall hear from me again.

HOUSE OF LORDS

20 *febry* 1772 $\frac{m}{55}$ *past* 5 P.M.

No. 1022—*The King to Lord North.*

[? *Feb.* 1772.]

LORD NORTH—I am much pleased at the very good division
at the out set of the business, and not less so with Your attention
in so immediately informing Me of it.

$\frac{m}{48}$. p^t 5. PM.

No. 1023—*The King to Lord North.*

[? 21 *Feb.* 1772.]

[The bill referred to in this and succeeding letters is the Royal Marriage
Bill.]

LORD NORTH—I have this morning received from Lord
Rochford the letter of Lord Mansfield enclosing a second proviso,
I shall certainly not [be] opiniatre, and therefore as the Cabinet
with Lord Mansfield the Drawer of the Bill think it right it
should be put into the Body of the Bill before presented to the
House this day, I find You have a Cabinet upon it this Morning,
I will certainly be at twelve at St. James's ready to receive You.

$\frac{m}{20}$. p^t 6 A.M.

No. 1024—*The King to Lord North.*

Printed. Donne I. 91.

LORD NORTH—I cannot say that the management of the Debate in the House of Lords this day has edified Me, I hope there will be a meeting tomorrow to settle the Mode of proceeding on Friday ; I do expect every nerve be strained to carry the Bill through both Houses with a becoming firmness, for it is not a question that immediately relates to Administration but personally to myself, therefore I have a right to expect a hearty Support from everyone in my Service and shall remember Defaulters.

QUEENS HOUSE
Feby 26th 1772.

$\dfrac{m}{3}$ p^t 11. PM.

No. 1025—*Lord Rochford to the King.*

Lord Rochford cannot give your majesty a greater proof of his sentiments having the good fortune to coincide entirely with your majestys than by sending your Majesty a copy of a letter he wrote this morning to Lord Mansfield before he was honored with your Majestys Note. Lord Rochford will have the honor to attend your majesty at St James's to report what passes at the Cabinet this morning

BERKLEY SQUARE

21 *feb^y* 1772 $\dfrac{m}{30}$ *past* 10 AM.

No. 1025A—*The King to Lord North.*

(See ADDENDA at end of Volume.)

No. 1026—*The King to Lord North.*

[? *Feb.* 1772.]

LORD NORTH—I desire to hear from You what has passed with Lord Mansfield.

$\dfrac{m}{46}$. p^t 10. PM.

No. 1027—*Lord Hertford to the King.*

SIRE—Your Majesty does me great honor in communicating your sentiments to me : You cannot convey them to any person whatever who has a more sincere zeal for your service, nor that can wish more warmly than I do to prove himself upon any and every occasion with personal attachment, your Majesty's most faithful and most devoted servant   HERTFORD.

GROS^R STREET
Feb^{ry} 28th 1772.

No. 1028—*The King to Lord North.*

Printed. Donne I. 93.

[Richmond Old Park had been settled upon Queen Charlotte on her marriage.]

QUEENS HOUSE *March 2^d* 1772.

LORD NORTH—There is a great difficulty if not impossibility of enfranchising the Copy holds at Richmond ; the Application of Lady Fitz Williams for a special Act to render Her Land a Free hold has given rise to an idea of applying to Parliament for empowering the Queen as Lady of the Manour during life to enfranchise such of the Copy hold Tenants as She may think proper, the true reason is that there are some purchases that may in time be agreable to Me which I could obtain on easier terms if that boon on such an occasion could be granted ; I have ordered Mr. Sayer to wait upon You and State it more fully, that if You see no objection to it a Bill may be prepared for that purpose, as it is an ease to the Subject it cannot I should think meet with difficulty.

No. 1029—*The King to Lord North.*

Printed. Donne I. 94.

[Mr. Montague's motion was to repeal a clause of an Act of Charles II., directing the 30th of January (King Charles Martyr's Day) to be observed as a day of fasting and humiliation.]

LORD NORTH—I am glad to find Mr. Montague's Motion has been rejected, as it will keep many worthy Men in good humour, besides the abolition of the day would not be very delicate

QUEENS HOUSE
March 2ᵈ 1772.

$\frac{m}{15}$. p^t 6 PM.

No. 1030—*The King to Lord Mansfield.*

LORD MANSFIELD—As Your time is now a little more in Your power, I am desirous of knowing whether tomorrow Evening will be convenient for Your coming here.

QUEENS HOUSE
March 4ᵗʰ 1772.

$\frac{m}{48}$. p^t 5. PM.

No. 1031—*The King to Lord North.*

Printed.   Donne I. 94.

[The King's mother had died intestate.]

LORD NORTH—I am desirous of seeing You at St. James's this day having seen Lord Mansfield last night, and being desirous of putting the Letters of Administration into forwardness.

QUEENS HOUSE
March 6ᵗʰ 1772.

$\frac{m}{30}$. p^t 7 PM.

No. 1032—*The King to Lord Bristol.*

[Lord Bristol was Lord of the Bedchamber. He had been Ambassador at Madrid, 1758-1761.]

QUEENS HOUSE *March 9ᵗʰ* 1772.

LORD BRISTOL—the attention shewn by the Spanish Ambassador on all occasions added to the very sincere good opinion I entertained of His late Brother Count Lavagno, makes me desirous You should just write a line of Condolance to the Ambassador on His misfortune, and mention how much I feel for him   GEORGE R.

Endorsed by the King.

No. 1033—*The King to Lord North.*

Printed. Donne I. 95.

[This again refers to the Royal Marriage Bill.]

LORD NORTH—Nothing can be more pleasant than Your Account of the long Debate, I am desirous of knowing more of it, and therefore wish You would call here at any time that suits You best this Evening.

QUEENS HOUSE
March 10*th* 1772.
8. *o'Clock* A.M.

No. 1034—*The King to Lord North.*

Printed. Donne I. 95.

QUEENS HOUSE *March* 12*th* 1772.

$$\frac{m}{37} p^t 8. \text{ A.M.}$$

LORD NORTH—The turn of Yesterday's Debate is most favourable as opposition, or at least the greatest part of it have been forced to change its Ground and admit that there ought to be some regulations made with respect to the Marriages of the Royal Family ; it is a known Maxim in all Military Operations that when the Enemy change positions that is the right moment to push them with vigour, the Rule I look upon as not less good in Parliamentary opperations, therefore a continuation of the Zeal and activity You have shewn in this Bill will carry it through with great eclat.

No. 1035—*The King to Lord North.*

Printed. Donne I. 96.

[Colonel John Burgoyne—later the victim of Saratoga—was Governor of Fort William in Scotland.]

Lord North's, Attention in correcting the impression I had that Col. Burgoyne and Lt. Col. Harcourt were absent yesterday is very handsome to those Gentlemen, for I certainly should have thought myself obliged to have named a new Governor in the room of the former, and to have removed the Other from my Bedchamber.

QUEENS HOUSE
March 12th 1772
$\dfrac{m}{48}$ p^t 7. PM.

No. 1036—*The King to Lord North.*

Printed. Donne I. 96.

[The division referred to was in favour of Ministers by 200 to 164, for going into Committee on the Royal Marriage Bill.]

LORD NORTH—I think You have advanced farther in the Committee than I expected the last Division was nearer than some Persons will have expected though not more than I thought, I hope every Engine will be employed to get those friends that staid away last night to come and Support on Monday if a good countenance is kept I doubt not but You will find Your Divisions encrease I wish a List could be prepared of those that went away and of those that Deserted to the Minority that would be a Rule for my conduct in the Drawing Room tomorrow. I wish You could bring the List a little before three.

QUEENS HOUSE
March 14th 1772.
$\dfrac{m}{2}$ p^t 8 AM.

No. 1037—*The King to Lord North.*

Printed. Donne I. 97.

[This division showed a majority for Ministers of 222 to 160.]

LORD NORTH—Your account of the good Majority of yesterday gives me much satisfaction, and is a great proof of the activity You have shewn in collecting persons together, I trust those You employ will not be less vigillant to get them to attend tomorrow when the Committee will certainly be closed, I desire You will call here about two that I may hear more on the Subject.

QUEENS HOUSE
March 17*th* 1772.
$\frac{m}{22} p^t$ 9 A.M.

No. 1038—*The King to Lord North.*

Printed. Donne I. 97.

[This refers to the persecution of Caroline Matilda, sister of the King, by her husband, Christian VII., King of Denmark.]

LORD NORTH—As two o'Clock is not convenient to You a little before three will do just as well ; I have dedicated this unpleasant Morning to going through the whole of the Danish Correspondence which by the Messenger's dispatches seem to be drawing to a conclusion, great rancour and inclination to blacken the affair as much as possible is not wanting, therefore the decision must be now finally taken.

QUEENS HOUSE
March 17*th* 1772.
$\frac{m}{55} p^t$ 10. A.M.

No. 1039—*The King to Lord North.*

Printed. Donne I. 98.

LORD NORTH—The very good Divisions You had on the last Debate, and the Committee having proceeded almost to the end of the last Clause but one, makes it evident the Committee will be finally closed tommorrow and I hope not very late ; I look on Your abilities and the zeal You have shewn in conducting this Bill through the different Stages as the means that have Brought it thus and that will crown it with Success. Mr. Dowdeswell's Clause of incapacitating any one of the family marrying without consent is infinitely more Subject to dangerous consequences than any that Opposition can with begging the question falsely pretend may at the remotest period be occasioned by any part of the Bill

QUEENS HOUSE
March 18*th* 1772.
$\frac{m}{2}$ p^t 9. A.M.

No. 1040—*The King to Lord North.*

LORD NORTH—Having learnt from Mr. Brudenell, that You had a feverish Complaint during yesterday's debate, I am anxious to hear how You bore the fatigue of the last night ; I find Lt. Col. D'Auvergne of the first Troop of Horse Guards is dead, as Lt. Col. Burgoyne could succeed to this without any expence, and as the being attached to a Corps in London may perhaps be agreable to Him I shall not fill up the Vacancy untill I know whether it might not suit him.

QUEENS HOUSE
March 18*th* 1772.
$\frac{m}{40}$. p^t 3 PM.

No. 1041—*The King to Lord North.*

LORD NORTH—By the enclosed Note I have this moment received from Lord Barrington, You will find that Lieut. Col. D'Auvergne is not dead.

QUEENS HOUSE
March 18*th* 1772.
$\frac{m}{47}$. p^t 5. PM.

No. 1042—*The King to Lord North.*

Printed. Donne I. 99.

LORD NORTH—I am much pleased at finding the Royal Marriage Bill has got through the Committee this Morning with Such handsome Majorities, I do not doubt but a continuation of

the Zeal You have shewn on this Occasion will carry handsome
Majorities on the Report, and on Mr. Fuller's provisoe, for two
days respite is allways more favourable to Administration than
to Opposition.

QUEENS HOUSE
March 21st 1772.

$\frac{m}{46}$. p^i 8. A.M.

No. 1043—*The King to Lord North.*

Printed. Donne I. 99.

[A clause in the Royal Marriage Bill, limiting its duration to the reign
of George III., was rejected by a majority of only 18.]

LORD NORTH—Though the Majority was smaller than I
should have expected this day, yet the division coming on so
early in the day very naturally accounts for it; I hope the
friends of the Bill will therefore attend in time tomorrow, that
the Majority May be greater at the third reading; but as You
have got through the Report without borrowing part of the
Night I am amply repaid any disappointment as it has less
fatigued You.

QUEENS HOUSE
March 23d 1772.

$\frac{m}{25}$ p^i 10. PM.

No. 1044—*The King to Lord North.*

LORD NORTH—The finding You have so early this day
finished the Royal Marriage Bill gives much satisfaction and I
shall at all times with pleasure reflect at the Spirit and Zeal You
have shewn in conducting it through its different Stages

QUEENS HOUSE
March 24th 1772.

$\frac{m}{43}$. p^i 6. PM.

No. 1045—*Lord Rochford to the King.*

Lord Rochford has for some time past wished for an opportunity to see your majesty alone in order to mention the uneasiness he is under with regards to Mr Sutton's late Conduct, too bad, though perhaps innocent, to be justified, there was a violence in his behaviour, that makes it necessary he should not remain in the Situation he is in, and Lord Rochford has been waiting for some plan to be proposed by Lord North, as a punishment to the opposers, to point out Mr Sutton as an object ; Lord Rochford is aware that it will be said, removing Mr Sutton, will be doing him a favor, as he will immediately have a pension of £500 a year for Life, this may be an object to the Treasury but in Lord Rochfords poor opinion, does not weigh against the Consequence of keeping a person in employment, who when he is most wanted, is determined to go against Government, and what is worse, against a Bill in which your Majesty is principally Concerned at the same time Lord Rochford would do what he hopes, he is incapable of, if he did not say that he does not beleive Mr Sutton is *designedly* connected with opposition ; Thuss far Lord Rochford thinks it became him to unburthen his mind to your Majesty previous to what he means to take an opportunity of saying when Lord Suffolk shall be present, and as it is expected from all Quarters that those who opposed the marriage bill will be noticed, Lord Rochford has humbly ventured to say, that no predilection for Mr Sutton, will prevent him from recommending strongly to your Majesty to make the most striking examples on this remarquable occasion.

BERKLEY SQUARE 29th *March* 1772 $\frac{m}{15}$ *past* 6 P.M.

No. 1046—*The King to Lord North.*

[? *March*, 1772.]

Lord North should send for the Advocate General and direct Him to draw up the form of a Warrant appointing Him Lord North My Commissioner for Administring the late Princess Dowager of Wales having died without leaving a Will.

The effects of my late Father ought to be seperated from those of my late Mother.

Then Lord North ought to have a reference made to the Attorney and Solicitor General, 1° to know whether the Assets of my late Father are not subject to his Debts and whether the Bond Debts are not to be satisfied in preference to all others.

2ᵈᵒ Whether Such of my Mother's Jewels as were given Her by my Father are not subject to His Debts.

Two copies, both in the King's handwriting.

No. 1047—*The King to Lord North.*

Printed. Donne I. 100.

LORD NORTH—The enclosed packet contains the Keys of the Scrutores at Carlton House, and of a press with Glass doors in the Tapestry Room at Kew that contains the Keys to all my late Mother's Scrutores in that Houses; I desire You will direct Mr. Martin to go and open them and any Papers that are in either House to seal them up and transmit them to Me, I shall this very evening examine if I have any Schedule of the Furniture taken at the death of my late Father, though I rather expect not to meet with it as I have already glanced them over; I desire no time may be lost with regard to Kew as I wish to begin to put things there into order

QUEENS HOUSE
March 30ᵗʰ 1772.
five o'Clock PM.

No. 1048—*The King to Lord North.*

Printed. Donne I. 101.

[The petition of the Dissenters was for relief from the restrictions imposed upon them.]

QUEENS HOUSE *April* 2ᵈ 1772.

LORD NORTH—As I understand the Petition of the Dissenters is to be presented tomorrow, I take this method of acquainting You, that I think You ought not to press those Gentlemen who

are brought on that Interest into Parliament to oppose this
measure, as that would be driving them out of those Seats on a
new Parliament ; but I think You ought to oppose it personally
through every Stage, which Will gain You the Applause of the
Established Church and every real friend of the Constitution, if
You should be beat it will be in doing Your duty and the House
of Lords will prevent any evil ; indeed it is the Duty of Ministers
as much as possible to prevent any alterations in so essential a
part of the Constitution as everything that relates to Religion,
and there is no Shadow for this Petition as the Crown regularly
grants a Noli prosequi if any over nice Justice of Peace encourages
prosecutions.

No. 1049—*Lord North to the King.*

[3 *April*, 1772.]

[A bill was this day brought in by Sir Henry Hoghton for relief of the
Dissenters. It was carried in the Commons.]

Lord North was prevented from paying his duty to his Majesty
yesterday at St James's by business which required his early
attendance at the House of Commons and detained him till near
five o'clock. He had the honour of his Majesty's commands
yesterday Evening, and had soon after a meeting of the principal
Members of Parliament concerning the Dissenters petition. The
Gentlemen continued till eleven o'clock in Downing Street, dis-
cussing the proper course to be held today. Lord North is sorry
to inform his Majesty, that upon the best information that he
has received there is not merely a possibility or a probability but
a certainty that he will be beat if he opposes this measure in the
House of Commons : The Opposition are all united in favour of
it, and one half of the friends of Government will either stay
away, or vote with the Opposition. The greater number of the
gentlemen, who were with Ld North last night strongly dissuaded
him from attempting to throw it out in the House of Commons :
Those, whose elections principally depend upon Presbyterians,
must vote for this petition ; Those, who have a few dissenting
constituents would avoid voting at all, as they are sure that their
Dissenting friends would resent it, and that their Church of
England would not thank them : Upon the whole, They look'd

upon it as one of those bills, which ought to be thrown out by the House of Peers and not by the Commons, and conceiving that they had given evident proofs of their attachment to the Church in two instances during the present Sessions, think it hard to be press'd a third time in a case, where their conduct may endanger their own seats, but where the Lords may act with perfect freedom, and without the least apprehension.

Lord North will not fail to attend his Majesty at St James's this morning, when he will explain the matter more at large.

DOWNING STREET *Friday morn:*

No. 1050—*Lord Rochford to the King.*

Lord Rochford has the honor to submit to your Majesty the Draught of a letter to the Duke of Richmond, which if it meets with your Majestys approbation, Lord Rochford will send it to night. Your Majesty will see by the letter from Mr Tindal that the rioters at Chelmsford are dispersed.

CLEVELAND ROW 16 *april* 1772

$\frac{m}{50}$ *past* 10 AM.

No. 1051—*The King to Lord Rochford.*

QUEENS HOUSE *April* 5th 1772.

$\frac{m}{-} p^t$ 10 PM.

LORD ROCHFORD—On carefully examining the proposed promotions on the Irish Establishment which I now return to You I cannot help refusing the four following proposals

1° In the 27th Regt. of Foot, Cornet Fox made a Cornet in the 1st Regt. of Dragoon Guards in Septr 1770. all the Lieutenants but two in this Regt. being older than Him.

2° In the 34th Regt. of Foot, Ensign William Norton of the 44th appointed in July 1770. is proposed to Succeed Lieut. Churchill in which five Ensigns are Older, though the eldest was appointed in 1770.

3^{tto} In the 48th Regt of Foot Lieut. Anstruther of the 7th appointed in January 1770. and probably never an Ensign as there are none in that Corps is recommended to buy a Company in the 48th where all the Lieutenants are older except three

4to In the 49th Regt. of Foot Major Mercer who obtained that rank in 1769. is proposed to Succeed Lieut. Colonel Roberts which would be hard on many Majors, on the English Establishment, the Lord Lieutenant must therefore find one Senior at least to Major Hawke to purchase this Lieut. Colonelcy.

The tacit permission of the Lord Lieutenant to Officers Selling for more than the price regulated about four or five Years ago tempts many good ones to quit the Service and if not prevented will so far advance the Irish Officers over those on the British Establishment that it will occasion well grounded dissatisfaction therefore the Lord Lieutenant must be apprised of this and that from henceforth I shall not agree to any Sale but where the purchaser declares on his Honour that neither directly nor indirectly he has engaged to pay more than the Regulated Price, therefore none of the remaining Commissions by purchase can be signed untill the Lord Lieutenant assertains that they are to be agreable to that price

No. 1052—*Lord Suffolk to the King.*

[The long-expected despatch was from Denmark, concerning Queen Caroline Matilda.]

[*April*, 1772 ?]

Lord Suffolk has this instant received the long-expected Dispatch from Col. Keith—it is all in cypher—But will be sent to Your Majesty to night, and the moment it is decyphered.

$\frac{m}{51}$ p^t 3. P.M.

No. 1053—*Lord Suffolk to the King.*

Lord Suffolk begs leave to submit to Your Majesty, whether, in consequence of the information received by S^r: Robt Keith's last Letter, it may not be proper to suspend the Equipment of the Fleet till further orders. Abundance of speculation and stock-jobbing will be prevented by this means ; and he beleives no material purpose, as matters now stand, obstructed, if Your

Majesty approves of this idea, he farther begs leave to lay before
Your Majesty the Dra^t of a Letter which, if it shall be Your
Majesty's Pleasure, he will send to the Admiralty to night that
Ld Sandwich may be authorised to give the necessary directions
without loss of time.

DUKE ST. WETM.
April 18. 1772
$\frac{m}{10}$. p^t 8. P.M.

This note wou'd have been with Your Majesty soon after
six o'clock, if the Messenger orderd to carry it wou'd have been
pleas'd to have found a Horse in all London.

No. 1054—*Lord Suffolk to the King.*

Lord Suffolk has the honour to transmit to Your Majesty a
Letter from the King of Denmark, and the note which accompanied it from Baron Diede. He trusts Your Majesty will not
attribute his failing to deliver a Packet of this Nature into Your
own Hands himself, to any inattention or Neglect. He has been
induced to convey it to Your Majesty in this manner from a
Reluctance to break into Your Majesty's Retirement, and an
apprehension that it is most agreable to Your Majesty that he
should not.

DUKE S^T WEST^R: $\frac{m}{55}$ p^t 10. A.M.
April 20. 1772.

Lord Suffolk also sends Your Majesty a Letter from S^r: Robt
Keith which he has this ins^t received from the office. The rest
of the Dutch mail is decyphering.

No. 1055—*Lord Suffolk to the King.*

Lord Suffolk takes the liberty of laying before Your Majesty
an Inclosure which he has this instant received from Lord
Sandwich ; It contains a pleasing proof of the alacrity and

expedition with which Your Majesty's orders wou'd have been, and will be, carried into execution, if the disagreable necessity had existed, or shou'd happen.

DUKE S^T WESTM^R

April 27. 1772. $\dfrac{m}{22}$ p^t 5. P.M.

No. 1056—*Lord Suffolk to the King.*

Lord Suffolk happening to dine in the Country today has but this ins^t: received the honour of Your Majesty's note ; And he cannot refrain from troubling Your Majesty with his dutyfull and gratefull acknowledgments for the most gracious manner in which Your Majesty is pleas'd to express Yourself in it. He begs leave to lay before Your Majesty an absurd kind of a note from Baron Diede : And means to see him tomorrow morning.

DUKE S^T WESTM

April 27. 1772. $\dfrac{M}{30}$ p^t 8. P.M.

No. 1057—*Lord Suffolk to the King.*

Lord Suffolk has the honour to transmit to Your Majesty the several Dispatches brought by the Messenger King who arrived about nine this morning. He would not disturb Your Majesty's jaunt into the Country today by sending them after You to Richmond, as the essential parts of their contents were already known. He has also sent Your Majesty the Charts which Sr Robt Keith has collected and refers to : But hopes Your Majesty wont give Yourself the trouble of making the Bundle up again—if Your Majesty will have the goodness to bring the contents of it with You to St James's tomorrow, Lord Suffolk will take care of them afterwards.

S^r. JAMES'S

April 28. 1772. $\dfrac{m}{37}$. p^t. 2. P.M.

Ld S. is going home to meet Baron Diede at three o'clock

No. 1058—*The King to Lord North.*

Printed. Donne I. 102.

[The debate was on the Budget.]

LORD NORTH—I am much pleased that Opposition took so absurd a part as to object to the very honorable proposition You made yesterday, it shews their ignorance of finances and that they have no other object but to find fault with whatever is proposed : I am certain this measure will do You the greatest credit and will shew that the Person I have thought most able to fill the Employment of Chancellor of the Exchequer fully answers the opinion I have of Him

QUEENS HOUSE
May 2^d 1772.

$\frac{m}{5}$. p^t 9 A.M.

No. 1059—*The King to Lord North.*

LORD NORTH—Having by some neglect omitted to Send to You Yesterday any answer to Your communication of the debate of friday, I upon finding it this morning still send it as it contains my fullest approbation of Your conduct.

ST. JAMES'S.
May 3^d 1772.

$\frac{m}{30}$. p^t 11. A.M.

No. 1059A—*The King to Lord North.*

(See ADDENDA at end of Volume.)

No. 1060—*Lord Suffolk to the King.*

Lord Suffolk has the honour to transmit to Your Majesty a private Letter, together with some Dispatches from S^r: Robt: Keith, and some Charts and Prints, just brought from Copenhagen by the messenger Long.

DUKE S^T WESTM^R
May 14. 1772.
9. P.M.

No. 1061—*The King to Lord Bristol.*

[The reference is to the bill for the relief of Dissenters.]

LORD BRISTOL—I write with the Queens consent to desire
You will not come on Tuesday Evening till the Debate is over in
the House of Lords, I have authorized Lord Rochford to say to
any others that are in the same situation the injunction put on
You which will I trust make a good attendance at that Debate ;
the question is a very short one, at the Revolution the Toleration
Act was established, the Dissenters have not been molested therefore why must now an alteration be made ; this I think contains
the sum of the Argument.   GEORGE R.

QUEENS HOUSE
  May 17*th* 1772.

Endorsed by the King.

No. 1062—*Lord Bristol to the King.*

SIR—I have this Instant been honor'd with your Majesty's
letter commanding my Attendance at the House of Lords instead
of paying my Duty on Tuesday at the Queen's House : Your
Majesty will I hope never have Reason to doubt of my implicit
Obedience to any Orders your Majesty condescends to honor me
with : I feel with the utmost Duty your Majesty's gracious
Manner of explaining the Reason of the Propriety of your
Majesty's Servants attending on so interesting a Point, at the
same Time I must flatter my-self that I shall be forgiven in
lamenting the Necessity of my Absence from your Majesty's
Presence.

I beg Leave to subscribe my-self with the most perfect
Respect, Sir, Your Majesty's Most dutiful most oblig'd and most
devoted Servant & Subject   BRISTOL

  half an hour after Six
  May the 17*th* 1772

No. 1063—*The King to Lord Bristol.*

LORD BRISTOL—Though I flatter myself You have taken my Note of yesterday in the Sense I meant, yet from an unwillingness of not seeing You tomorrow Evening I just add a line of explanation that it is hoped the House of Lords will be up early enough for You to come to the Queens House some part of the Evening though probably not so early as the hour appointed. You will at the House of Lords give the same hint to Lord Pembroke.

GEORGE R.

KEW. *May* 18*th* 1772.

Endorsed by the King.

No. 1064—*Copy of a Letter from Cap*^{t} *Cook of His Majestys Sloop the Resolution dated the* 19*th of May* 1772—*to M*^{r} *Stephens.*

SIR—In consequence of Lieu^t: Cooper representing to me that the Resolution Sloop under my command was found upon trial to be so Crank that she would not bear proper Sail to be set upon her ; I gave it as my opinion that it was owing to the additional Works that have been built upon her in order to make large accomodations for the several Gentlemen Passengers intended to embark in her, and proposed that she might be cut down to her original state which proposal I laid before you in my Letter of the 14th Ins^t and likewise attended the Navy Board who were pleased to inform me of the alteration they proposed to make which alteration I am of opinion will render her as fit to perform the Voyage as any Ship whatever. I understand that it has been suggested that I never thought her, or these kind of Vessels proper for the Service She is going upon ; I beg you will acquaint their Lordships that I do now and ever did think her the most proper Ship for this Service I ever saw and that from the knowledge and experience I have had of these sort of Vessels I shall always be of opinion that only such are proper to be sent on Discoveries to very distant Parts. I am . . . etc.

Enclosure.

Copy.   NAVY OFFICE 19*th* *May* 1772.

William Appleby Pilot of the Resolution Sloop attending was call'd in and discours'd on the qualities of the said Sloop. He acquainted the Board that he took charge of her at Deptford and Piloted her to the Warp below Sheerness. That she is very crank owing to her being over built with the additional Works raised on her. That he is well acquainted with these kind of Ships having served his time in them, and been Mate and Master of several of them, and that they are of a built for burthen and stowage. That he is of opinion if the additions were taken away, she will be as good as any Ship of that kind. That he never heard of her being esteemed Crank when a Merchant Ship or could say any thing to that effect having never seen or known the Ship before.

No. 1065—*Sir Joseph Banks to Lord Sandwich.*

Copy.

MY LORD—The present situation of Things regarding the proposed Expedition to the South Seas which it was my intention and inclination to have taken an active Share in will I trust render any other Apology to your Lordship for this intrusion unnecessary :

To avoid the appearance of inconsistency and to justify my Conduct in the Eyes of the Public and your Lordship, I feel it incumbent on me to state the reasons by which I am influenced to decline the Expedition

When it was first proposed to me by your Lordship to go to the South Seas again if His Majesty should think proper to send Ships to perfect the Discoveries that had been begun in the last Voyage, I joyfully embrac'd a proposal of all others the best suited to my Disposition and Pursuits. I pledg'd myself then to your Lordship and have since by the whole tenor of my Conversation and Correspondence pledg'd myself to all Europe not only to go the Voyage but to take with me as many able Artists as the Income of my Fortune would allow me to pay ; by whose means the learned World in general might reap as much benefit as possible from those Discoveries which my good Fortune or Industry might enable me to make

The Navy Board was in consequence ordered to purchase two Ships, to fit them up in a proper manner for our reception that we might be enabled to exert our utmost Endeavours to serve the Public, wheresoever the course of our Discoveries might induce us to proceed

Two Ships were accordingly purchased; but when I went down to see the principal Ship I immediately gave it as my opinion that she was very improper for the Voyage and went so far as to declare that if the alterations which I proposed would not be made I would not go in her.

In consequence of this the Surveyor of the Navy was sent to me with a Plan of the Ship; to him I stated my Proposals and laid down upon that Plan the quantity of room that I thought absolutely necessary to be allotted to me and my people for the carrying on our respective Employments

When these Alterations, and those which were judg'd necessary also for the Accomodation of the Captain and the People were made, the Ship in falling down the River was found absolutely incapable of pursuing her intended Voyage

The Navy Board have attributed this incapacity to the alterations that had been made and are of opinion that when the Ship is reduced to her original Situation, that in which I before refused her, she will be the fittest that can be had for answering the Nautical purposes of the Expedition. Without suffering myself to controvert this Opinion of the Navy Board that the Ship will be very fit for Sea although many able Seamen concur with me in doubting it, I must be allowed to say, that the Ship will thus be if not absolutely incapable at least exceedingly unfit for the intended Voyage

We have pledged ourselves my Lord, to your Lordship and the Nation to undertake what no Navigator before us has ever suggested to be practicable; we are to attempt at least to pass round the Globe through Seas of which we know no Circumstance but that of their being tempestuous in those very Latitudes, in passing through which, in Order to get round one Cape, the whole Squadron commanded by Lord Anson narrowly escaped being destroyed. We have done more we have undertaken to approach

as near the Southern Pole as we possibly can, and how near that
may be no Man living can give the least guess

In Expeditions of this nature the Health and Accomodation
of the People are essential to Success ; when Sickness and discontent are once introduced it will be absolutely impossible to
continue the discovery ; by the Alterations made the Accomodations of the People are very much reduced for the Spar Deck
being cut away 30 of the Crew are to be removed under the Gun
Deck, before sufficiently crowded, which being very low and
confined without a free Air must infallibly in so long a Voyage
produce putrid Distempers and Scurvy ; and what my Lord
ought more to be dreaded by a Discoverer than such a Calamity
which must soon oblige him to quit his Discovery and very
probably even put it out of his Power to bring Home any Account
of what he has done previous to its fatal influence

The Accomodations in the Ship are much lessened by the
Changes which have been made in the Equipment since the first
Plan, the House of Commons have thought the Undertaking of
so much importance as to vote the Sum of £4,000 to enable D^r
Lind to accompany Us and assist us with his extensive Knowledge
of natural Philosophy and Mechanics, the Board of Longitude
have also engaged an Astronomer to proceed in each Ship and an
extraordinary Establishment of Officers was thought necessary
on account of the difficulties and Dangers which we were likely
to experience in the course of our Voyage

Shall I then my Lord, who have engaged to leave all that can
make Life agreable in my own Country, and throw on one side
all the Pleasures to be reap'd from three Years of the best of my
Life merely to compass this undertaking pregnant enough with
Dangers and difficulties in its own Nature after having been
promised every security and convenience that the Art of Man
could contrive without which Promise, no Man in my situation
would ever have undertaken the Voyage, be sent of at last in a
doubtful Ship with Accomodations rather worse than those
which I at first absolutely refused, and after spending above
£5,000. of my own Fortune in the Equipment, upon the Credit
of those Accomodations which I saw actually built for me.   Will
the Public be so ungenerous as to expect me to go out in a Ship
in which my People have not the room necessary for performing
the different Duties of their Proffessions a Ship apparently

unhealthy and probably unsafe merely in conformity to the
official Opinion of the Navy Board, who purchased her without
ever consulting me, and now in no degree consider the part
which I have taken in the Voyage or the Alterations which on
my Remonstrance they concurr'd with me in thinking necessary,
but have now taken away, or should I embark could any thing
material be done by People under Circumstances so highly
discouraging ?

For my own part, my Lord, I am able and willing to put up
with as small Accomodations as any Man living can be content
with ; Six feet square is more than sufficient for all my personal
conveniences nor are any of my People desirous of a larger
Allotment. Tis our great Cabbin which is too small, and that is
in reality the Shop where we are all to work which if not sufficiently large will deprive the Workmen of a possibillity of following
their respective employments and prevent me from reaping the
Fruit earned by voluntarily exposing myself to danger and
incurring a material Expence.

Neither personal hazard nor expence however will I withold
when likely with their proper encouragement ; born with an
Attachment to a singular pursuit I have already performed two
Voyages, and in the course of them have merited, I hope, some
share of the Public regard, and though my Services are upon this
Occasion refused, I shall always hold myself ready to go upon
this or any undertaking of the same Nature when ever I shall be
furnished with proper Accomodations for myself and my People
to exert their full Abilities

To explore is my Wish ; but the Place to which I may be
sent almost indifferent to me, whether the sources of the Nile or
the South Pole are to be visited I am equally ready to embark
in the undertaking when ever the Public will furnish me with
the means of doing it properly, but to undertake so expensive a
pursuit without any prospect but Distress and disapointment is
neither consistent with Prudence or Public Spirit

As to the position of no other Ship being fit for the Voyage,
because no other could take the Ground I cannot omit putting
your Lordship in Mind that within these few weeks the Emerald,
one of our sharpest Frigates, lay on Shore on the Gun fleet a
much longer time than the Endeavour did upon the Coast of
New Holland after which she was got off. Sir John Lindsay also

hauled up the Stag another of our Frigates at Trincomaly and shifted her Rudder Irons during the course of his last Voyage :

What more my Lord did the Endeavour do or what more could any Ship have done in that particular point on which the opinion of the Navy Board so materially rests ?

If these then are capable of taking the ground how much more so, must the Launceston (the Ship for which we have petitioned your Lordship) be, as all Seamen know that the bottoms of that Class of Ships are flatter than any others employed in His Majestys Service. For my own part I can only say that was your Lordship to think proper to let us have her for our intended Expedition, I would gladly embark on board a Ship in which safety and Accomodation, both which must be consulted in a Voyage of this kind are more nearly united than in any other kind of Ship I am acquainted with, and well know that there are many Commanders in His Majestys Service of un- doubted Abilities and experience who would willingly undertake to proceed with her in the intended Expedition ambitious of shewing the World that the success of such an Undertaking depends more upon the Prudence and perseverance of the Commander than upon any particular Built of the Ship that may be employed

I cannot dismiss this Letter without thanking your Lordship for the many particular Favors which I have received at your Lordships Hands in the commencement and during the prosecu- tion of this my Favorite Undertaking of which I shall ever retain a most grateful sense. I do not doubt that was not your Lordship prevented by forms of Office I should still continue to receive the same Countenance and Assistance, and that if it should be thought proper to alter or enlarge the present Equipment your Lordship would still continue your Protection, As I am not conscious that by any part of my Conduct I have forfieted that Claim to it which your Lordships great condescention and goodness originally conferr'd upon me

I am with the utmost respect Your Lordships most obliged and most obedient Humble Servant   Jos: BANKS

May 30th 1772.

No. 1066—*Memorandum by Sir George Collier.*

The Appearance of some Russian Men of War lately in our Seas, and their Success in the Mediterranean against the Turkish Fleet, led me to consider the Naval force of that Nation with more Attention, than possibly I might otherwise have done : the Result, was a clear and perfect Conviction that with the Dominions (extensive as they are) which Russia at present possesses, She *never can* become a great Maritime Power ; and my Reasons for taking up that Opinion are these

The 1st: (and most principal) is their having no Merchant Ships, the inevitable Consequence of which is their having no Seamen ; their Method of manning their Men of War, is to seize upon as many of the Common People as will make up the Number wanted ; (no matter of what Occupation,) and these they send out in their Ships to make the Campaign, (as they call it,) which is a Cruize in the Baltic for a Month or Six Weeks in the Summer ; where if it happens to *blow fresh*, or they are bound to Revel or any other Port and the *Wind contrary*, they come to an Anchor under the Lee of some Island till the Weather is such as they like : at the return of the Squadron, the Crews are discharged, and perhaps 30 Men out of the whole Number never go on board a Ship again [*sic*] : hence it is very plain that few or no Seamen can be bred in the Imperial Navy ; and the Empress has the Misfortune besides, of not having any Officers (*Natives of Russia,*) who are capable of disciplining and forming the Men ; for from the Admirals downwards, they all know so little themselves of Sea Matters, that they are by no Means equal to convey Instruction to others.

The 2d: Reason is the general Dislike which the Officers have to the Sea Service ; this arises partly from their Ignorance in their Profession, and partly from a kind of Uncreditableness attending it ; for tho' in point of Rank they are on a Line with the Army, yet they are held in a much inferior Light both by the Empress, and every body else ; the little Encouragement they meet with from her Imperial Majesty, as well as the smallness of their Pay, must therefore make the Profession of a Sea Officer not the most Eligible, and prevent People of Distinction from breeding their Sons to the Naval Service.

3dly. The tedious progress of Equipments, from the *Manner* of carrying on the Service ; if a few Nails or a Coyl of Rope is wanted, it can't be procur'd (let the Squadron be in ever so much Haste,) till a Memorial to the Admiralty Colledge has been sent, and References and Answers have passed ; which inevitably wastes a great deal of Time.

4^{thly}. From their having no Arsenals and Storehouses furnished with Materials for the Equipping of Ships ; most of those Things when wanted, must be purchased of Merchants ; and to make it Still more inconvenient, they have no Contractor to furnish any of the different Articles.

5^{thly}. From their Sea Ports being absolutely lock'd up by the Frost, and useless at least 7 Months in the Year.

6^{thly}. From the want of proper Encouragement to Ship Builders and Artificers : From the bad Construction of their Ships most of whose Knees and Standards are made of *Fir* ; their Timbers all cut out of *Streight* Wood ; and all the Wood they build with at Petersburgh and Cronstadt brought from more than a thousand Miles distant : From their never keeping any Stock of Timber in their Dock Yards, so that what they use in Building is Green, and consequently must soon decay : The Ships built at Archangel (their principal building Port) are all of Larch and Fir ; which joined to their Fleet being constantly in *fresh* Water, makes them decay very fast ; they Launch Yearly, from 5 to 7 Ships of the Line, which is about the Number that is every Year unserviceable and has (from Peter the great's Time) kept their Navy at about 20 Sail of the Line ; which unless the Russians shou'd hereafter become possessed of *better* Sea-Ports, they can never much exceed.   GEO. COLLIER.

No. 1067—*Lord North to the King.*

Lord North has the honour of requesting his Majesty's permission to wait upon his Majesty at Richmond this Evening between nine and ten o'clock.

DOWNING STREET *Monday June* 1 [1772].

No. 1068—*The King to Lord North.*

LORD NORTH—Upon coming home, I have found Your note and shall be ready to receive You at the time that You have named

KEW.   *June* 1*st* 1772.

$\frac{m}{30}$ p^t 7. PM.

No. 1069—*The King to Lord North.*

LORD NORTH—Your Servant did not arrive till half hour past Six I had then been above an hour out ; at half hour past Seven the inclination to Rain drove Me home, where I found Your letter, and instantly dispatched him with the answer that I should with pleasure receive You at the hour You had proposed ; as by the note You have now sent Me I find he was not returned at nine o'Clock and that You wish to learn what time will suit me best tomorrow, as You are an early Man I desire You will call here by ten o'Clock in the morning

KEW, *June* 1*st* 1772.

$\frac{m}{10}$. p^t 11. P.M.

No. 1070—*Observations on Mr. Banks's Letter*
(*see* No. 1066).

Mr. Banks's first Objection to the Ship respected only the Conveniences for himself, and was then no more than this, " that the forepart of the Cabin was an Inch or two too low." As to the proper kind of Ship, and her fitness and sufficiency for the Voyage, his opinion was never asked, nor could have been asked with any propriety, he being in no degree qualified to form a right Judgement in such a matter ; and for the same reason his opinion now thereon is not to be attended to. As to what concerned himself, as he increased his Suite, and his Demands, every thing was done to satisfy him ; by which it happened that the Properties of the Ship were so much altered that it has been necessary to take away the additional works that had been done at his request; in doing which it was so contrived that the Difference occasioned thereby to him was simply this—The great

Feet. Ins.

Cabin (6. 6 high between Plank and Plank) was shortened from 22 to 16 feet long; and there was one small Cabin for his attendants taken away. After this small Reduction, there remained on the whole much better Accomodations than he had in the former Voyage in the Endeavour; and the great Cabin remained in Length and Height though not in breadth, equal to those in a 74 Gun Ship* for an Admiral, who frequently embarks in such Ships to command His Majesty's Fleets at Sea, whose Cabins are

*Bellona Superb Arrogant &c[a].

Feet. Ins.   Feet. Ins.

only 16. 2 long and 6 : 6 high.

Mr. Banks seems throughout to consider the Ship as fitted out wholly for his use; the whole undertaking to depend on him and his People; and himself as the Director and Conductor of the whole; for which he is not qualified, and if granted to him would have been the greatest Disgrace that could be put on His Majesty's Naval Officers.

His Assertion that the Ship is incommodious to the People, and made worse to them by the late alteration, has a very evil tendency, to raise Discontent amongst the People, and for defeating the Voyage; but it may be averred he is mistaken in the Fact; for the People will be better accomodated, a freer Circulation of Air throughout the Ship, and in all respects wholesome, and the Men better lodged than they are in any King-built Ship of the same Dimensions and Burthen.

His application of the Cases of the Emerald and Stag, and the Conclusion he draws therefrom, discover him to have less knowledge of Matters relating to Ships than might be expected in one who has associated and converesed so much with His Majesty's Sea Officers—The First was on shore in a smooth-Water Channel *at home*, not on a *distant, strange, desolate* or savage Coast at the Antipodes. Six Ships instantly anchored by her, hauled alongside, took out her Guns, Provisions &c., and immediate assistance of every kind was sent from one of the King's Dock Yards. The Stag, if she was hove up, or hove down, at Trincomaly, it was a Port where there were conveniences for fitting Ships of burthen, and where undoubtedly they had all the like Conveniences that could be had in the River Thames. Had either of those Ships been in the Endeavour's place, on the Coast of New Holland, they would never have been heard of again : Even if they had got off the Rocks, they could not have been hauled up to repair Damages, as was done by the Endeavour.

June 3ᵈ 1772.

No. 1071—*Lord Suffolk to the King.*

Lord Suffolk has the honour to lay before Your Majesty a Letter he received this evening from Sʳ John Moore, upon which he has told him he wou'd take Your Majesty's pleasure, and inform him of it.

Lord Suffolk has not yet heard a word from Baron Diede.

DUKE Sʳ WESTMᴿ:
June 5. 1772.   12. *o'clock at night.*

No. 1072—*Lord Suffolk to the King.*

Lord Suffolk has the honour to acquaint Your Majesty that he has just had a Conference with Baron Diede, in which he has received a copy of the Instrument by which the King of Denmark engages to restore the Queen of Denmark's Fortune, exactly in the manner it is stipulated in that which Sʳ Robert Keith transmitted, which corresponds with it word for word.

Baron Diede is to meet Lord Suffolk on Wednesday at one o'clock to sign and seal this Instrument, and to receive the Receipt for it which Your Majesty has already seen and approved. so that after the Levee on Wednesday next, Lᵈ Suffolk will have the honour and happyness of delivering the finally Conclusive Paper of this tedious transaction into Your Majesty's hands.

Lord Suffolk did not omit to converse with the Danish Envoy on the other Busyness : He represented the Share of the late Princess's effects which in strictness of Law wou'd devolve to the King of Denmark as of no consequence to Him, tho' it wou'd be a material addition to the Little his unfortunate Queen was possessed of ; And therefore, that it cou'd not be supposed His Danish Majesty wou'd do otherwise than relinquish his claim to it in her favour. Lord Suffolk told the Baron he did not speak official to him ; that the Busyness was in Lord North's hands ; Who, from the peculiarity of his situation of Administrator cou'd not throw out this hint, which wou'd be very becoming in him to reflect upon, and therefore that Lord Suffolk took upon him to do it. Baron Diede said he made no doubt of the King of Denmark's giving up his share to the Queen ; and all his language on the subject was in that strain. He will not fail to take the sense of his court upon the occasion.

Captain Keith, and Mr. Man (Sr Horace Man's nephew, and his intended Proxcy) will attend together with Cap^{tn} Parker, at St. James's on Wednesday next, to receive the honour of Knighthood, if Your Majesty does not express Your Pleasure to the Contrary.

St. James's
June 8. 1772.

$\frac{m}{20} p^t$ 4. P.M.

No. 1073—*Lord Suffolk to the King.*

Lord Suffolk is unwilling to loose a moment's time in Acquainting Your Majesty that The Frigates arrived at Elsinoor on Wednesday evening May 27 ; and that the Queen of Denmark was to go on a Board at six o'clock of the evening of the 30th., when the wind was favourable for Her Majesty's immediate Departure.

St. James's
June 10. 1772. M.

No. 1074—*The King to Lord North.*

Printed.   Donne I. 103.

Lord North—My not receiving the Duke of Cumberland being a matter publickly known, it would be absurd in the Bishop of Salisbury to Summon him ; as to General Paoli's desire of Seeing Me, You need not be supposed to have named the request to Me till next Wednesday, then I shall hear what has passed, and can with greater propriety fix the time for Seeing him.

Kew, *June* 11th 1772.

$\frac{m}{10}. p^t$ 8 PM.

No. 1075—*Lord North to the King.*

Lord North has the honour of informing his Majesty that he has [had] a visit from the Bishop of Salisbury this morning, who is under some perplexity, not knowing whether he ought to Summon the Duke of Cumberland to the Chapter on Thursday : If he receives no orders to the contrary he will issue the Summons to his Royal Highness as a matter of course ; but as the Chapter is to be held in your Majesty's palace and presence he is unwilling to take this step without previously apprizeing your Majesty, which Ld North has undertaken to do for him, and to let him know, if he finds your Majesty has any objection to it.

Gen. Paoli was with Lord North this morning, when Lord North inform'd him that the payment of £1000 a month could not be continued to the Corsicans who are in the Dutchy of Tuscany longer than a twelvemonth from this time. Gen. Paoli remain'd with Lord North a considerable time, and the conversation ended by General Paoli's desiring an audience of your Majesty, at any time which your Majesty will please to appoint.

DOWNING STREET $\frac{3}{4}$ p^t *six.* P:M: *Friday June* 12 [1772].

No. 1076—*Lord Suffolk to the King.*

Lord Suffolk hopes Your Majesty will approve his having directed the inclosed Letter from Sr: Robert Keith to be sent to Your Majesty early in the morning, without waiting 'till the Dutch Mail, which is just arrived, is ready for Your Majesty's Inspection.

DUKE S^T WESTM^R

June 12. 1772. $\frac{m}{15}$ p^t 11. P.M.

No. 1077—*The King to Lord Suffolk.*

[13 *June*, 1772.]

Lord Suffolk's Attention in instantly communicating to Me Sir Robert Keith's Account of the Arrival of the Queen of Denmark at Stade is not lost.

No. 1078—*Lord Harcourt to the King.*

PARIS *June the* 17th 1772

SIR—I take the Liberty to avail myself of Colonel Blaquier's Return to England to express My Sense of the very great Obligation which your Majesty has been graciously pleased to confer on me, that carries along with it such evident Marks of your Favour, as not only redound much to My Honour, but what is of much more Consequence, may I hope enable me to serve your Majesty with more Credit and Reputation, in the exalted Station you have been pleased to place me.

If it is not too much Presumption in me to mention Ireland, before I am invested with your Majesty's Authority, I would humbly beg leave to submit it to your Majestys Consideration, whether the Place of Commissary General of that Kingdom should it become vacant, might not contribute towards an Arrangement highly beneficial to your Majesty's Service.

Taking for granted that Ld Drogheda would readily exchange the Ordnance for the Commissary General's Place, your Majesty might then have it in your Power to give the Ordnance and the Command in Chief of your Irish Troops, to any officer you shall think worthy of that important Station, and If I mistake not the late Lord Molesworth held both those Employments. Till this or some other Additional Provision is made for a Commander in Chief, I fear the five Pounds pr Diem will be thought inadequate to the Charge and Expense of that Station, and be a very insufficient Inducement to tempt any Officer of Credit to sollicite that command. I can presume to suggest these Hints with the greater Confidence, as I can have no other View in so doing, than that of promoting your Majesty's Service. Should you be pleased to make any Alteration in the Command of your Irish Troops, it would be the farthest from my Thoughts to propose any Thing that might be deemed a Hardship to the poor Man who now Commands in Ireland. His bad state of Health and his Age make him respectable but ought at the same Time not to make him averse to relinquish a Command for which some Compensation may be easily found, without any considerable Burden to Government, or any additional Charge to your Majesty. Should what I have ventured to throw out become impracticable, either by the unexpected Recovery of Lord Belvidere's Health, or from any other Cause whatsoever, I am in Hopes your Majesty will excuse the Liberty I have taken, and impute it only to My Zeal for your Majestys Service which ought ever to be the chief Object of, Sir, Your Majesty's Most Dutyfull & Faithfull Servant

HARCOURT.

No. 1079—*Memorandum by* (?).

Lieutenant John James Gordon of the 9th Reg^t of Foot.

1st Sentence.
Guilty of behaving in a manner unbecoming an Officer and a Gentleman, tho' not in a Scandalous or Infamous manner.

Falls under the *3^d* Article of the *20th* Section. Suspended from Pay and Duty for 12 months, and to be Reprimanded by the Commanding Officer att the Head of the Regiment.

The Sentence ordered to be Revised, by.
The Lord Lieutenant.

2^d Sentence.
Guilty of a Breach of the *23^d* Article of the *15th* Section—by which article The Prisoner is Discharged from His Majesty's Service, but In consideration of the *Prisoner's youth*, and Some favourable Circumstances which appeared to the Court During the Course of the Proceedings, They Recommend him to The Lord Lieutenant for Mercy.

Lord Ligonier Recommends him for Leave to Sell In Consideration of his *Family*, of his having *Served the Last War*, and of having *purchased his Commission*.

Lord Ligonier's Recommendation from his having Served the *Last War*, and the Court Martial's Recommendation on Account of his youth contradict Each other, and a Court-Martial, after finding an Officer Guilty of behaving *unbecoming an Officer and a Gentleman* Recommending him for Mercy, contradict the Rules of the Service.

Having bought his Commission, is no manner of Reason That he Shou'd Sell, when proved Guilty of Criminal Conduct, and It is to be much feared, That There is a nice pity of Checking these Drunken Quarrels in Ireland, and which are Productive of Dishonourable Proceedings.

The Lord Lieutenant in his Letter, Declares, That He is of

Opinion, that a man who wou'd be Guilty of Such Scandalous behaviour, shou'd not bear a Commission in Your Majesty's army.

Its Hard That The Highest Devolved Power shou'd not undertake to punish Scandalous Offender's without appealing to Your Majesty, and It will be Difficult to agree with the Court-Martial's Definition, That a Man can act *unbecoming an Officer and a Gentleman*, and yett not be Guilty of *Scandalous behaviour*.

If Your Majesty thinks, That The Court-Martial has Erred in Recommending a man to mercy, who is found Guilty of behaving in a manner *unbecoming an Officer and a* Gentleman It may be productive of Good. If The Lord Lieutenant was to Acquaint The Court-Martial of your Majesty's Opinion, and I acknowledge I can't Join in the Good nature of Lord Ligonier That Your Majesty Shou'd permit the favour of Selling to be Granted to Such a man, which is frequently Denied to Deserving Officers.

30*th* *August* 1772.

No. 1080—*Note.*

[This evidently has to do with the administration of the estate of the King's deceased mother.]

Les Dettes contractees en Allemagne par S. A. R. Mgr. le Prince de Galles, pendant les dernieres Années de Sa vie, & acquitees en *1761.* en conformité des Ordres de Sa Majesté à Son Ministere & à Sa Chambre des Finances à Hannover, montent en tout a 338400 écus d'Allemagne, en espèces nommées Florins, qui excedent dans la proportion de 5. pour 100. la valeur de l'ecu ordinaire.

Outre cette Somme de 338400. ecus, il reste encore à payer aux Creanciers celle de 145752. ecus, pour les satisfaire sur les interrets, qu'ils avoient à demander au terme du Remboursement de leurs Capitaux.

Les Preuves authentiques des Susdits Payemens ont eté deposé en quatre Volumes aux Archives de la Chancellerie Privée Electorale ici, et peuvent etre produit sur le premier Ordre

De la Chancellerie privée Electorale
du Roi a S James *ce* 17. *Juin* 1772.

Charles Hinüber
Secretaire Privé.

No. 1081—*Lord Suffolk to the King.*

Lord Suffolk takes the Liberty of Acquainting Your Majesty that he has postpond making use of Your Majesty's Indulgence upon hearing of S^r: Robt: Keith's Arrival ; who he understand brings Letters to Your Majesty from The King as well as Queen of Denmark. If your Majesty has no Commands for him, Lord Suffolk means to make the excursion he mentiond yesterday, and to set out late this evening or early tomorrow morning But he will certainly not Stir 'till he has received Your Majesty's farther pleasure.

HAMPTON COURT
June 20. 1772.
$\frac{m}{42}$ p^t 10. A.M.

No. 1082—*Lord Suffolk to the King.*

The enclosed Letter from Captain McBride, of Your Majesty's Ship the Southampton, giving an account of his proceedings in consequence of his Instructions for conveying Her Majesty the Queen of Denmark from Elsineur to Stade, was received this morning at Eleven o'clock

ADMIRALTY OFFICE
20 *June* 1772

Enclosure.
Captain Macbride to the Admiralty.

SOUTHAMPTON—DOWNES
June 18th: 1772.

SIR—In Obedience to their Lordships Orders of the 5th of May I acquaint you of my proceedings which you will be pleased to lay before their Lordships. I sailed on the 16th of May from the Downes of which I informed you by letter of that date, the little wind we Sailed with just carried us clear of the North Foreland when it came again to the North East ; in consequence of their Lordships order of the 7th: I hoisted a Broad Pendant and hauled it down on my return to the Coast ;—the Seaford sailed badly and I was obliged to Tow the Cruizer when the Weather would permit notwithstanding which I arrived off the Castle of Cronenburgh in the Evening of the 27th: ; I immediately sent an Officer on shore to the Consul to enquire for Sir Robert Murray Keith, and to know if there was Access to Her Majesty (who I could plainly distinguish on the Platform of the Castle) and if She was treated with respect and Attention, to wait on the Governor and say I would salute the Castle, the Officer returned with the Captain of the Fort with a civil Message from the Commandant, saying a proper return would be made to the salute in consequence of which I fired Seventeen Guns which was returned ; My Officer likewise informed me that Sir Robert Keith was at Copenhagen but would be at Elsinore in the Morning ; I immediately went ashore to the Castle and was Introduced to the Governor, as soon as Compliments were over I desired to know who were the Officers in waiting on Her Majesty as I wanted it to be announced to Her that I was arrived to attend upon her and receive her Commands, I was then Introduced to the Compte De Holstein the Grand Maitre, I soon found that no Message was to be delivered to the Queen at that time, and apprehended some Instructions from Court were wanted, from what happened I believe my Conjectures were right ; the Compte said when he had the Honor to see the Queen that night he would inform Her Majesty and send me an Answer in the Morning, I waited 'till four next Evening and finding Compte Holstein did not send any Message agreeable to his promise, I sent Captain Davis of the Seaford to him, desiring to know if my Message was delivered to the Queen and to say that he had treated me with great rudeness in not sending me an Answer as he promised ; he made some Aukward excuses and said The Queen would see me next Morning ; at Night Sir Robert Keith came to Elsinore, from him I learn'd the Number of People the Queen was to take with Her, and it was agreed I shoud meet him in the Morning, in consequence of which I went on shore taking Captains Davis and Cumming with me, about Noon we were presented to Her Majesty by Sir Robert Keith. There was a Danish Commodore there with a Boat of the King's who wanted to consult about the Queen's Accomodation and Reception &c^a, as both the Governor and Grand Maitre had treated me very uncivilly, I made a very short reply ; that I had received the Queen's Commands and did not come there to consult them what was to be done, that if they would shew me the place where they meant to Embarque Her Majesty from, it was all I wanted, and that as soon as She came to the water side she was then under my care and consequently they had nothing further to say on the Occasion

The Evening of the 29th: and Morning of the 30th: were taken up in getting on board the Baggage of Her Majesty and Suite, about Noon the wind blowing fresh from the Southward, I got the Ships under sail and drop'd round the point on which the Castle stands, for the more convenient reception of Her Majesty ; at Five O'Clock I went on shore with all the Boats I could make up, and with the other Captains Joined Sir Robert Keith at His Hotel, from whence we proceeded to the Castle and found that Her Majesty was ready ; we walked before through one of the Sally Ports to the place where the Boats were waiting by a stage erected for the purpose ; As soon as Her Majesty came to High water mark led by the Compte Holstein, I took Her from him and Conducted Her into the Southampton's Barge which was steered by Mr. Davey the First Lieutenant ; along with the Queen went the Comptess Holstein and One of Her Maids of Honour, As soon as Her Majesty was seated in the Boat the Standard was hoisted, when the Ships immediately fired a Royal Salute ; Sir Robert Keith went with me in my Cutter which preceded the Barge Her Majesty was in, Captain Davis with the Compte Holstein kept on the starboard and Captain Cumming on the Larboard Quarters with our Pendants in the Bows of the Boats, in this form we rowed alongside the Southampton, as soon as Her Majesty was on board my Broad Pendant was hauled down and Her Standard hoisted, which was again saluted with Twenty-one Guns from the Seaford and Cruizer, the Castle saluted with Twenty seven Guns as did Two Danish Men of War that passed us next morning ; it continued quite Calm with a Current strong against us 'till about Noon of the 1st of June when I immediately Sailed : the Comptess Holstein and Madam Mastein with Five Maids and about Twenty others were on board the Southampton, Sir Robert Keith, Compte Holstein and another Gentleman of the Court were in the Seaford ; We had a most fortunate passage to the Elbe of three days and just got in time enough to escape a smart Gale of wind, at four in the

Evening of the 4th I anchored off Gluckstadt as did the Seaford, the Cruizer came in next Morning, about Noon we got under sail, and at four Anchored of Stadt; Her Majesty was then disembarqued in the same manner she came on board, with this difference only, that the Ships saluted twice as she went on shore, and when she left Stadt the day following I order'd Another salute with the Garrison.

Her Majesty was pleased to express Her Approbation of our Treatment and Attention to Her, and was so good to ask us to Accompany Her to the Palace of Goard, we returned the 11th Instant to Stadt; As the people of Fashion there had behaved in the Handsomest Manner to Her Majesty and all those who came with Her; and seemed Anxious to see the Ships, I gave them a General Invitation for the 12th: when About Forty Ladies and Gentlemen dined in the Southampton and went away highly pleased; I sailed next Morning, and have only to Add, that every contrivance that was possible to render the Ship Convenient and Agreeable was thought of, the want of Beds, Bedding, Linnen, and other necessaries I supplied in the best manner I could or the short warning I had would Admit

The Compte Holstein and the Ladies who Accompanied Her Majesty, prefer'd going to Altona in a Yatch from Stadt Sir Robert Keith is return'd to England with me, the Seaford is arrived in Company I parted with the Cruizer two days ago off the Texel

I am, Sir, Your most Obedient Humble Servant

JNO MAC'BRIDE

No. 1083—*Lord Sandwich to the King.*

AUGUSTA AT SEA OFF DARTMOUTH
June 20. 1772

Lord Sandwich has the honour to transmitt to Your Majesty his observations thus far. He allso sends a sketch of a letter in answer to that written to him by Mr Banks, which may possibly be proper to be printed in case the other is made publick. Your Majesty will observe that it is under a fictitious name, which for many reasons is most adviseable.

We are now in company with the four ships of the Line, but

as the wind is contrary it is not certain that we shall get to Plymouth to morrow. We sailed from Portsmouth last Wednesday Morning.

No. 1084—*Lord Suffolk to the King.*

Lord Suffolk is extreemly happy that Your Majesty is pleased and satisfyed with what passed when Your Majesty saw Sr Robert Keith, whose attention, Honour, and abilities nothing can surpass— He hopes Your Majesty will find the drat to Woodford prepared according to Your Orders.— He has this inst received the inclosed private Letter from Lord Rochford which he takes the Liberty of laying before Your Majesty— He hears sad accounts of the Bankruptcys and confusions in the City in consequence of Mr Fordyce's Failure— What a pity it is Sir, that the just Fate of a bad man shou'd involve numbers of honest People in Ruin !

Sᵀ Jamˢ's
June 23. 1772.

$\frac{m}{20}$ *pᵗ* 4. P.M.

No. 1085—*Lord Suffolk to the King.*

The inclosed letter from Mr. Morris is so extraordinary that Lord Suffolk takes the Liberty of accompanying it with a line from himself, to express his hopes that Your Majesty will approve of his sending it to the Chancellor with the Letter which he lays before Your Majesty for that purpose : it seems all that is necessary to be done on the occasion.

Hampton Court
June 27. 1772.

$\frac{m}{40}$ *pᵗ* 5 P.M.

No. 1086—*The King to Lord Suffolk.*

Lord Suffolk—The letter from Mr Morris is very extraordinary, but very suitable to the Company he has kept, who have never deemed a breach of trust as dishonourable, your letter

to the Chancellor is highly proper, and puts things into the right
Channel

KEW *June* 27*th* 1772.

$\frac{m}{8}$ *p*^t 8. PM.

*Draft, written on a page of Lord Suffolk's
letter of same date.*

No. 1087—*Lord Rochford to the King.*

[The Senate of Sweden on the death of Charles XII. had seized the
greater part of the Royal prerogatives. King Gustavus III. succeeded in
resuming them by stirring up an insurrection in Scania and a military
movement in Stockholm ; the Court of Versailles supporting him by a
subsidy. This happened in August ; but the English Foreign Office, as is
here shown, had early intelligence of what was coming. Sir John Goodricke
was British Minister at Stockholm.]

Lord Rochford has the honor to acquaint your Majesty that
on receiving your Majesty's note last night I got Mr. Fraser who
was in the way, and immediately wrote the inclosed letter to
Sr John Goodricke, which Lord Rochford flatters himself your
Majesty will approve and of his sending it by a messenger who
went away this morning at two o'clock, it was impossible to put
the whole letters in cypher in time, and there is now a possibility
of Booths arriving in time to prevent the mischeif, as he has
orders to use the utmost expedition Your Majesty will observe
Sr John Goodricke is strongly recommend[ed] to conceal the
Intelligence, and in sending him the copies, the names on the top
of each letter were left out ; I shall send the two letters by a
Messenger to Lord Suffolk this afternoon and acquaint him with
what I have done.

CLEVELAND ROW, 4*th July* 1772.

$\frac{m}{10}$ *past one* PM.

No. 1088—*Lord Suffolk to the King.*

Lord Suffolk, tho' always reluctant to give Your Majesty
trouble, cannot refrain from expressing how much he is vexed

to have been absent when the material Intelligence relative to Sweden was receiv'd. He finds that copies of Vergenne's and d'Aiguillon's Letters have been sent to Sr John Goodricke ; But wont conceal from Your Majesty that he does not see the absolute necessity for this Proceeding. The Story lay in a narrow compass, and might have been accurately related without risquing the Discovery of so important a channell of Intelligence. But he is apprised that it is not the first time that Sr John Goodricke has been thus confidentialy treated ; and therefore cannot suppose that any ill consequences will follow what has been done in this instance. It was certainly necessary that Your Majesty's Envoy at Stockholm shou'd have early and complete information of such an Enterprise—Lord Suffolk cannot help thinking it a very extravagant one, tho' it seems as if the King of Sweeden did not act without concert with France, however suddenly his Plans come upon the French Ambassador.

CHARLETON
July 5. 1772.

No. 1089—*The King to Lord Suffolk.*

LORD SUFFOLK—On receiving the very authentic account of an intended attempt to change the Constitution of Sweden by some desperate measures, I thought it highly necessary to transmit it instantly to You with directions that if You had left London it should be carried to Lord Rochford ; he unfortunately has sent Copies of the two Letters instead of putting their contents into another form ; there is a letter of Vergennes which confirms the former one, but states that the stroke will not be struck till the middle of this month, I therefore hope Sir John Goodricke will be apprized in time ; least the same imprudence should be repeated on this occasion, I have wrote directions to Mr Eden that the contents must only be sent to Sir John, not a Copy of the letter.

KEW *July* 6th 1772.

Draft, written on a page of Lord Suffolk's
letter of preceding day.

No. 1090—*Lord North to the King.*

Lord North has the honour of informing his Majesty, that Mr. Eden having come over this morning to Bushy, and brought with him Mr. de Vergenne's letters to the Duke of Aiguillon, Lord North has, in the absence of Lord Suffolk and Lord Rochford, ventured to advise Mr. Eden to send over by a messenger, to Sʳ John Goodricke, Mr. de Vergenne's second letter, by which it appears that the K. of Sweeden's plan of altering the Swedish Constitution by force is laid aside.   Lord North thinks that it is desirable that Sʳ John Goodricke should receive the second letter at the same time with the first, or as soon after as possible, least he should in consequence of the first letter, embark in measures which the alteration of the K. of Sweeden's plan would render improper or unnecessary.

Bushy Park.   *July* 6. 1772.

No. 1091—*The King to Lord North.*

Lord North—The advice given by You this morning to Mr. Eden was perfectly agreable to the contents of Mr. de Vergennes letter, but it certainly alluded to the Plan formed in April ; for the enclosed dispatch of a later date proves that the scheme of changing the Constitution of Sweden is to be attempted in the course of this month agreable to the dispatch I communicated to Lord Rochford on Friday, which caused the transmitting that account by that night's packet to Sir John Goodricke ; You will send the enclosed dispatch when You have perused it to Mr. Eden.

Kew, *July 6th* 1772.

$\frac{m}{5}$ p^t 3. PM.

No. 1092—*Lord Rochford to the King.*

Lord Rochford who was gone a few miles out of Town did not see the last interceptions untill this morning, and is humbly of opinion that it will be much the safest way to send a messenger and by a letter Mr. Eden has received from Lord North, his lordship seems to wish a messenger should be sent, and if your

majesty should approve of it he shall sent off as soon as your
majesty has approved of the inclosed Draught, in which your
Majesty will, it is hoped, think all the interceptions have been
fully analysed and that Sr. John Goodricke will have all the
requisite information.

CLEVELAND ROW 7 *July* 1772.

$\dfrac{m}{50}$ PM.

No. 1093—*Lord Barrington to the King.*

WAR OFFICE
July 17. 1772
½ *an hour past four.*

On looking into the Army book, I find that I reported errone-
ously to your Majesty, for which I most humbly ask pardon.
L. Col. Garth's commission is dated as Lieutenant in the first
Regiment of Guards in September 1758, which made him an
older Captain in the army than Mr. West by near ten months. I
have defer'd my letter to Lord Digby till I knew whether your
Majesty thinks Captain West's pretensions sufficient to exclude
Major Digby, notwithstanding Mr. Garth, lately promoted, *was
an older Captain than Mr. West.* I am much distressed that a
mistake of mine should occasion this trouble to your Majesty.

BARRINGTON.

No. 1094—*The King to Lord Barrington.*

LORD BARRINGTON—The having been incorrect in reporting
Lieut. Col. Garth as a Younger Capt. in the Army than Capt.
West, makes Your immediately rectifying it by the letter I have
just received perfectly right ; but it is not a reason for my
altering the determination of permitting Capt. West to purchase
the Company in the first Regt. of Guards ; these Corps are
certainly sensible that in the affair of rank, I leant to the Line,
therefore though I am not inclined to advance them in preference
to the rest of the Army, I must not without particular reasons too
often put persons upon them, When they are able to purchase,

besides Major Hawke is not yet a Lieut. Col. and I should not chuse to put any Major over his head.

KEW, *July* 17
     1772.

Draft, written on a page of Lord Barrington's
     letter of same date.

No. 1095—*Lord Rochford to the King.*

Lord Rochford takes the Liberty to trouble your majesty with the inclosed presentation for your majestys signing, as Lord Suffolk intended to do it but the affair presses as your majesty will see by Lord Marchmonts letters. Lord Rochford also begs leave to trouble your majesty by Lord North's desire for a dispensation for Mr. Stillingfleet.

CLEVELAND ROW
     18*th July* 1772.

No. 1096—*Lord Rochford to the King.*

Lord Rochford takes the liberty to inform your majesty that last night he wrote both to Lord Hillsborough and Lord North and having received the inclosed answer from Lord Hillsborough he ventures to trouble your majesty with it and also with a copy of his own letter to Lord Hillsborough. Lord North has as yet sent no answer.

CLEVELAND ROW
20 *July* 1772. $\frac{m}{40}$ *past* 11 AM.

No. 1097—*Memorandum in the King's Handwriting.*

[20 *July,* 1772.]

2^d Bat. of the Royals Reviewed 10th June 1767 at Inverness ;
               29th of Augt 1768. N. Berwick
4th Regt. of Foot 11th April 1767 at Cirencester.
               1768. 13th July at Edinburgh.

6th	11th of June 1767 at Fort George
	1768. 24th May at Inverness.
7th	4th June 1767 at Perth.
	1768. Fort George. 25th of May
8th	28th of Augt 1767. at Dover Castle.
	1768. 14th of April D^o
12th	26th of May 1767. at Chatham
	1768. 11th of May D^o
13th	26th of May 1767. at Chatham
	1768 12th of May D^o
22^d	30th of June 1767. at Chatham
	? 1768 3rd of Oct. at Stroud
	1768. 24th of May at Plymouth
23^d	28th of May 1767 at Edinburgh.
	1768. 27th of May D^o
25th	26th of June 1767. at Stirling
	1768. 13th of May at Chatham
35th	30th of June 1767 at Chatham
	1768. 31st of May at Salisbury
43^d	20th of April 1767. at Plymouth.
	1768. 21st of May at Exeter

*Written on the back of Lord Rochford's
letter of 20 July, 1772.*

No. 1098—*Lord Rochford to the King.*

Lord Rochford is under the greatest confusion at being
obliged to be so troublesome but the inclosed letter he has received
from Lord North is of too serious a nature for him to omit
communicating it to your Majesty. Lord Rochford takes the
Liberty at the same time to trouble your majesty with his answer
to Lord North and to inform your majesty that he purposes to
take no further steps in this business untill he hears again from
Lord Gower being desirous to do every thing to the utmost of his
power that he thinks most conducive to your majestys services

CLEVELAND ROW

21 *July* 1772 $\dfrac{m}{50}$ PM.

No. 1099—*Lord Suffolk to the King.*

Lord Suffolk presumes to trouble Your Majesty with a few lines in consequence of a communication he has received, on his return this evening, of some part of what has passed between Lord Rochford & Lord North & on the Ohio Report : But he does it with the utmost Diffidence, & if he shou'd seem to be guilty of any impertinent interference, he implores Your Majesty to attribute his conduct to the sole motive which actuated it, namely that of wishing this disagreable affair (which he had no conception cou'd have ever become serious) may terminate in the best manner for Your Majesty's own personal ease & satisfaction, & for Your Majesty's Government. He feels no other warmth than this on the occasion : And if his having been accidentaly absent, & of course a good deal out of the scrape, and not being (as he hoped) ill with any of the parties concerned, can give him the least chance of being able to accomodate matters between any of them, he is ready to devote himself to Your Majesty's commands in any shape without considering trouble or fatigue of any kind, however fruitless it may prove, & however well convinced he may be of the general Prudence in avoiding to get into Disputes which accident may have kept one out of. In the mean time he cannot refrain from most humbly expressing a wish that no farther steps may be taken in this Business before Your Majesty has had a conversation with Lord North, & learn'd from himself his real intentions & ideas. The not having a chance of seeing Your Majesty alone tomorrow induces Lord Suffolk to take this liberty : He is so much struck with what he has just heard has passed on the subject, that he cou'd not be easy without unbosoming himself confidentialy (if he may dare to use the expression) to Your Majesty ; and on this principle, & your Majesty's goodness he relies for pardon.

HAMPTON COURT
July 21. 1772. 10. P.M.

No. 1100—*The King to Lord Suffolk.*

LORD SUFFOLK—The handsome manner in which You have unbossomed Yourself to Me by the letter I have just received gives me great pleasure the more as I can perceive You take the affairs in the same light I do ; I shall but briefly mention what has passed that I may shew what has been the cause of the present very unpleasant state of affairs ; after Your departure into the Country Lord North wrote to Lord Gower to desire the report on the Ohio business might be postponed, to which he received an answer that consented to it if the Cabinet but particularly You and Ld. Rochford came into it ; but the latter was certainly cold, the debating at Cabinet whether a report directed by the Privy Council should remain dormant was a new idea ; Your Brother Secretary who though possessed of many amiable qualities is not very prudent on receiving Your letter, (wherein You thought this unnecessary but chose Lord North as he had got into the puzzle should extricate himself out of it) writes to the President that the two Secretaries were averse to the proposal, upon which Gower directs him to report it directly this he has communicated to Ld. Hillsborough who means to resign in a few days, but by the letter Lord Rochford sent me yesterday I find Lord North takes the thing much to heart and has certainly been actuated upon by Lord Hillsborough, whose natural suspicion is greatly encreased by the whole of this trans-action and if care is not taken may be productive of some personal unpleasant thing between Rochford and him, by this short state of the affair You must see Lord North's natural good nature and love of indecision, added to too much precipitation in Lord Rochford, and suspicion in Lord Hillsborough, with want of confidence in all the parties have brought this to the present strange situation which is rather difficult to be unravelled ; I directed Lord Rochford yesterday to take no further step till he had seen Lord North and reported to Me what has passed I desire You will this morning see Lord North and pave the way to his speaking openly to You, I know the share you have in his esteem, but while You shew him an inclination to ease his mind You must not forget that in trying to keep Lord Hills-borough care must be taken of the danger of offending Lord Gower, this must be touched on very lightly in the first con-versation

KEW, *July* 22^d 1772.

Draft.

No. 1101—*Lord Suffolk to the King.*

Lord Suffolk has the honour to lay before Your Majesty the
Letter he wrote yesterday to Judge Willes—one that he has
received this morning addressed to Lord Rochford from the
Duke of Richmond, and an answer to it ; which he humbly hopes
Your Majesty will approve of.

HAMPTON COURT
Aug. 1. 1772.   11. A.M.

No. 1102—*The King to Lord North.*

Printed.   Donne I. 105.

[Lord Stormont was Ambassador at Paris. The demolition of the
fortifications of Dunkirk was a provision of the Treaty of Utrecht, repeated
in the preliminaries of 1762, which France had never fulfilled.]

LORD NORTH—The dispatches that arrived last night from
France are of so serious a nature, that I am unwilling to be silent
on the subject untill Wednesday ; I therefore mean by this
method to convey my thoughts unto You, which will enable You
to revolve it in Your mind and to suggest what has occurred to
You when we meet next.   Were the Members of the French
Ministry well settled in their Employments, and their King well
instructed and able to weigh the consequences of the steps he
may take, the language of intending to continue the quai begun
the last year at Dunkirk would convince me that there was a
hidden desire to enter into a War ; but when I consider how very
unsettled every thing is in France and more to the Character of the
Monarch [*sic*], I am convinced that they do not forsee the danger
they are running of drawing themselves into discussions with us,
which if not conduct[ed] with the greatest temper may draw both
Nations into that which they ought assiduously to avoid.   I am
glad to see that Lord Stormont views it in this light also ; Lord
Rochford (whose zeal makes him rather in a hurry) by a note
I received with the Dispatches wanted to write him an answer
with strength to oppose the steps that are proposed to be taken ;
I wrote him in answer that with the heat Lord Stormont repre-

sents to be principal feature in the Character of the King, that too much fire might bring things to what no honest man can wish ; that therefore I thought the affair too delicate to give any directions untill I had received the opinion of such Ministers as shall be in town this week ; I do not mean that I am inclined to yield, but I am averse to make a point of honour of such a trifle as the quai of Dunkirk ; I would order Lord Stormont with temper, politeness, and candour to prove that what is proposed is contrary to the strict letter of Treaties, but I would at the same time consider whether he might not grant a part if not very material to put an end to this tiresome correspondence ; Lord Stormonts private letter to Lord Rochford seems to state a mode of doing it ; You may think Me prolix, but it is from not desiring that the heat of a Boy may throw me so much off my guard as to draw this Country into another addition of 50 Millions to the National Debt ; we must get the Colonies into order before we engage with our Neighbours

KEW, *Aug^t* 1*st* 1772.

No. 1103—*Captain Cook to* (?).

RESOLUTION, AT MADEIRA 1*st Aug^t*
1772.

SIR—I have now the pleasure to acquaint you that the Resolution answers in every respect as well, nay even better than we could expect, she steers works, sails well and is remarkably stiff and seems to promise to be a dry and very easy ship in the Sea ; In our passage from Plymouth we were once under our Courses but it was not wind that obliged the Resolution to take in her Topsails tho' it blow'd hard, but because the Adventure could not carry hers. in point of sailing the two Sloops are well match'd what difference there is is in favour of the Resolution I arrived here late in the evening of the 28th of last month and shall put to Sea again this evening having got on board all our Wine water &c^a—

Three days before we arrived a person left the Island who went by the name of Burnett he had been waiting for Mr Banks arrival about three months, at first he said he came here for the recovery of his health, but afterwards said his intention was to go out with Mr Banks, to some he said he was unknown to this Gentleman, to others he said it was by his appointment he came here as he could not be received on board in England, at last when he heard that Mr Banks did not go, he took the very first opportunity to get of the Island, he was about 30 Years of age, and rather ordinary than otherwise and employ'd his time in Botanizing &c^a—every part of Mr Burnetts behaviour and every action tended to prove that he was a Woman, I have not met with a person that entertains a doubt of a contrary nature, he brought letters of recomendation to an English House where he was accomodated during his stay. It must be observed that Mrs Burnett must have left London about the time we were first ready to sail

I am &c^a   JAM^S COOK

Copy.

No. 1104—*Lord Suffolk to the King.*

Lord Suffolk thinks it his Duty to submit to your Majesty a Letter he has just received from the Chancellor containing one from Lord Mansfield ; that alluded to, in the latter, from the Duke of Richmond, is an exact copy of his Grace's letter to Lord Rochford. From the Dispositions the chancellor is in, it seems unnecessary to lay the Recorders letter before Him. Lord Mansfield appears rather inclined against a hasty Execution ; and if Mr Justice Willes's answer does not come in time, Lord Suffolk presumes Your Majesty will please to delay it.

HAMPTON COURT

Aug. 3. 1772. $\frac{m}{55}$. *p^t* 3. P.M.

No. 1105—*The King to Lord Suffolk.*

LORD SUFFOLK—Nothing but Mr Justice Willes's answer not arriving in time can be a reason for delaying the execution for Jones ; I cannot say Lord Mansfield's letter to the Chancellor has changed my opinion on the contrary the Lady of fortune has every appearance of being fictitious as she has not produced Her name.

KEW, *Aug^t* 3^d 1772.

$\frac{m}{15}$ *p^t* 5. PM,

*Draft, written on a page of Lord Suffolk's
letter of same date.*

No. 1106—*Lord North to the King.*

[3 *August*, 1772.]

Lord North has received the honour of his Majesty's commands to which he will give all possible attention ; and has leave to acknowledge his Majesty's goodness in apprizing him of his sentiments upon the subject. He received Lord Stormont's letters from Lord Rochford today, & return'd in answer, that he thought the first question was how far the Quai at Dunkirk was a breach of Treaty ; That treaty must certainly be observed, But, if our treaty-rights are not affected, the Works carrying out Dunkirk did not appear to Lord North to be in themselves of great importance.

Lord North is convinced that this renewal of the measures respecting Dunkirk proceeds from Monsr du May, who is lately return'd from the command of Flanders, & is therefore, eager about every thing that relates to Dunkirk.

Monday Even^g

No. 1107—*Lord Suffolk to the King.*

Lord Suffolk has this instant received Mr Justice Willes's Report, which he has the honour to transmit to Your Majesty ; And for any Light that it throws on the affair, or satisfaction that it affords, the Reference might as well have never been made. Whether the Judge means any thing favourable to the Convict by reminding Lord Suffolk that the Execution is fixed for Wednesday next, is humbly submitted to Your Majesty's mercyfull Interpretation.

Upon the whole; it seems clearly the opinion of all the Lawyers, who are acquainted with the case, that *by Law* the Wretch ought to suffer; on the other hand, many sensible & honourable Men fear, that, whatever may be the Truth of the Fact, it is proved by a Testimony in its nature so suspicious, and so equaly applicable on any future occasion to the Innocent as to the Guilty, that the Judgement, in consequence of it, cannot be executed without great & general Danger to the Lives & Honour of Many.

HAMPTON COURT
August 3. 1772.

$\frac{m}{39}$ p^t 11. P.M.

No. 1108—*The King to Lord Suffolk.*

[The trouble in this case was that the woman who set the prosecution on foot was said to be insane. It was tried by Lord Mansfield, who in his charge to the jury dwelt on her sanity.]

LORD SUFFOLK—The Judges opinion on the case of Jones does not give the smallest assistance; I owne all that has passed since the Report, only confirms me in his being guilty; but that every room may be given to getting to the bottom of the affair, I do not object to Your humane wish for a short respit, but the wretch ought to know that he is not to build upon it. I cannot see great reason for apprehending that this case will give rise to attempts of charging persons with this crime without foundation, for both Judges and Juries ought to be very cautious on such occasions, and where there is no truth the tale cannot well be supported; but I think his being executed may allarm others who are I fear but too guilty of the same Vice, for they will see that it is difficult sooner or later not to be brought to Justice.

KEW, *Aug*^{t} *4th* 1772.

$\frac{m}{40}$. p^t 7. A.M.

*Draft, written on a page of Lord Suffolk's
letter of preceding day.*

No. 1109—*Lord North to the King.*

[4 *August*, 1772.]

Lord North has the honour of transmitting to his Majesty a letter which he received yesterday from Lord Weymouth, & of informing his Majesty, that he has, in obedience to his Majesty's commands, written to Lord Dartmouth, to offer him the American seal.

BUSHY PARK, *Tuesday morn*ᵍ.

No. 1110—*The King to Lord North.*

LORD NORTH—The manner in which Lord Weymouth expresses himself though he declines accepting is so very handsome that You ought to express to him my approbation of his sentiments of attachment to my Person ; I hope the answer from Lord Dartmouth will be more favourable, and I doubt not he will readily comply to any regulations that may be thought necessary to prevent jarrings in department that ever are hurtful to the Service.

KEW, *Aug*ᵗ 4*th* 1772.

$\frac{m}{35}$. p^t 4. PM.

No. 1111—*Lord Boston to the King.*

*Tuesday, August y*ᵉ 4*th* 1772.

Lord Boston with all due Respect, and submission begs Leave to present his most humble Duty to The King, and to inform His Majesty, That in obedience to His Royal Commands, Mr Le Grand, and he with Two Jewellers, and Mr Watt, went this Morning to The Bank, where The Two Boxes containing The Late Princess of Wales valuable Effects on the search after her Death were lodged, when Mr Castelfranc and Mr Romilly The Person Nominated to make an appraisment into the Value of Her Late Royal Highnesses Jewells, They did make a carefull examination into them, Lord Boston humbly conveys therefore for His Majestys Perusal the inclosed wrote out account, taken by the said Jewellers of them at a Middle Price, They Assert The Jewells may be of more Value, if they were to be disposed of to Persons not in their trade, but were They to be Purchased by Jewellers, they would not produce Even the Prices, which They have fixed on them in their appraisment £7481. . . . The Cash, Bank Bills &c &c placed in the Great Box answers to the amount, which His Majesty has had before the Intelligence. £7404–0– . There are likewise contained in the two Boxes a Number of Trinkets supposed to be of some Value, But the Jewellers could not pretend to set any value on them, but some other Person, who may better be acquainted with the Worth of them, when necessary, must be appointed to do it.

Lord Boston thus gives to His Majesty the account, of what Mr Le Grand, and he saw done at the Bank this day, and the examination of Jewells took up four hours, Lord Boston returns to the King the Keys of the Boxes, and the inventory of the Effects contained in them formerly taken by the Earl of Rochford, Mr Le Grand and by him which His Majesty was Most graciously Pleased and did him the Honour to send to him on Munday Afternoon.

No. 1112—*Lord Suffolk to the King.*

[7 *August,* 1772.]

It is humbly submitted that the Admiral or Commander of the Fleet on the American or West India Station should transfer His Correspondence from the Secretary of State for the American Department to the Secretary of State for Foreign Affairs for the Southern Department, Also that the Commander in Chief in America, as well as the different Governors should correspond with the Secretary of State for Foreign Affairs for the Southern Department on all Matters of a Political Nature which may arise between them & any Governor or other Officer of Foreign Powers. And that, as to all Military Arrangements or Operations in Time of War, the Commander in Chief in America should solely correspond with & receive His Orders from the Secretary of State for Foreign Affairs for the Southern Department.

Endorsed by the King. Paper delivered me by the E. of Suffolk Aug. 7th, 1772.

No. 1113—*The King to Lord North.*

Printed. Donne I. 106.

LORD NORTH—Having received with the Mail that arrived Yesterday the letter of Attorney signed by the Queen of Denmark, I take this method of returning it to You. I also transmit a sketch of such alterations in carrying on the American affairs as I think essential towards preventing future jarrings between the different departments ; You will see by it that patronage and every degree of emolument is by it left as amply to the American Secretary as whilst those Seals were held by Lord Hillsborough. I am certain the candour and good sense of Lord Dartmouth will see that I have no other object but to prevent any uneasiness that might arise in futurity, I have therefore looked also forward to a time of War ; the interior police, the trade and improvement of America are the points that require being taken out of the perplexed mode of a joint interference of the Southern Secretary and the Board of Trade ; and gave rise to that Department which cannot be in more proper hands than those of Lord Dartmouth.

KEW, *Aug* 9th* 1772.

Draft, endorsed by the King.

Another draft, much corrected, with slight variations. A fair copy of this draft in the King's handwriting.

Enclosure.

[In the King's handwriting.]

To prevent the possibility of jarrings in departments it is proposed on the present vacancy of the Office of Secretary of State for American Affairs,

1º That the Admirals or Commanders in Chief of the Several Squadrons in America shall for the future transfer their correspondence from the Secretary of State for the American Department to the Secretary of State for Foreign Affairs of the Southern Department, as they generally relate to Subjects of a Political Nature not the interior arrangements of America.

2⁰ That the Commander in Chief in America as well as the different Governors shall for the future correspond with the Secretary of State for Foreign Affairs of the Southern Department on all matters of a Political nature which may arise between them and any Governor or other Officer of Foreign Powers.

3ᵗⁱᵒ That all orders relating to Military Arrangements, or Operations in time of War shall be expedited to the Commander in Chief in America by the Secretary of State for Foreign Affairs of the Southern Department.

No. 1114—*Lord Suffolk to the King.*

Lord Suffolk has the honour to transmit to Your Majesty Lord Mansfield's answer, which he has this instant received—also a note to Mr. Fraser, with the Respit signed, He humbly hopes that in case your Majesty's Pleasure shou'd be contrary to what he has done, that your Majesty will give orders to the Messenger to return to him, & will immediately prepare fresh Directions to Mr. Fraser in exact conformity to Your Majesty's commands. if your Majesty approves of the Respit &c, he presumes to request Your Majesty to take out Lord Mansfield's Letter and destroy it, as his Lordship desires, or to be pleased to deliver it to Lᵈ Suffolk when he has next the honour to approach Your Majesty—and then to dispatch the Messenger with the remaining contents of the Box to the office. In any other case but where life is concerned he wou'd be incapable of imposing such trouble on Your Majesty.

HAMPTON COURT
August 10. 1772.

$\frac{m}{50}$ pᵗ. P.M.

No. 1115—*Lord North to Lord [Dartmouth ?].*

[The papers referred to are evidently the King's letter and enclosures of the 9th of August.]

BUSHY PARK *Aug* 10. [1772].

MY DEAR LORD—I received the inclosed papers yesterday but could not send them to you before this morning. The Writer is strongly impressed with the propriety and even necessity of the proposed alterations in the American department : With all the deference I have, & ought to have to his judgement, I own that I do not perceive the great inconveniencies of the present system, & believe that the proposed regulations themselves will be found liable to some difficulties, & require future amendment as much as the plan which is now to be corrected. I remember, however, that during the alarms of an approaching war the K: was much interested by the difficulties which were started by the Secretary of the Southern department about the interference of the American Secretary in the foreign & Military business arising in North America & the West Indies : There certainly was a little awkwardness in the manner of conducting that business, & some transactions were obliged to pass through two hands instead of one, but I always suspected that the Southern office aggravated every inconvenience beyond it's first magnitude in hopes of recovering the Patronage & emoluments which had been lost by it, when the Office of Secretary of State for America was created. I suppose His Maj: has often heard a repetition of the same complaints & expects to put an end to them by the proposed regulations. I do not know whether they will appear to you a detriment or an improvement to your Office. Be so good as to consider them, & to let me know if you have any or what objections to them. As for the Southern Department who have made these complaints they, I believe, will be hardly satisfied with them. They will find that they have shot at a pigeon, & kill'd a crow. I shall be in town on Wednesday morning, & shall be glad to hear your sentiments upon these papers before I go into the Closet.

I am, My dear Lord, most affec^{tely} & faithfully Yours.   N.

No. 1116—*Lord Suffolk to the King.*

[This evidently refers to the case of the convict Jones ; see No. 1108.]

Lord Suffolk was in hopes not to have been under a necessity of troubling your Majesty above once more upon the most disagreable of Topics. But as it is precarious whether an answer to a letter he wrote yesterday to Lord Mansfield (who is to-day on the circuit at Horsham) may arrive in time, he cannot avoid submitting it to Your Majesty whether in case it does not Your Majesty would not think a Respit proper to be granted. He incloses the Dra^t of the Letter he sent to Lord Mansfield, which was accompanied by your Majesty's note of Yesterday (there not appearing any thing in it that might not be communicated to Lord Mansfield) and Mr Burke's Letter. He will be happy to hear that Your Majesty is pleased not to disapprove the steps he has taken—He presumes to lay before Your Majesty a letter, entirely private, from the Solicitor General to Mr Eden, as part of it relates to the present Business also a Paper received from the unhappy wretch himself.

HAMPTON COURT
August 10. 1772.
$\frac{m}{10} p^t$ 3. P.M.

No. 1117—*The King to Lord North.*

Printed. Donne I. 108.

LORD NORTH—Having received Your letter recommending Doctor Vivian at the request of Lord Suffolk to succeed Doctor Kelly Regius Professor of Physick at Oxford, I impower You to direct a Warrant to be prepared in his favour; I am thoroughly resolved that these employments at both Universities shall be faithfully administered not held as Sinecures; therefore the Gentleman must be acquainted that He will be required to read such a number of Lectures as the Heads of Houses may think necessary.

I take this opportunity of enclosing to You a list of the Servants that I find absolutely necessary to place about My third and fourth Sons now I put two Preceptors to attend them; I have very carefully brought the expense as low as the nature of the thing would admit.

KEW, *Aug^t* 22^d 1772.

Enclosure. £

| | Mr. de Bude . . . . . . | 350. |
| Preceptors | Rev^d Mr. Hooke . . . . . | 300. |

Pages of the ⎱ Mannorlay each Sallary 80 . . .
Back Stairs ⎰ Miller   for Mourning 20 . . . 200.
Housekeeper . . . . 50.
for keeping three Housemaids each £20 . . . 60.
Porter . . . . 30.
Watchman . . . . 25.
Writing Master . . . . 100.

£1,115

No. 1118—*Lord North to the King.*

Lord North has the honour of transmitting to his Majesty the Warrant for the Establishment of their Royal Highnesses Prince William & Prince Frederick [Edward] the day, at which the Establishment is to commence, & the person, to whom his Majesty would have the money paid, are left in blank, & Lord North intreats to receive the honour of His Majesty's commands on those heads. Lord North is encouraged, by his Majesty's goodness in permitting him to go for a few weeks into Oxfordshire & Somersetshire, to hope that he will forgive his sending the Warrant to Kew, instead of waiting upon his Majesty with it at St James's. He has already sent his family into Oxfordshire, & was himself just stepping into the Post chaise when he received the Warrant. He begs to leave to accompany it by three other warrants which require dispatch. The first is an allowance to Mr. Sargent who has been obliged to quit the Secretary's office from great age & infirmity. He is not likely to live many months. Lord North heard of his case yesterday for the first time from the Secretary of State's office, where they are in a great hurry to have it done. The second is a reimbursement of a sum to Mr. Pownall, & the third is a warrant for £3000 secret service money, which is much wanted at present, as Mr. Calcraft died yesterday, & Mr. Hatten set out at night to offer himself a Candidate to succeed him at Rochester, He stands on the interest of Government, but, if he meets with opposition, will, I am afraid want pecuniary support ; If it were not for the Warrant for the Establishment of their Royal Highnesses, & this for Secret service which can hardly be delay'd even till Wednesday, next, Lord North would not have presumed to give his Majesty this trouble.

BUSHY PARK [*Monday*] *Aug* 24 [1772].

No. 1119—*The King to Lord North.*

Printed. Donne I. 109.

LORD NORTH—The Establishment for my Third and Fourth Sons ought to commence from Midsummer, as those put about them have been from about that time waiting till the House on Kew Green could be put into order ; I take it the Establishment of My Elder Sons is paid to Lord Holdernesse this will therefore be the same. The death of Calcraft will I trust bring the Borough of Rochester into its antient hands. I hope You and Your family will enjoy every kind of comfort during the stay in Oxfordshire and in Somersetshire ; if any thing should occurr during Your absence You may depend on hearing from Me.

KEW, *Aug^t* 24th 1772.

$\frac{m}{10}$ p^t 4 PM.

No. 1120—*Lord North to the King.*

[Lord Dartmouth was succeeding Lord Hillsborough as Secretary of State for the American Department.]

[27 *August,* 1772.]

Lord North has the honour of informing his Majesty that Lord Dartmouth told him yesterday, that he wish'd to kiss his Majesty's hands today after the Drawing Room He thinks that He mention'd it to his Majesty yesterday, but, not being absolutely certain of it, he takes the liberty of troubling His Majesty with this note.

He has just heard that Lord Dartmouth must take an oath of Office as Secretary of State in Council, of which he has apprized him, & which, as it will keep him in Town, will perhaps make him less in a hurry about kissing hands today, if it should be inconvenient to his Majesty.

Thursday. morn^g

No. 1121—*Lord Suffolk to the King.*

Lord Suffolk has the honour to lay before your Majesty the Dra^t of the Letter he wrote to Lord North in obedience to Your Majesty's commands, and very conformably to his own sentiments, And also to transmit to Your Majesty the Answer which he has this instant received to it.

HAMPTON COURT
Augt 30. 1772.
$\frac{m}{5}$ p^t 8. P.M.

No. 1122—*The King to Lord Suffolk.*

[For the business in Sweden see Nos. 1087-1092. There were two factions in that country, the *hats*, who were supported by France, and the *caps*, who leaned upon England and Russia.]

LORD SUFFOLK—Your letter to Lord North and his answer, are so agreable to the ideas I expressed in the letter I wrote Yesterday to You, that I can only express my approbation of them. Therefore if by tomorrow's Post we hear from Sweden that the States and Senate seem firm, it will be proper to empower Sir John Goodricke to draw to the extent of £15,000. provided that Sum can defeat the attempts of the K. of Sweden ; but otherwise that the Caps cannot expect any assistance from hence after having so little counteracted the intrigues of the Court, though so timely warned from hence ; my reason for only nam'ing the lesser Sum, is to keep something in hand, as Sir John is but too ready to go to the utmost extent of his credit.

KEW, *Aug^t* 30th 1772.
$\frac{m}{26}$ p^t 9. P.M.

*Draft, written on a page of Lord Suffolk's
letter of same date.*

No. 1123—*Lord Sandwich to the King.*

WOBURN *Aug*: 30. 1772.

Lord Sandwich has the honour to inform Your Majesty that Mr Olive for whom Your Majesty receives a commission herewith, is a Serjeant of Marines, & bears a remarkable good character. Lord North is very desirous he should have a commission on account of some connections that he has at Banbury ; I therefore thought that the best opportunity that could be taken would be to recommend him to your Majesty to be made an officer, to go and be left at Falklands Island ; which as it is a very severe service no other person would desire to employed in, & cannot give a claim for other new commissions, till all the half pay officers have been called to serve.

Copy.

No. 1124—*Warren Hastings to the East India Company.*

COSSIMBUZAR 1st *Sept*: 1772.

To the Secret Committee of the
Honble Court of Directors for the
Affairs of the Honble United
East India Company

GENTLEMEN—This accompanies a Duplicate of my Letter of the 24th April last.

Since that Date I have duly received the Duplicate and Triplicate of your Commands of the 28th August 1771.

The immediate Departure of the Colebrooke, which sailed (as I recollect) the Day after my Letter of the 24th April had reached her prevented my giving you further Intelligence of the Issue of the Measures which I had taken for the Arrest of Mahomed Rezza Cawn.—As your Commands were peremptory and addressed to myself alone ; I carefully concealed them from every Person except Mr: Middleton, whose Assistance was necessary for their Execution, until I was informed by him, that Mahomed Rezza Cawn was actually in Arrest ; and on his Way to Calcutta ; To have consulted the Board on a Point on which your authoritative Commands had left me without a Choice or to have desired their Assistance, when I had sufficient Power to act without it, would have been equally improper : But I will confess that there were other Cogent Reasons for this Reserve, I was yet but a Stranger to the Characters and Dispositions of the Members of your Administration I knew that Mahomed Rezza Cawn had enjoyed the Sovereignty of this Province for Seven Years past, had possessed an allowed annual Stipend of Nine Lacks of Rupees, the uncontrouled Disposal of Thirty two Lacks entrusted to him for the Use of the Nabob, the absolute Command of every Branch of the Nizamut, and the Chief Authority in the Dewaunee ; To speak more plainly, He was in everything but the Name the Nizam of the Province, and in real Authority more than the Nizam, I could not suppose him so inattentive to his own Security, nor so ill versed in the Maxims of Eastern Policy as to have neglected the due means of establishing an Interest with such of the Company's Agents, as by actual Authority, or by Representation to the Honble Company might be able to promote or obstruct his Views, I chose therefore to avoid the Risk of an Opposition to put the matter beyond Dispute, and then to record what I had done ; The same Reflections occurred to me when I proposed to entrust M^r: Middleton with the Execution of your Commands, which might with more Certainty have been effected by an Order to the Commanding Officer of the Brigade station'd at Burrampore ; But this would have been productive of much Disturbance I was convinced that I might securely rely on M^r: Middleton, and his Behaviour justified that Confidence ; Indeed I am bound in Justice to bear the same Testimony to his faithful Attention to your Interests, in many other Instances, which I have had occasion to experience of his Subsequent Conduct, in which he has shewn himself a zealous Asserter of your Rights and a Supporter of the Authority of your Government.

Your Public Records will inform you, that Mahomed Rezza Cawn was brought without Delay to Calcutta, where he has been detained ever since in an easy Confinement, that it was judged adviseable and consistent with the Tenor of your Commands, that Rajah Shitab-Roy should be arrested and brought likewise to Calcutta : For the Particulars of these Transactions and the Debates concerning them, I beg leave to refer you to the Proceedings themselves which will better explain than I can the Motives which influenced the Resolutions of the Board, and the opinions of the different members upon them, something more may be necessary to be said concerning my own Conduct, which as it was grounded solely on the secret instructions which you had been pleased to give me for my guidance become a proper Subject of this address

It may at first Sight appear extraordinary, that Mahomed Rezza Cawn and Rajah Shitab Roy have been so long detained in Confinement without any proofs having been obtained of their guilt, or Measures taken to bring them to a Trial Very valid Reasons for this Delay have been assigned in our Minutes. I beg leave to call to your recollection, that by a strange concurrence of unforeseen causes, your Administration had at this time every Object that could engage the Care of Government,—War only excepted—all demanding their instant attention ;—the Settlement of the Revenue of Bengal—the Dismission of the Naib Dewan, and Naib Subah of the Provinces ; the enquiry into his conduct for a course of Years preceding ; the Dismission of the Naib Dewan of Bahar, and the enquiry into his conduct ; the establishment of the Dewannee on the plan directed by the Hoñble Company ; the arrangement of the Nabob's Household ; the reduction of his allowance and expences ; the establishment of a regular administration of Justice throughout the Province ; the Inspection and Reformation of the Offices at the Presidency ; and independent of all these, the ordinary Duties of the Presidency, which from the amazing growth of your Affairs, were of themselves sufficient to occupy the whole time and applications which we could bestow upon them, and even more than we could bestow, from the want of a regular System, the natural consequence of the Rapdity with which these Affairs have accumulated. So circumstanced, we were under an absolute necessity to leave many affairs suspended, that we might give due dispatch to the rest. The first in immediate consequence, claim'd our immediate Regard. This was the settlement of the Revenue. It was late in the Season. The Lands had suffer'd unheard of Depopulation by the Famine and Mortality of 1769. The Collections violently kept up to their former Standard, had added to the distress of the Country, and threatened a general Decay of the Revenue, unless immediate Remedies were applied to prevent it. The farming System for a course of Years subjected to proper checks and regulations, seem'd the most likely to

afford Relief to the Country, and both to ascertain and produce
the real value of the Lands without violence to the Ryots. It
was therefore resolved, that this business should first take place,
and it was deemed necessary for this Purpose, that a Committee
composed of the Members of the Council, should be appointed to
carry it into execution. The arrangement of the Dewannee,
and the regulation of the Nabob's Household were added to the
Charge of the Committee, and as these comprehended the most
valuable Parts of your concerns, it was thought proper, that, I
as President should be joined with it. This render'd it necessary
to suspend the Trials of Mahmud Reza-Cawn and Rajah Shitab-
roy, and this reason is assign'd for it in our Minutes. Neither
Mahomed Reza Cawn, nor Rajah Shitabroy complain of the
delay as an hardship. Perhaps all Parties, as is usual in most
cases of a public concern, had their secret views, which on this
occasion though opposite in their direction, fortunately concurred
in the same Point. These had conceived hopes of a relaxation of
the Company's Orders ; Mahomed Rezza Cawn had even buoyed
himself up with the hopes of a restoration to his former Authority
by the interest of his Friends, and a Change in the Direction, and
his Letters and the Letters of his Dewan to the City, declared these
Expectations. I pretend not to enter into the Views of others.
My own were these. Mahomed Rezza Cawn's influence still prevailed generally throughout the Country : in the Nabob's Household, and at the Capital it was scarce affected by his present
Disgrace. His Favor was still courted, and his Anger dreaded.
Who under such discouragements would give information or
evidence against him ? His Agents and Creatures filled every
Office of the Nizamut and Dewannee. How was the truth of his
conduct to be investigated by these ? It would be superfluous to
add other arguments, to shew the necessity of prefacing the
enquiry by breaking his Influence, removing his Dependants, and
putting the Direction of all the Affairs, which had been committed
to his care, into the hands of the most powerful or active of his
Enemies. With this view too, the institution of the new Dewannee
obviously coincided. These were my real Motives for postponing
the Enquiry. Whether my precautions will have their effect, is
yet a question of doubt.

The same principles guided me, though not uninfluenced by
other arguments of great force, in the Choice of Munny Begum

the Widow of the Nabob Meer Jaffier, and of Rajah Goordass the
Son of Mahrajah Nund-Comar, the former for the Chief Administration, the latter for the Dewannee of the Nabob's Household ;
both the declared Enemies of Mohamed Reza Cawn To the latter
indeed I was principally inclined by your Commands, and I hope
it will appear that I have adopted almost the only expedient in
which they could be exactly fulfilled.—You directed that, " if the
Assistance and Information of Nund Comar should be serviceable
to me in my Investigating the Conduct of Mohamed Reza Cawn, I
should yield him such encouragement and Reward as his Trouble
and the Extent of his Services may deserve."—There is no doubt
that Nund Comar is capable of affording me great Service by his
Information and Advice, but it is on his Abilities, and on the
Activity of his Ambition and Hatred to Mohamed Reza Cawn that
I depend for investigating the Conduct of the latter, and by
eradicating his Influence for confirming the Authority which you
have assumed in the Administration of the Affairs of this Country.
The reward which has been assigned him will put it fully in his
Power to answer these expectations, and will be an Encouragement to him to exert all his Abilities for the accomplishment of
them.   Had I not been guarded by the Caution which you have
been pleased to enjoin me, yet my own Knowledge of the Character
of Nund Comar would have restrained me from yielding him
any trust or Authority which could prove detrimental to the
Company's Interest. He himself has no Trust or Authority,
but in the Ascendancy which he naturally possesses over his
Son. . An Attempt to abuse the Favor which has been shewn
him cannot escape unnoticed and if detected may ruin all
his hopes. The Son is of a disposition very unlike his Father,
placid, gentle, and without Disguise. From him there can be
no Danger.

    You will perceive by the Records that this Appointment has
not taken place without opposition from a Majority of the
Gentlemen who form the Committee now at this place. I know
not whether you will approve or disapprove of the Silence which
I have observed with respect to your Orders in the Arguments
which I have used in Support of my Recommendation. My
reason was that, I thought the measure in itself so proper that I
did not doubt of it's receiving the Confirmation of the Board at
large, and unless some material Advantage could be gained by It,

I did not think myself at Liberty to divulge your Secret Commands. I am at this time most firmly persuaded that no other measure whatever would have been likely to prove so effectual either for promoting the Enquiry which you have directed or giving strength and Duration to the new System.

I hope I shall not appear to assume too much importance in speaking thus much of myself in Justification of the Motives which led me to this Recommendation, that I had no Connexion with Nund Comar or his Family prior to the Receipt of your Letter by the Lapwing; that on the Contrary from the Year 1759 to the time when I left Bengal in 1764 I was engaged in a continued opposition to the Interests and Designs of that Man, because I judged them to be adverse to the Welfare of my Employers; and in the course of this Contention I received sufficient Indication of his ill Will, to have Made me his irreconcileable Enemy, If I could suffer my passions to supercede the Duty which I owe to the Company.—My Support of Nund Comar on the present occasion could not therefore proceed from partiality, It will be as obvious that my preference of him to other Competitors could not arise from interested Motives.—I may be charged with Inconsistency, but the Reasons which I have urged in the Minutes of the Committee in Support of this Measure will I trust, acquit me to my honble Employers and if my Conduct shall stand the Test of their Judgment, it is a Point of Duty to bear with the Reproaches of the uninformed part of the World. To the Service of the Company, and to your Commands I have sacrificed my own Feelings (pardon the presumption of this Repetition)—and I have combated those of others joined with me in the Administration of your Affairs, I claim your Approbation of what I have done, not as a Recompence of Integrity, but as the Confirmation of the Authority which you have been pleased to confide in me, and of your own, which is involved in it.

I with pleasure do Justice to the Committee, in declaring that, strenuously as they opposed the Measure while it was a Point of debate, it had no sooner received the Sanction of your Council, than they all concurred with me in supporting both that and the other Resolutions which were connected with it, as steadily as if they had never dissented from it.

The Appointment of Munny Begum I believe will require no

Apology.   It was unanimously approved, and if I can be a Judge
of the public Opinion, it is a Measure of General Satisfaction.

The only Man who could pretend to such a trust, was the
Nabob Yeteram o'Dowla, the Brother of Meer Jaffier, a Man
indeed of no dangerous Abilities, nor apparent Ambition ; but
the Father of a numerous Family, who by his being brought so
nigh to the Musnud would have acquired a Right of Inheritance
to the Subahship, and if only one of his Sons who are all in the
Prime of Life should have raised his Hopes to the Succession, it
would have been in his Power at any time to remove the single
Obstacle which the Nabob's life opposed to the Advancement of
the Family, The Guardian at least would have been the Nizam
while the Minority lasted, and all the advantages which the
Company may hope to derive from it, in the Confirmation of their
Power, would have been lost, or could only have been maintained
by a Contention hurtful to their Rights, or by a Violence yet more
exceptionable.   The Case would be much the same, were any
other Man placed in that Station.—The Truth is, that the Affairs
of the Company stand at present on a Footing which can neither
last as it is, nor be maintained on the rigid Principles of private
Justice.   You must establish your own power, or you must hold it
dependant on a Superior, which I deem to be impossible

The Begum as a Woman, is incapable of passing the Bounds
assigned her ;   Her ambition cannot aspire to higher Dignity,
She has no Children to provide for, or mislead her Fidelity.   Her
actual Authority rests on the Nabob's life, and therefore cannot
endanger it.   It must cease with his Minority, when she must
depend absolutely on the Company for Support, against her ward
and pupil, who will then become her Master ;   Of Course her
Interest must lead her to concur with all the Designs of the
Company, and to solicit their Patronage—I have the Pleasure to
add, that in the Exercise of her Office she has already shewn herself amply qualified for it by her Discernment, Œconomy, and a
patient Attention to Affairs.

In the Execution of your Commands of the 8th May 1771, I
hope I shall not appear to you to have been guilty of Remissness.
The enquiry therein directed I have been obliged to entrust to the
previous Consideration of a Committee, the many weightier
Affairs of your Government rendering it absolutely impossible for
me to enter on a Scrutiny of that Nature myself, which however I

mean to take up as soon as I conveniently can, after my Return to the Presidency.

I have the Honor to be, Gentlemen, Your most obedient, and faithful Servant,   WARREN HASTINGS.

No. 1125—*Lord Suffolk to the King.*

Lord Suffolk, by a mistake of the Messenger who instead of coming to him from Kew, return'd to the Office, has but this instant received Your Majesty's commands, and Booth's dispatches—cou'd Your Majesty find a few minutes license and permit him to wait upon Your Majesty upon this critical busyness, at any time tomorrow Your Majesty pleases to appoint ?

HAMPTON COURT

Sept. 5. 1772. $\frac{m}{15}$ p^t 7. P.M.

No. 1126—*Lord Suffolk to the King.*

Lord Suffolk has the honour to aprise Your Majesty that You will find your commands obey'd at the end of a private Letter to Sr John Goodricke, which [with] several other dra^{ts}: will be sent to Your Majesty from the Office in the course of the day. Amongst them Your Majesty will find quite a private Letter to Mr Gunning, which he must own is a little *à la Blaquiere*; However it may have its use. He has received answers from Lord Rochford and Lord North, which he has the honour to lay before Your Majesty. He wrote to the rest of the Cabinet, but cannot be informed of their sentiments yet. Upon Reflection, he thought it best to send a Messenger to Petersbourg, and accordingly means to do so.

HAMPTON COURT

Septr 8. 1772.

$\frac{m}{30}$ p^t 10. A.M.

No. 1127—*Lord Hertford to the King.*

SIRE—As Your Majesty was so gracious to approve the letter I wrote to Lord Townshend and to order me to add a postscript which I did litterally as You was pleased to dictate I think it my duty to lay before your Majesty the moment I receive it the answer which is just come to my hands that You may not impute any error to me if You do not approve it's being transmitted to Lord Rochford. I have the honor to be with the most perfect truth and attachment, Sire, Your Majesty's most faithful & most devoted humble servant   HERTFORD

LONDON
  Septr 8th
    1772

No. 1128—*The King to Lord Hertford.*

LORD HERTFORD—Previous to receiving Your letter enclosing the Lord Lieutenant's answer to Yours, I had seen his letter to Lord Rochford ; it is a strong representation against the promotion of Major Campbell as he has had that Rank so few Years. he also adds that unless he is positively commanded to forward this affair he cannot advise it as he has refused many more regular it is impossible for me to act contrary to known rules, I have at the same time the pleasure of thinking I have shewn You a desire of assisting You, but that, nor no other consideration can make direct what is represented as disadvantageous to the Army by the Ld. Lieut.

KEW, *Sept.* 8th 1772

$\frac{m}{20}$ p^t 7. PM.

Draft.

No. 1129—*Lord Hertford to the King.*

SIRE—As I propose going tomorrow with your Majesty's leave into Suffolk I think it my duty before I leave London to transmit to your Majesty a letter which Sr Robert Wilmot has put into my hands of his brother's, by which it seems probable that the objection made to the honor intended him by your Majesty comes from some female hand of the family, for it does not seem likely that any except persons so connected should distinguish Sr Robt Wilmot so farr as to think much about the birth of his Sons. Sr Robt has intreated me whenever I have opportunity to express his utmost gratitude to your Majesty for your great goodness to

him with his assurances of every return in his power whenever
he could be so happy as to find occasion or to receive directions
from your Majesty.

I take the liberty of acquainting your Majesty that I have
this day received a letter from the Bath by Lady Powis's directions to acquaint me that Lord Powis died there yesterday
morning of a stroke of the palsey.

Your Majesty will I hope permit me to close this letter by
repeating my utmost acknowlegements for the very gracious and
condescending part You have been pleased to take in regard to
my Daughters whose interest and establishment in life must
naturally be a very favorite object of their Parents. Your
Majesty's countenance and good opinion is an honor and credit
to them. They will I am persuaded behave in such a manner as
not to forfeit so valuable an acquisition, and the early impressions
they must have received in this house of regard and respect to
your Majesty will make such a mark of condescention and
attention in You highly satisfactory and encouraging to them.
I have the honor to be with the truest sentiments of duty and
attachment, Sire, Your Majesty's most faithful & most devoted
humble servant   HERTFORD

LONDON
Sept 11th
1772.

No. 1130—*Lord Suffolk to the King.*

Lord Suffolk is induced to trouble Your Majesty in consequence
of the Dispatches brought by the Flora, amongst which Captain
Collier's Letter cuts no small figure. This maritime negotiator
seems to have been treated with an unaccountable confidence
both by Lord Cathcart and Monsr D'Osten : The Latter (notwithstanding his curious panegeryck on Ld S.) certainly was not
entitled to the Respect and Attention which the captain paid to
him at the suggestion of Admiral Rommelin. The Project he
presumes is contained in the Letters from Mr Gunning which were
not delivered with those which have been transmitted to him ;
and is not a busyness which admits of or requires immediate
Determination. *The Testimonial* which Mr Gunning mentions in
his private Letter is a most extraordinary affair ; and if the

Transaction is such as is represented in that Letter, he is free to call it the wildest Idea that ever enter'd into a foreign Minister's head. The strange circumstances of it are not a little encreased by the Knowledge General Loyd and Captain Collier had of it. Your Majesty has already observed symptoms of Lord Cathcart's and M^r: Gunning's being on no very cordial footing together; therefore, whatever is insinuated from the one relative to the other ought to be received with a degree of Caution. But the bottom of this matter may be worth knowing; And perhaps Your Majesty may be able to draw the Truth of it out better and more easily than any of your Servants, when Lord Cathcart has his Audience.

Lord Suffolk has conceived it w^d: be proper to direct that M^r: Gunning's Letters, which are of a very secret and confidential nature, shall only be circulated to Lord Rochford and Lord North. He humbly hopes Your Majesty will approve of this Direction— and that Your Majesty will think it indispensably necessary that, in his absence, Ld Cathcart shou'd recapitulate all the Transactions of his Embassy, and enter into, and explain the whole of his correspondence, making ample Comments upon every individual Letter, to Lord Rochford.

ELFORD. *Sept^r* 15. 1772.

No. 1131—*Samuel Foote to the King.*

TO THE KINGS MOST EXCELLENT MAJESTY

The Humble Petition of Samuel Foote one of his Majestys Servants most humbly sheweth.

That your Majesty was most graciously pleasd at the intercession of his late Royal Highness the Duke of York: and in compassion to a misfortune occasioned by your Petitioners attendance on his Royal Highness, to grant him a Patent, for the opening a Theatre from the middle of May, to the middle of September, being a Season, when from the thinness of the Town, and the Warmth of the Weather, no other Theatre would venture to open:

That from your Petitioners productions, and Personal Labour, he has been enabled to erect a Theatre, and hitherto support with credit, not only your Majestys Servants under his direction, but to furnish the other Theatres with Dramatic Materials, of which they have not been spareing

But the Public Diversions during his Season are so multiplyd, and the exhibitions of the other Theatres particularly that of Drury Lane protracted to so unusual a Length : that your Petitioner from his advancd time of life is afraid to engage any performers, as if, from illness, or any other accident : he should be disabled from acting himself, he must be inevitably ruind

Your Petitioner therefore Humbly hopes, especially too as after Christmass the other Theatres constantly overflow that your Majesty out of your great goodness would be most graciously pleasd to extend the time limited by the Patent already granted by your Majesty To Your Majestys most Dutiful and Most Devoted Subject and Servant   SAM^L FOOTE

Sepr 21st 1772.

Holograph.

No. 1132—*Lord Barrington to the King.*

CAVENDISH SQUARE *Sep^t* 27. 1772.

Your Majesty's Commands have been obey'd : I have talked with Lord Rochford and Mr. Pownall, I have written to Mr. Bradshaw, and I hope to make next Wednesday to your Majesty in the Closet such a report of the whole as will answer your intentions.   BARRINGTON.

No. 1133—*Lord Suffolk to the King.*

Lord Suffolk being just informed by Lord Barrington of Your Majesty's goodness towards a son of Lord Aylesford's in appointing him an Ensign in the first Regiment of Guards, feels himself so sensible of Your Majesty's gracious Reception of his wishes in that Respect, that he cannot refrain from seizing the earliest opportunity of humbly expressing his Gratitude 'tho' he shall have the honour of doing it in person on Wednesday next.

ELFORD. *Sep^t* 27. 1772.

No. 1134—*Lord North to the King.*

[*2 Oct.* 1772.]

Lord North has the honour of t[ransmitting] to his Majesty
the state of the City [poll] as it stood today when it was close[d.]

Halifax	.	.	1356.
Shakespear	.	.	1238.
Townsend	.	.	1174.
Wilkes .	.	.	1171.

Much damaged ; some words lost.

No. 1135—*The King to Lord North.*

Printed. Donne I. 110.

LORD NORTH—It is with pleasure I find by Your note that
Alderman Halifax continues superior to his antagonists and that
Shakespear has also an advantage over them ; I hope I shall
continue receiving an account of each day's poll till the final
conclusion of the Election.

KEW *Oct*^r 2^d 1772.

$\frac{m}{10}$. *pt.* 6 PM.

No. 1136—*Lord North to the King.*

[Lord North was unanimously elected Chancellor of Oxford University
on the 3rd of October.]

[*3 Oct.* 1772.]

Lord North has the honour of transmit[ting] to his Majesty
the numbers of the [candidates at] Guildhall as they stood
today at the close of the Poll

Halifax	.	.	1588.
Shakespear	.	.	1444.
Wilkes .	.	.	1381.
Townsend	.	.	1381.

The Mob have not been so quiet today, as they were on the
preceding days. They Huzza'd all the Voters for Wilkes and
Townsend, and hissed all the others

Lord North takes the liberty of infor[ming] his Majesty, that the Friends of the D[uke of Beau]fort and Lord Radnor declined giving any [opposi]tion at Oxford this morning, so that the [choice ? o]f the Chancellor has probably [passed ?] unanimously.

Much damaged ; several words lost.

No. 1137—*The King to Lord North.*
Printed. Donne I. 110.

LORD NORTH—I trust by Your account of this day's poll that there can be no doubt that it will end favourably ; the Mob being less quiet this day is a proof that to riot not numbers the *Patriots* alone can draw advantage.

That there is an almost certainty of the Chancellorship of Oxford having been conferred this day unanimously gives me great pleasure as the Choise is a compliment to Me and a credit to that Antient Seat of Learning.

KEW, *Octr 3^d* 1772

$\frac{m}{59}$. p^t. 7. P.M.

No. 1138—*Lord Suffolk to the King.*

Lord Suffolk has the honour to acquaint Your Majesty that he has received to-day the late Lord Litchfield's *Stick* from the present Lord, whose Infirmities will not permit him to have the honour of returning it to Your Majesty himself. Lord Litchfield told him that he was desired by his late Nephew to deliver it to one of the Secretarys of State, and to express his wish at the same time, tho' he was conscious it was irregular, that Mr. Dillon (upon whom he has entailed his Estate) might be allowed to accompany him to Your Majesty when You received that ensign of office, in hopes that it might possibly prove an Introduction of the Young Gentleman to a Peerage one day or other. He has endeavour'd to repeat the very expressions of Lord Litchfield ; and will not fail to execute whatever commands Your Majesty is pleased to signify on the occasion.

HAMPTON COURT

Octr 4. 1772. $\frac{m}{30}$ p^t: 3. P.M.

Lord North has the honour of sending to his Majesty an account of the numbers as they stood today upon the final close of the Poll at Guild hall. It has ended as Lord North apprehended, but as Halifax poll'd 308 today, which is more than Mr Nash poll'd towards the end of his poll, and as Mr Halifax's total number of votes is 2126. which is within 73 of the total numbers of Mr Nash which did not exceed 2199, and as, on the other hand, Mr Wilkes has poll'd at this election, above 500 more than Crosby, and above 400 more than Sawbridge did at the last, there is the greatest reason to believe that many of his votes are illegal. The strange ragged figures whom he brought up today were such as were never seen at any poll before, except at his own when he stood for Sheriff. A Scrutiny has been demanded, and, if it succeeds for Mr. Halifax and Shakespear, will more effectually ruin Wilkes than any thing which has yet happen'd.

DOWNING STREET *Tuesday Even^g* [6 *October*, 1772].

No. 1144—*The King to Lord North.*

Printed. Donne I. 112.

LORD NORTH—By the account of this day's Poll, it has ended as You foretold yesterday, I hope the Scrutiny will be conducted with great exactness, which if it can be obtained when under the direction of such Sheriffs, I doubt not but Wilkes will not only not be returned but that his little regard to true Votes will come to light which must do him great injury even among his admirers

KEW, *Oct* 6th 1772.

$\frac{m}{20}$ p^t 10 P.M.

No. 1145—*Lord Barrington to the King.*

[It was the custom for the Sovereign's pages of honour to receive commissions in the Guards without purchase.]

BECKETT *October the* 16. 1772.

I have this moment heard of Lord Albemarle's death ; and beg leave humbly to submit to your Majesty whether to prevent Solicitation you would not give away the Regiment and Government now vacant, by signifying your pleasure to me in writing at this place. I have nobody to propose for either, knowing that your Majesty will make the most proper choice of Persons for both.

I am also informed tho' not with the same certainty, that Captain Smith, brother to the Duke of Dorset is dead : If this be true, there will be a troop vacant in the Queen's Regiment of Dragoon Guards. Perhaps it may be unnecessary to remind your Majesty that I had your orders two years ago to notify for the first vacancy that should happen, Captain Tancred who was reduced at the late Peace who is the eldest Captain on half pay who applys, and who has suffer'd more hardship than any man of his sort in the Army.

Lord Tyrawley acquaints me that Captain Dilkes of the Coldstream is dead : He recommends the eldest Ensign to succeed, and has *a friend* Mr. Henry Brown for whom he desires the Ensigncy. I have acquainted his Lordship that besides many applications of long standing from Persons of great consideration, the eldest Pages to your Majesty and to the Queen are past the Age when they are usually placed in the Army.

BARRINGTON.

I beleive the youngest Captain
in the Queen's Dragoon Guards
is on short pay, but Captain
Tancred does not object to
that Circumstance.

No. 1146—*Lord Rochford to the King.*

[Duke Ferdinand must be Prince Ferdinand of Brunswick, who commanded the British forces and their allies in Germany from 1759 to 1762. Sir Joseph Yorke was Minister at the Hague.]

Lord Rochford has the honor to return Your Majesty the two letters from Duke Ferdinand, together with a Draught which he submits entirely to your Majesty's superior Judgement, if approved of he proposes sending it on tuesday night, under cover to Sr Joseph Yorke. Lord Rochford would submit to Your Majesty whether it would not be proper to recommend to Lord

Harcourt prince Ferdinands pension as five or six of the principal pensioners in Ireland have allwayes had the preference in point of payment to the others.

BERKLEY SQUARE

17th oct^{er} 1772. $\frac{m}{15}$ P.M.

No. 1147—*Lord Suffolk to the King.*

Lord Suffolk begs to know whether Your Majesty wou'd be pleased to have the Papers referr'd to in Mrs Wolter's letter, or not—and he will give immediate Directions accordingly.

DUKE S^T WESTM^R
Novr 2. 1772.
1. P.M.

No. 1148—*Lord Rochford to the King.*

Lord Rochford has just received the inclosed Note from Lord North, and if your Majesty approves of the word *Ever* being left out, Lord Rochford must trouble your Majesty to send the speech back that that Word may be properly erased. Lord Rochford humbly begs leave to add he thinks with Lord North that it is better that Word was left out.

BERKELEY SQUARE
2^d *Nov^{er}* 1772
$\frac{m}{50}$ *past* 9 A.M.

No. 1149—*Anonymous letter to the King.*

SIR—Lord North has taken the resolution to support the present Administration, & he intends for that purpose to bring as many of his friends to Town as possible against the opening of the Session, He will probably also write to your Majesty, & will be at the Levee on Wednesday It is wish'd that in order to promote this good disposition in his Lordship Your Majesty wou'd be pleased to show him as much countenance as you can without creating jealousy in others the person who writes this knows too well that there are those who are naturally *of a very jealous disposition*—This comes from a dutifull Subject & Servant.

No. 1150—*Lord Suffolk to the King.*

Lord Suffolk begs leave to accompany the inclosed Dra^t to Lord Stormont with a few Lines to Your Majesty. He cannot help looking upon the Swedish Business as very likely to end most disagreably; and therefore humbly thinks that every measure & Precaution ought to be taken that has any chance to prevent the bad consequences which may be apprehended from it. Much may depend upon the conduct of Lord Stormont when he arrives at Paris. Therefore it may not be improper to explain the present state of the Business to him before he goes there: and Lord Rochford forgives the incroachment upon his Department which the Dra^t is undoubtedly guilty of. But Lord Suffolk earnestly beseeches Your Majesty to honour him with Your commands if in any respect it is not conformable to Your Majesty's Pleasure, which he is particularly anxious to learn as he is not yet able to approach Your Majesty, and some nice Points are touch'd upon in the Dispatch.

DUKE S^T WEST^R
Novr 5. 1772.
11. A.M.

No. 1151—*The King to Lord Suffolk.*

QUEENS HOUSE *Nov^r* 5th 1772.
$$\frac{m}{pt.}$$

LORD SUFFOLK—The draught to Lord Stormont meets with my thorough approbation, as it consists only [*sic*] general reasoning well adapted to the present state of things, and what will probably be the issue of the Swedish business. I am clear we cannot appear too cold, and too strongly point out to Mr Gunning the little real advantage that can accrue to Russia from new broils till recovered from the weak state to which she is now reduced by the waste of Men and Treasure; besides as we are not bound by any treaty of Alliance, I cannot see any reason for

joining with Russia in a declaration against the changes of the
Swedish Constitution ; though if Russia is attacked by France
views of general policy [will] not permit our remaining idle
Spectators ; the language to B. Diede ought to be civil but clear
of any engagement ; whilst great firmness must be shewn at
Paris, and that if France sends a fleet into the Baltick the
English Ships cannot remain at home ; indeed I wish to keep off
a War as long as possible, we are vulnerable in so many parts
that we cannot escape losses, and from the cause of the War it
[will] be a continental one, and from the little faith held in
liquidating the demands of the last, I fear a much more expensive
one, than as yet we may imagine.

Draft.

No. 1152—*The King to Lord North.*

Printed.   Donne I. 112.

LORD NORTH—I return to You the two Warrants which I
have signed, and the Letters from Lord Townshend ; I do not
pretend to be conversant enough in the Law to decide whether
the Patent authorizing the Commissioners of Customs and those
of Excise to join in appointing Collectors of Hearth Money is
legal but as the Chancellor of Ireland is so decided as to its
being so, and as there cannot be a doubt of the propriety of the
measure if free from that difficulty, I think I am justified in
putting my hand to the Warrant.

KEW *Novr 7th* 1772.

$\frac{m}{49}$ *p^t* 11. AM.

No. 1153—*Lord Rochford to the King.*

Lord Rochford has the honor to inform your Majesty that,
he concerted last night with Lord Suffolk the inclosed Draught
of the foreign article for your Majesty's speech, which is humbly
submitted to your Majesty for your approbation. The words
upon the margin are agreable to the Idea Lord Rochford had the
honor to mention yesterday to your Majesty, but as the *alterations*

that have happened in Europe is mentioned *The Event likely to happen* is alluded to and therefore Lord Suffolk thinks the words on the margin unnecessary, and Lord Rochford sees no objection to their being left out or put in, as it may please your Majesty.

CLEVELAND ROW
7th Nov^{er} 1772
$\frac{m}{30}$ PM.

No. 1154—*Lord Suffolk to the King.*

[? 7 *Nov.* 1772.]

Lord Suffolk has just received the long expected Dispatches from Mr Gunning ; & he presumes to trouble Your Majesty with the explanation (or rather the no explanation) about them which he has received from Fraser. He has taken the liberty of writing immediately to stop the Convicts, as the case was so strong & required Dispatch—

$\frac{m}{50}$. p^t 7. P.M.

No. 1155—*Lord Rochford to the King.*

Lord Rochford is informed by Mr. Fraser, that the late Recorder, is desired to make the next Report of the Convicts to your Majesty and the Recorder wishes your Majesty's indulgence to let him do it next wednesday. Lord Rochford has sent conformable to your Majesty's orders the draught of the foreign article to Lord North, and will take care that the peace officers be upon the Watch to morrow

CLEVELAND ROW
8 Nov^{er} 1772. $\frac{m}{15}$ PM.

No. 1156—*Lord Suffolk to the King.*

Lord Suffolk has the honour to submit a Dra'^{t} to Your Majesty in which there is a Decision that perhaps ought not to

have been expressed without the Opinion of Cabinet. But as
the state of his health of late has not allowed him to assemble
the Cabinet, and as he believes there are none of Your Majesty's
servants who wou'd wish other Instructions to be sent to Mr.
Gunning than those which the inclosed Dra^t contains, he has no
scruples of acting on this occasion without the Sanction of a
Meeting, if he is so fortunate to receive Your Majesty's approbation of what he has writte ; and Your Majesty does not think it
necessary that it should be previously considered in Cabinet. He
is going to Hampton Court, from whence he returns on Thursday,
in hopes of having the happyness to pay his Duty to Your
Majesty again on Friday.

DUKE S^T WESTM^R
Novr 9. 1772.
    2. P.M.

A great concourse of People attended the Lord Mayor to day
but there was no insult offerd to him, or any rioting.

No. 1157—*The King to Lord North.*

Printed.   Donne I. 115.

LORD NORTH—I do not doubt but very material reasons must
have occurred to make You desirous of altering the Article
regarding the East Indies ; I owne I think the wording of it is
very Cold, I therefore trust Lord Rochford has acquainted You
with the transposition which certainly would make it run better ;
though the Speech is softened I have no objection to that as I
know I may depend on Your remaining stiff in treating with the
Company ; till now the conduct You have held towards the
Directors is much to Your honour, but any wavering now would
be disgraceful to You and destruction to the Public, but I know
You too well to harbour such a thought.

QUEENS HOUSE
Novr 25th 1772.
    $\frac{m}{38}$ *pt* 6. PM.

No. 1158—*The King to Lord North.*

Printed.　Donne I. 115.

QUEENS HOUSE *Nov*^r 26th 1772

$$\frac{m}{25}. \ p^t \ 5. \ \text{P.M.}$$

LORD NORTH—It is with pleasure I learn that the Address passed this day without a Division, that a Committee of the whole House is appointed to examine into the high price of the Corn, and a Secret Committee into the present situation of the East India Company ; I cannot omit reminding You that though I trust when the Company finds the Committee has laid the true state before the House, that it cannot avoid coming into such an agreement as may be thought secure for its Creditors, and equitable for the Public and the Proprietors ; but that if this should not happen that You will be prepared with a plan for conducting those affairs, if You form it Yourself it will be just, and there are men of ability in Parliament will certainly support it well in the House ; but if You are open to their ideas nothing will be done for everyone will have schemes incompatible with those of the others You may consult.

No. 1159—*The King to Lord North.*

LORD NORTH—I cannot have any objection to Sir Charles Cox's Succeeding Mr Earle as Clerk of the Ordnance, and think M^r L'Anglois conduct at Vienna gives him very good pretensions to be Clerk of the Deliveries ; they may therefore kiss hands either tomorrow or Monday which ever suits best Your having their attendance in Parliament

QUEENS HOUSE
Novr 26th 1772.

$$\frac{m}{42} \ p^t \ 11. \ \text{PM.}$$

No. 1160—*The King to Lord North.*

LORD NORTH—The proposed answer to the Address is very proper ; I inclose the Warrants which You left this day with Me.

QUEENS HOUSE
 Novr 27th 1772
 $\dfrac{m}{}$ p^t 8 PM.

WARRANT FOR DELIVERING THE SWORD }
TO THE LORD LIEUTENANT OF IRELAND }

GEORGE R.—Right Trusty and Welbeloved Cousin and Councillor We greet you well.—Whereas We have by Our Letters Patent bearing Date the   Day of October last past constituted and appointed Our Right Trusty and Right Welbeloved Cousin and Councillor Simon Earl Harcourt to be Our Lieutenant General and General Governor of That Our Kingdom of Ireland, Our Will and Pleasure therefore is, and We do by these Presents require and authorise you forthwith upon Sight hereof, to render up to Our said Lieutenant General and General Governor The Earl Harcourt Your said Charge, by delivering to Him the Sword, being the Ensign of that Authority, with such other Ceremonies and Formalities as are accustomed to be used in transferring the said Charge, whereof You are not to fail ; And for so doing This shall be Your Warrant.   Given under Our Signet at Our Court at St James's the 4th: Day of November 1772.   In the Thirteenth Year of Our Reign.

By His Majesty's Command.
ROCHFORD

Enter'd at the Signet Office the
 7th Day of November 1772.
 MONT^U: WILKINSON.

Inrolled in the Office of the Rolls of His Majestys High Court of Chancery in Ireland the First Day of December in the Thirteenth Year of the Reign of King George the Third, and Examined by John Lodge D^y: Clerk & Keeper of the Rolls.

No. 1161—*The King to Lord North.*

Printed. Donne I. 115.

LORD NORTH—As Parliament has with so much dispatch gone through some of the Provision Bills, I should not act agreably to my Speech and the Answers to the Addresses of the two Houses, if I delayed passing them till Monday ; though I fear they may not lessen the distresses of the Poor, yet I would not have it supposed that any alievation had been delayed by Me ; I shall therefore certainly pass them tomorrow, and those that may be ready the next week can be passed by Commission.

Sᵗ JAMES'S
Decʳ 3ᵈ 1772
$\frac{m}{1}$ pᵗ 2. PM.

No. 1162—*Lord Rochford to the King.*

Lord Rochford would not trouble your Majesty with the inclosed, did not he think it incumbent upon him to let your Majesty be ignorant of no event that comes to his knowledge which he thinks interesting It appears by R—c's letter to Lord Clermont that all his friends are disposed to shew the greatest attention to the Lord Lieutenant Lord Rochford hopes Your Majesty will have the goodness to return this as Ld Clermont does not know the use Ld Rochford makes of it

BERKLEY SQUARE
7ᵗʰ Decʳ 1772 $\frac{m}{25}$ past 5 P.M.

No. 1163—*Lord North to the King.*

[7 *Dec.* 1772.]

Lord North has the honour of informing his Majesty that upon a motion made by Mr. Harley in the house today for leave to bring in a bill for restraining the E. India Company from appointing Supervisors for a limited time, Mr. Dempster moved the previous question, & a debate ensued which lasted till past six o'clock : Mr. Harley's motion was carried by a great Majority.

Ayes—114.

Noes— 45.

DOWNING STREET

$$\frac{m}{45} \; pt \; 6.$$

Enclosure.

7th Decr 1772. Speakers on the Motion for Leave to bring in a Bill to restrain the East India Company from send^g out Com^{rs}

Pro	C
Mr Harley	Mr Dempster
Mr Jenkinson	Mr Bolton
Mr Chas Fox	Ld John Cavendish
Mr Dyson	Mr Thos Townshend
Mr Stanley	Mr Hussey
Mr Sol^r General	Ld George Germaine
Lord North	Mr Rhumbold
Mr Prescott	Mr Dowdeswell
Mr Cooper	Edm^d Burke
	Wm Burke
	George Johnstone

Ayes—114.

Noes— 45.

No. 1164—*The King to Lord North.*

Printed. Donne I. 116.

LORD NORTH—Nothing could have been more advantageous to prosecuting the affairs of the East India Company than on the motion for a Bill to restrain the Company for a limited time from appointing Supervisors, a debate having ensued and on the division the Majority being so great. I trust that if You proceed with the same assiduity and temper this business though arduous will turn out to the security of the Company, the Advantage of the Public, and Your personal honour.

QUEENS HOUSE
Decr 7th 1772.

$\dfrac{m}{40}$ *p^t* 7. PM.

No. 1165—*Lord North to the King.*

Lord North has the honour of transmitting to his Majesty a paper of memorandums concerning the effects of her late Royal Highness the Princess Dowager of Wales, upon some of which his Majesty has already signified his pleasure, but as the paper contains likewise some points upon which Lord North has not yet spoken to his Majesty, He thought that his Majesty would permit him to send it to the Queen's House, and he will take his Majesty's pleasure upon the matters contain'd therein either on Wednesday next, or at any other time, which shall be more convenient to his Majesty.

BUSHY PARK, *Dec*: 12. 1772.

Enclosure.

MEMORANDUMS FOR LORD NORTH WITH THE KING.

[Copy in the King's handwriting.]

The Jewels, which belonged to Her late Royal Highness the Princess Dowager of Wales and were deposited at the Bank on Her demise, having been appraised in presence of Lord Boston and Mr. Legrand by Persons whom they appointed, it is now time to dispose of those Jewels for the benefit of Her Royal Highness Representatives ; since the Town is full and of course they are likely to be better sold than they would have been before the Winter Season.

But before they are exposed to sale it is proper to be known

1st Whether or no His Majesty is desirous of taking any of the Jewels at their Appraised value.

2^{ly} Whether or no His Majesty hath any objection to their being sold at Publick Auction, or to the Advertising of such intended sale with an express mention of the Jewels as having been the Property of Her Royal Highness at the time of Her demise ; because it is thought that this method of selling and of Advertising the sale will be most beneficial to the Parties interested ; and should be pursued, unless His Majesty should disapprove of it upon any other Account.

3dly Would His Majesty desire to be furnished with Lists of the Jewels, and also of the Trinkets both at the Bank and at the Queen's House, and if He should make choise of any thing in those Lists, He will be pleased to mark what he chuses ; that those Articles may be again appraised Seperately ; because the Appraisers Inventories, according to established usage, do not contain the values of the several Items One by One, but conclude with a lumping valuation of the whole together.

N3. The Trinkets at the Bank are not yet Appraised : the Jewellers who valued the Jewels, having declined the Appraisement of the Trinkets as not being within their Province ; and there seems to be some doubt whether the Trinkets at the Queen's House ought not to be appraised, having been Appraised by Common Appraisers, as Bradburne &c^a; whose skill in this peculiar bussiness is not relyed upon by some Persons concerned

4^{thly} When Bradburne and his Coadjutor attended last Summer to Appraise the Princess's Effects removed from Carlton House to the Queen's House, they were not shewn either the Plate or China. Wherefore these are yet unappraised. Will it be agreable to His Majesty to let the Appraisers finish those Articles at any time most convenient to Him, and to let some Person used to deal in Trinkets examine the things of that kind, which were carried from Carlton House

5^{thly} Lord Boston and Mr. Legrand having signed Lists of all the Effects which they sent from Carlton House to the Queen's House, it would be the shortest and surest way to the making of a compleat Appraisement, if His Majesty would be pleased to let Lord North have the use of those Lists.

6^{thly} Will His Majesty take the furniture of Brunswick House at an Appraised value, or shall it be sold for the best Price that can be got by Auction ?

Ditto Of the Princess's Furniture at Pall-Mall House ?

No. 1166.

LIST OF CLOATHS FOR THE BEDCHAMBER WOMEN, WHICH HAVE BEEN WORE.

[Effects of the Princess Dowager deceased.]

[? 12 *December*, 1772.]

Sacks.

A Grey and Gold with Colors.
A White Ground with Colors.
A Grey Striped with Colors.
A Purple and White.
A Crimson Sattin with Colors.
A Blue Damask.
A Crimson Taby.

Mourning.

A Black Velvet Gown and Coat.
Two black Silk Gowns and Coats.
Three black Silk Sacks.

One Hoop and an Apron Hoop and a Pocket Hoop.
Two White Sattin quilted Pettycoats.
One White Silk Under Pettycoat.
One Pair of Stayes.
Three Waistcoats.
Eleven Pair of Shoes.
Three black laced Handkerchiefs.
Three white blond and Shennel Ditto.
Two black Silk Ditto.
A black laced Hood and Two Crape Hoods.
Four Fans.
Two Old embroidered Short Aprons.
Four Tippets and Four Muffs and two Silk Muffs.
Two Hatts.

LIST OF CLOATHS, which have not been wore, to be divided between Mrs. Winter Mrs. Henniker and Miss Reynolds.

Three Pieces of Gold and Silver Silk not made up and designed for Gowns and Coats.

A Painted Lutestring for a Sack, not made up.
A White and Gold Sack, not wore.
A Moreene Colored Sack with Colors, not wore.
A Piece of India black Sattin worked with Colors.
A Piece of Purple and White Chintz, and about Six yards of blue
    Damask.

A Dress Hoop.
A Pair of Stayes.
Two Pair of Shoes.
Three Fan Mounts.
The Robes.
A White feathered Tippet Stomacher and Sleeve Knots.
Two Tippets and Two Muffs.
Two Cloaks lined with Ermine and a Sattin Cloak.
With the Laces and Linnen which have not been wore,
            Excepting the Lace Trimming.

                    To Miss Reynolds.
                    ————

Three travelling Gowns (One of them at Kew)
A Spotted Silk Morning Sack.
A Muslin Morning Sack.
Two Half Sacks and Pettycoats.

            No. 1167—*The King to Lord North.*

                                    [12 *December*, 1772.]

LORD NORTH—Previous to any steps towards selling any of
the effects of my late Mother it would be right to let my Sisters
and the Dukes of Gloucester and Cumberland have Copies of the
Appraisements of the Jewels and Trinkets the latter I should
think my Sisters would chuse to keep. I have a Copy of the
Appraised Jewels but none of the Trinkets You will therefore
let one be [made] out for Me, and also of the Plate ; the Gilt
Plate was my late Fathers and the Dresden Porcelain. As to the
Furniture of Park House and Brunswick I shall certainly think
it right that it be kept for My use.

No. 1168—*Lord Suffolk to the King.*

Lord Suffolk has the honour to transmit to Your Majesty a Letter which he has this ins^t: received from Mr. Woodford: it was directed on the outside, *to be open'd by himself*: And the contents of it indeed are such as require that Injunction And perhaps an Attention to what Mr. Woodford hopes for at the conclusion. But Lord Suffolk thinks it his first Duty to conceal nothing from Your Majesty; And, after all that has passed in this most unfortunate Affair, that it wou'd be a false Delicacy to have Scruples of laying before Your Majesty whatever farther may happen in the least connected with it : Tho' When Your Majesty has read the inclosed papers he sees no occasion to circulate them any where. He thinks Mr. Woodfor'd conjecture (which he has marked in the Margin with a pencil cross) very likely to be well founded.

He is much concerned to have been so soon again deprived of the honour of approaching Your Majesty, and receiving Your Commands : He will be most punctual in the execution of any Your Majesty may have for him on this occasion, or will not fail to submit his poor ideas to Your Majesty upon it, when he is able to goe abroad again ; which he trusts may be Tomorrow.

DUKE Sr WESTM^R:
Decem^r: 12. 1772.

$\frac{m}{10}$. p^t: 3. P.M.

No. 1169—*Lord North to the King.*

[The occasion of sending troops to St. Vincent was the so-called Carib War.]

Lord North has the honour of informing his Majesty that the General Court at the East India House determined yesterday upon a petition to be presented to the House of Commons against the Bill for restraining their power of appointing supervisors for a limited time, which petition is to be presented on Monday next.

Mr Thomas Townshend Junr moved yesterday in the House for all intelligence, laid before administration, and all applications to them upon which the resolution of sending troops to

St Vincents was taken, and all orders sent from hence relative to the employment of the said troops.

Mr Townshend said that it was not his intention to proceed in the enquiry before Christmas.

BUSHY PARK *Dec^r* 12. 1772.

No. 1170—*The King to Lord North.*

Printed. Donne I. 117.

LORD NORTH—I have answered the Papers of Memorandums as clearly as possible to give · You as little trouble as possible, I cannot enclose them without just adding a desire that if possible the Secret Committee may make some Report before the Recess, I am convinced that if they do not it will give some room to the insinuations of malevolent Persons that it is delayed that advantages may be made in the Stocks by knowing what will [be] the Report in January ; if a state of the Resources cannot be made out in time where would be the evil of stating the bad situation with a declaration that though the Committee has not advanced far enough to Report on the Resources, that they can already declare that they shall certainly be able after the Recess to make a Report on that head that will give more satisfaction

QUEENS HOUSE

Decr 16th 1772. $\frac{m}{2}$. p^t 8. AM.

No. 1171—*The King to Lord North.*

Printed. Donne I. 117.

LORD NORTH—I am infinitely pleased at finding that the East India Supervisor Bill passed by so great a Majority, but am rather Surprised that Lord George Germaine was in the Majority and a Speaker for what the Rockinghams alone opposed, and also that Tho. Townshend was silent

QUEENS HOUSE
Decr 19th 1772.
Eight o'Clock A.M.

No. 1172—*The King to Lord North.*

Printed. Donne I. 118.

LORD NORTH—I omit entering into the contents of Lord
Townshend's letter concerning the behaviour of Sir William
Osborne, as I shall see You tomorrow.

I have given notice that I shall tomorrow in person pass the
Land tax and the Malt, not chusing to neglect any business, and
not chusing without real necessity to be continually passing Bills
by Commission, those not ready for my Assent tomorrow will be
passed by Commission on Wednesday.

I have no objection to Mr. Charles Fox's vacating his Seat
tomorrow.

The extract of Mr. Lees's letter to Mr. Robinson shews the
Common Council of Dublin to be of the same metal as that of
London, and I trust will have as little weight on the minds of
the Irish at large, as Guildhall Patriots have on the sentiments
of this Island.

QUEENS HOUSE

Dec 20th 1772. $\frac{m}{40}$ p^t 6 PM.

No. 1173.

[21 *Dec.* 1772.]

Such a Scheme for Bengal as the
Proprietors would probably consent to.

1st THIRTY Directors to have large Salaries, one half to be
named by The King, one half by the Company, to be divided
into five Committees of *Government, Army, Shipping, Revenue,*
and *Trade* The Committees to sit at different times from each
other, and the Members of each Committee to be Members of the
others, if they please. The Kings Directors to remain during
Pleasure, the Company's for two years. The Directors to fill
the Chair and Deputy Chair week about.

Reasons for this Article.

1st the present nine Committees of the East India house
were a good mercantile Division, but will not apply to a mixed

mercantile and political Arrangement which is now become necessary.

2ᵈ One Commission of the India house has at present no Right to know what another is doing, the consequence of which is general Ignorance.

3ᵈ the Directors at present leave all to the Chairman and Deputy Chairman, whereas if they were shifted every week as is done in the Boards of Custom and Excise every Member would be forced to understand the Business and the King and Company would be forced to chuse only Men of Ability for Directors.

2 the President of Bengal either to be named by the King with a Negative in the general Court, or by the general Court with a Negative in the King, & to have the executive Power.

Observation.

In Holland, the Governor of Batavia is named by the Company with a Negative in the States. the advantage of these Negatives is, that no Man profligate in his Character would be offered, whether the nomination was in the King or the Company.

3. the Council of Calcutta named by the Directors to be the legislative Power with a Negative in the Supreme Court of Justice, as was done last year in the Bill sent to Parliament ; the Council also to be the President's consulting Council.

4 Provincial Judges with English and Indian to be established in the Bounds of the double Government, and a Supreme Court of Calcutta. The Judges of the Supreme Court with the Sheriff to be named by the King, and of the Provincial Courts by the Supreme Judges.

5 Judicial Proceedings in Bengal to be evidence in England.

6 A Board of Trade in Bengal for carrying on the Company's Trade, to be named by the Company's part of the Directors.

7 A Board of Revenue to be named by the Directors with a Power to establish a land Property as soon as Land will sell at twelve year's purchase.

8 The King to name all military Commissions.

9 the Delinquencies of the Company's Servants with regard to their Service and the penalties upon them to be specified in the

Act, and they from the highest to the lowest to be tried by a Jury in Bengal. the proceedings and Evidence to be in writing; the Action to be popular, that is, at the instance of anyone; the verdict of the Jury to be reviewable in England.

10 The Statute which hampered the splitting of Stock, & thereby weakened the strength of the Proprietors in general Courts in competition with the house Interest, to be repealed.

11 Liberty to any British Subject, upon finding Security for his good behaviour, to go to India and trade there, carrying with him all the privileges of an Englishman, so far as not altered by the new legislative Body, in order that future Ages may not complain of a Law, which barred the Ingenuity of Englishmen from exerting itself in the greatest Field for it in the world.

Observation

The only good reason assigned for restraining British Subjects, not in the Company's Service from trading to India is that they maltreat the Natives, but when regular Courts of Justice are established, this will cease.

12 Publick Officers not to trade, or receive Presents, or farm the Revenues, but to have Salaries.

13 The Accounts of the Company's Trade and Revenue to be kept separate from each other. An Average of the Profits of Trade to be struck for a certain number of years back. An Average of the Produce of the Revenue clear of all charges to be struck for the same number of years back. A per Centage upon the neat Revenues to be preferably secured to the Company, in such a proportion as added to the average profits of the Trade, the Company's Dividend at present may be £400,000. In future times all the profits of the Trade are to belong to the Company, and their per Centage upon the Revenue and Sales of lands is to rise or fall with the produce of the Revenues and Sales of Lands. The rest of the Revenues after deducting the charges of Government to be divided between the Public and The King, in order that The King may not be the only Person in the Kingdom who has not a private Interest in the prosperity of the Company. The Public in the first place to draw £400,000, and the remainder to be divided between The King and Public equally. The Shares

of the Public and of The King to be lent in India to the Company for a year without Interest to be repaid by the Company in England.

14 Every Year a State of the Company's Affairs to be published in the London Gazette, and the Vouchers of it to be open upon the application of nine Proprietors, as also all Papers relative to it, which they may call for, if they doubt of the Justice of it. A similar mode was made use of in France a few years ago.

15 To relieve the Company's present distress, the Stockholders to be allowed to subscribe £800,000 a new Capital, they paying £150 for each £100 of new Stock, which would raise one million two hundred thousand pounds. A Dividend of £400,000 upon the old and new Stock making together four millions, would make India Stock sell at above £200 because it would be more secure than the former Dividend was.

Observation.

Here then in return for the pretended encroachment made by Parliament upon the pretended Rights of the Company, two equivalents would be given, 1st the old Stock would rise from 170 to above 200, and 2dly the Proprietors would instantly get 200 for the new subscribed Stock for which they gave only 150—as these two equivalents would save the Proprietors from a *Loss* in the old Stock and give them a *gain* on the *new* Stock, it is probable that not fifty of them would refuse the Bargain if offered them. The above Scheme would be of advantage to the Company by relieving them from their present debts ; to the Stockholders by raising the value of their Stock ; to the Company by supplying them with money to trade upon without Interest ; to The King by giving him a probability of a Revenue where at present He has none, to the Public by putting the Direction of the Company into Hands where there is a chance of Success ; to Bengal by giving Government and Law to a Country which has neither ; and to the unwary in England by lessening the opportunity of Stockjobbing, seeing the London Gazette alone would be the Pole Star by which Sellers and Purchasers would steer.

The Scheme goes upon the same principle with the present bargain between Government and the Company, for if it be just that the Public should have one half of the Company's Dividend, it is just that the public Magistrate should name a part of the Officers who are to create it, & it is the past cruel Neglect in this respect which has occasioned the present Distress to both. The Scheme also leaves the Territorial Question as undetermined as ever.

If the Scheme is thought probable, the Committee of the House of Commons might enquire into the Average profits of the Company's Trade since the year 1766 the average neat produce of the Revenues of Bengal since that time, and the Savings which might be made upon it, and then it will be known whether Government is safe to adopt the Scheme.

The King's Ministers having at present the Directors and Proprietors equally dependant upon them, the question is, whether they shall only patch up holes like Tinkers, or make all the Vessel right and tight like the great Ministers of a great Nation.

N.B. A similar arrangement upon a smaller Scale will apply to the Circars which are within the Presidency of Madrass, and upon a still smaller Scale also to the Presidency of Bombay. These Regulations would be more forcibly executed, if the King named the Governors & Councils for the first three Years.

Endorsed, R. 21 Decr 1772 from Sir John Dalrymple.

No. 1174—*The King to Lord North.*

Printed. Donne I. 119.

LORD NORTH—I desire You will call here at eight this Evening when I will return the Warrants and the Charts, and will deliver the Bank notes and trifling cash that is in my hands belonging to my late Mother.

QUEENS HOUSE
   Decr 24th 1772.
   $\frac{m}{50}$ p^t 4. PM.

No. 1175—*Lord Rochford to the King.*

Lord Rochford has Just got the protest which he has the honor to send your Majesty what is asserted in the beginning of the 3ᵈ article is absolutely false, as Lord North can, I presume inform your Majesty, and I contradicted it yesterday flatly to the Duke of Richmond, it is therefore astonishing he should dare to put it in the protest as an uncontroverted matter of fact.

BERKLEY SQUARE
24 *Dec*ᵉʳ 1772.

$\frac{m}{20}$ *past* 9 P.M.

No. 1176—*Geo: Pitt to Lord North.*

MY LORD—If Your Lordship will condescend to employ a very little of Your Time in considering the very extraordinary State of my Pretentions to a Peerage, and the unparrallell'd Hardships I have for so many years been made to undergo in the Pursuit of them, I flatter myself You will lend a favorable Ear to my humble Request that Your Lordship would lay me at His Majesty's Feet, and obtain from His known Equity and Benevolence that I may *now* be releas'd from that cruel State of Anxiety and Suspence, in which I have been so unmercifully toss'd during yᵉ long Space of twelve Years.

The only Answers I have hitherto recᵈ: (I would not wish to reconsider them) cannot surely now be repeated, unless, at the same time, I am inform'd that I have been guilty of forfeiting a Claim to the least Regard, by some signal Misdemeanor, and must think no more of being put into Possession of that Right, which His Majesty was most graciously pleas'd to assure me, in the most solemn and benevolent Terms, should be confirm'd to me, if I made good the Allegations of that Petition, which I was encouraged to present, by such Expressions of Humanity, Indulgence, and Justice as I shall never forget.

As this is a very serious Business to me, and become much more so by the long delay it has undergone, I am sure Your Lordship will pardon the Trouble I give You, and grant my very just Request. I have the Honour to be, with great Respect, My Lord, Your Lordship's Most Obedient and Most Humble Servt GEO: PITT

Dec: 25th 1772.

No. 1177—*Colonel Dalrymple to Lord Barrington.* Copy.

S^T VINCENT *December* 26th 1772.

MY LORD—I was honored with your Letter by the Lynx, I most humbly acknowledge His Majesty's goodness, and shall endeavour to deserve the honor conferred on me by carrying into execution his Commands in the most effectual manner.

After surmounting a series of difficultys that are perhaps peculiar to this Island, the principal Corps of Troops are arrived at a place called Massiricau being the utmost extent of the road formerly marked out by the King's Surveyors, from thence to the Corps posted at *Grande Sable* may be near six Miles, I hope to effect a junction soon.

As there are but few Charts of this Island, I am writing to your Lordship of places unknown to you, I am endeavouring to send to His Majesty's Ministers some drawings that may serve to give a perfect idea of Our Operations.

If the Savages on being deprived of their habitations on the Sea Cost, retire to the Mountains in the Center of the Island, I fear, my Lord, they will change the nature of the War upon us, so as to spin the affair to a considerable length ; no white Man has ever been in their concealed places of retirement, the Inhabitants are intirely Ignorant of these quarters of the Island, neither guides nor intelligence can be procured, we move directed by our own Judgement.

Governor Leyborne very early established a Staff for this Service ; I have made no addition or alterations ; some public Officers are essentially requisite, and a Secretary particularly so, I have appointed Lieu^t Farley of the 68th to that trust ; the public business is more than can be done by one person.

Our losses by the Enemy and by this fatal Climate render it impossible to embark any of the Corps destined for Europe ; the 50th Regiment on its passage to *Jamaica* called here and in consequence of the Applications of the Legislature, as well as from the necessity I was under is detained for some little time until a blow can be struck.

This Opportunity being a very uncertain one, I do not trust the Returns of the Troops, fearing this will never reach your Lordship's hand.

To conclude there is great reason to believe that the Reduction of the Savages will be a work of time, and attended with great Expence my best diligence shall be used for his Majesty's Service.

I have the honor to be &c &c   W. DALRYMPLE.

No. 1178—*Lord Barrington to the King.*

[? 1772.]
WAR OFFICE *Friday afternoon.*

I have received the honour of your Majesty's Commands of this morning and am going to obey them.

By a visit I have lately had from Major Hawke, I find his father Sir Edward will soon apply to your Majesty for leave that his Son should succeed to the Lieutenant-Colonelcy of the old Buffs by *agreement* with L. Colonel Biddulph. Sir J. Wrothsleys promotion will not alter the good old Man's intention ; and it will not be easy to make him comprehend, that the brother in law of the Duke of Grafton and the late Duke of York's Servant has claims to your Majesty's favour which Mr. Hawke has not. I thought it my duty thus to prepare your Majesty for this application, as Sir Edward Hawke may probably have an Audience before me.   BARRINGTON.

No. 1179—*The Royal Academy to the King.*

[*December*, 1772.]

TO THE KINGS MOST EXCELLENT MAJESTY.

May it please Your Majesty.

The following Laws & Regulations agree'd to in the Gen¹ Assembly's of the Academicians of the Royal Academy, held on the 1st Day of Febry the 10th & 21st Days of December 1772, are most humbly presented for Your Majesty's Approbation.

At every Election of Visitors, four, or five, alternately of the Old Visitors shall go out by Rotation.

The Librarian shall attend, in the room of one of the Members of the Council.

The Library shall be open every Wednesday, during the Meetings of the Academy.

The Librarian shall attend in the Library from ten o'Clo: in the Morning, till three o'Clo. in the Afternoon. if he neglects attending himself, or appointing a Deputy from amongst the Academicians, he shall forfeit half a Guinea, to be deducted out of his Salary. No Student shall be admitted into the Library, but such as attend the Schools of Design, who at the Close of every Week, upon application to the Keeper, shall receive a Ticket of Admission.

Every Academician shall have free ingress at all seasonable times of the Day, upon Application made to the Librarian, or Keeper.

A Meeting of five Members of the Council, including the President, or his Deputy, shall be deemed a Quorum.

If at the Election of an Academician there shall appear three, or more Candidates, who have an equal Number of Suffrages ; a Ballot shall be taken of the Members present, to reduce them to two, previous to the second Ballot.

The Election of Associates shall be on the first Monday in November, and the Notice of the Vacancy of an Academician, shall be put up on the Monday following.

The Winter Academy shall begin at six o'Clo: in the Evening, except on Lecture Nights, when it shall begin at five o'Clo:. The Summer Academy to begin at five o'Clo: in the Afternoon.

That the following Regulations be repealed, viz.

There shall be two different Models each Week, each Model to sit three Nights.

That for the future the Model shall sit for three, or more Nights at the Discretion of the Visitor for the time being. No Student shall be permitted to stay in the Living, or Plaister Academy unless he is employed in Drawing or Modeling.

It is required of every Student that draws or models from the living Models, to deposit into the Hands of the Visitor for the Month, one Drawing, or Model, done in the Academy during that Visitor's Attendance ; which if he neglects doing without making a sufficient Apology in writing to the Visitor for his omission, he shall be disqualified from being a Candidate for any Premium during that Year.

If any Student neglects to draw, or model, at least three Figures in the Course of the Year, he shall no longer be considered as a Student in the Royal Academy, nor be admitted either to the Library, Lectures, or Exhibition.

In regard to the Students in Architecture, it is expected from them, only, that they attend the Library, & Lectures, more particularly those on Architecture, & Perspective; & whoever neglects to attend during the Season, without making a sufficient Apology to the Keeper, will not be admitted as a Candidate for a Premium, nor any longer considered as a Student in the Royal Academy.

The Students that may be sent abroad on His Majesty's Bounty, & are guilty of improper Behaviour, shall not be dismissed, or their Salary's taken from them, unless such Determination of the Council, is confirmed by the General Assembly of the Academicians & finally by His Majesty.

The Premiums of the Gold Medals shall be given only every other Year.

In the intermediate Year, three Silver Medals, only, shall be given. Viz^t.

One for the best Drawing of an Academy Figure. One for the best Model of an Academy Figure, & One for the best Drawing of Architecture, being a Copy from some noted Building.

Rules & Orders of the Exhibition

No Picture, Model or Design that has gained a Premium, No Needle Work, Artificial Flowers, cut Paper, Shell Work, or Models in colour'd wax, or any such Performances shall be admitted in the Exhibition.

Whoever exhibits with any other Society, at the time that his Works are exhibited in the Exhibition of the Royal Academy, shall neither be admitted as a Candidate for an Associate, nor his Performances be received the following Year.

NB. This Prohibition extends to one Year only.

The Law against admitting Copies, to extend to honorary Members.

The Exhibitors who only exhibit Drawings, · cannot be

admitted Candidates for being elected Associates, unless such Exhibitors are Architects by Profession.

The following Laws to be repealed. Viz^t.

All Academicians till they have attained the Age of Sixty, shall be obliged to exhibit at least one Performance, under a Penalty of five Pounds to be paid into the Treasury of the Academy, unless they can shew sufficient cause for their Omission, but after that Age they shall be exempt from all Duty

Every Associate shall be obliged to exhibit annually at least one Performance in the Exhibition, under a Penalty of two Pounds & ten Shillings.

The Following is the List of the Officers of the Royal Academy, elected in the General Assembly of the Academicians held on the 10th Day of December 1772 for the Year 1773.

Sir Joshua Reynolds, President.

Francesco Bartolozzi		Edward Burch	
Agostino Carlini		Agostino Carlini	
Mason Chamberlin		Charles Catton	
George Dance		J. Bap. Cipriani	
Dominick Serres	Council.	Nathaniel Dance	Visitors
Peter Toms.		Francis Hayman	
Samuel Wale		Edward Penny	
Richard Yeo.		Benjamin West	
		Joseph Wilton	

No. 1180—*Memorandum on the Partition of Poland.*

[In the King's handwriting.]

[1772.]

The very extraordinary phenomenon of a coalition of the Courts of Vienna, Petersburgh, and Berlin to take what may suit their Seperate conveniencies of the Kingdom of Poland, is so subversive of every idea of their mutual jealousies, and of the balance of Europe that it of necessity must give rise to very extraordinary Alliances amongst the other Powers ;

Poland carries on a considerable Trade with Great Britain for Stuffs and Cloth this must inevitably be greatly diminished as the above powers have manufactures and therefore will at least lay heavy duties on the importations of these manufactures if not entirely prohibit them.

The Dutch received a considerable quantity of Corn which they retailed to great advantage this must also cease.

France will find also a diminution of its trade but more particularly in the Levant if Russia obtains the Navigation of the Black Sea.

These three powers will certainly sooner or later be induced to unite and when opportunities arise which the jealousies of Austria and Prussia cannot fail perhaps within a short time to give birth to, then an Alliance may be formed which may extricate Poland from the Tyrany that now seems impending.

This plan may perhaps seem chimerical, but if Britain and France would with temper examine their respective situations the antient animosity would appear absurd and that they have by it agrandized other powers and weakened themselves ; Commerce the foundation of a Marine can never flourish in an Absolute Monarchy therefore that branch of grandeur ought to be left to England whilst the great Army kept by France gives Her a natural preeminence on the Continent

No. 1181.

INTELLIGENCE.

[1772.]

Accounts from France.

Accounts from India &c.

French Ships of Force at the Cape and in India 26 *Dec.* 1769, by Sir John Lindsay's Account :

		Guns
La Nourrice	King's Ship	20
Normandie	do. lent to Mch	20
Vigilance	K's S.	20
Africa	do	36
Garonne	do	54
Utile	do	54
Ambulante	do	36

N.B.—There is no account of these returning to Europe, as we should probably have heard of them from the French Ports, or the Cape.

Accounts from France.

Accounts from India &c.

Bound to France at that Time.

Phoenix   K's S.   64

Le Grand Choiseul

         Comp's S.   64

La Paix   Do   64

April 1770.

Landing at Mahie for Europe, Indienne & Dauphine, each 64.

1,000 Europeans & 1,500 Sepoys said to be at Pondicherri, the first to be encreased to 3,000, and the others in proportion.

April 1770.

Mr. Call, chief Engineer then at Mauritius, computed they could spare for an Expedition from Mauritius

     150 Artillery.

     1000 Royal Comptois.

     500 Legion.

     1650 Regulars.

     2000 Coffrees.

leaving for the Defence of Mauritius 1000 of the Legion.

Advices.

Jany 8, 1770.

Three ships sailed from Bordeaux for East Indies. Secd. Battn. Royal Compts. Men   682
another ship from L'Orient   271

April 1770.

Secd Battalion of Royal Comtoi's of 500 men arrived at Mauritius, probably in the Telemaque, Praslin and St. Florentin, which sailed from Table Bay at the Cape in March 1770.

Advices.

Jany. 27*th*, 1770.

Duras & Pondicherry sailed 7th inst from L'Orient with 950 Royal Comtois, including Recruits   950
Five Ships were to sail by the end of Feb. with   1200

     3049

June 1770.

Two Transports arrived at Mauritius with Men   800
Five more were expected.
Letters by Anson India Ship rec'd
     Octr. 13.
Five or Six Frigates at Mauritius.

Accounts from France.

Advices.

Mch 9th, 1770.

Triton, Mars & Massiac ready to sail from L'Orient, the two first freighted to carry Recruits   1200

Lord Harcourt, 12 *March,* 1770.

By Advices from Isle de France there were at that Place la Legion des Indes of 3 Battns of 10 Comp. each Company of 1000 Men, as also the Regiment of Royal Comtois of 2 Battns.

L'Orient 29 *Decr.* 1770.

Royal Dauphin of 74 Guns & the Bizarre of 64, destined for L'Isle de France, detained at Port Louis by contrary winds from coming to Brest.

N.B. No account whether they sailed.

Brest 16*th Jan.* 1771.

Union & Seine sailed with 4th Battn. of Normandy & 2nd of Artois on board 3 ships. Union & Seine certainly destined for the Isle de France. said 3 ships mentioned in advices of 22nd Dec, to be 3 great Merchant Ships, & that the 2nd Battn of Royal Vaisseaux was embarked on 3 great ships at Honfleur, & the destination of all was mysterious. That 2nd Battn of Limousin or at least 2/3 of it sailed in 2 large ships. The Instructions to be opened at Height of Cape Finisterre.

Accounts from India &c.

Letter from Sr. M. Lindsay from Bombay rec'd 18*th January* 1771.

Triton of 30 Guns arrived in Aug. with 200 men landed at Pondicherry Mars of 60, Comp. Ship landed 200 Soldiers at Mauritius Massiac, Comp Ship, arriv'd Sep. 1770

Letter from President & Council of Bengal *Oct* 31, 1770 & 12*th March* 1771.

French making military Preparations ; attempted to bring 700 Draught Bullocks, but prevented by the Government there.

St. Helena 6*th May* 1771 & 10 *July*

Captain Pelly of Europa informed that before he left the Cape 16th April arrived a French Man of War of 64 Guns, 800 Men, of which 400 Soldiers. French Captain said He left France in Company with 3 more of same rate & numbers of Men.

Letter from Capt. Lewin of the Vansittart 3*rd August.*

Three French Ships with a number of Troops had been at the Cape and sailed before Him. French Capt. said He did not know He was going to India, having sailed under Orders for West Indies.

Major Fitzgerald arrd. 10th Aug. 1771. One French Ship of War touched at the Cape for Mauritius with 900 Men, 4 Transports with 3 to 400 men each.

Accounts from France.

Accounts from India &c.

Major Prehin commanding Dutch Troops at the Cape affirmed that the French had sent that season 7,000 Men to India.

Great Quantities of Provisions were buying for them at the Cape confirmed by Major Prehin's letter to Mr. Ramsey.

Brest 13*th March* 1771.

M. de Monteil gone to L'Orient to take Command of the Actionnaire of 64 Guns, lower Ports not pierced, destined for l'Isle de France to carry recruits for Royal Comtois and Semestriers for 4th Battn of Normandy.

N.B. No news of Actionnaire sailing.

Paris, 8*th April* 1771.

A Dutch Ship has taken part of Clare's Regt. for l'Isle de France. The Experience to take the remainder.

Brest, 8*th April,* 1771.

Two Ships fitting out at l'Orient for King's Account & 2 Fleetes at Brest, the two first to be commanded by Messrs Monteil and Resquelin, two last by Messrs Lombard and Cramache. All four for l'Isle de France with Recruits.   1200

Brest, 8*th May* 1771.

The two Fleetes of Messrs Lombard & Cramache suspended till Septr.

Paris, 8*th July* 1771.

Advice from Rochefort that Experience was not sailed, & is destined to Goree for Negroes for the Colonies.

Accounts from France.

Paris, 29*th July* 1771.

Advice by *two rich Ships* arrived at l'Orient from Isle de France, dated 6th April, that the Regt. of Royal Comtois was in good condition, but great Dissensions among the Officers.

———

Brest, 31*st* July, 1771.

The Flute La Seine had put into Rio Janeiro.

———

Paris, 23*rd August* 1771.

Messrs Lombard & Cramache named to command two Ships at l'Orient.

———

Brest. 13*th Sept*, 1771.

Frigate, l'Enjouee fitting out to go to l'Orient to carry M. de Ternay to l'Isle de France.

———

Paris, 4*th Novr.* 1771.

Flutes, Fortunes, Gros Venture, Corisante & The Citoyen, Merchant Ship freighted by the Court, all sailed from Rochefort 5th February with Clare's Regiment for l'Isle de France, met with violent storms and put into the Bay of Simons, & were to proceed to India.

———

paris, 22*nd Novr.* 1771.

The Aurore sailed from Rochefort for Brest, but the Belle Poule destined to carry the Chevalier de Ternay to India.

———

Brest, 27*th Novr.* 1771.

Belle Poule ready to sail.

———

Colonel Blaquire 10*th Nov.* 1771.

Marqus de Monteynard & M. de Boien have been working for a week past with Engineers and with Chev.

Accounts from India &c.

———

Rio. Janeiro. 30*th July*, 1771.

Captain Stott mentions two or more sail of French ships had passed some time before, pretended for the Malouines, but He was convinced it was for the East Indies.

———

Tellicherry 5*th May* 17*th Nov.* 1771.

Mascarenhas French Europe, private ship 600 tons 22 guns arrived at Mahia from Goa with 300 Coffres Slaves for Mauritius, was to take in Pepper & return thither.

———

Accounts from France.

de Ternay lately made Governor of
Mauritius, upon a Plan strengthening and fortifying the Isle de France.
Chev. Ternay was to sail from
L'Orient in Janry. with three or
four Frigates. The work intended
to be considerable, & will take four
or five Years to complete, & that
Money may not be wanting, the
compleating Fort Garnier in Mar-
tinico to be suspended.

Colonel Blaquiere. 11 *Dec.* 1771.

New French East India Company
engages much attention. India the
great object. Isle de France not
only to have new fortifications, but
be the general Deposit. They say
the English are unprovided there
and that it is the heel of Achilles.
One ship from Bordeaux and two
from Nantz were to sail immediately
with 500 Soldiers each, besides 600
tons of warlike stores & between
five and six thousand Stands of
arms going directly from L'Orient.
It was thought that the famous
Count d'Estaign the great Adviser
of M. de Boien will be sent there as
Captain General. Circumstances
that confirm a Belief that the
present Ministry in France are pursuing with equal ardour the hostile
Projects of their predecessors.

Colonel Blaquiere. 30 *dec.* 1771.

Lord Harcourt's Man had informed him that the Chevr. de
Ternay had orders on his arrival at
the Isle de France to embark the
Legion de Bourbon of about 3000
men for Pondicherri to strengthen
and rebuild fortifications there, a
Project the more credible by their
unremitted attention to the re-
establishment of their new East
India Company.

Accounts from India &c.

Lowest Computation of French Ships in India as far as our Intelligence goes :

		Guns	
Union. King's Ship		64	
Mars, Company's Ship		60	
La Garonne. King's Ship		54	
Utile	do	54	
Africa	do	36	by French Deserter called 64 Guns.
Ambulante		36	
Triton		30	
Mascarenhas private ship		22	
Normandie		20	This lent to Merchants.
Vigilance	K's S.	20	

Highest Computation :

	Guns	
Dauphin Royal.	70	
Bizarre	64	
Actionnaire	64	Seems to have sailed from the circumstances of the Somestriers she was to carry.
Union	64	
Mars.	60	
La Garonne	54	
Utile	54	
Africa	36 or 64	This ship not to be found in any List of the French Navy.
Ambulante	36	
Triton	30	
Mascarenhas	22	
Normandie	20	
Vigilance	20	

FLEETES, ARMED SHIPS, & MERCHANTMEN, WHOSE FORCE DOES NOT APPEAR.

Telemaque.

Praslin . . . . . . Just returned.

St. Florentin ⎫
Massiac ⎬ . . . . . Company's Ships that may carry
Seine. ⎭ 64. Guns as since appears.

Fortune.

Gros Ventre.

Corisante.

Citoyen.

No. 1182—*The King to Lord North.*

Printed. Donne I. 121.

LORD NORTH—Having heard by the Dutch Mail of this day that the Great House at Amsterdam of Clifford and Company is declared Bankrupt, that fourteen other Houses have met with the same fate, I am desirous to know what effect it has had on Merchants in this Country ; I have been told three houses stoped payment this day ; is not Sir George Colebrooke in a very precarious situation

QUEENS HOUSE
  Jany 1^*st* 1773.
    $\frac{m}{3}$. p^t 11. PM.

No. 1183—*Lord North to the King.*

Lord North has not yet heard of the effect which the Bankruptcy of Clifford & Company has had in London, but he is afraid that it will cause a fresh stagnation of Credit : Lord North has been for some time past engaged to go tomorrow to Hill Park, but will, if your Majesty has any commands for him, put off his journey. Mr Cooper will go early into the City to-morrow, and will learn every thing that has happen'd, or is expected in consequence of this misfortune at Amsterdam, and will take care to inform Ld Suffolk of whatever he is able to learn, in order that it may be laid before your Majesty.

DOWNING STREET.
  $\frac{30}{m}$ p^t 11. *Jan:* 1^*st*

No. 1184—*George Pitt to Lord North.*

STRATFIELDSAY *Jan:* 3^*d*
1773.

MY LORD—I troubled Your Lordship with a Letter dated Dec: 25th, upon the very interesting Subject of my Claim to a

Peerage. A very short Answer being all that I desir'd, and being depriv'd of that Honour, I will not defer humbly intreating Your Lordship to condescend to employ a very few Minutes in ye attentive Consideration of my very extraordinary Case, with all the aggravating Circumstances that have happen'd since I was honour'd with Your Lordship's visit in Half Moon Street. These I am desirous of banishing from my Thoughts, and have the strongest Hopes, and Expectations that Your Lordship will lend me Your kind Assistance, by granting me that Justice, to which every Man is entitled, and to which I have ever been taught to think Your Lordship inclin'd.

The Age of my Son has for some late Years occasion'd my being less pressing for ye Completion of his Majesty's most gracious and solemn Engagements, nor was it my Intention to have mention'd them previous to my intended Embassy to Spain, had not Your Lordship express'd Your Desire that I should resign my post of Groom of the Bedchamber. By what means everything was lost at that Period I have already shewn my most ardent wish to forget; and shall proceed to tell Your Lordship that had I succeeded sooner in my Claim to the Peerage, the County I represent, in which I now hope to establish my Son, would have fallen into Hands ye most obnoxious to Government. He is of Age, and is returning from his Travels; and Your Lordship cannot be surpris'd that I should now use my utmost Endeavour to obtain for my Family, what they have so clear a Right to expect, and which, after so tedious a Delay, I am so perfectly authoris'd to continue to solicit by every Means in my Power.

I have the Honour to be with great Respect, MY LORD, Your Lordship's Most Obedient and Most Humble Servt:

GEO: PITT

No. 1185—*Lord Rochford to the King.*

Lord Rochford has so many proofs of Your Majestys great Goodness to him that he can never, much less on this sorrowfull occasion, express half what he feels, for Your Majestys most gracious enquirys after him to Sr Stanier porten; in order that my own private misfortunes may be no prejudice to Your

Majestys Service, Lord Rochford proposes being in Town to morrow Morning at a private Lodging where he will see Sr Stanier porten, letting nobody else know that he is in Town, and where he will be ready to obey any Commands Your Majesty may think fit to honor him with.

St Osyth 11th Jan^{ry} 1773.

No. 1186—*George Pitt to Lord North.*

HERTFORD STREET *Tuesday*
Jan: 12 1773.

MY LORD—I rec^d: the Honour of Your Lordship's Letter of the 7th, last Night, which would have reach'd me in due time, had I remain'd at Stratfieldsay.

Finding that I have been, and still am totally misunderstood, and persuaded of the utter Impossibility that any Injustice can be intended me, I must humbly intreat Your Lordship to suspend the Business of my Claim, and to defer taking His Majesty's Royal Pleasure upon the Subject of it, 'till Your Lordship shall have rec^d:, upon that Head, every necessary Information. This I shall take the first Opportunity of laying before Your Lordship, and I shall not enter upon the Contents of Your Lordship's Letter 'till You have had those Lights, without which I am persuaded Your Lordship would not wish to proceed in a Business, which is become of much more Consequence than my having a Seat in One, or the other of the Houses of Parliament.

I have the Honour to be, with the greatest Respect, MY LORD, Your Lordship's Most Obedient and Most Humble Servant

GEO: PITT

No. 1187—*Lord Rochford to the King.*

Lord Rochford humbly takes the Liberty to send Your Majesty one of the finest prints, he thinks he ever saw it has been done at the Joint expense of Mr Piercy (?) and a Brother of Mr Devismes two very Considerable Merchants of the English factory at Lisbon, as they have received many favors from Mr de Pombal out of Gratitude to him they had the picture and the engraving done which Cost them sixteen hundred pounds, as none of these are to be sold, and as Mr Devismes means to give them to the principal persons in Europe, he wished me to learn whether Your Majesty would vouchsafe to let me have the honor of presenting Your Majesty one, which I take the liberty to do, well knowing that if Your Majesty does not think it proper to accept of it that Your Majesty will have the goodness to return it me. the print is the 16th part of the sise of the picture, one part of the subject of it is a remarquable epocha for it is the embarcation of the Jesuits on their expulsion from portugall

DAVID STREET
13 *Jan^{ry}*
1773
$\frac{m}{50}$ P.M.

No. 1188—*George Pitt to Lord North.*

HERTFORD STREET *Jan*: 16th
1773.

MY LORD—I took the Liberty, in my last of the 12th, to intreat Your Lordship to defer taking the King's Pleasure upon my Business of the Peerage, 'till You should be fully inform'd of the true State of my Case. This earnest Request proceeded from the fair and manly Confession of Your Lordship's Sentiments, the Advice You seem inclin'd to give, and ye very disagreable Consequences that might proceed from any serious Misapprehension of the Facts upon which those Sentiments, and this Advice may be suppos'd to be founded.

I ventur'd to conclude my last letter by asserting that this Business was become of more Consequence than the Alternative of my sitting in one or the other of the Houses of Parliament : I despair not of proving to Your Lordship the Truth of this Assertion, from the very just, and unanswerable Expressions of your own Letter.

But before I proceed to this, I cannot but observe that Your Lordship takes not the least Notice of my Pretentions to two antient Baronies in Abeyance. I dare not, in this Letter, repeat the strong Expressions of Justice and Benevolence, the essential

Terms of gracious Encouragement, in which I was *order'd* to *present myself* the Petition for those Baronies, after I had fully made known that they were in Abeyance, and mention'd the Name of my Competitor. The Petition was referr'd to Sr Fletcher Norton, who reported my having a just Claim in Abeyance, and that His Majesty might lawfully confirm, and allow those Baronies to me. Thus, at a very heavy Expense, I obtain'd what I had reason given me to expect would insure me immediate Success. This, My Lord, was in ye Year 1765.

Surely this very material Circumstance, carried to this length, even by the Commands of The King Himself, distinguishes me very widely from every one of those Gentlemen who expect New Creations : For the present, however, I will dwell no longer upon this part of my Claim.

As Your Lordship confines Your Arguments to my other Pretentions, I will very readily join Issue with You, and most sincerely rejoice that I have an Opportunity of laying my most extraordinary Case before a Minister, who possesses such high, and just Conceptions of the Honour and Dignity of the Crown, and who greatly makes himself responsible, in such cogent Terms, for the inviolable Observance of His Majesty's sacred Engagements. Did I not cherish ye same Sentiments, with the same Ardour ; could I dare to doubt of the exact Performance of such Engagements, I should not have us'd the Term *Claim*, for an indefinite Expectation, nor have shewn all that Impatience (which however, Your Lordship does not blame) after having given such repeated Proofs, during so many Years, of a very contrary disposition.

As I plainly perceive that what I have said will stand in need of Explanation to Your Lordship, I must inform You that, on Account of the Difficulties, and Expense, which I suppos'd would attend the Claim of the Abeyance Titles, I became an humble Petitioner to the King for a New Creation. In the Year of His Majesty's Accession, I was honour'd, in answer, with ye following most benevolent, and satisfactory assurance, " that, tho' His Majesty did not incline to add, at the time, to the Number of Peers, for whom new Patents were making out, *I might firmly depend* upon being created with the very first who were to be honour'd with that Dignity." I give Your Lordship my Word of Honour that I rec^d: this verbal Answer from The King, thro'

the noble Lord, who did me the Honour to recommend me to
His Majesty, and I have besides, a Letter, dated several Years
after, under this noble Lord's own Hand, confirming what I have
said above, and bearing the most ample Testimony to the Truth
of this gracious, and most explicit Promise, with the precise Time
of it's intended Performance : I rec^d: this Answer in the beginning
of the Year 1761. In May 1762 Lord Holland, Lord Milton,
Lord Beaulieu, and Lord Vernon were created ; and this was
that second Creation of Peers, in which I had the absolute
Promise of being included. That I should have been disappointed
by being employ'd abroad in His Majesty's Service must appear
something more than unfortunate, but I could not have fail'd of
Success, had I been present to have enter'd my just *Claim*. Can
it's Validity be impair'd by it's having been so long due ? Ought
my sufferings to increase at this Date, because they commenc'd
in 1762 ? I depended, however, upon the Solidity, and Safety
of my Expectations, and therefore, was the less anxious for
the immediate Completion of what I had so serious, and so
indisputable a Right to expect upon the very first Occasion.

After what I have said, it would be an Insult to that good
Faith, which I am bound to depend on, and to reverence as well
as to Your Lordship's high Sense of it, to add another Word upon
the Events of so many years. I shall only add that upon my
coming from Turin, on leave of Absence (under the strongest
Hopes of being allow'd to return) I made out, as I have already
said, my Claim to the Abeyance Titles, in the year 1765, and in
1773 shall sign this Letter with my Family Name.

After what Your Lordship has just read may I not humbly
express my Fears that there must have been some Misapprehension either in, or of ye Information mention'd in the following
quotation from the Letter, with which Your Lordship has
honour'd me ? " Soon after I had rec^d the King's Commands to
serve Him in the situation, which I now occupy, I was inform'd
that Peerages had been promis'd to five or six Gentlemen, that no
Creation was to take place, in which they were not all compriz'd
and that You were one of the Number ; but I learnt, at the same
time, that His Majesty had not signified *when* He would proceed
to a new Creation, and that he was resolv'd to postpone it to a
distant Period." After ye Proofs I have offer'd, I should be the
most unworthy Wretch that ever approach'd Majesty, if I were to

harbour ye Shaddow of that Thought, which to say the Truth, is not even insinuated in the Words I have taken the Liberty to quote. The noble Duke, Your Lordship's immediate Predecessor, did me the Honour to communicate to me at St. James's in *June 1768*, a most gracious Message from The King, and that, too spontaneously, without my having, at that time, troubled either His Majesty, or His Grace with any Solicitation. This gracious Message absolutely convey'd His Majesty's kind Resolution to take *two* or *three* of *the first*, whom His Majesty intended to honour with Peerages, from ye Number of Expectants, and to order their Patents : Of the two, or three then selected, I was to be one, and 'tho' the Duke did not specify the Time, His Grace gave me reason to hope it would not be long deferr'd : This, My Lord was in 1768. The most emphatical Word in Your Lordship's Letter, upon which everything depends, the only Word that is underlin'd, which has cost me so many cruel Years of anxiety, the Loss of every thing with which His Majesty's Indulgence, and Bounty had honour'd me, in a Series of such unexampled Fatality as Your Lordship cannot conceive, or the most unworthy Wretch can have merited ; the Word *When*, I say, in the Sentence above quoted, would come next under Consideration, did it not receive it's final Extinction, as far as it expresses a doubt, by the very material Fact, insisted on above, which will no more admit of Contradiction than the most self-evident Truth.

In consequence of what I have said, let me earnestly conjure Your Lordship's known Judgement, and Candour to pardon my presuming to infer that some Misapprehension of this Matter must have occasion'd part of Your Lordship's Letter, and let me intreat that it may be render'd needless for me to enter farther into the Contents of it, or into the Merits of my strange Case. However innocent every succeeding Minister may be of the Omissions of his Predecessor, the whole of my just Complaints must fall somewhere, if by farther Severities, they are forc'd from a Breast, which, I will freely confess, is incapable of containing more. Lay not, I beseech You My Lord, to undue Impatience, or improper Warmth, what proceeds from the calmest Dictates of a Heart, capable of the most submissive Humility : If it possesses also the Requisite to correct a vitious Degree of that Quality, be persuaded that not a Word of this Letter is dictated by that Spirit, and that whatever may carry the Appearance of it, results from that Force, which Truth and Reason, however express'd, will alwaies carry with them.

As I have now stated this Matter, I will venture to affirm that no reasonable Man, who expects a Creation, can look upon himself as injur'd by my Success, back'd as it is, by the *authentick Vouchers* of every Administration since the Accession. My favourite Pursuit was undoubtedly the Claim in Abeyance, which by Sir Fletcher Norton's Report, His Majesty is authoris'd to confirm. If, after so many years cruel Suspence, and the necessary Expenses attending this Business, I am ready to accept a Creation in lieu of what is infinitely preferable, to which Creation also, by the Faith of the best of Kings, and Masters, I was absolutely entitled in the Year 1762, can any Man, at this time, pretend to murmur ? But, after all My Lord, why should I be repeatedly tantaliz'd (I mean not by Your Lordship) with the most solemn Assurances that the Door, when open'd, should be open'd for me, and, with such strong Pretentions, have ye Mortification again and again, to see it open'd for others, and shut against me ? Why is *my* Success to be so offensive, and *I* the only Person who am not to be offended at the Success of Others ?

But I am asham'd of taking up so much of Your Lordship's time upon what will not bear an Argument. If Your Lordship, which I cannot suppose, after having learnt, in part, what it is evident You did not know before, should still be inclin'd to advise, as " a wise, and impartial Observance of the King's Resolutions " that my Case should not be distinguish'd from the Expectations of other Gentlemen, and that my humble Request should be again " postpon'd to a distant Period ", I intreat Your Lordship to tell me so before You trouble His Majesty upon the Subject, with the same manly Freedom, with which Your Lordship has already express'd Yourself : I honour it, and will imitate it.

I know, from Experience, the Attention His Majesty lends to Men in Your Lordship's exalted Station, and I shall never forget the following Expression, which fell, not long ago, in the House, from a great Minister. " Whatever is good, and worthy of Praise in this Measure, is the King's ; if anything be reprehensible, it is Mine." A Minister capable of conceiving and uttering that Sentiment, is in no danger of offering improper Advice, and I desire to be under no better Protection. This Reflection affords me the most flattering Prospect, and I can most truly and sincerely assure Your Lordship, that the Pleasure attending my Success will be greatly increas'd by that of esteeming myself indebted for it to Your Lordship's obliging Assistance.

I have the Honour to be, with the greatest Respect, MY LORD, Your Lordship's Most Obedient and Most Humble Servant .

GEO: PITT

No. 1189—*Lord Cowper to the King.*

May it please Your Majesty

Though I am at a loss how to answer for the great liberty I am taking in addressing myself to your Majesty in this manner ; yet w^n I reflect upon the great goodness which Your Majesty formerly condescended to shew me, when our ages Suspended at certain hours that immense distance there is between a Sovereign and his Subject, I am encouraged to hope that your Majesty will both pardon this freedom and most graciously be pleased to accept of this box containing part of the famous Gallery of Painters at Florence, [all] done in miniature by one Macpherson ; What I have the honour of [sending] to your Majesty is only half the collection ; the other half as soon as finished I intend presenting to your Majesty in person ; As there is nothing of the kind to be found in any Cabinet whatever in Europe, as it is the first time they have ever been permitted to be copied, be so gracious, SIR, to accept this humble offering of veneration from him, who is with the most profound respect

Sir, May it please Your Majesty Your Majesty's most dutiful Servant and Subject,   NASSAU CLAVERING COWPER

FLORENCE *January ye 20th*
1773.

Much damaged ; some words lost.

No. 1190—*Lord Suffolk to the King.*

SIR—I fear Your Majesty will think the Busyness You have entrusted to me long a settling : But it is better to proceed upon sure grounds especially in these times, with regard to Money matters, than on precarious ones. Baron Diede told me this morning that two more Bills of Exchange wou'd be transmitted to England *properly indorsed,* as soon as it was known Whom

Your Majesty authorised to receive the Money at Hamburg, and to give a proper Receipt for it : The Bills already arrived are not for payment but acceptance of Baur's correspondent Here. This seem'd so roundabout a way that I told him the remaining Bills had better be sent here, and that if they were *properly indorsed* I shou'd by Your Majesty's command receive them for actual payment, as the Bank wou'd discount them immediately, and I cou'd give better than any body a regular Discharge. This has been accordingly agreed to ; and I hope Your Majesty Will approve of it. The 40,000 German crowns are ready to be paid in Specie by Baur to whomsoever Your Majesty is pleased to name. Baron Diede desired me to let him know the Person. If Your Majesty is pleased to appoint Mr. Mathias, I will not fail to send him the necessary Orders—if Your Majesty names any of Your German Servants, I presume You will give Your Commands to Mons[r] Alvensleben ; and in either case I cannot suppose but the Authority will be Acknowledged without farther forms.

Your Majesty's dutyfull Servant   SUFFOLK

DUKE S[T] WES[T]
Jan. 21. 1773.

No. 1191—*Lord Boston to the King.*

Lord Boston begs Leave with all due Submission, and with the greatest respect humbly to present his Duty to The King, and he takes the liberty to convey to His Majesty inclosed in this Box Several Minature Pictures found amonst the Trinkets belonging to Late Princess of Wales, and which he was directed to take out from the other Trinkets, before They were to be given up to M[r] Christie, which were thought to be improper for exposal at a Public Sale, Many of these Minature Pictures are supposed to be of the Royal Family, and of other Persons, some of them of Foreign Princes, & they may be agreable for His Majesty to keep them in his own Possession, They are set down at little value by the Jewellers, who made the appraisment of them, the fifteen first taken away Minature Picture[s] by order were only valued £4-4s-0 and which has been checked of from the List of the other Trinkets on the Dilivery of them to M[r] Christie, There are also contained in the Said Box Ten other small Minature Picture[s] much better done 3 of them in Particular imagined by Lord

Boston to represent the Late Prince Frederick His Majestys
Royal Brother & His Royal Sisters the Late Princess Louisa, and
the Present Queen of Denmark These Pictures, Lord Boston
humble presumes to beleive, That the King may chuse to keep.
There are amonst the Minature Pictures Several of them, which
are supposed to be of his Royal Father the late Prince of Wales,
Lord Boston would be much obliged, if he might be allowed to
have one of them, which would be most valuable to him, as he has
no Picture of his Late Royal Master, who he had the honour and
happiness to Serve for a number of years. the other Things contained in the Box now Sent to His Majesty are a very curious
Ivory Box Set in Gold, Put down by the Jewellers at Eight
£8-8s value, & a Tortoishell Snuff Box with the Late Prince of
Wales[s] Crest inlaid on the Top of it with his Picture, as supposed,
in it.

There is also another Tortoishell Snuff Box of the Same kind
without any Picture, but found Tho ommitted to be Set down in
the list taken by the Jewellers of the other Trinkets.

There is likewise to be found in the Box a Key, but whether
it was one of his Keys, or [to] what other Persons belonging, &
[whether] of his Majestys Royal Father[s] and of His Royal Mother[s]
Family, Lord Boston doth not know, nor How it got into the possession of her Royal Highness. The Padlock ordered to be taken
out from the Box containing the Trinket[s] Lodged at the Queens
Palace is also conveyed in the Box, but not of the Sort, as
described in the Lists made out by the Jewellers, it is only a Sort
of Padlock to be purchased at Many of the Ironmongers Shops in
London, & of no value, it requires no Key to it, but it is difficult
to be opened, if the word is not found out by Placing the letters
marked on it in a regular Manner, which will open it. Lord
Boston has also ventured to Send to The King a Small Pocket
Case with a Minature Picture on it & two Seals with the Present
Royal Family Arms and those of Saxe Gotha engraved on them,
and these may be proper to be kept out from the Public Sale.
These are the Several things contained in [the] Box and Lord
Boston hopes, what has been done on the occasion, it will meet
with The Kings Most gracious Approbation. Strict care has been
taken to have done all right, and agreable to His commands which
M[r] Le Grand, and he were honoured with.

GROSVENOR STREET *Friday Jan[ry] y[e] 22[d]* 1773.

No. 1192—*Geo*: *Pitt to Lord North.*

HERTFORD STREET *Jan*: 28
1773.

MY LORD—I attended Your Lordship's Levee this Morning
purely to pay my Respects, with^t: any Intention of taking up a
Moment of Your Lordship's time upon my Business, and, therefore, I only express'd my Obligation for your kind Intention of
laying my Letters before The King. I must now, My Lord,
take the Liberty earnestly to intreat that Your Lordship would
do this in a favorable Manner. I know perfectly the Effect,
which the small Part of my History, with which I have troubled
Your Lordship, must have produc'd upon Your equitable &
benevolent Mind, and I cannot hesitate to conjure that You would
give it free Utterance in the Closet. Without this, long, very long
Experience will not suffer me to hope ; With it, I can no more
doubt of immediate Success, than I can of that Justice, &
Humanity, which reside so sacredly, & so conspicuously in the
Royal Breast.

I have the Honour to be, with the highest Respect, MY LORD,
Your Lordship's Most Obedient and Most Humble Servant

GEO: PITT

No. 1193—*Lord North to the King.*

[9 *February*, 1773.]

Lord North has the honour of informing his Majesty, that
Lord Howe, having this day presented to the House a petition
from the Captains of the Navy for an increase of their half pay,
followed it by a motion for referring it to a Committee, which,
Lord North having opposed, a debate ensued at the end of which
The Motion was carried by a great majority, all the Navy, and
army, & Country Gentlemen and most of the placemen having
voted for it. Lord North has the honour to inclose the names of
the Speakers, & numbers of the division, by which his Majesty
will see, that the defeat was complete.

DOWNING STREET *Tuesday* $\dfrac{25}{m:}$ p^t 8.

Enclosure.

9th Feb^ry 1773—Speakers on the Motion to refer the petition of the Capt^ns of y^e Navy to a Committee

PRO	CON
Lord Howe	Lord North several times
Captn Pigot	Mr Ellis
Mr Phipps	Mr C: Fox
Sr George Saville	
Mr Barre	
S^r G: Elliot	Ayes 154.
L^d J: Cavendish	Noes 45.
Mr Hawke	
Genl Conway	
Mr. E: Boscawen	
S^r P: Brett	
Sr Wm Meredith	
Mr T: Townshend Junr	
Mr. Mackworth	
Mr. Grosvenor	
Mr. Dowdeswell.	

DIVISION 9th Feb^ry 1773—on the Motion for referring the Petition of the Captains of the Navy to a Committee.

PRO	CON	FRIENDS CON
Baldwyn	Allen	
	Adam	
	Aubrey	
Bacon E.	Baker	Bayley Sir N
Baldwyn	Barre	Bennet
Barne	Bayley N	Belasyse
Barrington	Bernard	Boscawen E. H.
Bradshaw	Boothe	Brett C.
Brudenell G. B.	Brett	Bunbury.
Buller Senr	Bullock	
	Bullock	
	Burke W	
	Byng	

PRO	CON	FRIENDS CON
Cooper	Cavendish	Cator
Caswall	Cavendish	Campbell Ld F.
Cockburn S^r J	Cavendish	Colleton
	Cavendish	Conway Genl
	Cholmley	Croftes
	Clarke	Congreve
	Conolly	Clive
	Cornewall M.	Clive
	Coke	
	Coxe.	
Durand	Dempster	Dolben
Dyson	Dowdeswell	Donegal
	Delaval Sr T.	Drake F W.
Edmonstone	Egerton Sr T.	Egerton W^m
Ellis		Elliot S^r G.
Fox	Fielde	Fife
Fuller Rose	Finch	Fellowes
	Fitzmaurice	Fitzroy
	Fletcher	Fox St—
	Foley E^d:	Fraser
	Folkestone	
	Frankland S^r T	
	Fuller R^d	
Gilbert	Germaine	Garden
Guernsey	Goddard	Grant
		Grenville Jn^r
		Grosvenor
Hare	Hamilton	Harcourt W^m
Hanmer	Honeywood	Hawke Jn^r
Harcourt	Hotham	Hill
Hinchinbrooke		Hopkins Rd
		Hopkins B.
		Hoghton
		Howe.
		Howe.

PRO	CON	FRIENDS CON
Jenkinson	Johnston	Jennings G.
Jenkinson	Juvin	
Jolliffe		
Keene		Kennedy
Legh	Lascelles Edwd	Livingstone
Lewis	Lascelles Danl	Long
Lisburne	Lenox	
McDowall	Martin Jos^h	Mackworth
Marsham	Meredith	Mackay
	Milles	Mauger
	Molesworth	Morton
	Montague	Melbourne
	Morgan C	Molyneux T.M
	Murray	
North		
Onslow	Oliver	
Onslow	Owen Col	
Palmerston	Penyman	Panmure
Poulet Ann	Penruddock	Pigot
	Percy	Prescott
	Phipps	Pringle Jn^r
	Popham Al^n	Penton
	Pownall	Powlett G.
	Pulteney	
Rice		Ross
Rigby		
Robinson		
Selwyn	Savile	Seaforth
Sloane	Sawbridge	Southwell
Stanley	Scrope	Stewart Keith
Stephenson	Seymour	Stewart Wm

PRO	CON	FRIENDS CON
Stephens	Skipwith	Sturt
Sutton S^r R	Sutton Ja^s	St John S^r H.
		Stepney
		Strachey
Townshend C.	Taylor	Thrale
Tucker	Tempest	
	Thompson	
47	Townshend Senr	
	Townshend Jn^r	
	Tyrconnel	
	Van	Vernon G.V
	Vincent	
	Walsingham	Waltham
	Williams S^r H	Warrender
	Williams Watkin	Wemyss
	Whitmore	Whitbread
	Wray	Whitworth R^d
		Wriottesley
		Yorke

No. 1194—*The King to Lord North.*

Printed. Donne I. 122.

LORD NORTH—I was never clearer of opinion than of the
impropriety of encreasing the half pay of the Captains of the
Navy, therefore am much better pleased that You should have
shewn a disapprobation to the measure and care must be taken
to throw it out if it requires a particular Bill in the House of
Lords. upon the whole You have done Your duty and that is a
consolation that must fully repay any disappointment the
division may this day have given.

QUEEN'S HOUSE
Feby 9th 1773.
$\frac{m}{13}$. p^t 9 P.M.

No. 1195—*Lord Rochford to the King.*

As Lord Rochford is to see the foreign ministers today he will not be able to pay his court to Your Majesty, but as his Duty to your Majesty admits of no reserve he would not defer one minute Communicating a letter he has this instant received, by which your Majesty will see the sentiments of a Splenatick Man, at the same time he begs leave to assure your Majesty, that Lord Hardwick has not the least foundation for the Report of the Town ; whilst there remains a Spark of Life in him Lord Rochford will devote it to your Majestys service and has but one ambition and one wish that is to live to see every subject your Majesty has as loyally devoted to Your Royal house as he is.

BERKLEY SQUARE
11 *febry* 1773

$\dfrac{m}{5}\, p^t$ 10 A.M.

No. 1196—*Lord Rochford to the King.*

Ld Rochford has not the least doubt of Lord Dartmouths being extremely reasonable and flatters himself your Majesty believes Ld Rochford will do every thing to prevent any uneasiness, he has nothing at heart in the whole but the honor of his department, and as he shall meet Lord Dartmouth to morrow hopes to settle it amicably with him.

BERKLEY SQUARE 12 *febry* 1773

$\dfrac{m}{5}\, p^t$ 8 PM.

No. 1197—*Lord Cathcart to the King.*

Feb. 12. 1773.

M. Poushkin informed Lord Cathcart in Conversation that he had Orders from the Empress of Russia to procure her the best whole Length Picture possible of the King, the Queen, the Prince of Wales and Prince Frederick, and that he found himself a good deal embarrassed, the Empress having already Ramsay's Pictures of their Majestys which are the best Originals from which Copys could be made, and it being very difficult if not impossible for a Painter of whatever Note to obtain a sitting of their Majestys.

Being asked if he had mentioned, confidentialy, the Situation to Lord Suffolk he replied that having no orders he could not do it.

It appeared to Ld Cathcart to be a Pity, if it could be avoided, that the Empress should either be deprived of the Pictures she so much wishes to have, or should receive such as would do no Credit to the British Artists, and what is worse, disgrace the Resemblance meant to be transmitted. It also appeared to him that this Circumstance afforded an Opportunity of his Majesty's showing in a less or in a greater Degree, if such should be his Pleasure, a personal and very agreeable and acceptable Attention to the Empress, either by simply permitting Sir Joshua Reinolds to draw the Pictures, should he make that Request in Consequence of M. Poushkin's employing him, or by ordering Sir Joshua to draw them and making a Present of them to the Empress, either in a direct or indirect Manner : Sir Joshua's Name and Reputation being well known at St Petersburg by his having been knighted and being at the Head of the Academy, by his Accademical Discourses, and by the Prints done from his Pictures, and as he has now adopted another method of Colouring upon Principles of Duration upon which he and many other good Judges are of opinion he may absolutely depend, the Objection, not unjustly made to his former Pictures, being removed.

From these Considerations L. Cathcart thought it right, in order to stop M. Poushkin from entering precipitately into Engagements with any inferiour Artists, and gain time to acquaint Lord Suffolk of the whole, (without in any degree committing his Lordship) in case his Lordship should judge it proper to interest himself in the affair and to mention it to his Majesty, to tell him (M. Poushkin) that he would inform himself of what were the best Originals, and who were the best Painters and let him know.

No. 1198—*Colonel Geo. Lane Parker to Lord Barrington.*

My Lord—Tho I have not as yet been informed of His Majesties determination with respect to the disposal of the 37th Regiment late Sr George Grays which my Brother very lately solicited in my favour, I hope your Lordship will not think I presume too much on your goodness if I trouble you with a fresh application as there is now a fresh vacancy. for I understand from good authority that Lt General Rufane was found dead in his bed yesterday morning. There is no need to repeat how much Lord Macclesfield has my promotion at heart and how happy I shall be to receive such a mark of His Majesties favour as this is well known to your Lordship. I will therefore say no more on this subject trusting you will be so kind as to mention me to the King on this occasion as one who with all submission to His Majesties pleasure hopes to be honoured with the command of a Regiment. I am with great truth your Lordships most Obedt Humble Servt   Geo. Lane Parker

Monday morning.
Feb. 15. 1773.

No. 1199—*Colonel S. Fraser to Lord Barrington.*

My Lord—I can never forget that the first time I appeared at St James's after my return from America in 1761, your Lordship was pleas'd in a circle of The Great Officers of State to do me the honor to say, you thought it incumbent upon you to thank me in that public manner for the services I had done with my Regiment to my King and Country, this is too creditable a testimony for me not to wish to rest upon it ; Your Lordship is not unacquainted with what has befallen me since ; As I desired to leave Canada only because the War was at an end there, my only request when I returned was to be again employed wherever there was actual Service, of which His Majesty was pleased to express his aprobation in the most gracious terms, and to name me to go to Portugal as Brigadier ; the situation I hold there proves that my service has not been unacceptable to The

King of Portugal and I was given to understand that it woud
be considered as British Service ; indeed I must humbly beg leave
to think, that the way I have been employed since the peace has
been more usefull to my Country, as well as more improveing to
myself in my profession, than if I had been upon half pay at
home ;—When my Regiment was reduced I had gracious assurances by command of His Majesty that I shoud not be forgotten,
the expressions of which were too flattering to be repeated here,
but when I considered the number of meritorious Colonels reduced
at the same time, many of them my Seniors, and that variety of
requests from faithfull Servants when few coud be attended to,
must be distressing to a good and gracious Master, I thought it
my duty not to trouble His Majesty with an early aplication for
a Regiment, but now at the distance of almost ten years since
the reduction of that which I had the honor to command, when
Regiments have been given to above twenty Junior Colonels,
very few of whom have been more upon actual Service however
they may have performed it better, I hope it will not be reckoned
presumption, if I take the liberty to beg of your Lordship to lay
at His Majesty's feet my most humble request, that he may be
graciously pleased to bestow upon me the Regiment now vacant
by the death of Lieu^t Genl Gray.

I have the honor to be with the most perfect respect MY LORD
Your Lordship's much Obliged and very faithfull Servant.

S. FRASER.

ARGYLL STREET 15th
feb^{ry} 1773.

No. 1200—HOUSE OF COMMONS.

15th February 1773—Speakers on the Questions respecting
the Expedition against the Charibbs.

For the Questions	Against
Mr Thos Townshend Junior	Mr Stanley
Lord Folkestone	Mr Fox
Mr Cornewall	Sr R^d Sutton
Genl Burgoyne	Mr Saml Martin
Lord John Cavendish	Mr Cooper
Lord George Germaine	Mr Ar Paulett

For the Questions	Against
Mr Barre	Gen¹ Conway
Mr Dowdeswell	Lord Barington as to the Military Officers being consulted.
	Gen¹ Hervey—as to being consulted and the proper Time for sending Troops to St Vincents
	Mr Rice
	Lord North
	Lord Barrington

On the first Question—
　　Ayes—88　　Noes 206—

On the second—
　　　Ayes—78　　Noes 199—

Endorsed by the King, In Lord North's Feb. 16ᵗʰ, 1773.
$\frac{m}{30}$ pt one A.M.

No. 1201—*The King to Lord North.*

Printed. Donne I. 123.

LORD NORTH—I am much pleased at the very handsome Majority last night, I am curious to know how people Voted on this occasion, therefore wish to see You this Evening at Nine that I may have an explanation of what passed ; but should there be defaulters it will be highly necessary to punish them ; the taking away Regiments I can never think adviseable but Governments are a very fair prey, but more of this when You come this Evening

QUEEN'S HOUSE
　Febʸ 16ᵗʰ 1773.

No. 1202—*Lord North to the King.*

Lord North has the honour of informing his Majesty, that, Sir Wᵐ Meredith having moved, " That the Speaker should leave the Chair," a debate ensued which lasted till half an hour after eight o'clock, when the Question was carried against Sir William Meredith's motion by a very considerable Majority, and the Committee was postponed for six months.

Ayes   .   .   . 67.

Noes   .   .   . 159.

DOWNING STREET $\frac{m}{5}$ p^t 9. *Feb*: 23.

Speakers on Sir W^m: Meredith's Motion for the Speaker's leaving the Chair February 23^d: 1773.

Pro	Con
Sir Wm Meredith.	Sir Wm Bagot.
Mr. Montagu.	Sir R: Newdigate.
Mr. R. Fuller.	Mr. Page.
Mr. Dowdeswell.	Mr. Jenkinson.
Mr. Graves.	Mr. Ellis.
Mr. C. Fox.	Mr. Cornwall.
Mr. Grenville.	Sir R^d Sutton.
Mr. Hotham.	Mr. T. Townshend Junr:
Lord J: Cavendish.	Mr. Fitzmaurice.
Sir George Savill.	Sir Wm Dolben.
	Lord North.
	Mr. Skynner.
	Mr. Thomas Townshend.

Division

Ayes — 63

Noes.   159

Majority.   96

No. 1203—*Lord Rochford to the King.*

Since Ld Rochford left Your Majesty he has seen Loguet the french engineer who he sent to Brest, and who has since returned to France, the inclosed account which he had from him, is rather material, and it may be worth while to get the plan of Mauritius, especially as Cap^tn Russel who lately returned from thence and

gave an account of it will be able to examine such a plan if
obtained   Loguet clears up the mistake of having said the
Battallions of Normandy Were returned to france, it was only a
detachment upon the whole Ld Rochford thinks this mans
intelligence may in great measure be depended on.   As Lord
Rochford may possibly be prevented from paying his Court to
your Majesty to morrow on account of the foreign ministers, he
humbly begs Your Majestys leave to go out of Town on Fryday
'till tuesday morning next, which he forgot to mention to Your
Majesty to day.

BERKLEY SQUARE
24 feb^y 1773
$\dfrac{m}{50}$ pas 3 PM.

No. 1204—*The King to Lord Rochford.*

[*February,* 1773.]

LORD ROCHFORD—Having very carefully examined the List
of Successions recommended by the Lord Lieutenant, You will
order the Commissions to be prepared in consequence except the
permitting Major Mungo Campbell of the 55th Regt. of Foot to
purchase of Lieut Colonel Duncan of the same Regt.   He being
appointed Major only on the 31st of March 1770, and my having
refused Majors who are his Seniors to purchase, as being too low
on the list.   Therefore Major Legge who is recommended in the
same list to purchase the Lieut. Colonelcy in the 57th may have
this as I cannot permit him to pay the family of the late Major
General Townsend ; Major Marsh to succeed Legge in the 46th ;
and Capt Lieutenant Broderick French of the 45th to have the
Company in the 46th.

No. 1205—*The King to Lord North.*

Printed.   Donne I. 124.

LORD NORTH—The hearing that the four resolutions sent me
this forenoon have passed the Committee without a Division is
so very favourable a commencement of the East India business

that I cannot help expressing the pleasure it gives me, and I trust
that with a constant inspection of those Affairs Parliament may
yet avert the ruin to which the Company has nearly been plunged
into by the ill conduct of its Directors and rapine of its Servants

QUEEN'S HOUSE
Mar^{ch} 9th 1773.

$\dfrac{m}{35}$ *p^t* 7. PM.

Two copies, both in the King's handwriting.

No. 1206—*Ja^s Sayer to* (?).

OLD PALACE YARD 11th *March* 1773.

D^R SIR—Having communicated to You, the proceedings of
the inhabitants of Richmond towards obtaining a bridge there ;
give me leave to explain myself further on this subject ; so far as
regards the part I have acted in it, in hopes for y^r advice and
assistance, how to conduct myself ; finding this business grows
more nice and difficult than I at first imagined, from the opposition of the owners of the land on the opposite shore ; the disappointment of the lessee of the ferry, in being prevented from
erecting a bridge so much to his advantage ; and the ill humour
of the inhabitants in not receiving support in their application to
Parliament. I own I did not thoroughly consider these difficultys, or probably I might have been deterred from interfering
in this business, indeed my motives for doing it, were from a
perswasion that a bridge wou^d be pleasing to their Majestys, and
of utility both to the town and public, and the more so, if it was
erected upon a disinterested and public spirited plan, and having
reason to believe their M: wished to have Kew foot lane shut up,
I thought the application to parliament for the bridge, wou^d be
a favourable opportunity to accomplish it, as I imagined the.
inhabitants might be induced, from the hopes of assistance in
their application, and a proper recompence, to join in a petition
to Parliament for leave to add a clause in the bridge bill, to enable
Her Majesty, Lady of the manor, to shut up this lane. For these
reasons, the beginning of last summer I called upon several of
the principal inhabitants to fullfill the promise they made me of

endeavouring to have an elegant stone bridge under their own direction, in case the Lessee of the ferry was prevented from erecting one. This they most readily complied with, and several general meetings of the inhabitants were had, to take the same into consideration, when they settled the plan, and appointed a Committee to carry it into execution. At these meetings I was often called upon to know if the town might expect the countenance and approbation of their Majesties ; to which I co^d only answer, that I had not the honour of knowing their M: sentiments, neither cou^d I presume to say how those high personages stood affected in the intended application for a bridge, but flatter'd myself that a bridge wou^d be agreeable, as it wou^d open a more easy communication into the county of Middlesex, in this I was contradicted by one or two, who took upon them to declare they believed a bridge wou^d not be agreeable, and this notion has been propogated and prevails among many. Sr Fra^s Vincent having a few days ago told me he met with Lord Pelham at court the sunday preceding, who assured him a bridge at Richmond was not agreeable to their Majesties, & therefore they wou^d not countenance the inhabitants in their application to Parliament, and that he Sir Fra^s had heard the same from several other persons of rank, and that a bridge was a mere whim of the lower inhabitants. This I durst not presume to contradict ; except the last, that all the settled inhabitants approved of the plan among whom were many persons of fortune and reputation and not the lower sort only. Hence you may perceive how disagreeable is my present situation, not knowing how to act or proceed. I did venture once or twice last summer, when I had the honour to be admitted into the presence of a great personage, to mention the intentions of the inhabitants relative to a bridge, but fearful I had been guilty of presumption in so doing, durst never afterwards take any further notice of it. I also by desire of the town had the honour of communicating the intentions of the inhabitants to Her Majesty, which met with a favourable reception, but even there, I have been fearful of saying anything further about it, till the other day, the inhabitants having desired me to know of Her M: if Her M: was desirous of having Kew foot lane shut up, if so, they wou^d call a general meeting of the town to take the sence of the inhabitants upon it, not doubting but it wou^d readily be complied with, on having a proper recompence for parting with it ;

and being inform'd it will be agreeable, they intend to mention it to the bridge committee, who meet on monday next, and then call a general meeting but what recompence they expect I can^t say ; they not having yet fully considered of it.   But if I might presume to give my opinion, as it now strikes me, and as the mode of obtaining a power for shutting up this lane, must be by a petition of the inhabitants to the house of Commons, taking notice that a Bill is depending there for building a bridge, and that the lane is become of little or no benefit to the inhabitants, and dangerous to persons passing along it, from its length and privacy, and that they having reason to believe the shutting it up wou^d be agreeable to Her M: Lady of the manor, who was willing to give such a recompence to the town for parting with it, which will promote and encourage the proposed plan of a bridge, therefore they pray that a clause may be incerted in the bill to enable Her M: to shut up the same.   I sho^d think if such recompence was the inheritance and lease of the ferry, as this will be connected with the subject matter of a bridge, intended by the bill, will promote the undertaking, by lessening the expence, and encourage persons to lend money towards building it, and support the Allegations in the preamble, that a bridge will be of utility to the town, and the sooner it is free, the more advantageous it must be to the inhabitants.   These are my present thoughts, which I throw out with great diffidence for further Consideration.

I find Mr. Windham has assigned his lease in the ferry to Mr. Holland but suspect it is only in trust for the former, that his name may not be made use of, and I am inclined to think there was some connection between Mr. Windham, Mr. Holland, Mr. William Robinson, Mr. John Phillips, and Mr. King the ferryman ; that if they cou^d have obtained a proprietary bridge, they were all to be part owner of it, but seeing themselves disappointed, and that a bridge is intended to be built upon a more liberal and disinterested plan, I sho^d imagine they will now part with the lease of the ferry for a fair and equitable consideration, and more particularly to Her M: was Mr. Robinson, who I apprehend has great influence over Mr. Holland, and who knows the value of the lease, to be directed to treat in Her M: name with him, for the purchase of it ; which I imagine he may easily accomplish. I think he once last summer was calculating the value of it and seemed to think it worth £2400 or 2500. supposing the clear profits of the ferry, after paying the rent, the charge of boats and men, to amount one year with another to £200. and 26 years of the term yet to come, however after obtaining a true account of the profits for twenty years past I shoᵈ think the value might easily be calculated by Mʳ Robinson, who is accustomed to things of this nature, which I shoᵈ think cannot come to so large a Sum and apprehend the lease ought to be valued according to the rent paid by the ferryman, and not according to his profits which arise chiefly by his care diligence and labour, however this I also submit to yʳ consideration. I have thus ventured to give you my sentiments relative to the proposed bridge & shutting up the lane, all which is submitted to your consideration; assuring you that my conduct in it proceeds from a zeal for their Majesties service, I hope this will find you better and that you will believe me to be Dᴿ Sɪʀ Yʳ most obedient and faithful humble Servant

Jaˢ Sayer

No. 1207—*Lord North to the King.*

Lord North has the honour of sending to his Majesty a Copy of the Remonstrance. As the attendance of the Livery at Guildhall was very small, those who were there were very quiet, and seem'd indifferent to the business. It was natural to expect that the remonstrance would not have been so violent, but it exceeds in violence, insolence and falsehood any that have gone before. The reason is that it was drawn by Mʳ Wilkes in order to put the Lord Mayor under the difficulty either of carrying to your Majesty a most scandalous and unjustifiable paper or of disobliging the factious part of the livery by refusing them a Common Hall. Mʳ Wilkes told a friend of his that he had given the Lord Mayor a Choaker, but that he had not yet done with him, and would give him a hearty dressing before his Mayoralty was out. The Lord Mayor told Mʳ Harley that the Remonstrance was a Strange heap of stuff, and held a language to some persons in the Hᵒ of Commons as if he was doubtful whether he should present it or no. It is most probable, however, that he will present it, and Lord North will take care to have an answer prepared by Monday next.

Dᴏᴡɴɪɴɢ Sᴛʀᴇᴇᴛ. *Mar*: 13. [1773].

Enclosure.

To The King's Most Excellent Majesty.

, The humble Address, Remonstrance and Petition of the Lord Mayor, Aldermen & Livery of the City of London in Common Hall assembled.

Most Gracious Sovereign,

We Your Majesty's dutiful & loyal Subjects the Lord Mayor, Aldermen & Livery of the City of London beg leave to approach the Throne with the Respect becoming a Free People, zealously attached to the Laws & Constitution of their Country, & the Parliamentary Right of Your Majesty to the Crown of these Realms.

We desire, with all Humility, in the Grief & Anguish of Our Hearts, to submit to Your Majesty, that the many Grievances & Injuries We have suffer'd from Your Ministers still remain unredressed, nor has the Publick Justice of the Kingdom received the least Satisfaction for the frequent atrocious Violations of the Laws, which have been committed in Your Reign, by Your Ministers, with a daring Contempt of every Principle Human & Divine. Your People have, with the deepest Concern, observ'd that their former humble Petitions & Remonstrances were received with a Neglect & Disregard very hardly brook'd by the high Spirits of a great & Powerful Nation ; but the Hopes of Redress still encouraging Us to persevere, We again supplicate Your Majesty to listen to the Voice of Your aggrieved Subjects, In Vindication of Your own, & the Nations Honour, against Your despotick & corrupt Ministers, who have perverted the Fountains of Publick Justice, & undermined the Foundations of our excellent Constitution. — Our Representatives, who were chosen to be the Guardians of Our Rights, have invaded our most sacred Privileges. — The Right of being represented in Parliament is the inherent, unalienable Privilege, as well as peculiar Glory of the Freeborn Inhabitants of this Country ; and a Person qualified according to Law, a Magistrate of this City, was duly elected a Knight of the Shire for the County of Middlesex by a great Majority of legal Votes, yet has been excluded from the House of Commons, by a Resolution of that House, & a Candidate who had only a few Votes declared the Representative of the said County, against their Consent, thro' the like corrupt Influence of the same Minister.—The Chief Magistrate, & One of the Aldermen of this City, were imprisoned for not obeying the illegal Mandates of an arbitrary House of Commons, & violating the solemn Oaths they had taken for the Preservation of the Liberties & Franchises of the Capital of Your Majesty's Dominions.—We recall to Your Majesty's remembrance with Horror that unparralel'd Act of Tyranny, the erasing of judicial Record, in order to stop the Course of Justice, to introduce a System of Power against Right, and to tear up by the Roots Truth & Law from the Earth.

We therefore, Your Remonstrants, again supplicate Your Majesty to employ the only remedy now left by the Constitution, the Exercise of that Salutary Power with which You are intrusted by Law, the dissolving the present Parliament and the removal of those Evil Counsellors who advised the Measures so generally odious to the Nation ; and Your Majesty, as the true Guardian of our Rights shall ever reign in the Hearts of a grateful People.

No. 1208—*The King to Lord North.*

Printed. Donne I. 125.

LORD NORTH—The Remonstrance according to the Copy You have transmitted to Me this day has undoubtedly the marks of being the most violent, insolent, and licentious ever presented, but when it is known how thin the meeting was that countenanced the proceeding and their indifference to it, a dry answer rather bordering on contempt than anger may not be improper ; I cannot help suspecting that Mr. Oliver has been advised to be ill which delays the bringing this flagrant piece of impertinence whilst the Lord Mayor consults what part he will take or at least to shew that the Irish party has not been the proposers of this absurd measure

QUEENS HOUSE *March* 13th 1773.

$\frac{m}{38}$. p^t 8 P.M.

No. 1209—*The King to Lord North.*

Printed. Donne I. 126.

LORD NORTH—Though Lord Townshend will certainly on the death of Lord Tyrawley receive a mark of my favour yet I cannot conferr the Regiment of Guards on him as his being so low on the list of Lieutenant Generals would give real dissatisfaction to many of his Seniors the having laid his letter before Me is all You are authorized to mention to him and nothing with regard to any favorable intentions I may have towards him; Mr. Robinson's intelligence from the City shews that the City Patriots are destroying themselves in the Snare meant for others, which is but too often the fate of those who have nothing in view but mischief.

QUEENS HOUSE
March 15, 1773
$\frac{m}{30} p^t$ 5. P.M.

No. 1210—*The King to Lord Cowper.*

LORD COWPER—The very curious and well executed copies of the Painters Portraits in the Florentine Gallery which You have sent me are much enhanced by the very genteel Epistle that accompanied them ; the remaining part of the collection will be still more agreable as You promise to be Yourself the bearer of it. I remember with great pleasure the moments I passed formerly with You and have been much disappointed at Your making so long absence from Your native Country.   G. R.

QUEENS HOUSE
March 16. 1773.

Draft.

No. 1211—*The King to Lord North.*

Printed. Donne I. 127.

[The Resolutions were for restraining the East India Company's dividends.]

LORD NORTH—It is very material that the two Resolutions passed this day without Division, and the General entering on the whole of the business in the Speeches will so far cast the fuel of opposition before the attack when Your whole plan is before the House that people will be tired of the subject and therefore not endure many long Speeches that would otherways be produced

QUEENS HOUSE
March 23^d 1773

$\frac{m}{46}$ p^t 8 PM.

No. 1212.

HOUSE OF COMMONS

23^d March 1773

Speakers on the East India Resolutions

Lord North	Mr Sullivan
Mr Jenkinson	Mr George Johnstone
Mr Dyson	Ld John Cavendish
Ld North several times	Mr Dempster
General Conway	Mr Cornewall
Sr Fletcher Norton	Mr E: Burke
Mr Cooper	Mr Barre
	Mr Mackworth

Conversation in General and not debate on the Question

No Division.

No. 1213—*Sir John Dalrymple to Lord Rochford.*

[26 *March,* 1773.]

I forgot to tell your Lordship yesterday that I had left for you with Sir Stanier Porten, a plan by the Transplantation of plants for raising in one or other part of the British dominions every article of commerce that depends upon vegetable production. I gave the idea to a botanical clergyman in Scotland who executed it exceedingly well. I gave the paper to Lord Bute when he was in power, if he did not shew it to his Majesty your Lordship may, for I am sure it will amuse him.

friday.

Endorsed, R. 26 March, 1773.

No. 1214—*Lord Rochford to the King.*

Lord Rochford has just received the inclosed letter but has not yet seen Monsr de Mortanges, nor will not see him without your Majestys approbation ; Lord Rochford presumes there can be no harm in hearing what he has to say and after reporting the whole to your Majestys Judgement, can after mature Consideration decide what answer it will be proper to give and how far it may be prudent to fall into his proposals, or reject them, and Lord Rochford humbly is of opinion that the Conduct of Mr de Guines has hitherto so much deserved approbation that the greatest attention ought to be shewn to him, which makes any transaction of this Nature infinitely more delicate than it would otherwise be

BERKELY SQUARE
28th *March* 1773
$\frac{m}{10} p^t$ 3 P.M.

No. 1215—*The King to Lord Rochford.*

LORD ROCHFORD—There cannot be any objection to Your seeing Monsr de Mortanges, nor to Your hearing what he is instructed to say ; but Your own delicacy has very properly suggested that the very attentive conduct of Monsr de Guines makes it the more proper that the meetings should be private and as void as possible of the appearance of any thing but the civility You naturally would shew to the recommendation of Mr de Forcalquier

QUEENS HOUSE
    March 28th 1773

$\dfrac{m}{50}$ p^t 5 PM.

*Draft, written on a page of Lord Rochford's
    letter of same date.*

No. 1216—*The King to Lord North.*

LORD NORTH—I intend to pass the Bills that shall be ready for my Assent on Thursday ; those that can be prepared between that day and the recess shall be passed by Commission on Holy Thursday.

ST. JAMES'S
    March 29th 1773.

$\dfrac{m}{46}$ p^t 2. PM.

No. 1217—*Lord North to the King.*

[*March*, 1773.]

Lord North has the honour of informing his Majesty, that the Committee has gone through the India Regulation Bill, which was reported tonight in order that it may be printed with the alterations made in the Committee. It is to be taken into consideration on Tuesday next, so that Lord North hopes he can now venture to say with confidence that it will be sent to the Lords in the course of next week.

DOWNING STREET $\frac{1}{4}$ p^t 11. *o'clock*. P:M.

No. 1218—*Lord Rochford to the King.*

Lord Rochford has the honor to send your Majesty the minutes, it went off extremely well, but Lord Mansfield not only divided against us, but spoke and carried off with him, Ld Trevor, the bishop of Lincoln and the D of Newcastle, The Duke of Athol was also in the minority as well as Lord Say & Seale and Lord Le Despencer

House of Lords
2^d *april* 1773
$\frac{m}{40}$ *past* 8 p.m.

No. 1219—*Lord Suffolk to the King.*

Lord Suffolk takes the Liberty to submit the inclosed Interception from Count Maltzhein to The King of Prussia once more to Your Majesty's Inspection, as it is so immediately Connected with the Busyness he is under a necessity to trouble Your Majesty upon. He thinks it will pretty clearly explain Monsr. Moussin Pouschin's note ; to which he has at the same time the Honour of proposing to Your Majesty an Answer. if what he has written is in the least disagreeable to Your Majesty, or different from Your Ideas, he most humbly assures Your Majesty, that in this, as in every other instance, his Inclination coincides with his Duty to pay entire obedience to Your Majesty's commands.

Duke Sr Westm^r
April 3. 1773.
11. p.m.

No. 1220—*Lord North to the King.*

[5 *April*, 1773.]

Lord North has the honour of informing his Majesty, that Mr Dowdeswell made a motion to recommit a part of the third report of the Secret Committee, which, after some debate, passed in the negative : Lord North afterwards made the motion concerning the territorial acquisitions and revenues, which pass'd in the affirmative, after two Speeches by Mr Dowdeswell and Mr. Burke.

Downing Street $\frac{m}{40}$ *pt*: 7. p:m.

No. 1221—*The King to Lord North.*

[The " Clouds in the North " were dark. The Russian Fleet was in the Levant, maltreating the Turks, and destroying the trade of France and Spain in that quarter. These two powers prepared armaments to expel Russia from the Mediterranean, against which England, as Russia's ally, protested. Simultaneously Prussia and Denmark were threatening to force Sweden into alliance with them against France. The King, as will presently be seen (No. 1228), acted with an energy which checked France, and so dispersed the clouds.]

LORD NORTH—I am much pleased at the Question on the Territorial Acquisitions and Revenues having passed this day without a division, and trust much less difficulty will be found in carrying Your East India Bill through Parliament than might have been expected ; I shall tomorrow Evening send You a paper containing my thoughts on the clouds in the North ; which I desire You will read over before I see You on Wednesday, which I hope may be of some utility in collecting for You the matter that will come under the consideration of the Cabinet on Wednesday Evening ; but I desire the paper may be only for Your perusal for I do not mean to communicate it farther

QUEEN'S HOUSE
April 5th 1773.

$\frac{m}{38}$ p^t 8. P.M.

No. 1222—*The King to Lord North.*

Printed. Donne I. 127.

LORD NORTH—The enclosed is the short state I promised to send You on the present state of Affairs in the North ; the speaking out is ever the best method and upon this occasion perhaps more so than any other ; when I see You tomorrow I will explain still farther why I think a firm language will prevent the Court of France from taking the Step that alone seems to oblige us to take a part

QUEENS HOUSE
April 6th 1773.

$\frac{m}{8}$ p^t 7. PM.

No. 1223—*Lord Cowper to the King.*

SIRE—I am extremely sensible of the great honour your Majesty has been pleased to do me by your gracious acceptance of the portraits which I took the liberty to present to your Majesty and for the most benign letter which, Sire, you have condescended to write to me : I have not words to express half what I feel upon this occasion ; and I can assure your Majesty, it shall be the business of my life to give your Majesty the most incontestable proofs of my gratitude for such instances of your Royal favour. I have presumed to put your Majesty in mind of a circumstance that happened no less than five and twenty years ago ; One evening being at Leicester house at play with your Majesty, then Prince George, and with the late Duke of York, then Prince Edward, I happened to put on Prince Edward's ribbon, and your Majesty smiling was so good as to say to me " Who knows if ever it is in my power, but I may give it you " ; perhaps Your Majesty may not recollect it, as it is so many years since, but it made so great an impression upon me, tho' so very young, that I have never forgot it : I am very conscious to myself of not meriting so high a mark of distinction, as on the contrary I have failed in my Duty to you, Sire, by staying abroad so long without coming back to pay my respects to your Majesty ; however if Your Majesty should think me worthy of the Garter, I recommend myself to your Majesty's goodness for it on my return to England ; or if the distinction should be too great for me, at least for the Thistle, as some mark of your Royal favour would make me the happiest man in the World.

Pardon me, Sire, if I have advanced too much in mentioning this anecdote, but both the honour of being the oldest acquaintance your Majesty has at present, and my ambition of getting some mark of your Royal favour ; have encouraged me to say more than I ought to have done upon this subject : Excuse me, Sire, if I have intruded upon your Majesty's time and believe me to be with the most profound veneration and respect,

SIRE Your Majesty's most dutiful Servant and Subject

NASSAU CLAVERING COWPER

FLORENCE *April ye 9th*
1773.

No. 1224—*Lord Suffolk to the King.*

Lord Suffolk received the Honour of Your Majesty's Commands last night ; and this morning communicated to Lord North the Letters from Paris, And Your Majesty's Ideas upon them, in which they both entirely concurr. He has accordingly prepared a Letter to Lord Stormont, (and alter'd the Memorial) which will be sent to Your Majesty presently ; And in order that no time may be lost, He has directed it to be transcribed for signing, instead of Dra^tways in the usual manner, in case Your Majesty shou'd think no time shou^d be lost in transmitting it to Paris. Otherwise a very small Delay wou'd happen by it's being first sent to Lord Rochford for his opinion, alteration, or correction. Your Majesty's Pleasure shall be exactly followd in either case.

Sr James's *April* 12. 1773.
3. P.M.

He is going back to Hampton Court where he will wait Your Majesty's orders.

No. 1225—*Lord Suffolk to the King.*

Lord Suffolk cannot help directing the Messenger to call at Kew in his way back, just to express to Your Majesty his satisfaction at the Letter from Paris, by which notwithstanding all the Duc d'Aiguillon's Duplicity (abundance of which appears in it) it is pretty clear he will not finally dare to set his Face against the Firmness which (very contrary to his expectations) has been shewn on this side the Water. Ld S. will get rid of the foreign Ministers tomorrow time enough to receive Your Majesty's Commands when the Drawing-Room is over. In the mean time he humbly wishes Your Majesty wou'd turn it in your thoughts, whether some Ships shou'd not be orderd to Spithead (where some might rendezvous without creating any new expence) immediately. Lord Stormont has so solemnly declared Your Majesty's sentiments and Determination to the french Minister, that perhaps a Delay of some appearance of naval Preparation, was it to be deferr'd no longer even than to the Receipt of the Answer to the Memorial, wou'd, after what has passed, encourage

Monsr d'Aiguillon, and induce him to indulge his hopes that Your Majesty is not in earnest.

HAMPTON COURT

April 14. 1773. $\frac{m}{15}$ p^t 9. P.M.

No. 1226—MEMORANDUM BY THE KING.

I have received from the Earl of Suffolk the amount of my Sister the Queen of Denmark's Portions of forty thousand pounds Sterling, and forty thousand German Crowns, with the interest thereon at the rate of five pounds per Cent p. Ann. calculated from the first of June to the thirty first of December one thousand Seven hundred and Seventy two both inclusive.

ST. JAMES'S *this* 14th *day of April*
  one thousand Seven hundred and Seventy three

G. R.

No. 1227—*Lord North to the King.*

[16 *April,* 1773.]

Lord North has frequently since he had the honour of his Majesty's commands on Sunday last, thought over the proper method of receiving and answering the City petition, and has talked with several persons upon the subject. The more general opinion of those whom he has consulted is that it is improper for his Majesty to signify his intentions either of giving or of refusing his assent in answer to the petition, and that the most desirable thing would be either that no answer should be given, or that the answer should consist in declaring that no answer can properly be given. Upon the whole, Lord North thinks the best course of proceeding would be for the Ld Chamberlain to be sent to the Lord Mayor and his attendants with this message.

"As your petition relates to a Bill agreed on by the two Houses of Parliament of which his Majesty can not take public notice except in Parliament, I am commanded by His Majesty to inform you, that you are not to expect an answer."

After this declaration, if the City choose to present their petition, it will be read but not answer'd. This Method is less harsh than declining to give an answer, without apprizing them of it, and at the same time it may prevent their attempting to draw from the Crown any other answer so improperly on a future occasion. Lord North has mention'd this to Lord Hertford, but has not been able to speak to any of the Cabinet, who all lie out of Town tonight.

Tuesday Even⁹ 11 o'clock.

No. 1228—*The King to Lord North.*
Printed. Donne I. 128.

LORD NORTH—I received yesterday the dispatch from Lord Stormont which convinces me when the Duc d'Aiguillon finds we make preparations that he will give up his *promenade*; which opinion I am the more confirmed in from a German interception I received also yesterday of a letter from Creutz the Swedish Minister at Paris to the King of Sweden, wherein he declares that Mr d'Aiguillon has told [him] that as England would certainly take umbrage if he sent a Fleet to the assistance of Sweden, that he therefore could not think of that mode of Succour for that *at all events he would avoid a war with England*; I instantly wrote to Lord Suffolk to Summon a Cabinet this Evening, Lord Rochford will by that time be also in Town; the measure to be taken seems clearly pointed out let *all* the Guard ships be ordered to Spithead let them be compleatly manned and 20. Ships of equal Strength be ordered to replace them, and let the Ambassador's conduct be approved of and ordered to remain silent till the French Court renew the conversation, and I trust that in less than three Weeks the whole of this Armament may be countermanded, I cannot conclude without expressing my approbation of Lord Sandwich's plan of having the Guard ships always ready for immediate Service that will I am persuaded prevent many Wars for by that means we have ever 20. large Ships ready before the Enemy can equip one, consequently about the start of three months which is an immense advantage in all Military Operations

QUEENS HOUSE
April 20th 1773.
$\frac{m}{15}$. p^t 8 A.M.

No. 1229—*Lord Suffolk to the King.*

Lord Suffolk has the Honour to lay before Your Majesty the remaining part of the correspondence which passed between him and the Magistrates &c, this morning on account of the expected Disturbance, in case Your Majesty shou'd choose to see it. He also takes the liberty to inclose a private note from the Solicitor General in answer to a Letter from Mr. Eden explanatory of the Plan which was submitted to Your Majesty this morning. He has desired to see the Attorney and Solicitor General together this evening, and will then, with Your Majesty's Approbation, settle the safe and proper method of proceeding.

DUKE S^T WESTM^R
April 23. 1773

$\frac{m}{47}$ p^t 4. P.M.

No. 1230—*The King to Lord Suffolk.*

LORD SUFFOLK—I am much pleased that the wicked attempt of collecting different bodies of men with an intent of disturbing the peace of this Town has through the becoming vigilance of the Magistrates been prevented ; nothing can be more proper than Your seeing this Evening the Attorney and the Solicitor General, that it may be thoroughly assertained what punishment can be inflicted on the Author of hand bills to encourage tumultuous assemblies ; it is impossible that in any Society which deserves the appellation of civilized, such a crime shall not meet with a very exemplary one ; the more I reflect on Your proposal of writing to the Lord Mayor and one of the Sheriffs, the more I think it proper

QUEENS HOUSE
April 24th 1773

$\frac{m}{48}$ pt 5 PM.

Draft, written on a page of Lord Suffolk's
letter of preceding day.

No. 1231—*The King to Lord North.*

Printed. Donne I. 129.

LORD NORTH—The letters arrived from Paris this day have proved agreable to what I have uniformly declared, that on the return of Mr de Mortanges the fleet would be countermanded, I have in consequence of the duc d'Aiguillon's saying that the fleet is postponed, directed the two Secretaries to say publickly *that the letters arrived from France this day give reason to think the fleet will be countermanded, that therefore it is hoped we may do the same in a few days* and I have ordered Lord Sandwich not to commission any Ships but merely fit out the fifteen for that I hope by this day Sevenight even they may be countermanded ; we must see what effect our arming has had at Versailles before we can properly give counter orders, and within that time we shall receive the Messenger.

QUEENS HOUSE *April* 25th 1773. $\frac{m}{12}$. p^t 7. PM.

No. 1232—*Lord North to the King.*

Lord North has the honour of informing his Majesty, that there have been two divisions in the House today : the first upon a Question moved by the Recorder.

" That Mr Wilkes be call'd in to state his complaint against the Deputy Clerk of the Crown for refusing him the certificate of his Election to represent the County of Midlesex."

Ayes: 124.   Noes 227.

The second division was upon Sr George Saville's annual motion for leave to bring in a bill to remove doubts concerning the elegibility of Members to serve in Parliament.

Ayes: 151.   Noes. 201.

The House went afterwards into the East India Committee, where they came into three resolutions, concerning the Exportation of Tea to America and foreign parts ; There was some debate, but the questions pass'd without a division at half an hour after six o'clock.

Lord North is sorry to find that the Weavers continue in motion, and may possibly come to our end of the Town tomorrow.

He received the inclosed note from Mr Eden at the H^o of Commons, and will consult some friends upon it. The misfortune is that their Bill is pressed in a very exceptionable manner, and is, it is much to be fear'd, more likely to hurt than benefit the petitioners. It is to be hoped that some other method of preventing the weavers from assembling may be devised.

DOWNING STREET. *April* 26. 1773.

Enclosure.

Speakers 26th April 1773

on the Motion to permit Mr Wilkes to make good his Charge ag^t the Clerk of the Crown

For	Against
Mr Serj^t Glyn	Mr Dyson in respect to
Mr Sawbridge	Order

Division—Ayes 124. Noes 227.

On Sir George Saville's Motion.

For	Against
Sr George Saville	Mr Dyson
Mr Dowdeswell	Ld North
Mr Thos Townshend	Mr E: Freeman
Mr E: Burke	
Serj^t Glyn	

Division   Ayes 151 — Noes 201

No. 1233—*The King to Lord North.*

Printed. Donne I. 130.

LORD NORTH—I am sensible of Your attention in sending to me two accounts concerning the conduct of the Weavers ; it seems to me as if they would have remained quiet after the care taken on Friday last, if the same framer of mischief had not a fresh exhorted them ; and I am sorry to find the Crown Lawyers do not well know that attempting to assemble riotous meetings is criminal ; it is no great credit to the laws of this Island if they do not provide against what is so detrimental to Civil Society

QUEENS HOUSE
   April 26th 1773.
   $\frac{m}{40}$. p^t 5 PM.

No. 1234—*The King to Lord North.*
Printed. Donne I. 131.

LORD NORTH—Nothing can be a greater proof of a want of grievances when so trite an affair as the Middlesex Election can be hashed up every Session and the dividing it into two questions shews that not reason but obstinacy dictated the conduct of Opposition.

The passing any Bill with a tendency to aleviate the Weavers if they previously assemble would be quite contrary to my ideas of propriety, for it would be an encouragement to every other body of Men riotously to combine as a sure means of obtaining what wild minds may dictate ; it is the quite [*sic*] Member of Society that deserves encouragement not the licentious.

QUEENS HOUSE
   April 26th 1773.
   $\frac{m}{2}$. *pt.* 8 PM.

No. 1235—*Lord Rochford to the King.*

Lord Rochford in Consequence of Your Majesty's orders has had a Conference with L^ds Suffolk and North, and found that they entirely agreed with what he proposed to them which was to write a short Note to the french ambassador desiring to see him in the course of the day, a copy of which Note Ld Rochford now troubles your Majesty with, to talk to the french ambassador, as if this contradiction in his language and the D. Daiguillon's must be owing to a mistake, and to tell him further that I should write to Lord Stormont to night, to give the french ambassador nothing in writing but to say everything that could possibly tend to take off any Idea of a wish to menace or even renew a business that is considered as over. The inclosed letter to Lord Stormont is agreeable to what appeared to be all our Ideas, 'though it has not yet been seen by either Lord Suffolk or Ld North, I propose sending it by a messenger if it meets with your Majesty's approbation.

CLEVELAND ROW
April the 27th
1773

No. 1236—*Lord Rochford to the King.*

Lord Rochford cannot let these dispatches go to your Majesty without observing upon them, that they are by no means conclusive, and that no resolution can be taken till the return of Slaughter. As your Majesty was rode out the dispatches have been communicated to Lord North, who sent word out by Mr. Robinson to Sir Stanier, as he is absorbed in India affairs, that he would talk to me to morrow, but agrees with me, that what is come is yet inconclusive. Both he & I were struck with the Spanish fleet being encreased 18 ships of the line in two years time. Mr. Robinson told Sir Stanier that he had seen a Confidential person on whom he could depend & to whom the french ambassador said, he did not know what to think of this business for one party in France informed him they were disarming whilst another Party told him the contrary, if this is true No one but a prophet can say how all this will yet end but I think I can venture to say the likelyest way to make it end soon, will be not to be too hasty in disarming. it is with the greatest diffidence Lord Rochford presumes to lay his sentiments before your Majesty.

CLEVELAND ROW
3 *May* 1773
$\frac{m}{10}$ *past* 2 P.M.

No. 1237—*The King to Lord North.*

Printed. Donne I. 131.

LORD NORTH—The finding that the East India Bill has been ordered without a Division is a very favourable circumstance I

hope it will be soon brought in and a daily progress be made in it ;
I received the draught of the Bill which seems to me to be as
perfect as the first attempt of redressing the dreadful evils that
the rapacity of individuals have occasioned, and by annual
additions may in the end in some degree curb if not eradicate
what otherways must render that trade the ruin, instead of a
source of restoring the finances of, this Country.

QUEENS HOUSE
 May 3ʳᵈ 1773

 $\frac{m}{15}$ p^t 10 PM.

No. 1238—*Lord Rochford to the King.*

Lord Rochford has the honor to inform your Majesty that he
has had the french ambassador with him, who has communicated
the orders he has received from his court to declare to me, *qu'on
avoit suspendu lavaenement* [?] *de Toulon que trois vaisseaux
devoient parter pour Brest et que le Reste devoit rester dans le port de
Toulon Jusq'ua nouvel ordre* he observed that this was as compleat
a proof of their disarming as could be given, and that although
he had no orders to tell it me, yet he would pledge his Life that
their fleet would not go out at all to exercise, that if we had a
mind to it we might with the greatest propriety disarm immediately, he added that this was very different from what he had
written me, and that it was after his Court knew we were armed.
he owned confidentially to me that they had committed a great
Sottise and that if he had been the D, Daiguillon, the fleet should
have gone out & have exercised although they had staid out but
a fortnight. I look now upon the affair as entirely over, but
humbly presume the waiting a day or two Till Slaughter arrives
cannot be of any great consequence particularly as the Count de
Guins said he had no orders to say any thing of our being armed,
or make any demands about it.

CLEVELAND ROW
 4 *May* 1773

 $\frac{m}{15}$ *past* 3 P.M.

No. 1239—*Draft of a Motion to be made in the East India Committee.*

That it is the Opinion of this Committee, that It may be for the mutual Benefit of the Public and the Company that the Territorial Acquisitions and Revenues lately obtained in India should, under proper Restrictions and Regulations, remain in the Possession of the Company during a Term not exceeding Six Years to commence from the expiration of the present Agreement between the Public and the Company :

That the Public should forego all participation in the Produce thereof until the Company shall have repaid such Sum of Money as shall be advanced by the Public for the Relief of the Company, and the Bond Debt of the Company be reduced to £1,500,000 ; and that from thenceforth, during the remainder of the said Term, Three fourth Parts of the Surplus Net Profits of the Company at home above the Sum of £8. p Cent per Annum upon Their Capital Stock should be paid into the Exchequer for the Use of the Public, and the remaining fourth part be applied either in farther reducing the Company's Bond Debt, or for composing a Fund to be set apart for the Use of the Company in case of extraordinary Emergencies.

No. 1240.

Resolutions moved in the House of Commons by Gen[l] Burgoyne & seconded by Sir W[m] Meredith. May 10th. 1773.

1. That all Acquisitions made under the Influence of a Military Force or by Treaty with Foreign Princes do of right belong to the State.

2. That to appropriate Acquisitions so made to the private Emolument of Persons intrusted with any Civil or Military Power of the State is illegal.

3. That very great Sums of Money and other valuable Property have been acquired in Bengal from Princes and others of that Country by Persons entrusted with the Military and Civil Powers of the State by means of such Powers ; which Sums of Money and valuable Property have been appropriated to the private Use of such Persons.

10th May 1773   Speakers on the Motions made by
General Burgoyne.

For	Con
Genl Burgoyne	Mr Sol General
Sir Wm. Meredith	Lord Clive, to justify himself
Mr. Ongley	Lord George Germaine for the
Mr Dyson	principle but objecting to
Mr Vane	the Words of the Motion.
Mr Cornewall	
Lord North	
General Conway	
M^r. Barré	
M^r. Attorney General	
M^r. Dunning	

Mr Dempster for the Resolution but to explain
why he voted.

M^r. Henry Cavendish

Division on what day to proceed

For Friday   Ayes 142—Noes—*None.*

No. 1241—*Resolutions of the East India Committee.*

[10 *May*, 1773.]

That it is the Opinion of this Committee that in case a Sum
of Money shall be advanced by the Public for the Relief of the
East India Company, the Company ought to be restrained from
increasing their Dividend beyond 6 Per Cent per Annum until
such Money shall have been repaid.

That in case a Sum of Money shall be advanced by the Public
for the Relief of the East India Company the Company ought
to be restrained from increasing their Dividend beyond £7 Per
Cent per Annum until their Bond Debt shall be reduced to
£1,500,000.

No. 1242—*Lord North to the King.*

Lord North has the honour of informing his Majesty that the Committee upon India affairs came today to two resolutions, the intent of which was to prevent the proprietors from making any Dividend unless by accepting the Loan or by some other method they provide for the present deficiency ;   There was some debate but no division ; Lord North intends tomorrow in the Committee of Supply to vote the Loan of the £1,400,000, & on Thursday to order in the Loan Bill.   The India Company will be heard against the Bill of Regulations on Friday, & the House will, probably, make a sufficient progress to go through the Committee the next day that they sit, or at most the day after.

Speakers.

Pro.	Con.
Ld North.	Govr: Johnston.
Mr Prescott.	Mr Dempster.
Mr Poulet.	Mr Sulivan.

No. 1243—*The King to Lord North.*

Printed.   Donne I. 132.

LORD NORTH—The resolutions the House came to last night are such known Axioms of Government that it seems to me rather unwise in the friends of any of the fleecers of the East Indies to have combatted them though they may attempt when they are applied to particular persons to evade them ; but I believe though the House has very properly come to these resolutions that the many favours obtained by particular gentlemen will prevent much National Justice being obtained.

QUEENS HOUSE
May 11th. 1773.

No. 1244—*Lord Suffolk to the King.*

Lord Suffolk has the honour to suggest to Your Majesty an Idea which he cannot presume to accompany either with a wish or an opinion.   He submits it only from a sense of Duty as what might possibly engage Your Majesty's attention if it had happened to occur to you. He knows that Lady Erskine has long ambition'd the honour of serving the Queen as a Woman of Her Majesty's Bedchamber, and has heard that She was formerly thought of for that employment. If it could be conferr'd on her in this moment of affliction he is confident it would be considered by the Solicitor General as the greatest of obligations, and leave an Impression on his mind never to be erased. At the same time he begs leave to aprise Your Majesty that he hazards this suggestion without the least communication with any one, or in any degree as an Application ; that if, on the one hand, Your Majesty should think the measure either ill timed or inexpedient, it will never be known by any person to have been made ; and that on the other hand, if it should engage Your Majesty's attention, it should appear to be a spontaneous mark of Your Majesty's and the Queen's benevolent consideration for a sister who has lost her brother in the public service. At all events he hopes Your Majesty will pardon the Zeal which has occasioned You this Trouble.

DUKE S^T WESTM^R

May 13. 1773. $\frac{m}{20}$ *pt.* 10 P.M.

No. 1245—*The King to Lord North.*

Printed. Donne I. 133.

QUEENS HOUSE *May* 15th. 1773.

LORD NORTH—I have just heard from Lord Rochford that the Ballot has ended 319. for the Question & 149. against it ; I trust Your whole conduct which has in the East India business been alone guided by a desire of acting right will prompt You from this check with redoubled zeal to go forward. I am convinced the House of Commons will so strongly feel the absurdity of the Proprietors, that they will be the more inclined to come to the question of right ; if You on consulting the ablest of Your Counsellors in the House of Commons, chuse to avoid coming yet to that, Continue the Bill of regulations, and as the Company do not chuse to be assisted with money, pass an Act to prevent their having any dividend for the next three Years they must then come on their knees for what they now seem to spurn.

No. 1246—*Lord Barrington to the King.*

CAVENDISH SQUARE, *May* 17. 1773.

Your Majesty's goodness to me is without bounds: It is impossible to be more grateful than I am, but my duty and devotion have been long incapable of being increased.

I will obey your Majesty's Commands without delay; & I will inform Lord Westmoreland and Mr Cosmo Gordon's other noble friends and relations that he was promoted immediately by your Majesty's express command before I could have the honour to attend you.

The list herewith inclosed contains the applications which have been made for me for Ensigncies in the Guards. Tho' the Duke of Beaufort's is the last in point of time, perhaps your Majesty may think it deserves a preference to the others, on account of his extraordinary and amiable Virtue in publick and private life; as well as of his high quality, and near relation to Lord Botetourt whose attachment to your Majesty was noble and generous in the highest degree.

Mr Rigby reminded me today of Mr John Douglas proposal that if his son could have an Ensigncy in the Guards, his brother who is a Captain in the third Regiment would be well satisfy'd to sell his Company at the regulated price, tho he bought it at the high rate of 5000£ with the Duke of Gloucester's approbation. Your Majesty who forgets nothing, must remember the applications you have had on this subject from Lord Rochford, Colonel Hudson, and I believe others. I gave Mr. Rigby no encouragement; but I determin'd to mention the matter to your Majesty, because Mr. Douglas is a constant attender and Voter, and because a favour shewn to him will much oblige Lords Gower, Weymouth, Rochford, Mr. Rigby the Attorney General and others. BARRINGTON.

No. 1247—*The King to Lord North.*

Printed. Donne I. 134.

LORD NORTH—I am sorry You have been detained so long this day on an affair quite out of Season. I was in hopes the

East India Bill would have been read the first time this day, the longer it is delayed the more people will be trying to move vexatious questions to postpone the business; but I trust Your candour will not let them carry this too far ; and where intentions are so just as Yours with Spirit and perseverance the end will be obtained.

QUEENS HOUSE,
  May 18*th* 1773.

$\frac{m}{23}$ *pt.* 10 P.M.

No. 1248.

HOUSE OF COMMONS.

19th May 1773

Speakers on the East India Questions—

Genl. Burgoyne
Sir Gilbert Elliot
Mr. Sol. Genl.
Sr. Rich. Sutton
Ld. Geo: Germaine
Mr. Ongley
Ld. Clive
Mr. Strachey
Mr. Cornewall
Ld. Folkestone
Mr. Walsh
Mr. Rose Fuller
Mr. Sawbridge
Mr. Chas Fox
Mr. Barré
Mr. Vane
Sr. John Turner
Mr. Seymour
Sr. Wm. Meredith
Mr. Rigby
Mr. Ellis
Mr. Dyson
Mr. Morton

Mr. Bootle
Mr. Hotham
Mr. H. Cavendish
Mr. Gascoigne
Mr. Graves
Mr. Jenkinson
Mr. Baldwin
Mr. Mackworth
Mr. Sykes
Mr. Stanley
Sr. Chas. Bunbury
Mr. Byng
Mr. Grosvenor
Mr. Van
Mr. Hen. Townshend
Mr. Ryder

Division on Question whe[t] to
    adjn. the further Consn. of it
    till tomorrow or *Friday*.

For tomorrow—Ayes— 81.
For Friday   Noes —116.

No. 1249—*Lord North to the King.*

[19 *May*, 1773 ?]

Lord North was detained so long in the House today, that he was prevented from paying his duty at the Queen's House this Evening. The day, however, in the House of Commons was neither amusing, nor instructive, it was spent in disputes about the necessity of having *viva voce* evidence to corroborate the report of the Select Committee, and ended with adjourning the consideration of the reports to Friday, and appointing several gentlemen to attend to give evidence on that day.

DOWNING STREET. $\frac{1}{4}$ *pt.* 11 *o'clock.* P.M.

No. 1250—*Lord Rochford to the King.*

Lord Rochford is this instant come from the Duke of Gloucesters to whom he has delivered your Majesty's message, a very long Conversation ensued, which shall be faithfully related to morrow to your Majesty. his Royal Highness appeared at last tolerably satisfied, but said I should hear from him to morrow morning if any material Difficulty occurred but Ld. Rochford left his Royal Highness fully understanding that the Council was summoned for to morrow, and that whatever steps he took afterwards, your majesty would proceed without any variation from what your Majesty had finally resolved, Ld. Rochford thought it prudent to fix this beyond the power of alteration. The inclosed Message Lord Rochford meant to deliver to his Royal Highness the Duke of Cumberland to morrow morning but understands he is out of town and will not be here till to morrow night, would Your Majesty in that case have me leave the message to be delivered to his Royal Highness at his return, or sent early by a messenger to Windsor to morrow morning. the inclosed is what will be read by the Clerk to morrow in Council does your majesty think it necessary to have the archbishop and Bishop of London to attend.

BERKLEY SQUARE
20th of may 1773
$\frac{m}{10}$ *past* 9 P.M.

No. 1251—*The King to Lord North.*

Printed. Donne I. 134.

LORD NORTH—I cannot refrain having the pleasure of acquainting You that there is just arrived a letter from Lord Stormont dated May 18th that on saying to the Duc d'Aiguillon that our fleet is *Suspended* he had instantly answered ours is *countermanded*, *Les Matelots sont renvoyés ce n'est pas une suspension mais une cessation totale*, there is to be no fleet of evolution this Year ; this so very decided that no farther doubt can be had, and the Admiralty must now restore things to a state of Peace, but the Ships had better remain at Spithead.

QUEENS HOUSE
May 21st 1773.

$\frac{m}{55}$ *pt* 12

No. 1252.

HOUSE OF COMMONS.

Speakers 21st May 1773 on the Motion against Lord Clive.

Speakers as to the Examination of Witnesses.	Speakers during Mr. Beechers Examination and when he was ordered to withdraw.
Genl. Burgoyne	Mr. Dempster
Mr. Stanley	Mr. Dyson
Mr. Rd. Hopkins	Mr. Speaker
Mr. R. Whitworth	Mr. Popham
Mr. Attorney General	Sr. Wm. Meredith
Lord North	General Conway
Mr. Ellis	Ld. Clive
Mr. Seymour	Mr. Chas Fox
Mr. Mackworth	Mr. Sawbridge
	Sr. Rd. Sutton
	Mr. Cornewall
	Mr. Ward
	Mr. Solicitor General
	Mr. Attorney General
	Sr. George Saville
	Ld. Palmerston
	Mr. Mackworth

Speakers as to the Examination of Witnesses.

Speakers during Mr. Beechers Examination and when he was ordered to withdraw.

Mr. Graves
Mr. Franklyn
Lord Folkestone
Genl. Burgoyne
Mr. Seymour
Mr. Ongley
Mr. Prescot
Sr. Ewd. Blackett
Mr. Johnstone
Sir Gilbert Elliot.
Mr. H. Cavendish
Mr. Henr. Townshend
Mr. Hussey

On Mr. Burgoyne's Motion.

For	Against
Genl. Burgoyne	Mr. Stanley
Sir Wm. Meredith	Mr. Fuller
Mr. Dyson	Lord Clive
Lord North	Mr. Soll. General
Mr. C. Fox	Lord Pigot
Mr. Cornewall	Mr. Grenville
Mr. Attorney General	Sr. Chas. Saunders
Lord Palmerstone	Mr. Rhumbold
Mr. Ongley	Ld. G: Germaine
Mr. Vane	Mr. Norton
Mr. Ellis	Ld. Barrington
Mr. Barre	Mr. Byng
	Mr. Henr. Townshend
	Mr. Hotham
	Mr. Dowdeswell
	Lord F: Campbell
	Genl. Conway
	Mr. Carnac
	Sr. Gilbert Elliot
	Mr. E: Burke

Division—Ayes   95
Noes   155.

No. 1253—*Lord Rochford to the King.*

Lord Rochford has the honor to inform your majesty that the Archbishop of Canterbury called on him this morning in his way to Gloucester house, where he was going to fix with the Duke the time that the Committee should wait on him to take the examination, the Archbishop had a doubt whether he could go to Gloucester house without your majestys leave, but I ventured to tell him that in my opinion there could not be a doubt about it, as he was ordered by your majesty in Council to investigate his Royal Highnesses marriage in order to have it authenticated, and that naturally the means of doing it were left to the Committee. Lord Rochford humbly presumes that he did not give improper advice and as your majesty is not in Town had not time to take your majestys previous approbation.

CLEVELAND ROW
22d *may* 1773

$\frac{m}{20}$ p 11.

No. 1254—*Lord North to the King.*

[The underlined words refer to Lord Clive.]

[22 *May*, 1773.]

Lord North has the honour of informing his Majesty, that after a long examination Mr. Stanley moved to separate Mr. Burgoyne's question, dividing the matter of fact from the words of censure. This the Hs. agreed to, but Mr. Rose Fuller moved afterwards to leave out of the Question of Fact these words " by the influence of the powers with which he was interested as Commander in chief and Member of the Select Committee ". a long debate ensued which lasted till five o'clock in the morning when Mr. Fuller's motion was carried by a great Majority. Ld. North had the misfortune to be in the minority.

Ayes. 95.
Noes. 155.

The Question was, that the Words mark'd under do stand part of the Question.

DOWNING STREET $\frac{1}{2}$ *pt.* 5 A.M.

No. 1255—*The King to Lord North.*

Printed. Donne I. 135.

LORD NORTH—The Vote carried this Morning is a very strong proof of the propriety of Your leaving to private Gentlemen the punishing the Servants of the East India Company, and by that wise conduct You as an individual have been in a Minority that with every Man of honour must do You Credit at the same time that the Minister had nothing to do with it ; but I owne I am amazed that private interest could make so many forget what they owe to their Country, and come to a resolution that seems to approve of Lord Clive's rapine, no one thinks his services greater than I do but that can never be a reason to commend him in what certainly opened the door to the fortunes we see daily made in that Country. I cannot conclude without adding Your conduct has given the greatest satisfaction

QUEENS HOUSE
May 22d. 1773.

$\frac{m}{5}$ *pt.* 8 A.M.

No. 1256—*Lord Rochford to the King.*

Lord Rochford humbly begs leave to represent to your majesty that he thinks it would be advisable to put off the Recorders report till wednesday sennight, if it shall meet with your majesty's approbation, as the Committee of Council intend with your majesty's permission making their report on that day relative to the marriages, which Report will take up some time reading. Lord Suffolk also wishes the Recorders Report put off as he is not able to attend it, and there may possibly be applications upon it during my absence. The inclosed letter and plan is this instant come.

BERKLEY SQUARE
24 *May* 1773

$\frac{m}{5}$ *pt* 3 P.M.

On the back, in the King's handwriting.

Lieut. Oliver De Lancey of the 14th Drag. to be Captain in the 17th. Drag in the room of George Ramsay by purchase
Cornet John Browne to be Lieut in the 14th. Drag.
Hon: John Cunnyngham to be Cornet in the 14th Drag.

These Commissions bear date May 15th 1773.

No. 1257—*Lord Rochford to the King.*

Lord Rochford humbly takes the Liberty of troubling your majesty with the inclosed papers which he has had Copied for your majestys own use, apart from that he ventured to think your majesty would like to see them, as they are pretty long, before they were read in Council.

BERKLEY SQUARE.
  25th May 1773
  $\frac{m}{20}$ *pt* 2 P.M.

No. 1258—*The King to Lord North.*

LORD NORTH—You have been acquainted by Lord Dartmouth of the unpleasant message I have this day received. I have just Seen the Archbishop and the Bishop of London, and desire You will call here for five minutes

QUEENS HOUSE
  May 27th. 1773.
  $\frac{m}{59}$ *pt* 8 P.M.

No. 1259—*The King to Lord North.*

Printed. Donne I. 137.

LORD NORTH—The hearing that the raising the Qualification from £800. to £1,000. Stock has been carried by so large a Majority, gives a very good opinion of the concluding the East

India business with propriety this Season, and of introducing a continual inspection from Parliament into the State of the Company which alone can save it from destruction.

KEW, *May 29th* 1773.

No. 1260—*Lord Suffolk to the King.*

Lord Suffolk thinks it his Duty to submit to Your Majesty the inclosed note which Mr. Fraser has received from Mr. Duval. And he takes the Liberty to inclose Mr. Eden's Remarks upon it. Mr. Duval's Paragraph seems extreemly exceptionable ; And if Any is to be printed in the Gazette, one of the nature of that which Your Majesty will find drawn up on Mr. Eden's paper, seems most proper. He trusts he need not add that Your Majesty's Pleasure shall be strictly obeyed ; And the moment he has the honour of knowing it he will return to London and give Directions accordingly.

HAMPTON COURT
June 1. 1773.
$\frac{m}{10}$ *pt.* 4. P.M.

No. 1261—*Lord North to the King.*

[2 *June,* 1773.]

Lord North has the honour of informing his Majesty that the whole of this day in the House of Commons was consumed in the Committee on the India Bill, in which a considerable progress has been made but another day at least will be spent in the Committee. There were two divisions in the course of the day : The first upon the appointment of the Governor General and Council by Parliament.   Ayes. 161.

Noes.   60.

The second upon the appointment of the Judges by the Crown.   Ayes. 108.

Noes.   60.

DOWNING STREET. 1 *o'clock* A.M.

No. 1262—*The King to Lord North.*

Printed. Donne I. 137.

[Lieut.-General Monckton had been one of Wolfe's brigadiers at the battle of Quebec, and was wounded in the action. Later he commanded an expedition to the West Indies and captured Martinique.]

LORD NORTH—I wish You could contrive to be at St. James's at half hour past twelve as it is inconvenient the coming after the Drawing Room these late days and I wish to talk to You concerning a Petition I have received from Lieut. General Monkton who though an honest Man I cannot think so fit for go through the difficulties of the East Indies as Lieut Gen. Clavering.

QUEEN'S HOUSE
  June 4th. 1773.

$\dfrac{m}{46}$ *pt.* 10. A.M.

No. 1263—*Lord Sandwich to the King.*

[The name Fubbs for a royal yacht dated from King Charles II.'s time, being his pet name for one of his mistresses.]

ADMIRALTY *June* 7. 12 *o'clock.*

Your Majesty will observe by the enclosed letter that the Captain of the Pomona has done his business expeditiously and effectually.

Last night the French ambassador talked a great deal to me concerning the pleasure he should have in his expedition to Portsmouth, and among other things asked me whither there would not be a capital piece of work in hand in each branch when your Majesty went round the Dock Yard; I told him yes, but that those sort [of] things were very common and had been seen by most people; and that Your Majesty I knew would chuse to be as private as possible when in the Dock Yard, and meant to be attended only by those whose duty it was to be near your person. he made no reply, and I said nothing more, but I am perswaded he thoroughly understood my meaning.

I will take care to find Lodgings for all the Cabinet Council, your Majesties suite and the Admiralty and Navy Boards within the walls of the Dock Yard, and would submitt it to your Majesty whither [*sic*] orders should not be given that no other persons should be admitted into the yard while you are in it.

Your Majesty has I believe one of our small red boxes in your possession.

I am just now going to embark on board the Augusta, and shall sail with the William and Mary Yacht in the afternoon, the Fubbs I fear will not be ready before Wednesday.

No. 1264—*Lord Sandwich to the King.*

ADMIRALTY *June* 7. 1773.

Lord Sandwich is extremely mortified at the mistake about the plan of the House, which he fears was owing to his own inaccuracy in the hurry of writing; he has however written again to Major Archer for a draught of the Governors house, and desired him to send it to Mr. Stephens, who is directed to transmitt it to your Majesty as soon as it comes to hand : if it should be thought that any more furniture is wanting than that allready sent, there will be full time enough to send for it after Lord Sandwich's arrival, or in consequence of any orders your Majesty may think proper to give after having seen the plan of the House.

The Ocean and Raisonable arrived at Spithead on Friday from Plymouth, and the Triumph and Marlborough sailed thro' the Downs the same day.

No. 1265—*The King to Lord North.*

Printed. Donne I. 138.

KEW *June 8th* 1773 $\frac{m}{32}$ pt 9 AM.

LORD NORTH—Till the Parliament is up I shall continue coming to Town of a Sunday. I am rather surprised that Lieut. Gen. Monkton has not looked upon the contingency of the command in North America as more suitable to his affairs and constitution, than going Second in Council to Bengal, and I am clear from this that he is instigated by others to act as he does, not by his own feelings which have ever made him accommodating. I am sorry for it as his name may catch in the House and make the Division nearer than Clavering's delicacy will like ; but I am certain that the latter is most fit for the different sorts of business he must enter upon, but I hope the command of all the Troops in India is clearly given to him by the Bill, for from the beginning he declared without that He could not think of going ; I am much pleased at Colonel Monson's going third in Council. I have ever found him desirous of Service, and though not a shewy Man, has excellent Sense ; Major Gen. Frazer's conduct is very proper. If any of the Council at Bengal have acted in conjunction with Mr. Hastings, the naming one of them will be right ; but if otherways, I can see no reason for putting he who has done his duty, and those who have not on a foot ; as to the other Gentlemen that have applied to You, I do not know any thing of their personal qualifications except Mr. Francis who is allowed to be a Man of tallents ; as to Mr. Andrew Stewart I should think it wrong to take him into the Council when Monkton (very properly) is refused. I owne I think if the nomination had been made as in all other cases by the Executive Power, not a branch of the Legislature it would have prevented the disputing on Names this day which can never please the persons concerned, the only name that will not succeed and probably have many names will be Monkton, perhaps the Scotch may make a party for Andrew Stewart.

No. 1266—Lord Rochford to the King.

Lord Rochford has the honor to send your Majesty the inclosed papers that Mr. Ainslie has procured from the french Bureau. The *Doutes et Questions* were drawn up at the beginning of the Duke of Choiseuls administration under the inspection of Monsr. Dargenson, with an intent of having them seen by the french King, but that did not then succeed. They have now lately been read by him, by the intrigue of the Broglio party, in order to shew his most Xtian majesty that the Duke Daiguillon is following the same impolitical plan. And the *Conjectures raisonnées* have been written under the direction of the Broglios, and are given to the french King to read by a *cahier* at a time in order not to tire him. This information Lord Rochford believes may be depended on, and that the papers are genuine, they are in his humble opinion well drawn up and serve to shew at least what the ablest men in France think of their present situation. Mr. Ainslie has promised to do his best endeavours to get the suite of them.

BERKLEY SQUARE
8 *June* 1773

$\frac{m}{40}$ *pt* 9 A.M.

No. 1267—*Lord North to the King.*

[8 *June*, 1773.]

Lord North was prevented from paying his duty yesterday at St. James's by a misinformation which he had received that his Majesty was in the country, & that there was no drawing room.

Ld. North, when he saw Lt Genl: Monkton, found him much hurt, & complaining that, if he should not be sent to India, he should be disgraced, & unable to shew his head. Ld. North mention'd to him his Majesty gracious intention of conferring upon him the command of the Troops in North America, upon the first vacancy but the General did not appear to him desirous of that appointment but eager to go to India

Col: Monson is willing to go to Bengal as third in Council, upon condition of succeeding Lt. Genl: Clavering as Comr in chief in India in case he should quit the command. Majr: Gen:l Frazer, when Lord North mentioned this to him very handsomely & without the least hesitation relinquished his pretensions.

Lord North has been advised to nominate one of the present Council in Bengal that, if any accident should happen to Mr Hastings, there may be some person in the Council already acquainted with the country ; It is thought also to be right not to discourage the Gentlemen at present there too much, by totally excluding any of them from the Council

The Senior Counsellor whose abilities are spoken of as considerable is one Mr Richd Barwell, His name, therefore, will be proposed. •

For the remaining seat in the Council, the following gentlemen have offer'd themselves at different times. Sr Geo: Macartney,

Mr. Peter Lascelles, Dr Ferguson the author of a celebrated treatise on Civil Society, A Mr Francis who was lately in the War Office. The latter gentleman is highly extoll'd by those who know him, for his abilities, his industry, & his integrity. The objection against him is, that he was so lately a Clerk in an Office.

Lord North has just received a letter from Mr Grosvenor, by which he learns that Mr Grosvenor intends to move the House tomorrow to name Mr Andrew Stewart. Many Gentlemen will certainly support that nomination ; Ld North's only objection to Mr. Andrew Stewart is, that he wrote a little while ago those celebrated four letters to Ld. Mansfield ; In other respects, he is, I believe, in point of Knowledge, abilities, integrity & resolution as fit for the office as can be desired

Tuesday Morn 1 *o'clock* [perhaps a mistake for Wednesday, *see* No. 1265].

No. 1268—*Lord North to the King.*

[8 *June*, 1773.]

Lord North has the honour of informing his Majesty, that the Bill was reported to day and order'd to be ingross'd, & is to be read tomorrow for the third time, when it will be pass'd.

There were two divisions in the course of the day. One upon an amendment respecting the persons qualified to be judges, and the other upon putting the previous question upon Genl Clavering's name in order to insert Genl Monkton's.

The Debate was very handsome to them both. but the question was carried for Genl. Clavering by a great Majority. Ayes. 115
Noes 60.

No. 1269—*Lord North to the King.*

[9-10 *June*, 1773.]

SIR—Although I am convinced, that I have done my duty to the Publick in proposing Lt Gen: Clavering for the second in the Council of Bengal, and that I should have deserved much blame if I had done otherwise, yet I own I feel deeply for the disappointment and distress of Lt Gen: Monkton, and submit to your Majesty whether you would consent to my making him such an offer as would afford him a compensation for what he might reasonably have expected from his India Commission such a pension for the life of himself and two of his children, or for the lives of three of his children, as would, when sold at a market price, produce 12 or 15000£ would be more than adequate to any sum that he would probably have received during his life from the Commission in India, and would, at the same time, leave him free and open to all the promotions and honour which he might expect in the course of his profession. This proposal I humbly submit to your Majesty, as what would be very agreable to the Publick though nine in ten must consider Gen. Clavering as the better qualified for the employment in India. The Irish revenue, and the four and a half per Cent are both certainly much burthend, but to secure to the Public Gen: Clavering's abilities, without hurting a man of the merit of Gen: Monkton seems to me to be a sufficient cause for an additional charge on either. If your Majesty does not disapprove this proposal, it should be soon carried into execution. It might then facilitate our other transactions with the E. India Comp. where we [are] still likely to meet with storms. The inclosed note from Lord Rochford will convey to your Majesty an idea of their present temper. The proposal mentioned in it, though it would give us at first much trouble, would, probably, in the end lead to a much more useful, satisfactory, and effectual settlement of India affairs than any we have yet thought of. I trust in your Majesty's great and long experienced goodness to me that you will pardon this intrusion, and permit me to subscribe myself your Majesty's most devoted and most dutiful subject   NORTH.

No. 1270—*The King to Lord North.*

Printed. Donne I. 139.

KEW, *June* 10*th.* 1773.

LORD NORTH—If a proof was wanting of the goodness of Your heart, Your anxiety at the disappointment of Lieut. Gen. Monkton must for ever entitle You to a great share of that first of good qualities ; I am not wanting in compassion for the imprudence of that good natured Man, and am very ready to give him any reasonable assistance ; but I do not think myself in a situation to give such a Royal present as You suggest. Should that be done, Sir Jeffrey Amherst would come with a like demand ; but an idea suggests itself to Me it is Parliament that has with great propriety preferred Clavering to Monkton ; why cannot they in Return as a testimony of the services of the latter recommend him to a Grant of some of the unsold lands in the Ceded Islands his conquest of Martinique would be a sufficient grounds and that would make it particular ; besides he could then assist his Children, who being unlawful are more proper to be mentioned in a public Grant ; You will see by this proposition how desirous I am to forward on all occasions Your wishes but my income cannot bear great drains, besides the door that it would open for other applications as indeed Monkton's declining the handsome offer of the Command in America is also against him. As to an Irish Pension after the rawle about Dyson I cannot approve of that, and indeed the Pension on My Sister the Queen of Denmark must be made out before I can think of giving one to any other person.

I am certain Lord Rochford's intelligence will prove true not as a thing intended to be come to, but it may give room for delay which is the sole object of the D. of Richmond. Should they really resign their Charter it may occasion some difficulty, but in that case I should think the Military ought to be taken quite out of the hands of a new Company and the Supreme Council which ought to have powers to control the inferior Governments, and I fear whilst the Company can carry on Wars they will ever encline from interested motives to it.

No. 1271—*The King to Lord North.*

Printed.   Donne I. 141.

LORD NORTH—I am much pleased at hearing that the East India Bill has passed this morning by so great a Majority, and trust that it will prove a remedy to some of the many evils that if not corrected must soon totally prevent any possibility of preserving that great branch of Commerce ; besides it lays a foundation for a constant inspection from Parliament into the Affairs of the Company which must require a succession of Regulations every year ; for new abuses will naturally be now daily coming to light, which in the end Parliament alone can in any degree check ; for the Directors from Views of Self Interest, must Court their Servants who make rapid fortunes, from the desire of remaining at the Head of the Company. I suppose their [*sic*] can now be no doubt of the business in the House of Commons being totally finished so that I may prorogue the Parliament on Saturday the 26th of this month.

KEW, *June 11th.* 1773. $\frac{m}{33}$. *pt.* 7. A.M.

No. 1272—*Lord Sandwich to the King.*

PORTSMOUTH *June 12.* 1773
nine at night.

I am fearfull of offending your Majesty by troubling you about trifles ; but my desire that everything at this place should give satisfaction when you honour us with your appearance, inclines me to ask some few questions how things shall be conducted, & to submitt to your approbation some part of the plan of our intended proceedings, in addition to what has been allready honoured with your Majesty's sanction. I arrived here last night, & have employed myself this morning in settling the apartments in the Commissioners house, where there will be the room prepared for your Majesty which you pointed out on the plan, which is extremely quiet, & tho' low and by no means spacious, is well aired & warm.

The Lord in waiting, the Gold Stick, & the Groom in waiting will be properly accommodated in the house with your Majesty ; & the Garetts will be appropriated to their servants ; & the other orders recieved by me in the note written in your own hand will be duly executed with regard to the Commissioners house, stabling, & lodging for the Clerk of the stables & stablemen.

I have secured beds in the Dockyard for such of your Majesties servants in your Naval department whose duty requires their attendance when you visit the Dockyard ; & for such of your

Cabinet Council as have applied to me for accommodation ; &
I presume that I am not to concern myself for any who do not
apply ; & to tell any who do not apply & are not included, in
the above description that the beds in the Dockyard are allready
destined. the Cabinet Council who have applied to me for beds,
& to whom I have given answers that I have provided for them
are

Ld Gower   Duke of Grafton   Ld Hertford   Ld Suffolk
Ld Rochford   Ld Dartmouth   Ld North.

It will be proper that I should know your Majesty's pleasure
who shall have the honour of attending you in your barge when
you go to Spithead, I think there should on no account be more
than two besides your Majesty ; I would humbly submitt whither
the Lord in Waiting & the First Lord of the Admiralty should
not be the persons to be honoured with attending on your Royal
person. proper barges will be prepared for the Cabinet Council,
& the rest of your Majesties Suite.

A new red cloak (cloaks being allways used in boats belonging
to men of War) is prepared for your Majesty ; it seems to me
that a Star of the order of the Garter of a larger than the ordinary
size should be on the outside of the cloak, if this is thought
necessary Your Majesty must trouble yourself to order such a
star to be sent down before your arrival.

I have been this afternoon with Major Archer to view the
Governors house, there are fires in all the rooms in the ground
floor, & they are scouring & cleaning the apartment ; but if I
might venture to go a step out of my own department I could
wish that orders were given to hasten this part of the business ;
for tho' Major Archer is indefatigable in doing everything in his
power, I do not find that he has recieved any particular instructions from his superiors what steps he is to take, I enclose a copy
of the plan of this house, which your Majesty has I am persuaded
some time ago recieved from Mr. Stephens, and you will find
written down the destination of the several rooms according to
our ideas ; but it seems to me absolutely necessary that some
one belonging to your Majesties bedchamber should be here a
day or two before your arrival, that this matter should be settled
to your entire satisfaction.

Some Transports are arrived here to day with a regiment from

Jamaica, possibly they might be of use on this occasion, when a number of infantry will be extremely serviceable, as the concourse of people will undoubtedly be very great.

Does your Majesty mean that more than one Page shall lye in the room contiguous to your own ?

I have been on board the Barfleur with Mr Khuff to settle your Majesties table, and upon the most mature consideration & with the concurrent advice of Admiral Pye & the Comptroller of the Navy, I submitt it to your Majesty whither a horse shoe table will not be the most commodious. If there is to be only a common long table it must be across the ship, & I fear will not hold a sufficient number of those persons within the line which Your Majesty intends to admitt in their turns to the honour of dining at your table ; all the Captains of the Guardships, the Yatchts & frigates have the rank of Collonell ; and as the number of the Cabinet Council is encreased since I had the honour of seeing your Majesty, it is to be wished the table should hold more than thirty otherwise many must be left out. that this matter may be properly settled I submitt for Your Majesties determination the plan of the table proposed, with the number it will hold in case your Majesty should think proper to allow three to sit on your right, & three on your left hand.

As the Lord of the Bedchamber will not be here I imagine before Your Majesties arrival, I must beg to recieve your particular commands who shall be asked to dine the first day, and how they are to be invited.

No. 1273—*The King to Lord North.*

[*June,* 1773.]

LORD NORTH—I have desired both Lord George Germain and Lord Amherst to lay before the Meeting this day, the letters and whole conduct of the D. of Richmond ; I am certain everyone of You will on hearing it be shocked that any Man of Rank and Property, and indeed I might use the expression of anyone born in this Island [*unfinished*].

No. 1274—*The King to Lord North.*

Printed. Donne I. 142.

Kew, *June 12th* 1773.

Lord North—I return You the Minutes of the East India Court of Yesterday ; which shews the Duke of Richmond's blackness if it wanted any elucidation, and that his whole conduct is dictated by malevolence not a desire of preventing the Company from any Evils he might pretend to foresee ; but this will greatly delay the Session, for I suppose he will fight the loan Bill through its several Stages in the House of Lords that till the first Week in July Parliament cannot be prorogued.

The strange conduct of the Court in nominating Lieut. Gen. Monkton will certainly give a thorough reason for Parliament's preventing Clavering's becoming useless, and the former after the kindness expressed towards him will if You speak to him I trust decline the nomination, so that Clavering can then on Monday be named by a short Act of Parliament, without another discussion on the merits of these two Men ; and I should think that a very good reason for the House of Commons to propose a Grant out of the lands ceded by the Charrybs in St. Vincents for Lieut. Gen. Monkton's services at Martinique.

No. 1275—*Lord North to the King.*

[13 *June*, 1773.]

Lord North has received the honour of his Majesty's commands. As it is impossible for the new Council to act in Bengal before this time twelvemonth, there is no probability that Lt. Gen[1] Clavering will be prevented from enjoying the chief command of the Troops in India, but if there should be the least doubt, the Lords by a short clause may set all right ; & this method appears the most eligible. Lord North has not yet received any letter from Mr. Rigby.

Lord North had a meeting of merchants on friday night, who all dissuaded him from a Lottery this year, assuring him that he could not make £150,000 of it. Ld. North for that and other reasons thinks it better to let one year pass without a Lottery.

BUSHY PARK. *Sunday Even^g*

$\frac{m}{25}$ *pt* 7 *o'clock.* P.M.

No. 1276—*Lord North to the King.*

[13 *June*, 1773.]

Lord North has the honour of transmitting to his Majesty a fair copy of the E: India Regulation Bill, together with a letter he received yesterday evening from Lieut: General Monckton. He ought in justice to inform his Majesty, that it was not written in consequence of any application from Lord North, & does not doubt but his Majesty will consider it as a fresh proof of the good intentions of the General, & of his desire of shewing his attention to his Majesty's wishes upon all occasions. In the present instance this resolution of Mr. Monckton will be of the greatest use.

BUSHY PARK *Sunday morn^g*.

No. 1277—*The King to Lord North.*

Printed. Donne I. 145.

LORD NORTH—I am much pleased at the conduct of Lieut. Gen. Monkton, and hope You will soon settle his affair in St. Vincents. Mr. Rigby told Me he had sent You word that he thought it would save much time if You would get the Lords as an amendment to Your Bill for Regulations to add when they name Lieut. Gen. Clavering a Counsellor and Commander in Chief of all the Troops of the East India Company, least this should not yet have reached You, I think it right to mention it, but am not clear whether that or the Short Act You propose to Me on friday is best.

KEW, *June* 13*th* 1773.

No. 1278—*Lord Rochford to the King.*

Lord Rochford has the honor to trouble your Majesty with the inclosed Minute of the house of Lords, Lord Shelburne was there and voted against us but did not speak. I think the Duke of Richmond means to put an end to this business this week, everybody of our side to day was sanguine. Lord Rochford has had a visit to day from Coll Rainsford with a message from his R Hs the Duke of Gloucester, desiring Lord Rochford to attend upon him to morrow, Lord Rochford answered that he could not do it without your majestys special leave, but that he would take your majestys pleasure upon it. Lord Rochford therefore waits your majestys commands; by what fell from Coll Rainsforde Lord Rochford has reason to suspect that the message his Royal Highness wants to convey, is, to desire your Majesty and the Queen to be sponsors for his Royal Highnesses Daughter. The inclosed letter from Lord Sandwich Lord Rochford thinks it his Duty to trouble your Majesty with.

BERKLEY SQUARE 14*th June.* 1773

$\frac{m}{25}$ *past* 5 P.M.

No. 1279—*Lord Sandwich to the King.*

PORTSMOUTH *June* 14. 1773.

Lord Sandwich is very fearfull of being too troublesome to your Majesty, but he cannot avoid mentioning things that occurr which may tend to your Majesties ease & convenience while you are at this place.

I much fear that one morning will not suffice to see the Dockyard; We have been on our visitation full four hours this morning & have not yet gone thro' the whole; & yet as there is nothing that is new to us, we have not examined things so minutely as your Majesty would chuse to do, nor has there been one capital piece of work in hand to detain us; even in our manner of visiting I think we have full employment for two hours more in the afternoon; if your Majesty could allow us a fourth day, you would have full time to see everything at your leisure.

The Table for your Majesty is ordered according to the

amended plan which I recieved this morning, & which is certainly infinitely better than in the original idea.

Would your Majesty have me give notice to Admiral Pye that he is to dine with your Majesty the first day with the captains of his Divisions of the Fleet ? they will be obliged to hurry from the Levee the moment they have made their bow in order to have time to range their boats to attend you to Spithead ; & if you please I may inform the two senior Lords of the Admiralty that the same honour is intended them ; if I understand your Majesty right, the Cabinet Councillors and the other persons mentioned in the note with which I am honoured this day would recieve their invitation at the Levee from the Lord in Waiting.

I have reexamined your Majesties barge and there is full room for four sitters without incommoding your Majesty, my only reason for mentioning this again, is, that unless the first Ld. of the Admiralty has the honour of being with you there will be no one who can answer any question you may think proper to ask concerning the fleet ; and in rowing up the harbour among the Ships in Ordinary, which is a part of the business in which I think your Majesty will find much amusement, without some person who can give you some account of the state & character of each ship, you will see that part of Your fleet very imperfectly. of this branch the captain who will have honour of steering your barge can give you no information, as it is quite out of his way, & known by very few even of those who have the honour to serve your Majesty in the civil department of the Navy.

No. 1280—*The King to Lord North.*

LORD NORTH—I am infinitely pleased at the Opening of the Budget having met with no opposition, but am not surprised at it for Your abilities and integrity must meet with Success ; at the Review this morning I saw Clavering who seems rather disheartened at the difficulties the India Company throw in his way, but I answered him that I knew his probity, and that when nothing is in view but doing right all difficulties will with steadiness soon vanish.

KEW. *June 14th* 1773.

$\frac{m}{2}$ *pt* 9 P.M.

No. 1281—*A Letter of Intelligence.*

SIR—I dislike writing for fear of an accident or should by that method have communicated what I had to offer—the dispatch I mentioned was sent by Madm. Heinel, there remained for me to take the parcel I left at your house, which I have opened and found it to contain books only—I shall be believed when I say it was opened by the Custom House officers.

Having been in the country I did not receive your note till just now, as what follows may, or may not merit attention, I thought it necessary to receive instructions on the subject. I more particularly thought it necessary, having received injunctions very unusual to preserve it most inviolably secret. The Duke D'A[iguillon] is coming over to observe the fleet when his majesty is at Portsmouth, an express arrived on Friday with orders if I could answer for keeping him concealed, in case of any accident compelling him to go on shore, that he should immediately be informed of it, and I should be on the 20th at Fakeham where he would come unattended and embark in a vessel that, I am to hire for that purpose—I have wrote for the vessel, but not knowing if I can have that I formerly used, I cannot describe her, if you chuse to know her, I want to fix on some private signal that would mark her, and which might be unknown to any other person—my friend being out of town on Saturday morning I received my instructions from his representative and Twenty guineas on account—my personal concerns are some of them necessarily blended with those of the public I am told it will not be necessary for me to return and that I am to be fixed to some regiment, what am I to do Sir ?—I will chearfully encounter every risque to be serviceable, but I ought surely to have some certainty of protection where matters come to an extremity which will necessarily happen on the declaration of a war—I must say I never undertook a journey with so much reluctance yet I hope it is not necessary for me to repeat that my wishes to serve are superior to every other consideration. The hope of recompence diminishes danger, and inclination attaches me to your interest which in this case I consider as my own . . . You said you would speak to Lord N[orth] on the subject of a late requisition, it is probable it will be the last trouble of the kind for some time, if I am to remain, but you may be assured I will find some means of informing you of every occurrence that may be worth your knowing. I shall remain where I am till seven o'clock, if you chuse to write ; at ten this evening I will call at your house if I do not hear from you before, when I shall hope to receive your commands, or at least to morrow, for the time will not alow me to stay much longer in England.

SUN TAVERN ST. PAULS CHURCH YARD.
½ *past two o'clock. June 16th. 1773.*

Endorsed by Mr. John Robinson,

Private

16th June 1773

Mr M[ant ?]
Intelligence
Recd. same Afternoon—and
saw him same Night soon
after Ten o'Clock—J R—

No. 1282—*Thomas Mant to* [? *John Robinson*].

[17 *June*, 1773.]

SIR—I last night thought myself possessed of money sufficient for my present purposes or I should have asked you for more than you offered me. This morning I was striped of my whole stock by a *ne exeat regnum* [*sic*]. That I would not on my part hinder the service I am engaged in I am immediately going to Arundell This is to beg the favour of You to send by this evening's post which I shall recieve to morrow morning fifty pounds which I must consider as money paid me in advance. I trust you will not neglect speaking to my Lord North on the subject of last night which so very materially concerns me. I shall write to you from Arundell with the proper descriptions &c. and every other opportunity when it may be necessary to convey any intelligence that may be interesting.

I have the honour to be Your faithful Ser.   THO. MANT

Thursday Morning,
  eleven o'clock.

No. 1283—*Lord Sandwich to the King.*

PORTSMOUTH *June* 18. 1773.

Lord Sandwich hopes that this is the last trouble he shall have occasion to give his Majesty before his arrival at this place.

The four days with which we are to be honoured with your Majestys company, will enable you to see everything that can deserve attention without fatigue, hurry or inconvenience : & there comes with this a new arrangement where the plan is calculated for four days instead of three ; parts of which may be varied according to the weather, or to your Majesties inclination when you are on the spot.

It is now proposed that only Lord Edgecumbes Squadron should sail while your Majesty is here, there being some difficulties about sending Admiral Spry to sea at the same time, and he could at no rate go further than St: Helens, as he must have waited there some days for the Barfleur which is to belong to his Squadron.

Your Majesty will recieve herewith the account of the visitation of the Yard, which will serve to shew the State of things here at the time of your arrival, & we flatter ourselves that the encrease of the timber since last year will give your Majesty some satisfaction.

As the Defiance is a new ship, with some new contrivances on board, possibly your Majesty may not dislike to see her as well as the Britannia.

Your Majesty will find in this box, an account of the particular works that will be in hand when you visit the yard ; and I have been extremely firm in keeping all persons out of the Yard while your Majesty is in it, that you may not be incommoded with unnecessary attendants ; it is proposed that an order should be stuck up at the Gate notifying what persons are to have ingress & egress ; a copy of that order I send herewith, & I must beg your Majesty to inform me whither it is right, & whither any addition or alteration should be made ; with these regulations I flatter myself your Majesty will be as private as you can wish to be.

The two Yatchts are intended for Lady North with her

family, and the Nobility & others of your Majesties attendants ; & will follow the Augusta when your Majesty is on board her ; by which plan they will see everything to the greatest advantage ; I must beg to recieve your Majesty's Commands who shall be with you in the Augusta Yatcht, & would submitt it whither any other should be there than those who have the honour to attend you in your barge, & Admiral Pye, who being the commander in chief next to the Lord High Admiral, must be there to carry any orders into execution that your Majesty may think proper to give thro' the channel of the first Lord of the Admiralty ; if there are many more your Majesty will be crowded, & there will be full accommodation in the other yatchts for all your Majesties other servants & attendants : this matter however rests intirely with your Majesty for your determination, & pleasure upon it.

Your Majesties orders to me are at present that Admiral Pye shall invite the 6 senior captains of the fleet to have the honour of dining at your Majesties table ; but there are some circumstances to be submitted to you on this subject which did not occurr at first & on which I must recieve your Majesties pleasure before the orders are given finally.

Admiral Pye should by all means attend every day to recieve your commands thro' the first Lord of the Admiralty, tho' the Barfleur is no longer his ship ; for the Admiralty flag is now flying aboard her, and when your Majesty is on board & the Standard hoisted, the command of the Fleet will rest in yourself, and the Vice Admiral must be at hand to execute your commands and order the proper signals to be made. Admiral Pyes flag is on board the Royal Oak. There are three persons on board the Barfleur in a particular situation, Captain Vernon the Captain of the Ship, Captain Bickerton who steers the barge, & Coll: Smith of the Marines, who will be constantly on duty on your Majesty's person while you are in the ship ; & I do not know whither it would not be right that they should dine with your Majesty each day on that account : Coll: Smith will command one hundred Marines who will be your Majesties guard. That I may be sure to do nothing wrong on this matter I now transmitt to your Majesty two schemes of invitation. That you may decide between them. No: 1 is upon the idea of not considering the three above mentioned persons differently from the rest, and upon a supposition that your Majesty may not think it improper to allow the Vice & Rear Admiral to be twice at your table as Admiral Pye will be there every day. in this you will observe that Norton, Bickerton, & Percival tho' old Post Captains stand last in the list; the meaning of this is, that while they are at sea in a Yatcht their rank is suspended, & they will be commanded by the youngest Post Captain : but I do not apprehend that their rank of Collonell subsides; they continue to wear the Collonells uniform, command all Masters & Commanders at sea, tho' the commissions of the latter are of an earlier date than the Post Commissions of the former ; therefore they are more properly to be considered, even at sea, as the youngest Post Captains, than as Masters & Commanders ; & it would be a grievous disappointment to them to be deprived of availing themselves of their rank of Coll: which they have had many years, so as not to have the honour of dining with your Majesty.

It seemed necessary to be thus prolix, in order to give your Majesty a full insight into the merits of these questions, that you may give such orders upon them as your wisdom shall direct. Among the several papers, your Majesty will find a sketch of the Line of battle; you will percieve that the Thames frigate is among them but she is not here, & possibly may not arrive in time, in which case her place must be filled up by one of the Sloops. There is allso a sketch of the order in which the boats are to be ranged when they attend your Majesty to Spithead ; there is at present some little doubt about the placing the Navy Boards barge, but I hope to settle that matter (which is a dispute about precedency with the Captains) without your Majesty's hearing anything about it.

No. 1284—*Mr. Francis to Mr. Robinson.*

Mr. Francis presents his Compliments to Mr. Robinson: He has made the Search desired and finds, that there has not been a Writ of Ne exeat Regno issued aga^t any person for upwards of a Month last past.

CHANCERY LANE
   19*th June* 1773.

No. 1285—*Thomas Mant to Mr. Robinson.*

A Cutter, somewhat less than twenty Tons very short for her burthen, her gunwale painted blue, two painted windows in her stern. The colours a saint Georges Ensign and Jack; on the starboard shroud a Dutch Ensign, on the larboard shroud a Swedish Ensign—The vessel is now in dock and she will have a clean bottom—she will be ready to go to sea on Monday, I shall sail about five o'clock in the afternoon—I send this by an express, in the same manner There will be time for me to hear from You, as I hope you will send me a little money—If I can land I will, and you shall know it as soon as possible—If I judge right, the cause that I embarked in, will be attended with glory to the minister, advantage to my country and I trust some emolument to myself, impressed with this idea, I hope I shall not incur any blame for the present expence—I address this to Lord North, as it may be the means of a quicker conveyance, it being almost impossible to get horses on the road, owing to the multitude of people going to Portsmouth.   T. M.

THE POST HOUSE
ARUNDELL
one o'clock in the morning 20th. June 1773.

No. 1286—*Lord North to the King.*

Lord North has the honour of transmitting for his Majesty's approbation, a Warrant appointing Lord Leven, a Commissioner of the Police in Scotland in the room of Lord Napier. According to all the enquiries Lord North has been able to make, he appears to be as proper a successor to Lord Napier as any of the other candidates, and his promotion will vacate a pension of £400 pr ann: on the Civil List. Ld: North has the honour of transmitting at the same time a Warrant to revoke the pension, for his Majesty signature, if he approves of appointing Lord Leven a Commissioner of Police.

Lord North would not have troubled his Majesty with these Warrants before his return to London, were it not necessary that Lord Leven's appointment should have passed through all the requisite forms before the fifth of next month, when there is to be an Election of a Cashier of the Police, at which Lord Leven's presence will constitute a quorum ; It is very rare that a quorum of the Board of Police can be assembled ; It may be accomplished now, while Ld Cathcart is in Scotland ; Should he leave Scotland, it may be many years before such another opportunity will offer itself. BUSHY PARK. *June* 20: [1773.]

No. 1287—*The King to Lord North.*

LORD NORTH—I think the appointment of Lord Leven very proper and have in consequence signed the two Warrants and send them back to Bushy

KEW, *June 21st.* 1773

$\frac{m}{16}$ *pt. one* P.M.

ADDENDA

No. 1025A—*The King to Lord North.*

QUEENS HOUSE *Feby* 27*th* 1772

$\frac{m}{55}$ *pt* 5 P.M.

LORD NORTH—I am glad You have rejected Sir George Saville's motion with so little trouble. I have seen Ld Denbigh, who tells Me that the Country Gentlemen were at first hurt they were not Supported in defending Dr Noel but that now they are appeased ; You ought to consider of the best mode of rejecting Mr Fred Montague's proposition of no longer keeping the 30th of January.

Your having seen Ld Mansfield will I hope enable You to give good advice to the Lords this Evening for the Management of tomorrows Debate and whatever is agreed upon will I hope be decisive for altering the mode of proceeding when in the House never answers. I hope I shall either from You or one of the Secretaries receive a line concerning what passes, even to night for You may guess how much I am anxious to see this measure well carried through

No. 1059a—*The King to Lord North.*

Lord North—I have just received the Keys which Mr Martin has returned to You. Lord Rochford told Me that You have perfectly satisfied his mind as to Mr Fountayne. I desire You will finish the affair of the Glamorgan Shire Lieutenancy for the great delay that has arisen undoubtedly much lessens the favour. I find Lord Hardwicke is to come and recommend His Brother the Dean of Lincoln for a Bishoprick, I shall certainly explain it cannot be the first given to Cambridge for Dr Hurd will undoubtedly meet with general Approbation; he means also to press that Lord Breadalbane be restored to a Seat in the House of Lords on explaining his resolution to Support administration this is worthy of consideration but must require much explanation.

Queen's House *May 8th* 1772. $\frac{m}{55}$ p^t 9 pm.

INDEX

END OF VOL. II

Printed in Great Britain by R. & R. CLARK, LIMITED, Edinburgh.